WATER IN
THE CULTIC WORSHIP OF
ISIS AND SARAPIS

ÉTUDES PRÉLIMINAIRES
AUX RELIGIONS ORIENTALES
DANS L'EMPIRE ROMAIN

PUBLIÉES PAR

M. J. VERMASEREN

TOME QUATRE-VINGT-SEPTIÈME

ROBERT A. WILD

WATER IN
THE CULTIC WORSHIP OF
ISIS AND SARAPIS

LEIDEN
E. J. BRILL
1981

ROBERT A. WILD

WATER IN
THE CULTIC WORSHIP OF
ISIS AND SARAPIS

WITH 32 FIGURES, 30 PLATES, AND 1 MAP

LEIDEN
E. J. BRILL
1981

ISBN   90 04 06331 5

To My Mother
In Memory of My Father

TABLE OF CONTENTS

Figures in the Text   IX
Acknowledgements   XIII
Abbreviations and General Bibliography   XV

Introduction   1

   I. Overview of the Evidence   9
      The Questionable Sites   10
      Sanctuaries with Cultic Water Facilities . . . .⸴.   23

   II. The Nile Water Crypts   25
      More Proximate Egyptian Antecedents   28
      Evidence from Outside of Egypt   34
         1. Delos A   34
         2. Delos B   36
         3. Delos C   38
         4. Thessalonica   39
         5. Gortyn   40
         6. Pompeii   44
      Changes in the Roman Period: Sabratha   48
      The Purpose of the Crypts   49

   III. Other Types of Fixed Nile Water Containers   54
      The Nile Water Containers   55
         1. Eretria   55
         2. Cyme   57
         3. Pergamum   57
         4. Frauenberg   59
      The Typology of Nile Water Containers   60
      Nile Water and Rain Water   63
      A Shift within the Ideology of the Cult.   65

   IV. Why Nile Water? 1. Evidence from the Crypts   71
      Statuettes of Cows from the Crypt at Gortyn   72
      The Reliefs at Pompeii   76
      Conclusions   84

    V. Why Nile Water? 2. Evidence from Outside the Cult   86
        General Perceptions   88
        Properties of Nile Water   89
        Benefactions of Nile Water   92
        Life after Death and Nile Water   97
        Conclusions   99

   VI. Why Nile Water? 3. The Osiris Evidence 101
        The Cultic Pitcher 103
        The Images of Osiris Hydreios 113
        The Osiris "Cool Water" Inscriptions 123
        Conclusions 126

  VII. Ablution Facilities and Rituals 129
        The "Sprinkling Basins" 130
        Ablution Basins for the Ministers of the Cult 134
        Ablution Practices and Their Historical
        Antecedents 143

 VIII. Egyptianizing the Cult of the Egyptian Gods 149

Appendix 1. Survey of the Sites 161
        Table of the Sites 161
        Dating and Identification 162
        A So-Called "Serapeum" 188

Appendix 2. Other Types of Crypts Associated with the Cult 190
        A Crypt for Cultic Assembly 190
        Storage Crypts for Cultic Equipment 194
        Various Tunnels and Passageways 197
        Conclusions 205

Notes 207

Indices 281

List of Plates 301

Plates I-XXX and Map of the Known Isis-Sarapis Sanctuaries

FIGURES IN THE TEXT

Fig. 1. The Iseum at Ras el Soda, Egypt. Ground plan of sanctuary and adjoining areas. Source: Adriani, *Annuaire*, fig. 61 (modified) 11

Fig. 2. The Serapeum at Luxor. Ground plan of the sanctuary and surrounding area. Source: Abdul-Qader Muhammad, *ASAntEg* 60 (1968), pl. cvi (detail) 12

Fig. 3. Sanctuary of Sarapis and Isis at Thera. Ground plan. Source: F. Freiherr Hiller von Gaertringen, *Thera*, vol. 3, Berlin, 1904, figs. 70-71 13

Fig. 4. Late Hellenistic Sanctuary of Isis at Soli ("Temple D") and adjoining Sanctuary of Aphrodite. Ground plan (above) and reconstructed sketch of Iseum (below). Source: Westholm, *Temples*, pp. 87, 90, 91 15

Fig. 5. Roman-period Sanctuary of Isis at Soli ("Temple E") and adjoining Sanctuary of Aphrodite. Ground plan (above) and reconstructed sketch of Iseum (below). Source: Westholm, *Temples*, pp. 87, 91, 92 16

Fig. 6. The Sanctuary of Isis (?) at Industria. Ground plan. Source: Barra Bagnasco *et al.*, *Scavi*, Tavv. ii and iii 18

Fig. 7. The Sanctuary of Isis and Sarapis (?) at Ampurias (Emporion). Source: J. Puig y Cadafalch, "Els temples d'Empuries," *AIEC* 4 (1911-12), 39, fig. 2 (detail) 19

Fig. 8. Sanctuary of Isis and Sarapis at Philippi. Ground plan. Source: Collart, *BCH* 53 (1929), pl. 1 19

Fig. 9. The Sanctuary of Sarapis and Isis at Priene. Ground plan. Source: T. Wiegand and H. Schrader, *Priene*, Berlin, 1904, 166, Abb. 158 21

Fig. 10. The Iseum in the Precinct of Apollo at Cyrene. Source: Pernier, *Tempio*, Tav. 4 (detail) 22

Fig. 11. The Sanctuary of Isis at Philae. Ground plan showing location and general design of the four Nilometers. Source: Henry G. Lyons, *A Report on the Temples of Philae*, Cairo, 1908, pl. iv 27

Fig. 12. The Serapeum at Alexandria. Ground plan showing the Ptolemaic sanctuary and portions of the Roman reconstruction. Source: Rowe, *ASAntEg*, Suppl. 2 (1946), pls. vii and xvii (modified and simplified)   30

Fig. 13. The Serapeum at Alexandria. Plan of the "Lower Terrace" area showing the Ptolemaic Nilometer. Source: Rowe, *BArchAlex* 35 (1942), pl. xliv (modified and simplified—lower portion of Nilometer added on the basis of other information)   31

Fig. 14. Serapeum A at Delos. Ground plan. Principal features: A - Central Temple; B - Access opening to water from the Inopus; C - Portico; D - Shrine to various gods (?); E - Cultic dining room. Source: Roussel, *CE*, pl. 1   35

Fig. 15. Serapeum B at Delos. Ground plan. Principal features: A - Central Temple; B - Enclosed room; C - Portico; D - The Nilometer crypt; and G - A room with small shrines, perhaps the gathering place for one or more cult associations. Source: Roussel, *CE*, pl. 2   37

Fig. 16. Serapeum C at Delos. Ground plan. Principal Features: A - Main entrance; C - Temple (formerly a Metroon); D - *Dromos*; E - Fore court; F - Temple of Sarapis; G - Altar; H - Small temple; I - Temple of Isis; K - Entrance; L - Shrine of Anubis (?); P - Shrine or exedra; Q (and the three rooms to the west) - Rooms below the sanctuary courtyard, perhaps not connected with it; S, T - Rooms with access to the lower street, perhaps not part of sanctuary; V, X, Y - Shrines or exedrae; Z - Former Escharon. Source: Dunand, *Culte d'Isis*, 2.88, fig. 5   38

Fig. 17. The Sanctuary of Isis and Sarapis at Gortyn. Ground plan. More of the portico in front of the temple has been excavated than is shown here. Source: Salditt-Trappmann, *Tempel*, plan 6 ...   40

Fig. 18. The Iseum at Pompeii. Ground plan. Source: Elia, *Pitture*, 2, fig. 2   45

Fig.19. The Sanctuary of Sarapis and Isis at Sabratha. Ground plan showing features discussed in this work. Source: Pesce, *Tempio*, tav. 1   48

Fig. 20. The Sanctuary of Sarapis and Isis at Eretria. Ground plan. The principal features include: A - Cella; B - Pronaos; C - Enclosed courtyard in front of the central temple; D - Main courtyard; E - A surrounding portico; G - Room for ablutions; X - The Nile water container; and Z - Entrance to the precinct. Most of the rooms to the north of E and G were used for living quarters. Source: Bruneau, *Sanctuaire*, pl. xxxvi   56

Fig. 21. The Iseum at Pergamum. Ground plan. In the central temple are found a low, flat basin (M), the Nile water container (N), and a place of access (P) to an underground cistern. On either side of the temple are annex structures (B, D, E, G) and twin court-yards surrounded by porticoes. Each courtyard has an ornamental basin (Q). There are also underground chambers (D', E', and H') and a system of tunnels indicated by the lower case letters. Source: Salditt-Trappmann, *Tempel,* plan 2 .Between 56-57

Fig. 22. The Sanctuary of Isis (?) at Frauenberg. Ground plan of the sanctuary and other structures found within its vicinity. Source: Modrijan, *Frauenberg*, Abb. 7   59

Fig. 23. Saqqarah, Egypt. Detail from an embroidered tunic of the second cen. AD. A long-spouted cultic pitcher stands upon a stylized offering table. Loaves of bread are to the left; on the right is also bread (?). Source: Dunand, *BIFAO* 67 (1969), 35, fig. 9   107

Fig. 24. The Sanctuary of Isis (?) in the State Agora of Ephesus. Ground plan showing present remains. Source: Hölbl, *Zeugnisse*, 28, Plan 1   133

Fig. 25. The Serapeum at Leptis Magna. Ground plan. Source: Le Corsu, *Isis*, 246, fig. 18   134

Fig. 26. The Serapeum at Alexandria. Plan of the ablution basins and their drainage system. Source: Rowe, *BArchAlex* 35 (1942), pl. xxxii (detail—modified and simplified)   137

Fig. 27. The Serapeum in the South Stoa of the Agora at Corinth. Ground plan. Source: Broneer, *South Stoa*, pl. xviii (detail)   138

Fig. 28. The Iseum in the Campus Martius at Rome. Ground plan (reconstructed) showing at what locations the major finds were recovered. Source: Roullet, *Egyptian Monuments*, fig. 348 . . Between 178-179

Fig. 29. The Santa Sabina Iseum at Rome. Ground plan of the sanctuary and the rooms around it. A person entering into the area in which the worshippers met (III) had to pass first through Room IV and then through a gap in the Servian Wall. The paintings and graffiti were mostly found in the north corner of Area IV. Source: C. Descemet, "Mémoire sur les fouilles exécutées a Sainte-Sabine, 1855-57." *Mémoires présentés par divers savants a l'Académie des Inscriptions et Belles-Lettres,* ser. 1: *Sujets divers d'érudition* 6.2 (1864), pl. iii. 1 (detail)   182

Fig. 30. The Sanctuary of Sarapis and Isis at Thessalonica. Approximate ground plan. This illustrates the various structures mentioned in the reports and their approximate relationship to one another as far as this can be ascertained. Illustrations exist for those architectural elements marked with solid lines. Source: author, with assistance from an earlier plan by D. Fraikin, ''Note on the Sanctuary of the Egyptian Gods in Thessalonica,'' *Numina Aegaea* 1 (1974), 5 187

Fig. 31. The Serapeum at Ostia. Ground plan. Source: Squarciapino, *Culti*, 20, fig. 2 195

Fig. 32. The Serapeum at Miletus. Ground plan. The crypt under the cult platform is indicated with dotted lines. Source: Salditt-Trappmann, *Tempel*, plan 4 (modified) 196

ACKNOWLEDGEMENTS

This study of the use of water in the rituals of the Isis-Sarapis cult makes extensive use of various types of archaeological data. My interest in utilizing this kind of evidence in the exploration of Graeco-Roman religious movements was first enkindled by the enthusiasm of my teacher, Prof. Helmut Koester of Harvard University, for his own investigation of religiously-oriented material remains from Greece. The excitement of this work led a number of us to consider research projects of a related character. In the company of Prof. John Hanson of Wellesley College, a good friend and knowledgeable colleague, I made an inspection of some of the most important sites in the eastern Mediterranean area and became convinced that these remains still have much to tell us.

As my research progressed, various individuals offered generous assistance. Profs. Dieter Georgi (New Testament and Christian Origins), David Mitten (Classical Art and Archaeology), and Zeph Stewart (Greek and Latin) read earlier versions of this work and offered helpful criticisms from the perspective of their various disciplines. I also benefitted much from discussions with Prof. Richard Pervo and Rev. Thomas Tobin, S. J. More recently, I have been aided by the vast learning and insight of Prof. Maarten J. Vermaseren, the general editor of this series. The preparation of this work was much assisted by various staff members of the libraries at Harvard and at Marquette University and by the editorial and technical skills of Ms. Camilla Sieveking, Ms. Camille Slowinski, Mr. Guy Carter, Ms. Joyce Little, and Mr. Roberto Goizueta. Mrs. Milada Součkova, a specialist in the art and literature of Czechoslovakia, assisted me with the translation of reports written in various Slavic languages. Very special thanks are due to Mr. J. J. V. M. Derksen and to Mrs. Franca Derksen-Janssens for their excellent and careful work in preparing the figures and plates for the press.

Financial aid for this project was forthcoming from the Alexander Campbell Fund of Harvard Divinity School, from Marquette Jesuit Associates, and especially from the Chicago Province of the

Society of Jesus. Simply put, their generous assistance made my work possible.

During the long period of research and writing I received much-needed emotional support and encouragement from many people. I would single out especially my parents, my sister Ann, the priests and people of the Sacred Hearts Parish, Malden, Mass., and my Jesuit brothers at Marquette University, at John La Farge House, Cambridge, and in Chicago. To all of them I owe a very special debt of gratitude.

R.W.

Marquette University
Milwaukee, Wisc., U.S.A.
July 12, 1979

ABBREVIATIONS AND GENERAL BIBLIOGRAPHY

In Appendix One there is a complete bibliography for each of the sanctuary sites discussed. Only the more frequently cited of those works are listed here.

AA = *Archäologischer Anzeiger.*

Abdul-Qader Muhammad, M., "Preliminary Report on the Excavations Carried Out in the Temple of Luxor, Seasons 1958-1959 & 1959-1960," *ASAntEg* 60 (1968), 227-79.

AbhBerlin = *Abhandlungen der Deutschen (Preussischen) Akademie der Wissenschaften zu Berlin, Phil.-hist. Klasse.*

AbhLeipzig = *Abhandlungen der (Königlich) Sächsischen Gesellschaft der Wissenschaften. Phil.-hist. Klasse.*

ActaAnt = *Acta antiqua Academiae Scientiarum Hungaricae.*

ActaArch = *Acta archaeologica Academiae Scientiarum Hungaricae.*

ActaOrient = *Acta orientalia Academiae Scientarium Hungaricae.*

Adriani, Achille, "Sanctuaire de l'époque romaine à Ras el Soda," *Annuaire du Musée Gréco-Romain (1935-39),* Alexandria, 1940, 136-48.

Adriani, Achille, *Repertorio d'arte dell' Egitto greco-romano,* 4 vols., Palermo, 1961-66.

AeR = *Atene e Roma.*

AICorrArch = *Annali dell' Istituto di Corrispondenza Archeologica.*

AIEC = *Anuari del Institut d'Estudis Catalans.*

AJA = *American Journal of Archaeology.*

Almagro, Martin, "Manifestaciones del culto de Zeus Serapis y de Sabazios en España," *CuadEERoma* 8 (1956), 201-12.

AM = *Mitteilungen des Deutschen Archäologischen Instituts. Athenische Abteilung.*

ANRW = *Aufstieg und Niedergang der römischen Welt,* ed. H. Temporini and W. Haase, Berlin, 1972-

AntChrist = *Antike und Christentum.*

AntCl = *L'antiquité classique.*

AntK = *Antike Kunst.*

AnzWien = *Anzeiger der Akademie der Wissenschaften, Wien. Phil.-hist. Klasse.*

AO = *Der alte Orient.*

ArchCl = *Archeologia classica.*

ArchD = *Archaiologikon Deltion.*

ARW = *Archiv für Religionswissenschaft.*

ASAntEg = *Annales du Service des Antiquités de l'Egypte.*

ASAtene = *Annuario della Scuola Archeologica di Atene e delle missioni italiane in Oriente.*

Assmann, Jan, "Aretalogien", *LÄ* 1.425-34.

Auberon, P. and K. Schefold, *Führer durch Eretria*, Bern, 1972.
BA = *Bulletin archéologique du Comité des Travaux Historiques et Scientifiques.*
BABesch = *Bulletin van de Vereniging tot bevordering der kennis van de Antieke Beschaving.*
Baechler, J., "Recherches sur la diffusion des cultes isiaques en Italie," Diss., Strasbourg, 1959.
Baege, Werner, *De Macedonum sacris*, Halle, 1913.
Balil, A., "El culto de Isis en España," *CuadEERoma* 8 (1956), 213-24.
Baltrušaitis, J., *Essai sur la legende d'un mythe: la quête d'Isis*, Paris, 1967.
BArchAlex = *Bulletin de la Société Archéologique d'Alexandrie.*
Barra Bagnasco, M. *et al.*, *Scavi nell' area dell' antica Industria* (Memorie dell' Accademia delle Scienze di Torino, Cl. di Scienze Morali, Storiche e Filol., 4.13), Turin, 1967, 11-39.
BCH = *Bulletin de correspondance hellénique.*
Beaujeu, J., *La religion romaine à l'apogée de l'empire*, vol. 1: *La politique religieuse des Antonins (96-192)*, Paris, 1955.
Bell, H. Idris, *Cults and Creeds in Graeco-Roman Egypt*, Liverpool, 1957.
Berciu, Ion and Constantin Petolescu, *Les cultes orientaux dans la Dacie méridionale* (EPRO, 54), Leiden, 1976.
Bergman, Jan, *Ich bin Isis: Studien zum memphitischen Hintergrund der ägyptischen Isisaretalogien*, Uppsala, 1968.
Bernand, Etienne, *Inscriptions métriques de l'Egypte gréco-romaine*, Paris, 1969.
BIE = *Bulletin de l'Institut Egyptien.*
BIFAO = *Bulletin de l'Institut Français d'Archéologie Orientale.*
Bissing, F. von, "Ägyptische Kultbilder der Ptolemaier-und Römerzeit," *AO* 34 (1936), 1-37.
Bissing, F. von, "Das Heilige Bild von Kanopus," *BArchAlex* 24 (1929), 39-59 and 25 (1930), 97-98.
Bisson de la Roque, F., "Le lac sacré de Tôd," *ChrEg* 12 (1937), 157-62.
BJRL = *Bulletin of the John Rylands Library.*
Blackman, Aylward, "Sacramental Ideas and Usages in Ancient Egypt," *PSBA* 40 (1918), 57-66, 86-91 and *RecTrav* 39 (1921), 44-78.
Bleeker, C. J., *Die Geburt eines Gottes*, Leiden, 1956.
Bleeker, C. J., "Guilt and Purity in Ancient Egypt," *Proceedings of the XIth International Congress of the International Association for the History of Religions, Claremont, 1965*, vol. 2: *Guilt or Pollution and Rites of Purification*, Leiden, 1968, 47.
Bleeker, C. J., "Isis as a Saviour Goddess," *The Saviour God: Comparative Studies in the Conception of Salvation Presented to E. O. James*, Manchester, 1963, 1-16.
BlHeim = *Blätter für Heimatkunde* [Graz].
BMetrMus = *Bulletin of the Metropolitan Museum of Art.*
Bohm, R. K., "The Isis Episode in Apuleius," *Classical Journal* 68 (1972-73), 228-31.

Bonneau, Danielle, *La crue du Nil, divinité égyptienne, à travers mille ans d'histoire (332 av.—641 ap. J-C)*, Paris, 1964.
Bonneau, Danielle, *Le fisc et le Nil*, Paris, 1971.
Bonnet, Hans, *Reallexikon der ägyptischen Religionsgeschichte*, Berlin, 1952.
Bonnet, Hans, "Die Symbolik der Reinigungen im ägyptischen Kult," *Angelos* 1 (1925), 103-21.
Borchardt, Ludwig, "Nilmesser und Nilstandsmarken," *AbhBerlin* 1906, pt. 1, 1-55.
Borchardt, Ludwig, "Nachträge zu 'Nilmesser und Nilstandsmarken'," *SBBerlin* 1934, 194-207.
Borchardt, Ludwig, "Zu den biem Gebel Silsile neu gefundenen Nilmessern," *ZÄS* 72 (1936), 137-39.
Borhegyi, Etienne, "Statuettes égyptiennes en terre cuite au Musée des Beaux-Arts," *Bulletin de Musée Hongrois des Beaux-Arts* 2 (1948), 5-10.
Bosticco, Sergio, *Musei Capitolini: i monumenti egizi ed egittizzanti*, Rome, 1952.
Botti, G., *L'acropole d'Alexandrie et le Sérapeum*, Alexandria, 1895.
Botti, G., *Catalogue des monuments exposés au Musée gréco-romain d'Alexandrie*, Alexandria, 1900.
Botti, G., *Fouilles à la Colonne Théodosienne (1896)*, Alexandria, 1897.
Botti, G. and P. Romanelli, *Le sculture del Museo Gregoriano Egizio*, Vatican City, 1951.
Brady, Thomas, *The Reception of the Egyptian Cults by the Greeks (330-30 BC)* (University of Missouri Studies, 10), Columbia, Mo., 1935.
BRAH = *Boletín de la Real Academia de la Historia*.
Breccia, Evaristo, *Terrecotte figurate greche e greco-egizie del Museo di Alessandria* (Monuments de l'Egypte gréco-romaine, 2), 2 vols., Bergamo, 1930-34.
Breton, Ernest, *Pompeia décrite et dessinée*, 3rd ed., Paris, 1870.
Broneer, Oscar, *Corinth*, vol. 1, pt. 4: *The South Stoa and Its Roman Successors*, Princeton, 1954.
Bruneau, Philippe, *Recherches sur les cultes de Délos à l'époque hellénistique et à l'époque impériale*, Paris, 1970.
Bruneau, Philippe, *Le sanctuaire et le culte des divinités égyptiennes à Erétrie* (EPRO, 45), Leiden, 1975.
BSA = *Annual of the British School at Athens*.
Budge, E. A. Wallis, *Egyptian Magic*, London, 1901.
Budge, E. A. Wallis, *The Gods of the Egyptians*, 2 vols., Chicago, 1904.
Budge, E. A. Wallis, *The Mummy*, New York, 1974.
Budischovsky, Marie-Christine, *La diffusion des cultes isiaques autour de la Mer Adriatique*, vol. 1: *Inscriptions et monuments* (EPRO, 61), Leiden, 1977.
BullCom = *Bullettino della Commissione Archeologica Comunale di Roma*.
BullFarU = *Bulletin of the Faculty of Arts, Farouk I University*.
Burel, Joseph, *Isis et isiaques sous l'empire romain*, Paris, 1911.

Castiglione, L., "Zur Frage der Sarapis-Kline," *ActaAnt* 9 (1961), 287-303.

Castiglione, L., "Griechisch-Ägyptische Studien," *ActaAnt* 5 (1957), 209-27.

Castiglione, L., "Hérodote II 91," *MélMichałowski*, 41-49.

Castiglione, L., "Kunst und Gesellschaft im römischen Ägypten," *ActaAnt* 15 (1967), 107-52.

Castiglione, L., "Die Rolle des Kyathos im ägyptischen Kult: ein Beitrag zur Deutung des vatikanischen Prozessionsreliefs," *ActaAnt* 8 (1960), 387-404.

Cat. gén. Caire = Catalogue général des antiquités égyptiennes du Musée du Caire.

Cayeux, Lucien, *Description physique de l'île de Délos* (EAD, 4), Paris, 1911.

CE = Pierre Roussel, *Les cultes égyptiens à Délos du IIIe au Ier siècle av. J.-C.*, Paris, 1916.

Charbonneaux, Jean, "Prêtres égyptiens," *MélPiganiol* 1.407-20.

ChrEg = *Chronique d'Egypte.*

CIL = *Corpus inscriptionum latinarum.*

ClRev = *Classical Review.*

Collart, Paul, *Philippes ville de Macédoine depuis ses origines jusqu'à la fin de l'époque romaine*, 2 vols., Paris, 1937.

Collart, Paul, "Le sanctuaire des dieux égyptiens à Philippes," *BCH* 53 (1929), 70-100.

Corsu, France le, *Isis, mythe et mystères*, Paris, 1977.

CRAIBL = *Comptes rendus de l'Académie des Inscriptions et Belles-Lettres.*

CuadEERoma = *Cuadernos de trabajos de la Escuela Española de Historia y Arqueologia en Roma.*

Cumont, Franz, *Oriental Religions in Roman Paganism*, Chicago, 1911.

DAGR = *Dictionnaire des antiquités grecques et romaines*, ed. C. Daremberg and E. Saglio, 5 vols., Paris, 1877-1919.

Daressy, Georges, "L'eau dans l'Egypte antique," *MIE* 8 (1915), 201-14.

Daressy, Georges, *Statues de divinités* (Cat. gén. Caire, 28-29), Cairo, 1905-6.

Darsy, Félix, *Recherches archéologiques à Sainte-Sabine* (Monumenti dell' antichità cristiana, 2.9), Vatican City, 1968.

Dattari = Dattari, G., *Monete imperiali greche: numi augg. alexandrini*, Cairo, 1901.

Daux, Georges, "Trois inscriptions de la Grèce du nord," *CRAIBL* 1972, 478-93.

DenkschrWien = *Denkschriften der k. Akademie der Wissenschaften, Wien. Phil.-hist. Klasse.*

Deonna, W., "Croyances funéraires: la soif des morts—le mort musicien," *RHR* 119 (1939), 53-81.

Deonna, W., "Terres cuites gréco-égyptiennes," *RArch* 5.20 (1924), 80-158.

Derchain, Philippe, ed., *Religions en Egypte hellénistique et romaine*, Paris, 1969.
Derchain, Philippe, "Un sens curieux de ἔκπεμψις chez Clément d'Alexandrie," *ChrEg* 26 (1951), 269-79.
Dibelius, Martin, "Die Isisweihe bei Apuleius und verwandte Initiationsriten," *SBHeidelberg* 1917, pt. 4.
Dieterich, A., "Der Ritus der verhüllten Hände," *Kleine Schriften*, Leipzig-Berlin, 1911, 440-48.
Dobrovits, Aladár, "Az egyiptomi kultuszok emlékei Aquincumban," *Budapest Régiségei* 13 (1943), 45-75.
Dölger, Franz Joseph, "Esietus: Der Ertrunkene oder zum Osiris Gewordene," *AntChrist* 1 (1929), 174-83.
Dölger, Franz Joseph, "Nilwasser und Taufwasser," *AntChrist* 5 (1936), 153-87.
Donaldson, Thomas and William Cooke, *Pompeii*, 2 vols., London, 1827.
Dow, Sterling, "The Egyptian Cults in Athens," *HTR* 30 (1937), 183-232.
Drexler, Wilhelm, "Isis," *LM* 2.373-548.
Drexler, Wilhelm, *Mythologische Beiträge*, vol. 1: *Der Cultus der ägyptischen Gottheiten in den Donauländern*, Leipzig, 1890.
Düll, Siegrid, "*De Macedonum sacris*: Gedanken zu einer Neubearbeitung der Götterkulte in Makedonien," *Ancient Macedonia*, ed. B. Laourdas and C. Makaronas, Thessalonica, 1970, 316-23.
Dunand, Françoise, *Le culte d'Isis dans le bassin oriental de la Méditerranée* (EPRO, 26), 3 vols., Leiden, 1973.
Dunand, Françoise, "Les représentations de l'Agathodémon. A propos de quelques bas-reliefs du Musée d'Alexandrie," *BIFAO* 67 (1969), 9-48.
Dyer, Thomas, *Pompeii: Its History, Buildings, and Antiquities*, London, 1867.
EAD = Exploration archéologique de Délos.
Edson, Charles, "The Cults of Thessalonica," *HTR* 41 (1948), 153-204.
Eitrem, S., "Tertullian *de baptismo* 5: Sanctified by Drowning," *ClRev* 38 (1924), 69.
Elia, Olga, *Le pitture del tempio di Iside* (MPAI, 3.3-4), Rome, 1942.
Engberding, Hieronymus, "Der Nil in der liturgischen Frömmigkeit des Christlichen Ostens," *OrChr* 37 (1953), 56-88.
Engelmann, Helmut, *The Delian Aretalogy of Sarapis* (EPRO, 44), Leiden, 1975.
Engreen, Fred, "The Nilometer in the Serapeum at Alexandria," *Medievalia et humanistica* 1 (1943), 3-13.
EPRO = Etudes préliminaires aux religions orientales dans l'empire romain, ed. M. J. Vermaseren, Leiden, 1961- .
Erman, Adolf, *A Handbook of Egyptian Religion*, New York, 1907.
Festugière, A. J., "A propos des arétalogies d'Isis," *HTR* 42 (1949), 209-34.

Feuillatre, Emile, *Etudes sur les Ethiopiques d'Héliodore,* Poitiers, 1966.
FF = *Forschungen und Fortschritte.*
Floca, O., "I culti orientali nella Dacia," *Ephemeris dacoromana* 6 (1935), 204-49.
Fouquet, A., "Quelques représentations d'Osiris-Canope au Musée du Louvre," *BIFAO* 73 (1973), 61-69.
Frankfort, Henri, *Ancient Egyptian Religion,* New York, 1948.
Fraser, P. M., "Current Problems Concerning the Early History of the Cult of Sarapis," *OpAth* 7 (1967), 23-45.
Fraser, P. M., *Ptolemaic Alexandria,* 3 vols., Oxford, 1972.
Fraser, P. M., "Two Studies on the Cult of Sarapis in the Hellenistic World," *OpAth* 3 (1960), 1-54.
García y Bellido, A., "El culto a Sárapis en la península ibérica," *BRAH* 139 (1956), 293-355.
García y Bellido, A., *Les religions orientales dans l'Espagne romaine* (EPRO, 5), Leiden, 1967.
Gardiner, A. H., "The Baptism of Pharaoh," *JEA* 36 (1950), 3-12; 37 (1951), 111; and 39 (1953), 24.
GazBA = *Gazette des Beaux-Arts.*
Geissen = Geissen, Angelo, *Katalog alexandrinischer Kaisermünzen der Sammlung des Instituts für Altertumskunde der Universität zu Köln,* Opladen, 1974-
Gilbert, P., "Un trait de parenté entre les Serapeia de Délos et l'Egypte," *La nouvelle Clio* 7-9 (1955-57), 296.
Girard, P. S., "Mémoire sur le nilomètre de l'île d'Eléphantine," *Déscription de l'Egypte: antiquités, mémoires,* vol. 1, Paris, 1809, 1-47.
Gonzenbach, Victorine von, *Untersuchungen zu den Knabenweihen im Isiskult der römischen Kaiserzeit,* Bonn, 1957.
Graindor, P., *Terres cuites de l'Egypte gréco-romaine,* Antwerp, 1939.
Grandjean, Yves, *Une nouvelle arétalogie d'Isis a Maronée* (EPRO, 49), Leiden, 1975.
GRBS = *Greek, Roman and Byzantine Studies.*
Grenier, Jean-Claude, *Anubis alexandrin et romain* (EPRO, 57), Leiden, 1977.
Gressmann, Hugo, *Die orientalischen Religionen im hellenistisch-römischen Zeitalter,* Berlin, 1930.
Griffith, F. Ll., "Herodotus II 90—Apotheosis by Drowning," *ZÄS* 46 (1910), 132-34.
Griffiths, J. Gwyn, *The Isis-Book of Apuleius* (EPRO, 39), Leiden, 1975.
Griffiths, J. Gwyn, *Plutarch's De Iside et Osiride,* Swansea, 1970.
Grimm, Günter, *Die Zeugnisse ägyptischer Religion und Kunstelemente im römischen Deutschland* (EPRO, 12), Leiden, 1969.
Gsell, Stéphane, "Les cultes égyptiens dans le nord-ouest de l'Afrique," *RHR* 59 (1909), 149-59.
Guarducci, Margarita, *Inscriptiones creticae,* vol. 4: *Tituli Gortynii,* Rome, 1950.

Guimet, E., "Les isiaques de la Gaule," *RArch* 3.36 (1900), 75-86; 4.20 (1912), 197-210; and 5.3 (1916), 184-210.

Gusman, Pierre, *Pompéi, la ville, les moeurs, les arts*, 2nd ed., Paris, 1906.

Hamilton, William, "Account of the Discoveries at Pompeii," *Archaeologia* 4 (1776), 160-75.

Handler, Susan, "Architecture on the Roman Coins of Alexandria," *AJA* 75 (1971), 57-74.

Harris, E. and J. R. Harris, *The Oriental Cults in Roman Britain* (EPRO, 6), Leiden, 1965.

Helck, Wolfgang, "Osiris," *RE*, Suppl. 9 (1962), 469-513.

Hermann, Alfred, "Die Ankunft des Nils," *ZÄS* 85 (1960), 35-42.

Hermann, Alfred, "Antinous Infelix," *Mullus: Festschrift Theodor Klauser (JAC* Ergänzungsband, 1), Münster, 1964, 155-67.

Hermann, Alfred, "Ertrinken," *RAC* 6 (1963), 375-80.

Hermann, Alfred, "Der Nil und die Christen," *JAC* 2 (1959), 30-69.

Hermann, Werner, *Römische Götteraltäre*, Kallmünz über Regensberg, 1961.

Hicks, Ruth, "Egyptian Elements in Greek Mythology," *TAPA* 93 (1962), 90-108.

Hill, Dorothy, *Catalogue of Classical Bronze Sculptures in the Walters Art Gallery*, Baltimore, 1949.

Hölbl, Günther, *Zeugnisse ägyptischer Religionsvorstellungen für Ephesus* (EPRO, 73), Leiden, 1978.

HomVermaseren = Boer, M. B. de and T. A. Edridge, ed., *Hommages à Maarten J. Vermaseren* (EPRO, 68), 3 vols., Leiden, 1978.

Honigmann, Ernst, "Nil," *RE* 17.1 (1936) 555-66.

Hopfner, Theodor, *Fontes historiae religionis aegyptiacae*, 5 vols., Bonn, 1922-24.

Hopfner, Theodor, *Plutarch über Isis und Osiris* (Monografien des Archiv Orientalni, 9), Prague, 1940.

Hopfner, Theodor, "Der Tierkult der alten Ägypter nach den griechisch-römischen Berichten und den wichtigeren Denkmälern," *Denkschr-Wien* 57 (1914), pt. 2.

Hornbostel, Wilhelm, *Sarapis: Studien zur Überlieferungsgeschichte, den Erscheinungsformen und Wandlungen der Gestalt eines Gottes* (EPRO, 32), Leiden, 1973.

Hornung, Erik, "Seth: Geschichte und Bedeutung eines ägyptischen Gottes," *Symbolon: Jahrbuch für Symbolforschung* NF 2 (1974), 49-63.

HTR = *Harvard Theological Review.*

IBIS = Leclant, Jean, *Inventaire bibliographique des Isiaca* (EPRO, 18), Leiden, 1972-

I Délos = *Inscriptions de Délos.*

IG = *Inscriptiones graecae.*

ILS = Dessau, H., ed., *Inscriptiones latinae selectae.*

JAC = *Jahrbuch für Antike und Christentum.*

Janssen, J., *Annual Egyptological Bibliography/Bibliographie égyptologique annuelle,* Leiden, 1947-

Janssen, J., "Over de Canope van Smetius," *OudhMeded* NR 29 (1948), 3-4.

JAsiat = *Journal asiatique.*

JdI = *Jahrbuch des Deutschen Archäologischen Instituts.*

JEA = *Journal of Egyptian Archaeology.*

Jéquier, Gustave, "Les nilomètres sous l'Ancien Empire," *BIFAO* 5 (1906), 63-64.

Jéquier, Gustave, *Les temples ptolémaïques et romains,* Paris, 1924.

JHS = *Journal of Hellenic Studies.*

Jong, K. H. E. de, "De Apuleio isiacorum mysteriorum texte," Diss., Leiden, 1900.

Jorio, André de, *Plan de Pompéi,* Naples, 1828.

JRS = *Journal of Roman Studies.*

JS = *Journal des savants.*

JWCI = *Journal of the Warburg and Courtauld Institute.*

Kater-Sibbes, G. J. F., *Preliminary Catalogue of Sarapis Monuments* (EPRO, 36), Leiden, 1973.

Kater-Sibbes, G. J. F. and M. J. Vermaseren, *Apis* (EPRO, 48), 3 vols., Leiden, 1975-77.

Kaufman, Carl Maria, *Gräco-ägyptische Koroplastik,* 2nd ed., Leipzig, 1915.

Kees, Hermann, "Apotheosis by Drowning," *Studies Presented to F. Ll. Griffith,* London, 1932, 402-5.

Kenner, Hedwig, "Die Götterwelt der Austria romana," *ÖJh* 43 (1958), 57-100.

Kenner, Hedwig, "Das Luterion im Kult," *ÖJh* 29 (1935), 109-54.

Klauser, Theodor, "Taufe in lebendigem Wasser," *Pisciculi: Festschrift Franz Joseph Dölger,* Münster, 1939, 157-64.

Knackfuss, Hubert, *Der Südmarkt und die benachbarten Bauanlagen* (Milet, 1.7), ed. T. Wiegand, Berlin, 1924.

Köberlein, E., *Caligula und die ägyptischen Kulte,* Meisenheim am Glan, 1962.

Kobylina, M. M. and O. J. Neverov, *Représentations des divinités orientales sur le littoral nord de la Mer Noire aux premiers siècles de notre ère* (EPRO, 52), Leiden, 1976.

Kraus, Theodor, "Archäologische Zeugnisse der alexandrinischen Kulte aus Mittel- und Oberägypten," *Christentum am Nil,* ed. K. Wessel, Recklinghausen, 1964, 95-106.

Kraus, Theodor et al., "Mons Claudianus—Mons Porphyrites: Bericht über die zweite Forschungsreise, 1964," *MDIK* 22 (1967), 108-205.

LÄ = *Lexikon der Ägyptologie,* ed. W. Helck and E. Otto, Wiesbaden, 1975-

Lafaye, Georges, *Histoire du culte des divinités d'Alexandrie hors de l'Egypte,* Paris, 1884.

Lafaye, Georges, "Isis," *DAGR* 3.577-86.

Lakatos, P., "Beiträge zur Verbreitung der ägyptischen Kulte in Pannonien," *Acta Universitatis Szegedinensis: Acta antiqua* 4 (1961), 1-31.

Leclant, Jean, "Fouilles et travaux en Egypte, 1950-51, I," *Orientalia* 20 (1951), 453-75.

Leclant, Jean, "Histoire de la diffusion des cultes égyptiens," *Problèmes et méthodes d'histoire des religions,* Paris, 1968, 87-96.

Leclant, Jean, "Notes sur la propagation des cultes et des monuments égyptiens, en Occident, à l'époque impériale," *BIFAO* 55 (1956), 173-79.

Leclant, Jean, "Osiris en Gaule," *Studia aegyptiaca* 1.263-86.

Leclant, Jean, "Les rites de purification dans le cérémonial pharonique du couronnement," *Proceedings of the XIth International Congress of the International Association for the History of Religions, Claremont, 1965,* vol. 2: *Guilt or Pollution and Rites of Purification,* Leiden, 1968, 48-51.

Lederer, P. "Ägyptisches Theoxenion des Jahres 167 auf einer bisher unbekannten Münze des Marcus Aurelius," *Deutsche Münzblätter* 56 (1936), 201-11.

Legge, F., "The Greek Worship of Serapis and Isis," *PSBA* 36 (1914), 79-99.

Lehner, H., "Orientalische Mysterienkulte," *Bonner Jahrbücher* 129 (1924), 47-50 and 76-79.

Leospo, Enrica, *La Mensa Isiaca di Torino* (EPRO, 70), Leiden, 1978.

Lepsius, Karl Richard, *Denkmäler aus Ägypten und Äthiopien,* 12 vols., Berlin, 1849-59.

Lepsius, Karl Richard, *Denkmäler aus Ägypten und Äthiopien, Text,* ed. E. Naville *et al.,* 5 vols., Leipzig, 1897-1913.

Lévy, Isidore, "Les inscriptions araméennes de Memphis et l'épigraphie funéraire de l'Egypte gréco-romaine," *JAsiat* 211 (1927), 281-310.

LF = Listy filologické.

Lindsay, Jack, *Men and Gods on the Roman Nile,* London, 1968.

Lloyd, A. B., *Herodotus, Book II* (EPRO, 43), Leiden, 1975-

Lloyd, A. B., "Perseus and Chemmis (Herodotus II 91)," *JHS* 89 (1969), 79-86.

LM = Ausführliches Lexicon der griechischen und römischen Mythologie, ed. W. Roscher, 6 vols., Leipzig, 1884-1937.

Lyons, Henry G., *Report on the Island and Temples of Philae,* London, 1896.

Magie, D., "Egyptian Deities in Asia Minor on Inscriptions and Coins," *AJA* 57 (1953), 163-87.

Makaronas, C. I., "'Ανασκαφὴ παρὰ τὸ Σαράπειον," *Makedonika* 1 (1940), 464-65.

Malaise, Michel, *Les conditions de pénétration et de diffusion des cultes égyptiens en Italie* (EPRO, 22), Leiden, 1972.

Malaise, Michel, "La diffusion des cultes égyptiens dans les provinces européennes de l'empire romain," *ANRW* 2.17.2—forthcoming.

Malaise, Michel, "Documents nouveaux et points de vue récents sur les cultes isiaques en Italie," *HomVermaseren* 2.627-717.

Malaise, Michel, *Inventaire préliminaire des documents égyptiens découverts en Italie* (EPRO, 21), Leiden, 1972.

Manganaro, G., "Richerche di epigrafia siceliota. Pt. 1: Per la storia del culto delle divinità orientali in Sicilia," *Siculorum Gymnasium* 14 (1961), 175-91.

Marcadé, J., *Au Musée de Délos: Etude sur la sculpture hellénistique en ronde bosse découverte dans l'île*, Paris, 1969.

Marin Ceballos, M. C., "La religion de Isis en las Metamorfosis de Apuleyo," *Habis* 4 (1973), 127-79.

Mau, August, *Pompeii, Its Life and Art*, 2nd ed., tr. F. Kelsey, New York, 1902.

Mazois, François and François Gau, *Les ruines de Pompéi*, 4 vols., Paris, 1824-38.

MDIK = *Mitteilungen des Deutschen Archäologischen Instituts. Abteilung Kairo.*

Medini, J., *The Egyptian Cults in Dalmatia* (EPRO), Leiden—forthcoming.

Meeks, Dimitri, "Harpokrates," *LÄ* 2.1003-11.

MélMichałowski = *Mélanges offerts à Kazimierz Michałowski*, Warsaw, 1966.

MélPiganiol = *Mélanges d'archéologie et d'histoire offerts à André Piganiol*, Paris, 1966.

Merkelbach, Reinhold, *Isisfeste in griechisch-römischer Zeit: Daten und Riten*, Meisenheim am Glan, 1963.

Merkelbach, Reinhold, "Der Isiskult in Pompeii," *Latomus* 24 (1965), 144-49.

Merkelbach, Reinhold, *Roman und Mysterien in der Antike*, Munich-Berlin, 1962.

MIE = *Mémoires présentés à l'Institut Egyptien.*

Milne, J. G., *Catalogue of Alexandrian Coins, University of Oxford, Ashmolean Museum,* Oxford, 1933. Supplement by C. M. Kraay, London, 1971.

Modrijan, Walter, *Frauenberg bei Leibnitz: Die frühgeschichtlichen Ruinen und das Heimatmuseum*, Leibnitz, 1955.

Modrijan, Walter, "Frauenberg bei Leibnitz—seit alters ein 'Heiliger Berg'," *BlHeim* 27 (1953), 56-68.

MonPiot = *Fondation Eugène Piot. Monuments et mémoires.*

Moore, C. H., "Oriental Cults in Britain," *Harvard Studies in Classical Philology* 11 (1900), 47-60.

Morenz, Siegfried, "Ägyptische Nationalreligion und sogenannte Isismission," *ZDMG* 111 (1961), 432-36.

Morenz, Siegfried, *Die Begegnung Europas mit Ägypten*, Berlin, 1968.

Morenz, Siegfried, "Die orientalische Herkunft der Perseus-Andromeda-Sage," *FF* 36 (1962), 307-9.

Morenz, Siegfried, "Zur Vergöttlichung in Ägypten," *ZÄS* 84 (1959), 132-43.

MPAI = *Monumenti della pittura antica scoperti in Italia.*

MPAIBL = *Mémoires présentés à l'Académie des Inscriptions et Belles-Lettres.*

Müller, Dieter, "Ägypten und die griechischen Isis-Aretalogien," *Abh-Leipzig* 53 (1961), pt. 1.

Müller, H. W., *Der Isiskult im antiken Benevent und Katalog der Skulpturen aus den ägyptischen Heiligtümern im Museo del Sannio zu Benevent,* Berlin, 1969.

Neroutsos-Bey, T. D., "Inscriptions grecques et latines recueilles dans la ville d'Alexandrie et aux environs," *RArch* 3.9 (1887), 198-209.

Niccolini, Fausto and Felice Niccolini, *Le case ed i monumenti di Pompei disegnati e descritti,* vol. 1, pt. 2: *Il tempio d'Iside,* Naples, 1854.

Nilsson, *GGR* = Nilsson, Martin P., *Geschichte der griechischen Religion,* 2 vols., 3rd ed., Munich, 1974.

Nilsson, Martin, *A History of Greek Religion,* 2nd ed., New York, 1964.

Nissen, Heinrich, *Pompeianische Studien zur Städtekunde des Altertums,* Leipzig, 1877.

Nock, Arthur Darby, *Conversion,* Oxford, 1961.

Nock, Arthur Darby, "Early Gentile Christianity and Its Hellenistic Background," *Essays on Religion and the Ancient World,* ed. Z. Stewart, 2 vols., Cambridge, Mass., 1972.

Ohlemutz, Erwin, *Die Kulte und Heiligtümer der Götter in Pergamon,* Würzburg, 1940.

ÖJh = *Jahreshefte des Österreichischen Archäologischen Instituts in Wien.*

Oliverio, Gaspare, "Santuario delle divinità egizie in Gortina (Creta)," *ASAtene* 2 (1916), 309-11.

Oliverio, Gaspare, "Scoperta del santuario delle divinità egizie in Gortina," *ASAtene* 1 (1914), 376-77.

OpAth = *Opuscula atheniensia.*

OrChr = *Oriens christianus.*

Otto, Walter, *Priester und Tempel im hellenistischen Ägypten,* 2 vols., Leipzig, 1905-8.

OudhMeded = *Oudheidkundige Mededelingen uit het Rijksmuseum van Oudheden te Leiden.*

Overbeck, Johannes and August Mau, *Pompeii in seinen Gebäuden, Altertümern und Kunstwerken,* 4th ed., Leipzig, 1884.

PAH = *Pompeianarum antiquitatum historia,* ed. G. Fiorelli, 3 vols., Naples, 1860-64.

Panofsky, Erwin, " '*Canopus Deus.*' The Iconography of a Nonexistent God," *GazBA* 57 (1961), 193-216.

Papadakis, N. G., "'Ἀνασχαφὴ Ἰσείου ἐν Ἐρετρίᾳ," *ArchD* 1 (1915), 115-90.

Parlasca, K., "Osiris und Osirisglaube in der Kaiserzeit," *Les syncrétismes dans les religions grecque et romaine,* Paris, 1973, 95-102.

Peek, Werner, *Griechische Vers-Inschriften,* vol. 1: *Grab-Epigramme,* Berlin, 1955.

Peek, Werner, *Der Isishymnus von Andros und verwandte Texte,* Berlin, 1930.

Perc, Bernarda, *Beiträge zur Verbreitung ägyptischen Kulte auf dem Balkan und in den Donauländern zur Römerzeit,* Munich, 1968.

Perdrizet, Paul, *Bronzes grecs d'Egypte de la Collection Fouquet,* Paris, 1911.
Perdrizet, Paul, *Les terres cuites grecques d'Egypte de la Collection Fouquet,* 2 vols., Nancy, 1921.
Pernier, Luigi, *Il tempio e l'altare di Apollo a Cirene,* Bergamo, 1935.
Pernier, Luigi and Luisa Banti, *Guida degli scavi italiani in Creta,* Rome, 1947.
Pesce, Gennaro, *Il tempio d'Iside in Sabratha,* Rome, 1953.
Petrie, W. M. Flinders, *Kahun, Gurob, and Hawara,* London, 1890.
Pfister, R., "Nil, nilomètre et l'orientalisation du paysage hellénistique," *Revue des arts asiatiques* 7 (1931-32), 121-40.
PGM = Karl Preizendanz and Albert Henrichs, eds., *Papyri graecae magicae—Die griechischen Zauberpapyri,* 2 vols., 2nd ed., Stuttgart, 1973-74.
Picard, Charles, "Les dieux de la colonie de Philippes vers le 1ᵉʳ siècle de notre ère d'apres les ex-voto rupestres," *RHR* 86 (1922), 117-201.
Pietrzykowski, Michal, "Sarapis—Agathos Daimon," *HomVermaseren* 3.959-66.
Pippidi, D. M., "Sur la diffusion des cultes égyptiens en Scythie mineure," *Studii clasice* 6 (1964), 103-18.
Poole = Poole, R. S., *Alexandria and the Nomes* (Catalogue of the Greek Coins in the British Museum, 16), London, 1892.
Popesco, D. O., "Le culte d'Isis et de Sérapis en Dacie," *Mélanges de l'Ecole Roumaine en France* 1927, 157-209.
Porter, B. and R. L. B. Moss, *Topographical Bibliography of Ancient Egyptian Hieroglyphic Texts, Reliefs, and Paintings,* 9 vols., Oxford, 1927-72.
PSBA = *Proceedings of the Society of Biblical Archaeology.*
RAC = *Reallexikon für Antike und Christentum.*
RArch = *Revue archéologique.*
RdE = *Revue d'égyptologie.*
RE = *Paulys Realencyclopädie der classischen Altertumswissenschaft.*
Reallexikon = Bonnet, Hans, *Reallexikon der ägyptischen Religionsgeschichte,* Berlin, 1952.
RecTrav = *Recueil de travaux relatifs a la philologie et a l'archéologie égyptiennes et assyriennes.*
REG = *Revue des études grecques.*
REg = *Revue égyptologique.*
Rehm, Albert, "Nilschwelle," *RE* 17.1 (1936), 571-90.
Reichel, C., *De Isidis apud Romanos cultu,* Berlin, 1849.
Reitzenstein, Richard, *Die hellenistischen Mysterienreligionen nach ihren Grundgedanken und Wirkungen,* 3rd ed., Leipzig, 1927.
RendPontAcc = *Atti della Pontificia Accademia Romana di Archeologia. Rendiconti.*
RevPhil = *Revue de philologie, de littérature et d'histoire anciennes.*
RHR = *Annales du Musée Guimet. Revue de l'histoire des religions.*
RM = *Mitteilungen des Deutschen Archäologischen Instituts. Römische Abteilung.*

Roeder, Günther, *Ägyptische Bronzefiguren* (Mitteilungen aus der Ägyptischen Sammlung, 6), Berlin, 1956.

Rohde, Erwin, *Psyche*, 2 vols., 8th ed., New York, 1966.

Rolley, Claude, "Les cultes égyptiens à Thasos: à propos de quelques documents nouveaux," *BCH* 92 (1968), 187-219.

Roullet, Anne, *The Egyptian and Egyptianizing Monuments of Imperial Rome* (EPRO, 20), Leiden, 1972.

Roussel, *CE* = Roussel, Pierre, *Les cultes égyptiens à Délos du IIIe au Ier siècle av. J.-C.,* Paris, 1916.

Roussel, Pierre, "Un nouvel hymne a Isis," *REG* 42 (1929), 137-68.

Roussel, Pierre, "Les sanctuaires égyptiens de Délos et d'Erétrie," *REg* NS 1 (1919), 81-92.

Rowe, Alan, "Discovery of the Famous Temple and Enclosure of Serapis at Alexandria," *ASAntEg*, Suppl. 2 (1946), 1-94.

Rowe, Alan, "Short Report on Excavations of the Graeco-Roman Museum Made During the Season 1942 at 'Pompey's Pillar'," *BArchAlex* 35 (1942), 124-61.

Rowe, Alan and B. R. Rees, "A Contribution to the Archaeology of the Western Desert: IV. The Great Serapeum of Alexandria," *BJRL* 39 (1956-57), 485-520.

Rusch, A., *De Serapide et Iside in Graecia cultis*, Berlin, 1906.

Salač, Antonin, *Isis, Sarapis a božstva sdružená dle svědectví řeckých a latinských nápisů*, Prague, 1915.

Salditt-Trappmann, Regina, *Tempel der ägyptischen Götter in Griechenland und an der Westküste Kleinasiens* (EPRO, 15), Leiden, 1970.

el-Samman, Achmed, Ἀι αἰγυπτιακαὶ λατρεῖαι ἐν Ἑλλάδι, Athens, 1965.

Sauneron, Nadia, *Temples ptolémaïques et romains d'Egypte: études et publications parues entre 1939 et 1954—répertoire bibliographique*, Cairo, 1956.

Sauneron, Serge, "Le Nil et la pluie," *BIFAO* 51 (1952), 41-48.

SBBerlin = *Sitzungsberichte der Akademie der Wissenschaften zu Berlin. Phil.-hist. Klasse.*

SBHeidelberg = *Sitzungsberichte der Heidelberger Akademie der Wissenschaften. Phil.-hist. Klasse.*

SCE = Einar Gjerstad *et al., The Swedish Cyprus Expedition: Finds and Results of the Excavations in Cyprus, 1927-31,* 4 vols., Stockholm, 1934-56.

Schaaffhausen, H., "Über den römischen Isis-Dienst am Rhein," *Bonner Jahrbücher* 76 (1883), 31-62.

Schauenburg, Konrad, *Perseus in der Kunst des Altertums*, Bonn, 1960.

Schede, Martin, "Isisprozession," *Angelos* 2 (1926), 60-61.

Schmidt, V., *Choix de monuments égyptiens, Ny Carlsberg Glyptothek*, Brussels, 1910.

Schmidt, V., *De graesk-aegyptiske Terrakotter i Ny Carlsberg Glyptothek,* Copenhagen, 1911.

Schneider, H. D., "Osiris-Canope from the Time of Hadrian," *BABesch* 50 (1975), 8-9.

Schwartz, J., "Le Nil et le ravitaillement de Rome," *BIFAO* 47 (1948), 179-200.

Schweditsch, Elizabeth, "Die Umwandlung ägyptischer Glaubensvorstellungen auf ihrem Weg an die Donau—ihre Kenntnis in Rhaetien, Noricum, und Pannonien," Diss., Graz, 1951.

Selem, Petar, "Egipatski bogovi u rimskom Iliriku," *Godisnjak: Akademija Nauka i Umjetnosti Bosne i Hercegovine* 9 (1972), 5-104.

Selem, Petar, *Les religions orientales dans la Pannonie romaine* (EPRO), Leiden—forthcoming.

Sfameni Gasparro, Giulia, *I culti orientali in Sicilia* (EPRO, 31), Leiden, 1973.

SIG = Dittenberger, W., ed., *Sylloge inscriptionum graecarum.*

Simpson, William, ed., *The Literature of Ancient Egypt,* New Haven, 1973.

SIRIS = Vidman, Ladislav, *Sylloge inscriptionum religionis isiacae et sarapiacae,* Berlin, 1969.

Smith, Dennis, "The Egyptian Cults at Corinth," *HTR* 70 (1977) 201-31.

Solmsen, Friederich, *Isis among the Greeks and Romans,* Cambridge, Mass., 1980.

Sourdille, Camille, *Hérodote et la religion de l'Egypte,* Paris, 1910.

Squarciapino, Maria Floriani, *I culti orientali ad Ostia* (EPRO, 3), Leiden, 1962.

Stillwell, Richard, ed., *Princeton Encyclopedia of Classical Sites,* Princeton, NJ, 1976.

Stricker, B. H., "Een egyptisch cultusbeeld uit de Grieks-Romeinse tijd," *OudhMeded* 24 (1943), 1-10.

Stricker, B. H., *De overstroming van de Nijl* (Ex oriente lux, 11), Leiden, 1956.

Studia aegyptiaca = L. Kákosy, ed., *Studia aegyptiaca: Recueil d'études dédiées à Vilmos Wessetzky à l'occasion de son 65e anniversaire,* 3 vols., Budapest, 1974-77.

Susini, Giancarlo, "I culti orientali nella Cispadana," *HomVermaseren* 3.1199-1216.

TAPA = *Transactions of the American Philological Association.*

Taylor, Lily Ross, *The Cults of Ostia,* Bryn Mawr, PA, 1912.

Todorov, J., *Paganizmat v Dolna Mizija—The Pagan Cults in Moesia Inferior,* Sofia, 1928.

Toussoun, Omar, *Mémoire sur l'histoire du Nil* (*MIE*, 8-9), 2 vols., Cairo, 1925.

Toutain, J., *Les cultes païens dans l'empire romain,* Pt. 1: *Les provinces latines,* vol. 2, Paris, 1911.

Tran Tam Tinh, *Culte/Campanie* = Tran Tam Tinh, Vincent, *Le culte des divinités orientales en Campanie* (EPRO, 27), Leiden, 1972.

Tran Tam Tinh, *Culte des divinités* = Tran Tam Tinh, Vincent, *Le culte des divinités orientales à Herculanum* (EPRO, 17), Leiden, 1971.

Tran Tam Tinh, Vincent, *Essai sur le culte d'Isis à Pompéi*, Paris, 1964.
Tran Tam Tinh, Vincent and Y. Labrecque, *Isis lactans* (EPRO, 37), Leiden, 1973.
Tschudin, Peter, *Isis in Rom*, Aarau, 1962.
Vallois, René, *L'architecture hellénique et hellénistique à Délos*, vol. 1: *Les monuments*, Paris, 1944.
Vandier, J., *La religion égyptienne*, Paris, 1949.
Velde, Herman te, *Seth, God of Confusion*, Leiden, 1967.
Velkov, Velizar, "Zum Kult der ägyptischen Gottheiten in Mesambria Pontica (2.-1. Jh.)," *HomVermaseren* 3.1293-95.
Vidman, Ladislav, *Isis und Sarapis bei den Griechen und Römern*, Berlin, 1970.
Vidman, Ladislav, "Die Isis- und Sarapisverehrung im 3. Jahrhundert u.Z.," *Neue Beiträge zur Geschichte der Alten Welt*, vol. 2: *Römisches Reich*, Berlin, 1965, 389-400.
Vidman, Ladislav, "Navarchos im Isiskult," *LF* 89 (1966), 270-77.
Vidman, SIRIS = Vidman, Ladislav, *Sylloge inscriptionum religionis isiacae et sarapiacae*, Berlin, 1969.
Vidman, Ladislav, "Träger des Isis- und Sarapiskultes in den römischen Provinzen," *Eirene* 5 (1966), 107-16.
Visser, C. E., *Götter und Kulte im ptolemäischen Alexandrien*, Amsterdam, 1938.
Vogliano, Achille, *Primo rapporto degli scavi condotti dalla Missione Archeologica d'Egitto della R. Università di Milano nella zona di Madinet Madi*, Milan, 1936.
Vogliano, Achille, *Secondo rapporto degli scavi condotti dalla Missione Archeologica d'Egitto della R. Università di Milano nella zona di Madinet Madi*, Milan, 1937.
Vogt, J., *Die alexandrinischen Münzen*, 2 vols., Stuttgart, 1924.
Vogt, J., *Terrakotten* (Expedition Ernst von Sieglin: Ausgrabungen in Alexandrie, 2.2), Leipzig, 1924.
Vollgraff, Wilhelm, "Fouilles et sondages sur le flanc oriental de la Larissa à Argos," *BCH* 82 (1958), 516-70.
Wace, A. J. B., "Greek Inscriptions from the Serapeum," *BullFarU* 2 (1944), 17-26.
Wagner, Günter, *Pauline Baptism and the Pagan Mysteries*, Edinburgh, 1967.
Wainwright, G. A., "Some Celestial Associations of Min," *JEA* 21 (1935), 152-70.
Weber, Wilhelm, *Aegyptisch-griechische Götter im Hellenismus*, Groningen, 1912.
Weber, Wilhelm, *Die ägyptisch-griechischen Terrakotten* (Mitteilungen aus der Ägyptischen Sammlung, 2), 2 vols., Berlin, 1914.
Weber, Wilhelm, *Drei Untersuchungen zur ägyptisch-griechischen Religion*, Heidelberg, 1911.
Weinreich, Otto, *Neue Urkunden zur Sarapis-Religion*, Tübingen, 1919.
Wessetzky, Vilmos, *Die ägyptischen Kulte zur Römerzeit in Ungarn* (EPRO, 1), Leiden, 1961.

Wessetzky, Vilmos, "Die Probleme des Isis-Kultes in Ober-Pannonien," *ActaArch* 11 (1959), 265-82.

Westholm, Alfred, *The Temples of Soli*, Stockholm, 1936.

Wijngaarden, W. D. van, "De grieks-egyptische Terracotta's in het Rijksmuseum van Oudheden," *OudhMeded* NS 39 (1958), Suppl.

Wild, Robert, "The Known Isis-Sarapis Sanctuaries of the Roman Period," *ANRW* 2.17.2—forthcoming.

Wilson, John A., *The Culture of Ancient Egypt*, Chicago, 1951.

Witt, R. E., "The Egyptian Cults in Ancient Macedonia," *Ancient Macedonia*, ed. B. Laourdas and C. Makaronas, Thessalonica, 1970, 324-33.

Witt, R. E., *Isis in the Graeco-Roman World*, Ithaca, NY, 1971.

Wittmann, W., *Das Isisbuch des Apuleius*, Stuttgart, 1938.

Woodward, Jocelyn, *Perseus, a Study of Greek Art and Legend*, Cambridge, Eng., 1937.

ZÄS = *Zeitschrift für ägyptische Sprache und Altertumskunde.*

ZDMG = *Zeitschrift der Deutschen Morgenländischen Gesellschaft.*

Zotović, L., *Les cultes orientales sur le territoire de la Mésie supérieure* (EPRO, 7), Leiden, 1966.

ZPE = *Zeitschrift für Papyrologie und Epigraphik.*

INTRODUCTION

The last twenty-five years of scholarly work on the Graeco-Roman cult of Isis and Sarapis have been marked by a renewed interest in the study of the archaeological data. Spearheaded by the editor and writers of the *Etudes préliminaires* series, numerous investigators have been collecting, cataloguing, and studying this type of information[1] just as their predecessors in the nineteenth and early twentieth centuries were once so concerned to do.[2] Much of this work continues to be linked with efforts to determine where and how this cult spread. However, a smaller group of scholars has begun to utilize this material more extensively in order to understand better the religious practices and perspectives of those who took part in Isis-Sarapis worship.[3] To be sure, not all archaeological data is of equal value. Pierre Roussel long ago stressed the importance of studying "assemblages of monumental evidence from actual sanctuary sites,"[4] and more recently Jean Leclant urged investigators to seek out "coherent ensembles" of material remains.[5] Of limited use is evidence of unknown temporal and/or geographical derivation.

Scholars have long recognized that water played an important role in the rituals of this cult but have been less certain how it was utilized. In order to answer more precisely this latter question, I undertook a study of the various permanent water facilities found at the fifty or so known sanctuaries.[6] As indices for studying the internal life of the cult these installations proved to be of considerable value. Not only did they appear to have a significant function within the cult but they had a far better chance of surviving the vicissitudes of time than most other monumental evidence. This is true because very often these facilities were situated below ground level or were supplied by buried pipes or were emptied by surface or sub-surface drains. If just a few of these features survive on a site, it often becomes possible to reconstruct the appearance of the original water installation. On the other hand, when such a sanctuary site has been reasonably well excavated and no evidence for such facilities has been encountered, there is a high probability that the site never had them. Consequently, from an investigation of such structures we can expect reasonably controlled results.

For help in interpreting these water facilities I investigated not only all pertinent literary and epigraphical evidence but also several groupings of archaeological small finds which had an apparent link with the water rituals of the cult. These groups of materials are particularly important because they can be linked with assurance to actual known sanctuaries and because a significant number of member objects in each group can be situated in definite temporal, geographical, and cultic contexts.

My purpose in undertaking this study was two-fold: first, to determine as far as possible both what participants in the cult did with water in their rituals and how they understood such practices and, secondly, to see what light this entire body of data might shed on the question of the overall development of Isis-Sarapis worship.

With regard to the first of these concerns, it may prove helpful to the reader if I indicate at the outset the various theses I will be advancing in the chapters to follow:

1. The surviving cultic water facilities are all either containers for the sacred Nile water or basins for ablutions.

2. The nine or more known fixed containers for Nile water are typologically distinctive and were designed to allow for a symbolic re-enactment of the Nile flood.

3. With only one exception, the fixed Nile water containers built in Hellenistic times were designed in imitation of the Nilometers found in many parts of Ptolemaic Egypt. I believe it possible that the inspiration for converting this measuring device to more purely religious purposes first occurred at the Serapeum of Alexandria.

4. Sanctuaries of Isis and Sarapis built in Roman times show no evidence for the Nilometer-type crypts typical of the Hellenistic era and, for that matter, rarely afford evidence for any sort of fixed structure to contain Nile water.

5. The long-spouted pitcher commonly believed to have been used everywhere during the Imperial period for containing Nile water is instead restricted to a limited group of sanctuaries chiefly located in northern Egypt and central Italy. The Osiris Hydreios (Canopus) statue and the Osiris ''Cool

Water'' inscriptions share the same regional and temporal distribution and are related in function and significance to the cultic pitcher.

6. Various myths and images were utilized to expound the significance of the Nile water rituals. Well-attested examples of such myths are "The Finding of Osiris" and "The Rescue of Andromeda by Perseus."

7. Devotees of Isis and Sarapis most typically valued Nile water as a sign of the prosperity, fertility, and familial well-being offered them in this life by their gods. Only in that segment of the cult which made use of the pitcher and the other related Osiris materials is there clear evidence that people associated this water with hopes of life beyond the grave.

8. Ideological influences from Egypt are a key causal factor for the shifts in ritual practice related to Nile water which are observable beginning in early Imperial times. Whereas Hellenistic cultic observance tended to stress the power of the Egyptian gods in creating the Nile flood, liturgical practice in Roman times more often focussed on the presence of the god—normally Osiris—in the sacred substance.

9. Besides the "sprinkling basins" (περιρραντήρια) found at most Graeco-Roman sanctuaries, many precincts of Isis and Sarapis also had an ablution basin of special design for the purification of the clergy. An important part of all ablution rituals within this cult was the purification of the head.

As is apparent, in constructing these theses I have not limited myself to evidence from outside of Egypt. This practice, regularly adhered to since the time of Georges Lafaye,[7] is simply not valid.[8] Not only Alexandria (which usually does receive some attention) but also a variety of other sites in Egypt show configurations of data that can only belong to the Graeco-Roman cult.[9] Such sanctuaries differ sharply in architectural form, in iconography, and in the grouping of associated divinities from the "traditional" Egyptian sanctuaries of Isis built in Pharaonic, Ptolemaic, and Roman times.[10] Not that there is a total discontinuity between the two groups of sites. Many Greek-speakers made pilgrimages to Philae and to lesser known shrines such as Koptos, Maharaqah, and Qasr Dush and left in their inscriptions and graffiti a memorial of their presence. Nonetheless, two quite different configurations of material remains are found, and the clarity of this distinction allows me to include the Graeco-Roman sites and related remains and to exclude, except for purposes of comparison, the "traditional" sites.

The positions taken in my various theses have implications for scholarly efforts to reconstruct the various "phases of evolution"[11] through which this cult passed. The most important recent effort to present an overall description of its development is that of Ladislav Vidman. In his *Isis und Sarapis bei den Griechen und Römern* (1970) he argued that there were four major developmental stages. A purely Egyptian cult (1) was gradually modified (2) by an *interpretatio graeca*. In this second phase the various groups of Isis-Sarapis worshippers adopted the practices of Greek cult associations and rotated their priesthoods on an annual basis. In general, this phase presents itself as *strongly Hellenized*.[12] The rise of national feeling experienced in Ptolemaic Egypt after the Battle of Raphia (217 BC) affected finally the form of the cult which spread to Italy and the West. Although Vidman refers to this phase of development (3) as an *interpretatio romana*, what principally characterized it is a much stronger emphasis on purely Egyptian or Graeco-Egyptian elements. Vidman dates this set of developments to the first and especially the second century AD.[13] Characteristic of this third phase were colleges of priests who, like their colleagues in Egypt, had their heads shaven. These priests were not normally state officials. In addition, practices such as the daily washing and dressing of the cult statues, the celebration of the *Navigium Isidis* festival, the appointment of navarchs, and the wearing of "Horus-locks" by young boys were adopted. The emergence of a new titulature for Sarapis is also attested.[14] A final phase (4) continued this Egyptianizing tendency but also manifested a wide-spread syncretism with other cults. Emperors such as Commodus, Septimius Severus, and Caracalla were actively involved in the affairs of the cult during this last period, the late second and the third century.[15]

The principal evolutionary moment noted by Vidman and the one upon which he lavishes the most attention is the shift from the *interpretatio graeca* phase to that of the *interpretatio romana*. This transition he situates in the first century AD and observes that in the middle of this century a notable upsurge of devotion begins.[16] My own more specialized investigations support the hypothesis that this was indeed a crucial moment in the historical development of Isis-Sarapis worship. In this study, as I indicated in Thesis 8, I am arguing that the cultic water facilities and practices of the Hellenistic sanctuaries and those attested at Roman period sites differed significantly from one another. In my judgment, however, Vidman's own model for this development, a simple transition from one thing to another, from *interpretatio graeca* to *interpretatio romana*, is too simplistic. The results of my research point to a series of more complex developments. These begin to emerge at the very end of the first century BC and are readily observable in the following century.

There are several indicators beyond those cited by Vidman which support the hypothesis that in this period the cult was undergoing a major transformation. One of these is the construction of new sanctuaries. A survey of all the known Graeco-Roman sites as to the date of their foundation produces the following figures:[17]

3rd cen. BC—7	2nd cen. AD —22
2nd cen. BC—5	3rd cen. AD — 1
1st cen. BC—4	Unknown — 4
1st cen. AD—4	Doubtful sites — 6

The significantly larger number of sanctuaries from the second century AD—many from the reigns of Trajan and Hadrian—is indeed striking and cannot easily be explained away by appealing to factors such as the chance character of archaeological discoveries. These new sanctuaries, which in number represent a quantum increase over those known to have been constructed in the previous century, did not spring forth, as it were, full-panoplied from the brow of Zeus. As large scale projects requiring in the normal course of events the cooperation and involvement of fairly large numbers of people, they must represent the culmination of a religious movement rather than its incipience. Surely the preceding period of gestation must have extended well back into the first century.

Pausanias' guidebook for visitors to mainland Greece provides in its multitude of references to the various temples and shrines seen by the author (late second century AD) some further corroboration,

at least on a limited scale, for the popularity of Isis-Sarapis worship
during this period. Pausanias recorded no fewer than 19 sites
dedicated either to Sarapis or to Isis or to both together.[18] While
such a figure hardly compares with the number of sanctuaries
belonging to such gods as Artemis, Athena, Demeter, Dionysus,
Hera, and Zeus (in each case 50 or more sites) and is only about
half the number of those dedicated to Asclepius (45) and to
Poseidon (35), it sets the Egyptian divinities ahead of a number of
indigenous Greek gods and heroes and far out in front of any other
of the "oriental divinities." For example, Pausanias mentions only
14 precincts of Heracles,[19] 9 of the Dioscuri, 2 of the Cabiri, 2 of
Attis, 2 of the Syrian Goddess, and none at all of Mithra. As a
somewhat romantic tourist and antiquarian, Pausanias probably
was not much inclined to hunt out "store-front" shrines of exotic
gods in the poorer sections of various Greek towns. Rather, he
appears much more interested in cataloguing the architecturally
noteworthy centers of the more established cults. While as a result
the picture he then offers may not reflect with full accuracy the
degree of penetration actually achieved by these foreign cults, it
does provide some assurance that Isis-Sarapis worship enjoyed not
only a fair degree of popularity during this century but also a certain social status and respectability.

Votive inscriptions provide still another measuring device, if only
a somewhat crude instrument, for assessing popular interest in the
various deities worshipped in the Graeco-Roman world. I made an
examination not only of the eight hundred or so texts found in
SIRIS but also of the recently published body of inscriptions from
Thessalonica[20] and the multitude of texts found on Delos[21] to see if
a similar pattern as that for the sanctuaries would emerge. A great
many factors intervene both in the creation and in the subsequent
preservation through the centuries of such inscriptions. Economic
vicissitudes, political turmoil, local needs for building stone or even
for lime, etc., etc., all contribute to render one site rich in votive
texts and another barren. Consequently, in the following table it is
not the number of known Isis-Sarapis inscriptions for a given century that is important but the ratio of difference between one century and another. For those inscriptions which can only be dated
within a two hundred year period, I have adopted the expedient of

assuming that half of each group actually derived from one of the two centuries in question, half from the other. The following set of figures results:[22]

4th cen. BC —   2
3rd cen. BC — 68 (Delos: 19)
2nd cen. BC —269 (Delos: 164)
1st cen. BC —113 (Delos: 34)
1st cen. AD — 72
2nd cen. AD —189
3rd cen. AD —123
4th cen. AD —   9
Unknown date —295 (Delos: 31)

The relative mass of data for the second century BC and the second century AD suggests that religious interest in Isis and Sarapis may well have peaked at those periods. On the other hand, the reduced volume of votive texts from the first century AD and especially the first century BC provides some indication that this era marked a period of decline for the cult. Some explanation is surely required for the fact that then in the second century AD large numbers of people were moved to inscribe their vows and prayers to these gods and even to build numerous new sanctuaries. It is possible, of course, that these individuals simply turned to a traditional cult which had survived more or less intact through Hellenistic times. Yet the outburst of religious enthusiasm which the above statistics would seem to indicate suggests that not only a changing public mood but also internal developments within the cult during the previous decades led to a revival of popular interest. The present study is in part an effort to verify the presence of such new developments.

CHAPTER ONE

OVERVIEW OF THE EVIDENCE

Twenty-seven sanctuaries of Isis and Sarapis or almost sixty percent of all those known reveal evidence of some sort for the presence
of permanent water facilities. The table below lists all of the known
sites (see also Map) and indicates which of these possibly or certainly had water facilities which were utilized in the rituals of the cult.
Each sanctuary is listed under the name of the principal divinity or
divinities to which it was dedicated. A line separates those cult
centers of Hellenistic origin (above) from those of the Roman
period:[1]

SARAPIS	SARAPIS & ISIS	ISIS	ISIS & SARAPIS
Alexandria	*Eretria*	*Ephesus:*	Ampurias (?)
Delos A	Priene	State Agora (?)	Argos (?)
Delos B	Thera	*Pompeii*	*Gortyn*
Delos C	*Thessalonica*	Soli: Temple D	
Sabratha:			
Forum (?)			
Tauromenium			
Antinoopolis	*Sabratha:*	Aquileia (?)	* Cyrene:
Carthage	*East End*	Cyme	Acropolis (?)
Corinth:		Cyrene:	Philippi
South Stoa		Apollo Precinct	Rome:
Leptis Magna		Faesulae (?)	Regio III (?)
Luxor		*Frauenberg* (?)	
* Miletus		Industria (?)	
Mons Claudianus		Lambaesis (?)	
* Mons Por-		* Mons Por-	
phyrites:		phyrites:	
Serapeum		East Iseum	
* Ostia		*Pergamum*	
Thysdrus (?)		Ras el Soda	

<u>Timgad</u>   = Rome:
Virunum (?)   Campus
York   Martius
                          = Rome:
                            Santa Sabina
                        *   Savaria
                            <u>Soli: Temple E</u>

CODE: Italics   Cultic water facility probably or certainly present
         Underlined   Cultic water facility possibly present—status to be determined
            =   No cultic water facility yet discovered; evidence present for the
                      ritual use of water
            *   Site almost certainly did not have a permanent cultic water facility
           (?)   On the basis of available evidence possibly an Isis-Sarapis sanctuary

If a site had been incompletely excavated or inadequately reported, there necessarily remains some doubt as to whether the sanctuary in question had a water installation for its ritual needs or not. In the table I have tried to be fairly cautious in indicating the sanctuaries which lacked such facilities. Beyond those sites marked with an asterisk, three other sites, Mons Claudianus; Rome: Santa Sabina; and Sabratha: Forum, are strong candidates for inclusion among this group. In these cases, however, the condition of the extant remains renders a definitive judgment impossible.

This sub-grouping is larger yet, for additional sites can be added to the list of those lacking fixed cultic water facilities. In the table I have designated fourteen sanctuaries as certainly or almost certainly having such installations. The evidence supporting this will be set forth in the chapters to follow and the reader can make a judgment on that basis. At this point I wish to consider the more questionable cases, the sites I have underscored. All of these sanctuaries show evidence for some sort of water facility, and in many cases this evidence has led investigators to conclude that such a structure served *cultic* purposes. While this is true in some cases, in the majority of instances it is not. What follows is, therefore, an effort to clarify these more problematic situations and to produce a final list of those sites which had water facilities which were utilized for the ritual activities of the cult.

The Questionable Sites

There is a natural tendency among investigators to connect any water facility which is situated in the vicinity of an Isis-Sarapis sanctuary with the liturgical observances of that cult. For example, containers for water found in the neighborhood of the sanctuary of Isis at Ras el Soda, a town very close to Alexandria, were interpreted by their discoverer in this fashion. Here Adriani uncovered a series of rooms just to the east of the temple (Fig. 1). He described them as follows:

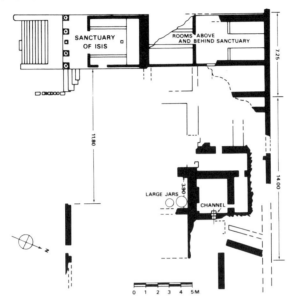

Fig. 1. The Iseum at Ras el Soda, Egypt.
Ground plan of sanctuary and adjoining areas.

Il s'agit de petites pièces qui étaient en si mauvais état de conservation qu'une description détaillée en serait impossible et inutile. On peut cependant affirmer que nous avions ici des annexes du petit sanctuaire. Dans une pièce on a reconnu les restes d'un canal, dans une autre deux grands vases en terre cuite ordinaire, destinés probablement à être remplis d'eau.[2]

It is regrettable that Adriani deemed the task of providing a detailed description as "impossible and useless," since no other information on this site is available anywhere else. Presumably, if the logic of his presentation is a proper guide, he concluded from the presence of the water facilities that these rooms formed an annex to the temple. Yet large pottery vessels for storage have not been found at any other Isis-Sarapis site, and the water channel or drain has not been described well enough to allow any certain conclusions to be drawn. It may have served, as at Eretria,[3] to drain off waste water from a room used for ablution rites but it may just as well have served some secular function. Given the fact that these structures are situated about twenty meters from the entrance to the temple, I think the latter possibility much the more likely.

In front of the small Serapeum at Luxor was found "un bassin de briques cuites, profond d'un mètre environ. Près de là a été ramassée une stèle de Tibère" (Fig. 2).[4] Perhaps the stele from the reign of Tiberius had something to do with this structure, perhaps not—I have seen no mention of its publication. The basin served either the needs of the temple, perhaps as a facility at which to perform an ablution rite before entering, or else the needs of pilgrims on the sacred way from Luxor to Karnak which passed in front of this building. Without more information than we presently possess, a firm conclusion one way or the other is difficult to obtain. For the present the matter can be left undecided; later, in the course of my

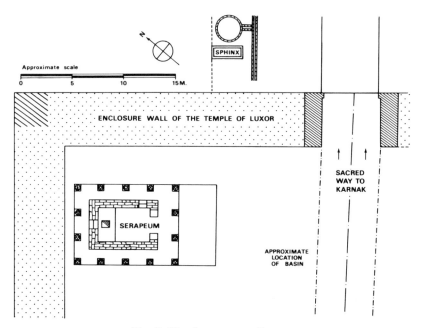

Fig. 2. The Serapeum at Luxor.
Ground plan of the sanctuary and surrounding area.

formal analysis of the ablution facilities (Ch. VII), I will investigate
the matter further.

At Timgad a temple to Sarapis is one of a group of three temples,
all facing north, which share a mammoth common precinct.[5] The
central building, dedicated to the Dea Africa, has in front of it a
spring, the *Aqua Septimiana Felix*, which seems to have had healing
powers and was probably the focal point of the entire complex. The
Sarapis temple lay just to the southeast of this spring. Perhaps this
god found a place within the precinct because of his reputation as a
healing deity. However, whether the spring served the cultic needs
of his temple or whether the temple had its own water facilities or
even whether water was a regular requirement for its cult remains
quite uncertain at present.

In the eighteen-nineties F. Hiller von Gaertringen and his
assistants excavated the sanctuary of Sarapis and Isis at Thera and
just outside of it near its north corner found two large cisterns (Fig.
3). Close to the northwest wall, the wall along which the cult statues
were possibly placed, is a cistern which measures c. 3.8 × 1.0 m.
The second tank, larger and more irregularly shaped, measures
c. 4.0 × 1.5 m;[6] it is located close to the northeast wall. Leading up
from this side of the precinct somewhat in the direction of the larger
cistern is a stairway cut into the natural rock of the mountain slope.
The location of these stairs led the excavators to conclude that
"ohne Frage" the sacred water for the cult was drawn from these
two reservoirs.[7] This theory presents some problems. Since cisterns
are found in great quantity all over Thera,[8] to establish a connec-

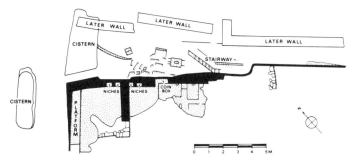

Fig. 3. Sanctuary of Sarapis and Isis at Thera.
Ground plan.

tion between one or more of them and the sanctuary, something more is needed than mere spatial proximity. In addition, the excavators failed to notice that the larger cistern, i.e., the reservoir closest to the staircase, clearly had been dug before the construction of the sanctuary and at best can only have been re-used for cultic purposes. For, as the builders of the shrine cut away the rock from the slope of the hill to form the northeast wall, they found it necessary to curve this wall inwards c. 0.30 m at its north end. The reason seems evident: if the wall had been continued in a straight line it would have come close to cutting into one corner of the large cistern. By curving the wall inwards, the builders kept at least 0.50 m of rock separating the cistern from the sanctuary. More would have to be known about the depth of the cistern, the state of the natural rock at that point, etc., to determine whether even this thickness would have allowed the tank to be filled without endangering the sanctuary through collapse of the wall, seepage, etc. If this, the cistern closest to the staircase and to the sanctuary, was constructed earlier and therefore for some secular purpose, it need not have been taken over by the devotees of the Egyptian gods for their own needs. Perhaps both it and the smaller cistern had simply been abandoned. Clearly not enough evidence is at hand to allow the conclusion that the Thera precinct had or needed permanent water facilities.[9]

Despite Dunand's belief that the cistern found to the south of the sanctuary of the Egyptian gods at Argos is a part of that complex and that it supplies further proof for the identification of the site,[10] no real evidence exists to support such conclusions. Indeed, the cistern was not discovered until seven years after the original excavation.[11] At Thera there was at least a stairway leading in the general direction of the cisterns but here there is nothing. Since cisterns are common enough in the dry Mediterranean climate of Argos and were used for all sorts of purposes, I conclude that the supporting data is too meager to permit the inclusion of Argos in the table of sites with permanent water facilities.

The earlier of the two sanctuaries at Soli, so-called Temple D, is apparently an Iseum and was built at approximately the same time as an adjoining temple to Aphrodite (Fig. 4).[12] Westholm examined the description of Soli provided by Strabo (14.6.3), noted that in the

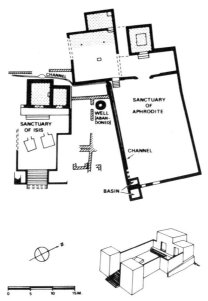

Fig. 4. Late Hellenistic Sanctuary of Isis at Soli ("Temple D")
and adjoining Sanctuary of Aphrodite.
Ground plan (above) and reconstructed sketch of Iseum (below).

late first century BC this ancient investigator had made mention of
the presence of a joint precinct of Aphrodite and Isis (ἱερὸν Ἀφροδίτης
καὶ Ἴσιδος) to the west of the town, and drew the conclusion that he
had indeed uncovered this very precinct.[13] There is no reason to
believe that this assessment was incorrect.[14] Between the Iseum and
the temple of Aphrodite runs a channel which carried water to two
large interconnected basins at the southeast corner of the latter
building (Fig. 4).[15] These basins are arranged in peculiar fashion.
One of them is inside the precinct wall of the Aphrodite sanctuary
while the other is outside the wall and close to the northeast corner
of Temple D. If Temple D and the Aphrodite sanctuary actually
shared a common precinct, perhaps the builders were content to
construct a single water channel to fill the inner basin for the needs
of the worshippers of Aphrodite and the outer for those frequenting
the Iseum. The same arrangements may have prevailed when the
new Iseum (Temple E) was constructed on the site of the old in the
second century AD (Fig. 5). However, because this second sanctuary was more elaborate and because it is not clear that it con-

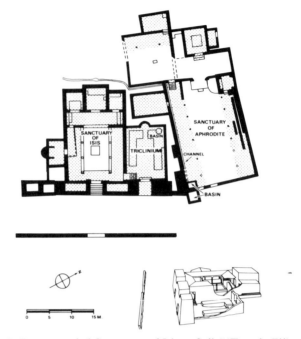

Fig. 5. Roman-period Sanctuary of Isis at Soli ("Temple E")
and adjoining Sanctuary of Aphrodite.
Ground plan (above) and reconstructed sketch of Iseum (below).

tinued to enjoy such a harmonious relationship with its next-door neighbor, I am more hesitant to believe that the outer basin served its cultic needs. Perhaps it did. Yet, since there had been a break in continuity of almost a century between the older Iseum and its replacement, it is surprising that the builders of the new edifice did not construct their own channel and basin if they needed water for the cult. That they constructed no such installation is quite certain.

Westholm also discovered a much older well (Fig. 4) in the open area between the Aphrodite precinct and Temple D.[16] In antiquity the well shaft had been closed off with a square stone block and the area above it covered over with soil and debris.[17] Since the pottery fragments found in this layer of fill belong only to the earliest types in the Soli pottery sequence,[18] this well probably had been abandoned even before Temple D was built.

The remaining sites to be considered all reveal clear evidence for some sort of water facility within their confines. In each case, however, questions arise concerning its precise nature and function. The sanctuary at Cyme provides an example of this. Here the major problem is the virtual absence of published reports. Soon after Salač carried out his excavations even the very location of the sanctuary became covered over and was obliterated. Later searches were unable to locate it. Fortunately, P. Knoblauch has recently gained access to Salač's papers and has promised to disseminate some of this information.[19] In the short account that we presently possess it is stated that in front of the sanctuary the excavators located "une vaste citerne creusée dans le roc, recouverte d'un enduit épais, et un distributeur d'eau avec des tuyaux d'argile conduisait l'eau dans toutes les directions."[20] No more than this is known, and the only published plan of the site is too small to be of any help.[21] The cistern *may* appear in the extreme foreground of an illustration in Salač's summary report.[22] If so, it lies directly in front of the temple. As for the system of pipes, if what Salač found was truly a system which brought water to various localities from a central source, he discovered something seen at no other Isis-Sarapis sanctuary. Perhaps, as at the Sabratha sanctuary,[23] what he actually uncovered is a water *collection* system with its network of pipes serving to channel rainwater from either the roofs or the courtyard floor into a central tank. If the cistern mentioned was fed by a system of pipes and if it is located right in front of the main temple, it may very well have served certain cultic needs of this precinct.

In the southwest corner of the precinct at Industria (Fig. 6), a site located near modern Turin, archaeologists discovered a circular well which has an outside diameter of 2.50 m.[24] After the fill had been removed, fill which included thin polychrome marble fragments, small pieces of various statues, and three coins from the era of Constantine, the excavators discovered water at a depth of 7.10 m below the ground level of the ancient sanctuary. They offered the view that this well had once supplied water for various ablution rites, including those related to initiation.[25] For several reasons I believe that this facility served a more mundane role. To begin with, the well existed before the construction of the sanctuary in the second century AD.[26] Even after this, it was at first situated outside the precinct but next to rooms identified by the ar-

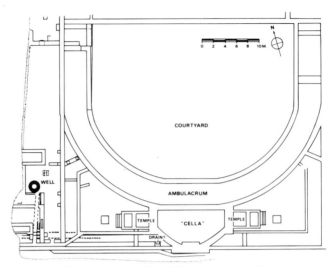

Fig. 6. The Sanctuary of Isis (?) at Industria. Ground plan.

chaeologists as quarters for the priests. Only at a later date was this area connected by walls to the sanctuary proper.[27] Even then the well still remained almost twenty meters from the central cella. While this facility may have supplied water for rituals in the temple, it is much easier to suppose that it served the daily needs of the priests and did not have a primarily sacral purpose.[28]

A series of sanctuaries have drains which may once have been connected to some sort of cultic apparatus. In two cases I believe this was the case but in two others the evidence is dubious at best. Least compelling of all are the finds from Ampurias (Fig. 7). Here a water channel extends around at least three sides of the portico which surrounds the courtyard.[29] The western portion of this drain is entirely preserved where it passes under the cella area of the temple. However, nothing was found that linked it to any facilities within the temple, and Puig y Cadafalch believed that such an arrangement indicated only that the temple was constructed somewhat later than the portico.[30] On the south side a drain leads from the main channel toward the outer wall of the sanctuary. Despite the unusual arrangement with respect to the central temple, this channel appears to be nothing more than an ordinary drain of the type found along the floor on the open side of almost every portico structure.

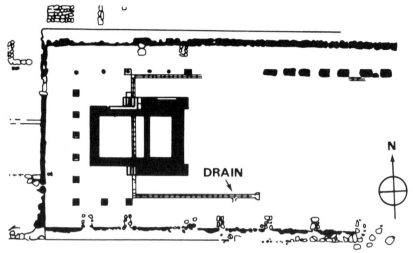

Fig. 7. The Sanctuary of Isis and Sarapis (?) at Ampurias (Emporion).

At Philippi the evidence is no more promising. On the north end of the raised terrace which supports the five temple cellae the excavators discovered a large room with entrances on the south and east sides (Fig. 8). The south door leads directly out into the cellae area while the east door opens onto a narrow corridor at the back of the terrace. The threshold of the south door was found *in situ*; its situation indicates that the floor of this large room was somewhat higher than that of the cellae area.[31] "Beaucoup plus profondément" than the level of the threshold Collart located a drain made

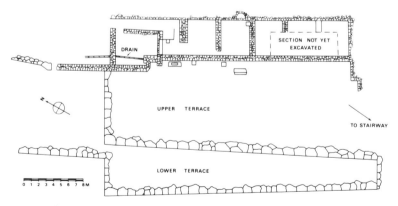

Fig. 8. Sanctuary of Isis and Sarapis at Philippi. Ground plan.

out of sections of terracotta pipe.[32] He traced this pipe beginning from a point c. 3.25 m north of the outer wall of the large room. From there the pipe ran under the foundations of this wall and below the room to a point where it encountered the butt end of the retaining wall for the cellae terrace.[33] Collart does not indicate whether it then continued buried in the masonry of this wall. Nor does he report any outlet either in this wall or in the terrace area above. Therefore neither the original point of inflow nor the outlet of this drain have been located. The section which Collart managed to trace is uninterrupted by coupling points for feeder lines, etc.

Collart hypothesized, first of all, that this pipe must have brought in the Nile water for the cult.[34] Secondly, he believed that below the large room had been a crypt from which this water was drawn.[35] Yet his sole evidence for this latter feature is the presence of the water pipe at a deep level below the room.[36] He reported no stairway down into this so-called *sous-sol* and provided no proof that there had been a concrete or stone ceiling for the lower area. The tile pipe itself certainly affords no evidence that there was any place for drawing water in this supposed "basement." It is continuous and uninterrupted in its entire course (c. 3.9 m) across the western end of the area. In short, Collart's entire hypothesis is a matter of grasping at straws. It is not clear that the drain bears any relationship to the sanctuary, much less what that relationship might have been.[37] Therefore the Philippi sanctuary cannot be included among those sites which are known to have had permanent water facilities.

However, at Priene the situation is more promising even though, once again, only a drain was discovered (Fig. 9). This drain, located to the east of the great altar, begins at a point about 5.2 m from the altar and continues in a straight line up to and under the east wall of the precinct. There it empties into the street outside.[38] The distance from the beginning of the drain to the east wall is c. 5.8 m. For four meters of that distance it runs along the south side of a wall which juts out from the exterior wall of the precinct into the courtyard.[39] This drain probably served other purposes than carrying off waste water from the floor surface. Since no other drain was encountered in this very large open area, its off-center location in one corner argues against its having been a floor drain. On the other hand, it is almost precisely centered with respect to the north-

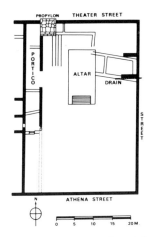

Fig. 9. The Sanctuary of Sarapis and Isis at Priene.
Ground plan.

south line of the altar,[40] and, as remarked above, its western ex-
tremity is approximately centered in the space between the altar
and the east wall of the precinct. Such a spatial arrangement
strongly suggests that the drain bore some relationship to the cultic
activity carried on in connection with the altar. My guess is that an
ablution basin, now vanished, once stood at the western terminus of
the drain.

On the south side of the precinct of Apollo at Cyrene stands a
small temple of Isis. According to the plan of the precinct published
by Pernier, an open tile drain is found on the floor in front of the
cult platform of this Iseum (Fig. 10). It begins at a point almost on
the central axis of the temple and extends c. 1.25 m to the northeast
corner of the platform where it makes a sharp right turn in order to
continue on to the rear wall of the building.[41] No published explanation of this feature seems to exist, and it may be only a simple
floor drain. However, given the fact that it begins slightly to the left
of the central axis, there is a reasonable possibility that a basin,
perhaps of metal, once stood in the center directly in front of the
cult platform. A detailed examination of the floor in this area might
determine whether this had been so.

This temple is situated just to the right of a Hellenistic fountain
which had been constructed as a part of the Apollo precinct.[42] Later

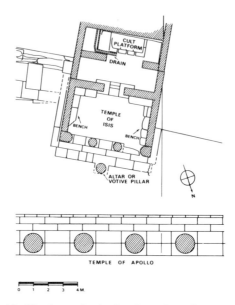

Fig. 10. The Iseum in the Precinct of Apollo at Cyrene.

this fountain was partially covered over by a small temple to Apollo
Musagetes and by other late Roman structures. It may not have
been operational when the Isis temple was built. Even if it did
remain in working condition, the location of the Iseum near it need
only be a matter of coincidence.

The final water facility to be considered has no parallel at any
other Iseum or Serapeum, and so I have deferred consideration of it
to this point. Connected to Temple E at Soli is a triclinium. In this
room, an annex to the main precinct which was constructed
sometime after 250 AD, there are two large L-shaped benches (Fig.
5). At the north corner of the right-hand bench are the remains of a
water container or basin. Westholm described this as having a con-
cave bottom with sides built up of rubble covered over with stucco.
The upper housing has been destroyed but the diameter of the surviving bottom portion is c. 1 m. An outlet on the southeast side may
have allowed water to flow through a channel and down into a *pithos*
sunk into the floor of the room.[43] It is altogether unlikely that this
cistern served the cultic needs of the main sanctuary since it is so
removed from it and so awkwardly placed in relation to it. Instead,

it probably provided water in the triclinium either so that those who dined there could purify themselves or else for more mundane purposes.

Sanctuaries With Cultic Water Facilities

From this preliminary sifting of the evidence there now survives the following working list of sanctuaries:

SARAPIS	SARAPIS & ISIS	ISIS	ISIS & SARAPIS
Alexandria	Eretria	Ephesus:	Gortyn
Delos A	Priene	State Agora	
Delos B	Thessalonica	Pompeii	
Delos C		Soli D	
Corinth:	Sabratha:	Cyme (?)	
South Stoa	East End	Cyrene:	
Leptis Magna		Apollo	
Luxor (?)		Precinct (?)	
		Frauenberg	
		Pergamum	

Archaeological evidence survives at all these sites except Delos C and Thessalonica. For these two cases there is clear epigraphical attestation for the presence of a water facility.[44]

Some preliminary observations are in order. At one time I had thought that Sarapis sanctuaries might show a different pattern with respect to water facilities from those sites dedicated to Isis. As is clear from the table, this is not the case. Rather, the more striking difference is between the Hellenistic and Roman periods. Despite the fact that almost twice as many Roman sanctuaries have been found as those established in Hellenistic times, proportionately far more Hellenistic sites are known to have had some sort of permanent water facility. This already points to some sort of shift in practice having taken place during Imperial times.

Secondly, despite a rather widespread view that such water facilities characterize Isis-Sarapis sanctuaries,[45] a great many sites show no evidence for such installations. Of course, in some instances facilities no doubt existed but were destroyed so completely that they have left no discernible remains. Nonetheless, a great number of Roman sites in particular afford no evidence whatever. This is also the case in Egypt both at the "traditional" sanctuaries of Isis and at the Graeco-Roman shrines of Isis and Sarapis. Of the twenty-seven sanctuaries in that country which I surveyed in the course of research for this study, only the Serapeum of Alexandria, the Temple of Min and Isis at Koptos, the temple at Madinet Madi dedicated to Sebek and Renenutet (= Ermouthis-Isis), the great sanctuary to Isis at Philae, and possibly the small Serapeum at Luxor provided evidence for such installations. Granted, in many cases the complete precincts of these sanctuaries have been only partially disinterred. Even those more completely excavated were explored, at least in many cases, by people who preferred treasure hunting to careful and painstaking investigative work. The point might even be made—and correctly—that the Nile River was close at hand in virtually every case. I would simply observe that there does not appear to have been a clear and fixed tradition for such facilities which then compelled the Graeco-Roman devotees of the Egyptian gods to follow a particular set of practices. My discussion in the next few chapters will make it clear that they did look to Egyptian antecedents in designing such structures. Yet they apparently were not bound by a rigid tradition of Isis worship inherited through the centuries but were able to borrow from a wider Egyptian context in their search to conduct their rituals in a proper setting.

CHAPTER TWO

THE NILE WATER CRYPTS

In Egypt at many of the major sanctuaries along the Nile River are found relatively small underground structures called Nilometers. The primary purpose of these is clear from their name: they measured the rise and fall of the Nile. No doubt such measuring devices were introduced at a very early date in Egypt's history since even a difference of half a meter in the height of the annual flood had a significant economic impact on the Nile valley.[1] In the first century AD Pliny observed how the area around Memphis was affected by varying amounts of flood water:

> The Nile flood normally rises about 12 meters. A smaller quantity of water does not irrigate all the land and a larger one by withdrawing too slowly retards agriculture. The latter gives less time for sowing because the soil is soaked with water while the former gives no opportunity at all for planting because the soil is too dry. The province makes the following computation with regard to these conditions: with a rise of 6 meters it senses the onset of starvation and even with $6^{1}/_{2}$ m it is still hungry. But 7 m brings joyfulness, $7^{1}/_{2}$ m freedom from care, and 8 m sheer delight.[2]

In short, a change of forty or sixty centimeters in the rise of the annual flood was able to make the difference between a year of well-being and a year of bare subsistence or even of starvation. Because of this, efforts were undertaken to measure day by day the upward movement of the water. Such an enterprise was especially important in Upper Egypt since the flood crested there well before it reached the Faiyum and the Delta. Information could then be sent northwards to help those areas prepare for the expected quantity of water.[3]

In Pharaonic and Ptolemaic times most Nilometers were constructed in conjunction with a temple precinct.[4] Typically these structures consisted of a covered stairway leading down from high ground to a depth equal to the local low-water level of the Nile. River water was channeled in at an opening at the bottom either directly or by means of infiltration through the soil; it was then able

to rise freely along the enclosed staircase until it reached the same
height as the river outside. Very often scales on the walls above the
steps served to measure the height of the water more precisely. In
most cases, if a person wished to descend into the Nilometer, he or
she first passed through an entry and vestibule and then down a
first flight of steps to a landing. Here a second flight of stairs
branched off at a ninety degree angle either to the right or to the left.
Often there was then a second landing and still another set of stairs
running down at a right angle to the previous descent (Pl. I). At
Edfu a spiral staircase of at least forty-five steps replaced this third
set of stairs. Less commonly—examples are found at Esna, Luxor,
and Philae—the Nilometer stairway made a single, straight-line
descent (Fig. 11). Because all of these structures were enclosed and
dark, their designers often provided light slits in the walls above
ground and niches for lamps in the subterranean sections.[5]

This general type of Nilometer continued to be constructed
during the whole Ptolemaic period and also in Roman times. However, during the early Imperial period it began to be replaced by a
new and simpler measuring device, a well with a column set into it
to serve as a measuring stick.[6] Perhaps the best known pictorial
representation of this new type is found on a mosaic from Leptis
Magna which dates from the second century AD.[7] Since it appears
here as a typical Egyptian motif, we can safely assume that it began
to be utilized in the early Roman period if not even in late
Hellenistic times.

Although Nilometers were primarily designed to measure the
Nile flood, they also served as sources of water. Because virtually
all known Nilometers have an evident connection with a sanctuary,
H. W. Fairman suggested that they were intended to provide pure
Nile water for liturgical rites and were not utilized for more ordinary needs.[8] Several factors offer some support for this viewpoint.
First of all, because the entrances to these Nilometers are usually
situated inside the precinct, these installations in effect served to
bring the Nile within the sacred area.[9] Secondly, at Edfu and
apparently also at the Temple of Amun at Karnak, the Nilometer is
situated directly to the right of the central adytum, a location
perhaps intended to underscore the importance of this facility for
the sacred rites. A most significant factor is the relationship of these

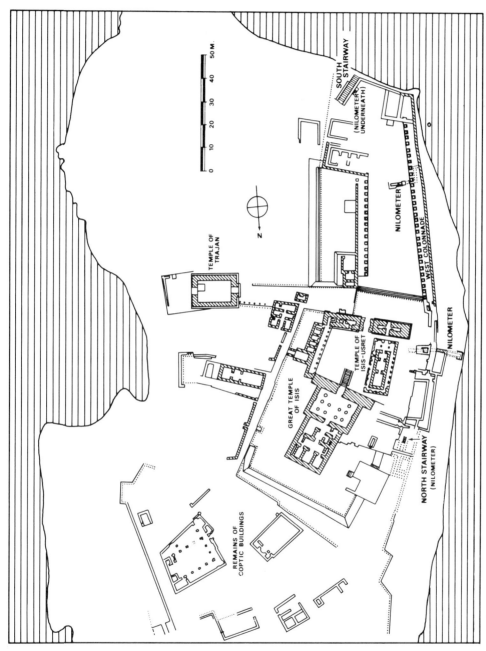

Fig. 11. The Sanctuary of Isis at Philae. Ground plan showing location and general design of the four Nilometers.

Nilometers to the Nile flood. While Egyptians considered water drawn from the Nile during any season to be sacred, it enjoyed this character only by extension. The sacred Nile water *par excellence* was the water of the annual inundation.[10] The flood represented a "renewal" or even a "rebirth" of the river; as early as the Old Kingdom its waters were called "the new water."[11] Even the name of the Nile god, Hapi, did not originally refer to the river in general but to its flood water.[12] Consequently, it was customary to draw water for all ritual needs at the time of the inundation.[13] Because of their special connection with the flood, the Nilometers perhaps served as facilities which conveyed this water to the sanctuaries with which they were associated. Indeed, they may have provided water for no other purpose but this. However, here some caution is required. At Luxor, for example, the Nilometer is not situated within the actual precinct but just outside where it is built into a quay which connects with the west outer wall of the precinct. This location appears somewhat more public, and so the facility found here may have been open to a variety of people and its water may have served more general purposes.

I have spent time describing these Egyptian installations and their functions because of my conviction that the Ptolemaic Nilometer is closely related both in structure and in purpose to a group of crypts found at several Isis-Sarapis sanctuaries of the Hellenistic period. The structural similarities are extensive, and I believe that I can demonstrate them clearly in the descriptions of the crypts which will follow. This typological similarity points in turn to the primary purpose of these crypts: they served as places in which the Nile flood (symbolically) recurred and from which this sacred flood water could be drawn out for the needs of the cult.[14] Different scholars have assigned other functions to this group of structures. In my judgment, all such proposed functions are at best only secondary. Indeed, in many instances the physical arrangements of the crypt do not provide sufficient space for the supposed ritual activity.

More Proximate Egyptian Antecedents

Two sites in Egypt, one an actual sanctuary of the Graeco-Roman cult of Isis and Sarapis and the other a "traditional" Egyp-

tian temple, offer evidence that these Nilometers could assume a
significance that was primarily religious and symbolic. The first
example, the Nilometer found at the Serapeum of Alexandria, in
many respects appears to function as a link between the traditional
Nilometers described above and the crypts discovered at some of
the Isis-Sarapis sanctuaries outside of Egypt. The former, as we
have seen, had a definite economic purpose while the latter clearly
functioned only within the domain of the cult. In design the
Nilometer at Alexandria looks like any other example of this type
of structure. However, it is my contention that, unlike the others, it
had no real economic role but served only a purely religious
function.

On the slope just to the east of the enclosed portion of the
Serapeum, Alan Row and his workers uncovered a long straight
stairway of at least forty-one steps, some of which had been carved
out of the bedrock (Fig. 12 and Pl. II).[15] This staircase, which had
once been covered over with a vaulted roof, is situated on a north-
south axis and runs down underground to a pit or basin. A channel
ran from the east side of this basin to connect with a nearby
underground aqueduct. This led in turn to the Canal of Alexandria
which lay 570 m south of the Serapeum, and which itself received
water from one of the branches of the Nile. Water could therefore
enter at the bottom of this stairway and could rise and fall as the
Nile rose and fell.[16] Even though Rowe did not report the discovery
of any measuring scales on its surviving walls, the stairway itself
would have served as a crude means for determining the water
level. About halfway down the surviving set of stairs is a door or
opening. However, the location of the upper entrance of this facility
remains uncertain. Perhaps the "Ptolemaic Stairway" which appears on Rowe's plan (Fig. 13) and which runs down from west to
east somehow provided access to it from the top of the plateau. The
difficulty for this hypothesis is that the two stairways appear to have
crossed rather than to have connected. In Roman times the north-
south stairs and the basin of the Nilometer were filled in and a wide
stairway leading up to the sanctuary was constructed over part of
the site.[17]

Despite the absence of measuring scales, scholars are in agreement that this structure should be called a Nilometer.[18] Yet it is

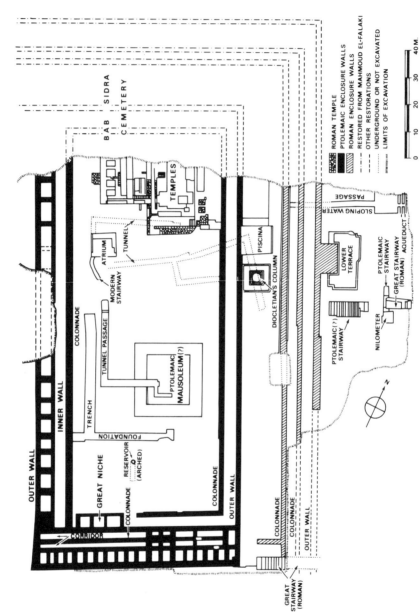

Fig. 12. The Serapeum at Alexandria. Ground plan showing the Ptolemaic sanctuary and portions of the Roman reconstruction.

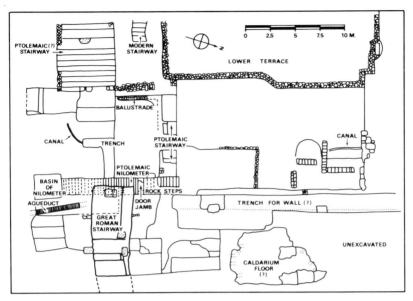

Fig. 13. The Serapeum at Alexandria. Plan of the "Lower Terrace" area showing the Ptolemaic Nilometer.

very hard to believe that it was built for any economic purpose. Alexandria lay at the very end of the Nile's long course at a point at which the flood's great volume of water had already largely dispersed itself over the wide alluvial plains of the Delta. Here the difference between high water level and low water level was only a meter.[19] F. E. Engreen is therefore surely correct when he observes that the Nilometer at the Serapeum must have had little scientific or economic importance. Instead, he remarks, its significance was probably only "local or symbolic."[20] The apparent absence of measuring scales is another probable indicator that this facility was not intended to provide precise scientific data even for local consumption. In addition, if it is supposed that the structure was designed to provide water for a variety of purposes, it is clear from evidence on the site that far simpler ways were known and employed.[21] I therefore believe that the structure's primary purpose was symbolic and that its builders constructed it within the Serapeum complex as an expression of the nature and concerns of their god.

Though scholars have generally assumed that a new Nilometer must have replaced this older structure after it had been filled in, the remains of this have never been found. It may lie still buried somewhere on the site. Some sections of the Serapeum have not yet been excavated, notably the north end of the site which has never been accessible to investigators since it is buried under the Bab Sidra cemetery. If we cannot yet be certain, I nonetheless think it quite possible that a different object, the sacred cubit, assumed in Roman times the symbolic role held formerly by the Nilometer.[22] We know that portable measuring rods were used, often in conjunction with a fixed Nilometer, to measure the height of the Nile on a scale of cubits, palms, and fingers.[23] In addition, we know that in Pharaonic times various individuals dedicated one-cubit sticks in wood, stone, or bronze as votive offerings to the gods.[24] Such objects had, of course, a symbolic rather than a directly pragmatic role. While examples of such "votive cubits" are not known from the Graeco-Roman period, such objects probably were the forerunners of the "sacred cubit" which became such a sign of contention between pagans and Christians in Alexandria during late Roman times. This latter object was certainly small enough to be transferred back and forth from Serapeum to Christian church at various intervals during the fourth century.[25] In addition, either it or a replica of it was regularly born in procession on festive occasions, a further indication of its compact size.[26] Since it was not itself an image of a god, it could pass readily from pagan to Christian possession and then back again. The purpose of all this shuttling back and forth, as the Christian historian Socrates makes clear, was to express the power and dominance of one god over another with respect to the Nile flood: "When the Greeks said that, inasmuch as the cubit was conveyed to the temple of Sarapis, it was that god who made the Nile to rise for the irrigation of Egypt, he [Constantine] commanded that the Alexandrian cubit be transferred to the church."[27] I believe that the Nilometer played the same role at an earlier date. Its presence at the Serapeum served to assert in symbolic fashion the lordship of Sarapis over the Nile flood and therefore, as will be discussed in later chapters, over life itself. Perhaps once the sacred cubit began to be used in the rituals of the sanctuary, there was no need to rebuild the old Nilometer.[28]

This symbolic role played by the Nilometer at Alexandria might help to explain the multiplicity of these facilities found at the Temple of Philae at least during its late Ptolemaic and Roman stages. Normally those sanctuaries in Egypt which have Nilometers have only one of them. However, at Philae, besides the well-known Nilometer to the west of the Temple of Isis Usret (Pl. I) and a second Nilometer with a Coptic scale located by the West Colonnade, there are also two other installations whose structural design suggests that they, too, were built as Nilometers (Fig. 11).[29] The "South Stairway" is a second set of stairs which made two ninety degree turns and finally reached an opening to the Nile at low water level. Because the opening is located so low, the stairs could not have been used as the means of access to a boat except during a small portion of the year.[30] Consequently, the structure probably served for drawing water from the river and perhaps also as a crude measuring gauge for the rise of the flood, both of these being functions proper to a Nilometer. Henry Lyons investigated its interior and reported that its steps showed little sign of wear. This indicates either that the facility was rarely entered or that it was constructed late in the history of the sanctuary, i.e., in Roman times.[31] The second installation which looks like a Nilometer even though it is without measuring scales is the so-called "North Stairway" located close to the west side of the main temple. It was constructed in much the same general fashion and so could not have been used as a means of exit from the island. Instead, it too probably served those purposes normally associated with Nilometers. Like the facility under the South Stairway, its steps are also very little worn.[32]

Let me advance a hypothesis to explain the presence of all these Nilometer-like structures. The facility used for obtaining precise measurements of the level of the river was the Nilometer by the Temple of Isis Usret. The steps of this show signs of heavy use, and it has no fewer than three different sets of measuring scales on its walls, the oldest of which goes back to the fifth century BC.[33] Perhaps in Coptic times the Nilometer in the West Colonnade replaced the older installation; its scale, which is certainly from this period, need not indicate the actual date of construction of the facility itself.[34] Its steps are quite worn, but this is in part due to its continued use as a Nilometer even down into the twentieth century.[35] Perhaps both this structure and those at the North and South Stairways were originally designed to be symbols of Isis' power and authority over the Nile flood. The very multiplicity of such structures would be a sign to those who frequented the temple that this goddess had full control over the annual inundation. Philae is not one of the Graeco-Roman sites and so is not directly pertinent to this present study. Yet it is fair to ask whether the symbolic use of a Nilometer as found, for example, at the Graeco-Roman sanctuary of Sarapis at Alexandria perhaps influenced in some fashion late Ptolemaic or Roman practice at Philae. The sheer number of Nilometers, some of which were little used, suggests that this is a definite possibility.[36]

Evidence from Outside of Egypt

Having established, as I hope, the symbolic character of these Egyptian Nilometers, I would like to turn to what I believe are corresponding structures found at several Isis-Sarapis sanctuaries outside of Egypt. Each of these facilities will receive a rather complete description since in most cases they have been accorded rather inadequate treatment in the past.

1. Delos A

The first example, the crypt located below the temple in the precinct of Delos A, is relatively familiar from Roussel's account of the sanctuaries on that island.[37] This temple, of which only the podium walls and floor survive, is situated at the east end of the narrow courtyard and is oriented almost due west (WSW). In the south wall of its podium is an entrance to a stairway of five steps which descends into a rectangular crypt, 2.30 × 1.10 m (Fig. 14 and Pl. III, 1). The height from floor to ceiling is 1.65 m, perhaps a sufficient height to allow most people of that period to stand upright. In the rear of the crypt, the area very probably under the cult statue in the temple above,[38] the floor drops off to form a deep basin, 1.10 × 1.10 m, into which water flowed. Roussel was unable to determine the precise depth of this basin, and no one since his time has excavated it completely to its bottom. Sometime around 1970 Regina Salditt-Trappmann visited the site, checked the facili-

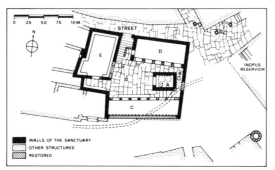

Fig. 14. Serapeum A at Delos. Ground plan. Principal features: A — Central Temple; B — Access opening to water from the Inopus; C — Portico; D — Shrine to various gods (?); E — Cultic dining room.

ty, and indicated her belief that the basin was about one meter deep.[39] This figure may well be correct although it is possible that she could have mistaken a layer of silt and sediment for true bottom. The basin was supplied with water by a "wide and well constructed channel" which led into it from the east. Roussel traced only the western portion of this inflow pipe but believed that it very likely originated at the Lower Reservoir of the Inopus, a large collection tank situated about 11 m east of the temple.[40] Roussel also discovered a place of access to this channel at ground level, a hole, c. 0.50 × 0.50 m, cut into the courtyard floor just behind the temple. Apparently a person did not always have to descend into the crypt to obtain water at the site.

This installation gives every appearance of having been designed as a small Nilometer. It has a covered stairway running down below ground level to a water source. As in the case of many of the Nilometers found in Egypt, a person descending into it has to make a sharp ninety degree turn before reaching the water. Furthermore, the source of this water is the Inopus River. A widespread tradition attested by the Alexandrian poets and by other writers in antiquity viewed this river as physically linked in some manner with the Nile itself.[41] The builders of the sanctuary took extensive pains to connect the underground crypt directly with the river.[42] As a result, the water in the basin rose and fell in harmony with the Inopus-"Nile."[43] This appears to have been an important consideration for its designers. If they had simply aimed at providing a source of water within the precinct, they presumably would have rested content with the inflow pipe and the connecting shaft behind the central temple. They chose instead to construct in addition an underground facility in which the rise and fall of water from the river would be readily apparent. Even though measuring scales have not been found within this facility, there are indications that it was designed to mark those moments at which the river flooded. The top of the nearby reservoir of the Inopus is about two meters higher than the courtyard of the sanctuary.[44] We do not know whether water ever rose close to the top of this reservoir during Hellenistic times.[45] Yet, given the considerable differential in height between the top of the reservoir and the top of the basin, water probably overflowed out of the basin into the rest of the crypt when the Inopus reached high water level. If so, the upper edge of the basin effectively served as a measuring gauge. When water rose above it, the "Nile" inundation was at hand. All of these observations point to a single conclusion: the crypt was designed to imitate on a small scale the Ptolemaic Nilometers of Egypt. Since this sanctuary was founded by an Egyptian priest and continued to maintain ties with Egypt,[46] those who planned the construction of the site must have had some acquaintance with the type of Nilometer in use there during Ptolemaic times.

At Alexandria the Nilometer very likely served as a symbol of Sarapis' power over the Nile flood just as the sacred cubit certainly did in a later age. The same appears true of this crypt as well. Its very location directly under the place where the cult statue of the god was erected afforded a very clear visual connection between Sarapis and the water over which he had power. Each time the water flooded over in the crypt, his saving might was revealed once again to his devotees.[47]

2. *Delos B*

A crypt similar in many respects was discovered in Serapeum B on Delos, a sacred precinct built just a few years after Serapeum A.[48] It is situated in front and to the east of the central temple under the floor of what Roussel termed a portico (Fig. 15).[49] Here also there are five steps which descend to one end of a flat, rectangular floor surface, c. 1.8 × 0.7 m, situated at a right angle to the stair-

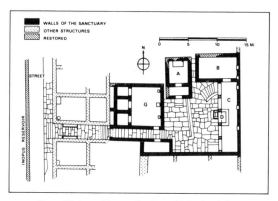

Fig. 15. Serapeum B at Delos. Ground plan. Principal features: A — Central Temple; B — Enclosed room; C — Portico; D — The Nilometer crypt; and G — A room with small shrines, perhaps the gathering place for one or more cult associations.

way. Very little of the upper housing of the crypt has survived (Pl. III, 2). Roussel noted that the remaining portions of the walls rise above ground level and suggested that the structure very probably was roofed over.[50] No basin was found within the crypt, and there is no sign of any inflow pipe or of any drain. Yet both its walls and its floor had been plastered over with a thick layer of stucco, a rather clear indication that the facility was designed to hold water.[51]

While a number of these features resemble those found in connection with the crypt at Delos A and so suggest that this facility, too, was built in imitation of a Nilometer, one major element is missing, a direct connection with a water source. Delos B is situated well above the Inopus River on a steeply rising grade. A person ascending to it from the street which ran by the Lower Reservoir of that river had to climb about thirty steps. Therefore any direct connection with the river itself was utterly infeasible. Instead, the crypt apparently had to be filled by artificial means.[52] Perhaps when the Inopus was in flood, servants or devotees of the sanctuary carried up this "new water" in jars to fill the basin. As an alternative, Roussel considered the possibility that rain water might have been channeled from the roof of the portico above the crypt into the underground area. He came to the conclusion, however, that the runoff of water would probably have been insufficient for this purpose.[53]

If, as I believe, this crypt imitates the structural plan of a Nilometer, a certain amount of stylization has assuredly taken place. There is no direct source of water and no measuring gauge. Yet those who constructed this sanctuary took pains to follow the pattern established at Delos A even though their facility could not actually be connected to a source of flowing water. If all they had wanted was a container for water, they hardly needed to build such an elaborate underground structure. Therefore, what was apparently important to them was the symbolism of this type of installation. They constructed their Nilometer-like facility high on a rocky hillside as a sign of the power of their god, Sarapis, over the Nile and its flood.

3. Delos C

Given the fact that both Delos A and Delos B had this type of water facility, we might suppose that Delos C would have had one as well. However, no such structure has been found within its precinct. Roussel asked whether the four rooms found two meters below the level of the courtyard in the northwest corner might have served this purpose (Fig. 16, rooms to the west of Q). As he recognized, the difficulty here is that no water basin was found in any of these rooms.[54] Even though there is no evidence that these

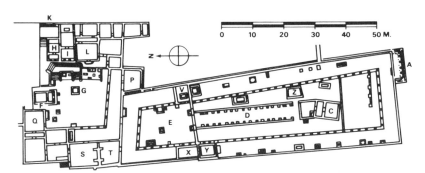

Fig. 16. Serapeum C at Delos. Ground plan. Principal features: A — Main entrance; C — Temple (formerly a Metroon); D — *Dromos*; E — Fore court; F — Temple of Sarapis; G — Altar; H — Small temple; I — Temple of Isis; K — Entrance; L — Shrine of Anubis (?); P — Shrine or exedra; Q (and the three rooms to the west) — Rooms below the sanctuary courtyard, perhaps not connected with it; S, T — Rooms with access to the lower street, perhaps not part of sanctuary; V, X, Y — Shrines or exedrae; Z — Former Escharon.

rooms had been filled in with soil and debris as were some of the other areas under the sanctuary, there is equally no evidence of any access to them from the courtyard above. As a consequence, their relation to the precinct remains quite uncertain.

However, Roussel also discovered a set of inscriptions which apparently were related to the repair of a ὑδρεῖον belonging to Serapeum C.[55] These fragmentary texts, the find spots of which are unknown, record long lists of subscribers to this project; these individuals are termed θεραπευταί. While at a later period the word ὑδρεῖον or its Latinized form, *hydraeum*, was used to refer to a particular type of water pitcher used in the cult of Isis and Sarapis,[56] in this case the Hellenistic date of the texts, the reference to the carrying out of repairs, and the large number of donors participating in the project all combine to suggest that a much larger facility was involved.[57] Roussel believed that such a large permanent facility may have been located below the sanctuary in an area close to the Inopus River where a maze of unexcavated structures still remains.[58] One of the factors that led him to this view was the discovery of a dedication to Artemis Hagia made by a certain priest of Sarapis.[59] Its presence at that location *may* be an indication that Serapeum C possessed annex structures in the vicinity.[60] If the designers of this sanctuary actually constructed such a facility close by the Inopus, this would have represented their solution to the problem faced at Delos B. Since they could not bring the water to the sanctuary, they would locate their crypt close to the water. If the word ὑδρεῖον actually refers to this type of facility, as I believe it does, presumably such a structure built in this period would have taken the form of a Nilometer. All of this is, of course, fairly speculative—further verification will have to wait until that area of Delos is systematically excavated.[61]

4. *Thessalonica*

A recently published inscription from the sanctuary of Sarapis and Isis at Thessalonica appears to be related to these texts from Delos C and so deserves attention at this point. It records the dedication of a ὑδρῆον to Isis by a certain priest of Sarapis and Isis and his son in the late first century BC.[62] While it is possible that the term ὑδρῆον refers only to a cultic water pitcher, such objects were just beginning to come into use and only in certain limited areas.[63] Therefore I suspect that just as the term ὑδρεῖον/ὑδρῆον referred at Delos to a large and permanent water facility, so also here. Given the fact that the priest and his son had this facility constructed in late Hellenistic times, it may have been a further example of a Nilometer crypt such as have been found at Delos A and Delos B.

5. *Gortyn*

At the same time that Roussel was excavating the sanctuaries of Sarapis on Delos, Gaspare Oliverio had begun to uncover the remains of a temple of Isis and Sarapis at Gortyn on the island of Crete (Fig. 17). Here he discovered a crypt similar in many ways to those found at Delos A and Delos B.[64] It is situated in a separate

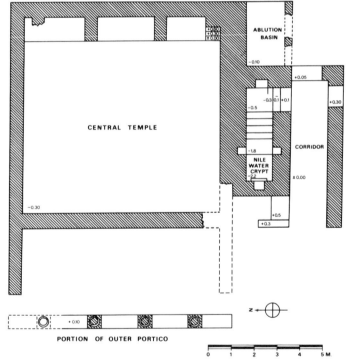

ABLUTION
BASIN

CENTRAL TEMPLE

CORRIDOR

NILE
WATER
CRYPT

PORTION OF OUTER PORTICO

0   1   2   3   4   5 M.

Fig. 17. The Sanctuary of Isis and Sarapis at Gortyn. Ground plan. More of the portico in front of the temple has been excavated than is shown here.

building which was constructed right up against the south wall of the central temple. The two buildings do not share a common wall, a fact which probably indicates that they were not constructed at the same time.[65] Salditt-Trappmann argued that the crypt was built before the temple now found on the site, a building known to have been reconstructed "from its foundations" in the first or second century AD.[66] She is very probably correct. The lower portions of the crypt walls are composed of carefully fitting ashlars, a type of masonry widely utilized in Hellenistic times. However, the upper sections were rebuilt with unworked stone (*opus incertum*).[67] The arches over three of the niches in the crypt have also been restored in brick (Pl. IV). Probably when the temple was reconstructed, it proved necessary as well to rebuild the upper portion of the crypt housing. Oliverio reported that he had discovered two Hellenistic inscriptions, one of them a dedication originally from the sanctuary, re-used as building material in the crypt.[68] The first of these had been cut down to serve as a tread for the stairs[69] and the second seems to have come from the upper portion of the crypt's north wall.[70] On the face of it, the presence of one or both of these stones suggests that the crypt had been constructed in Roman times. Yet the one stone definitely known to have come from this facility was re-used as a stair tread, certainly a portion of the structure likely to have required periodic repair. Given the type of masonry utilized in the lower portion of the crypt and the fact that this facility apparently antedated the restored temple, these re-used blocks must have made their way into the fabric of the crypt during a refurbishing in Roman times, not during its original construction.

There is no entrance to this underground structure from the central temple. Just as in the case of Delos A, this temple is oriented to the west, and there is a separate entrance to the crypt on the south side.[71] Apparently a person had to pass through a corridor to reach this door.[72] Just on the other side of this entrance, which is 1.00 m wide, are three steps which descend in a northerly direction to a landing, 0.95 × 1.05 m in size. This landing is 0.60 m below the top step but only 0.50 m below ground level.[73] In the east wall above the landing is a niche, 0.55 m wide and 0.33 m deep.[74] After reaching the landing, a person descending turned ninety degrees to the left and went down five more steps to reach a second landing

which measures 1.10 × 0.64 m.[75] Above the lower landing at its
west end are two arched niches, one in each of the side walls. These
are 0.34 m wide, 0.35 m deep, and 0.68 m high (floor to peak of
arch). At the extreme west end of the crypt the floor drops off
0.40 m below the landing to form an almost square basin, 1.10 ×
1.15 m.[76] This basin, which apparently lacked any sort of drain,
was filled by means of a rather large pipe—its inner diameter is
0.11 m—set high in the west wall, 2.10 m above the floor of the
basin.[77] Perhaps this pipe was connected to a large nearby
aqueduct[78] by way of one of the several water lines discovered in the
area around the southwest corner of the temple.[79] It may also have
been fed by rain water collected from nearby roofs or from the
courtyard floor by means of drains. These remain hypothetical
possibilities, for no one has yet traced the course of the pipe which
fed the crypt. Just below this pipe is a niche whose base is formed by
a stone slab, c. 0.80 m wide and 0.14 m thick, which projects out
0.14 m from the face of the wall. The niche is 0.45 m wide, 0.39 m
deep, and 0.80 m high (floor to peak of arch).

A few small finds were recovered from the crypt, the only facility
of this type to yield such objects. In the north niche Oliverio
discovered a terracotta statuette of a female figure wrapped in a
rather full cloak. Unfortunately, the figure's head was missing.[80]
The statuette remains unpublished and its present whereabouts is
unknown.[81] It may possibly have represented Isis, but nothing in
Oliverio's meager description permits any definite identification.[82]

The excavators also discovered broken fragments of several terracotta statuettes of cows or bulls lying in the basin. Out of some of
the pieces Oliverio managed to reconstruct a complete animal; this
rests on its knees with its head upraised.[83] Once again he did not
publish the restored object, and it, too, is lost.[84] He did offer the
opinion that these figurines had once occupied the wall niches.[85]
These niches very probably were not designed to receive such
objects—they are quite tall while an animal resting on its knees is
necessarily long and low. The only likely possibility is that the
niches were re-utilized as receptacles for these statuettes at some
late date. I prefer to suppose that the images were placed in or on
the edge of the water basin (as offerings?) and were later smashed to
pieces perhaps in the collapse of the upper portions of the crypt. In

all events, these bovine figures appear to offer an important clue for understanding what Nile water might have meant to the worshippers of Isis and Sarapis. They will therefore be accorded fuller treatment in a later section of this work.

Finally, a small marble head, not further described, was found "close to" (da presso) the terracotta statue.[86] This vague reference to the find spot does not really indicate whether the excavators found it in the niche, in the fill near the niche, or elsewhere in the crypt area.

As in the case of the two crypts found in the sanctuaries at Delos, this underground water facility is also comparable in many respects to the Ptolemaic Nilometers of Egypt. Granted, it probably did not serve to measure the rise and fall of an actual river. Yet its builders undertook to construct a covered stairway leading down almost two meters below ground to a basin into which water flowed. As in the case of many of the known Nilometers, the stairway in this crypt does not make a straight descent but has a ninety degree turn before reaching the water source. I suspect as well that the niches were intended to imitate those found in a number of the Egyptian Nilometers.[87] Those, for example, in the Nilometer at Elephantine are fairly comparable in size to the niches in this crypt.[88] Therefore, these niches may have held lamps rather than, as is usually suggested, images of various gods.[89]

The primary purpose of a Nilometer was to measure the Nile flood. The question therefore arises in this case: did any sort of flooding take place in the crypt at Gortyn? Its basin is not connected directly with a river. An aqueduct may have provided a more tenuous connection, although it is also possible that the basin was fed by rainfall channelled into it. If we do not know precisely how the basin was filled, we do know that it is not very large—it held at most only 0.7 m³ of water. Further, no drain was discovered within it. Yet the water main which fed it is quite sizeable indeed. If water began to flow under any pressure at all through this pipe, a small "flood" would take place in the crypt. Water could not have flowed steadily into the basin or the very sanctuary would soon have been deluged. Instead, there must have been certain times when water coursed through the large main and splashed down into the basin to cause it (probably) to overflow. Worshippers at this sanctuary very

likely looked upon such moments as a symbolic renewal of the Nile
flood, a visible manifestation of the power of their god over the
forces of life. They probably then collected this water and used it for
the ritual needs of the sanctuary—the absence of a drain in the
basin meant that the water which gathered there either had to
evaporate or had to be removed by hand.

6. *Pompeii*

The final crypt in this series is found in the Iseum at Pompeii.
This structure has been the source of much speculation and discussion ever since its discovery in 1765. Yet the various reports of the
site concentrate on interpreting this facility rather than on providing an exact description. In addition, features once observed by
older witnesses have been "removed" or destroyed in the course of
two hundred years of tourist traffic to the Iseum.[90] I therefore
believe it necessary to provide as complete a description as my
various sources of information will allow.[91]

The crypt found here is situated in the southeast corner of the
courtyard in front of the temple (Fig. 18) and has a large upper
housing (Pl. V, 1-2).[92] This building, which measures on the outside c. 3.2 × 2.8 m, has a single doorway set in the center of its
north wall. This entrance, 0.75 m wide, is arched and was originally provided with a wooden door.[93].

The rest of the north wall is decorated with an intricate set of
reliefs done in stucco.[94] In the tympanum over the door the central
feature is a large pitcher (Pl. VI, 1). On either side of it a figure
kneels in adoration. Further to the left and right are female figures
carrying banners on staffs; they are flying through the air and
pointing in the direction of the vessel with their hands. All of these
figures were painted white on a green background.[95] In the frieze
below the tympanum are nine figures, five to the left of the arch
over the entrance and four to the right. One of the figures to the
right is Anubis or an Anubis-priest; he bears a caduceus in his left
hand and a long stick decorated "with ribbons and a flower" (a
thyrsus wand?) in his right.[96] The three other figures on the right
carry respectively a serpent, a *situla* and a palm branch, and an object thought to be a fish. All four of these individuals face toward
the center. On the opposite side four of the five figures face toward

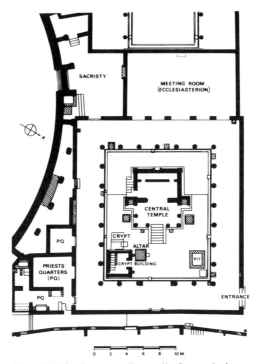

Fig. 18. The Iseum at Pompeii. Ground plan.

the center and appear to be reaching out with their hands in supplication and prayer toward the pitcher. One of these persons is kneeling and stretches forth both his hands. The figure fourth from the left faces forward and appears to be rattling a sistrum. All five of these individuals, who are otherwise dressed in white, have a red band looped across their left shoulder. The background of this entire scene was painted blue. The frieze rests upon four pilasters of which the outer two have shafts decorated with various symbols pertinent to the cult (a sistrum, a *situla*, a *uraeus* serpent, etc.) and the inner two each have a relief of a male figure standing upon an extravagant architectural structure and supporting a leafy stalk, a type of design found frequently in Pompeian art from the period of Style IV. At the top of each of the panels between these pilasters is a relief of a cupid frolicking with a dolphin. Below this design is the central figure of the panel: the goddess Isis with an Egyptian headdress, breasts bare, and arms stiffly at her sides. In her left hand she appears to carry an *ankh* emblem. The artist chose a very Egyptian iconographic style for depicting this divinity.[97]

Stucco reliefs also are found on the two side walls (Pl. VI, 2-3). The central figures on the east side are Perseus, who has winged sandals and a winged helmet, and Andromeda. They appear ready to embrace.[98] A cupid to the left carries a closed box (for the Gorgon's head?) while a cupid to the right looks away and appears, at least from the gesture he makes with his right hand, to be giving a command.[99] The central figures on the west wall are Mars and Venus; they are embrancing one another. To the left by Mars is a cupid with a tall lighted candlestick while at the right another cupid carries a shield and sword. I believe both of these side panels to be important for the interpretation of this crypt and will analyze them thoroughly in Chapter IV.

By contrast the inside of the crypt housing is quite bare. The door jambs in the entryway have been extended 0.70 m into the interior to form a kind of vestibule. At the rear of this inner area, which measures c. 2.5 × 2.2 m, is a narrow stairway, 0.65 m wide, which descends 2.5 m to the crypt proper. A low wall, 0.25 m wide, extends 1.4 m in a straight line from the west wall of the upper housing to form a guard rail just in front of the stairway.[100] A person desiring to go down into the crypt entered the upper housing, walked across the room to the staircase, and then turned ninety degrees in order to descend a flight of nine (?) steps to the underground chamber.[101] The entrance to this lower area is in its southeast corner. It leads into a room, 2.0 × 1.5 m, which has a vaulted ceiling whose highest part is about 1.9 m above the floor.[102] Just to the right of this doorway is a small base or platform variously described as a seat or as a place for setting a water jar.[103] The principal feature visible in this chamber is a basin measuring 0.85 × 1.5 m. This facility is not located below floor level but has a front wall, c. 0.30 m thick and c. 0.65 m high. Given this height of the wall, the maximum volume of water that the basin could contain is 0.83 m³. Apparently this basin lacked any sort of drain. If any small finds were recovered from this area, they have not been recorded.

In the early nineteenth century Mazois and Gau discovered that the rain water which collected in the channel cut into the stylobate of the portico flowed from there through subterranean pipes into the crypt.[104] Niccolini has a drawing of the cross section of the crypt which shows such a pipe running downward at an angle from the channel to the roof over the basin.[105] Such an arrangement makes it clear that the basin was intended to serve as a container for water. Since there apparently was no drain, whatever water flowed into the basin probably had to be removed by hand.

As in the case of the other crypts, this facility, which was constructed in Hellenistic times,[106] reveals many features parallel to those found in the Ptolemaic Nilometers. Even though the upper housing may not have had a roof,[107] the stairway itself is covered and descends to a water source well below ground level. A person wishing to reach the crypt had to make a ninety degree turn before beginning the actual descent. Furthermore, with every heavy rain a symbolic ''flood'' must have taken place in the crypt. Water would have risen in the basin, which is, after all, not that large, and would have then overflowed onto the floor. Since the whole facility resembles an Egyptian Nilometer, the overflowing water must have been looked upon as Nile flood water.

The four crypts found at Delos A, Delos B, Gortyn, and Pompeii share so many common features that they all must be examples of a single type. This type took its inspiration from the Egyptian Nilometers constructed during Ptolemaic times, structures which had already been utilized symbolically at the Serapeum of Alexandria, if not also at Philae. Even though two of these crypts, those at Gortyn and Pompeii, were refurbished during Imperial times, no such structure is known to have been constructed outside of Egypt after the Hellenistic period. This was not simply a matter of the Graeco-Roman sanctuaries of Isis and Sarapis reacting to the change in Nilometer design which began to take place in Egypt, for not a single site has produced an example of the well-and-column structure which became popular in the Nile Valley. We can only guess that with the advent of the Roman period the Nilometer crypts gradually ceased to be meaningful within the Isis-Sarapis cult.

Changes in the Roman Period: Sabratha

The presence of a water facility revealing some resemblances to this older type at the sanctuary of Sarapis and Isis at Sabratha, a precinct constructed during the second or third century AD, serves to illustrate the change in practice which had transpired. Under the steps leading up to the pronaos of the central temple the builders of this sanctuary constructed an ambulatory, c. 1.5 m high, running north to south from one end of the steps to the other (Fig. 19).[108] Access to this ambulatory, which measured 13.21 × 1.78 m, is had through doorways, c. 0.9 m wide, at either end.[109] Precisely in the center of the ambulatory and therefore directly on the east-west axis

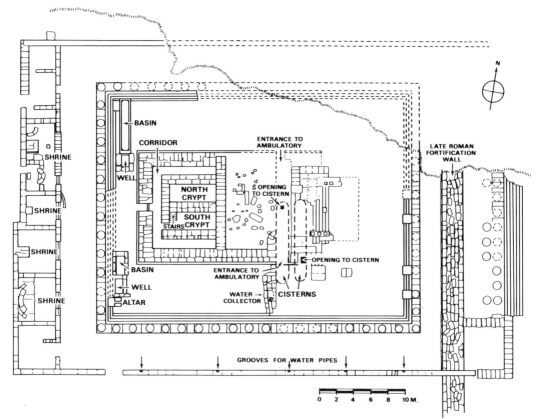

Fig. 19. The Sanctuary of Sarapis and Isis at Sabratha. Ground plan showing features discussed in this work.

of the temple is an opening, 0.37 m in diameter,[110] which extends 0.52 m through a concrete floor to reach the extreme north end of a gigantic vaulted cistern.[111] Both this cistern and an adjoining and interconnecting companion facility of the same size were filled by means of a system for collecting rain water. Rain flowed off the roofs of the porticoes which surround the sanctuary and into a series of pipes of which portions are still extant.[112] From there it ran into a drain which led in turn to the south end of the cistern.[113] Consequently, the water level in the cistern rose and fell according to the abundance of rainfall. Rope marks were found around the rim of this opening, a clear sign that the cistern was in use. At a later date, perhaps after the cessation of worship at the site, a new opening leading down into the east cistern was cut into the south side of the temple steps. This afforded much easier access to the water contained in both tanks. Perhaps at this same time the ambulatory was closed off—the archaeologists discovered that its entrances had been blocked off with stones at a late period.

This ambulatory crypt is structurally quite unlike the four examples discussed above. There is no staircase and no descent below ground. Yet care was taken to situate the opening of the cistern precisely on the main axis of the temple in a dark and windowless place which offered rather inconvenient access. The arrangement is reminiscent to some degree of the older Nilometer crypts—a person had to pass through a long, dark, enclosed passage to reach water which must have risen dramatically in the cistern on those occasions when rainstorms swept across the desert countryside. (The average annual rainfall in the area around Sabratha is about 40 cm.) I therefore suspect that this facility served as the Nile water container for this sanctuary. Probably the specialized design utilized for such containers in Hellenistic times is not repeated here because those who frequented this precinct no longer understood its significance.

The Purpose of the Crypts

As is clear from the previous discussion, I believe that these various crypts were not only designed in imitation of structures used to measure the Nile flood but also served as places in which this flood symbolically but "really" recurred from time to time. In

Egypt the Nile's inundation took place with regularity in early summer and this event was celebrated with a great festival.[114] Perhaps the sanctuaries with these "Nile water crypts" also celebrated festive rites when the winter rains (first?) caused the crypt basins to overflow, although no evidence for such rituals has yet been discovered.[115] Just as in Egypt, the flood water must have been viewed as a sign of the beneficent power of the Egyptian deities. If at one time this life-giving substance had been generally available only to inhabitants of the Nile valley, now all devotees of Isis and Sarapis could share in it even if they lived many hundreds of miles from Egypt.

Ancient Christianity offers parallels for this manner of dealing with sacred water. First of all, we know that in the sixth century AD certain Christian communities had the practice of blessing the Nile flood waters as the river began to rise. In localities close by the Nile, the people assembled at the river's bank. However, other communities lived too far from the Nile and so would bless a basin filled with water in place of the actual river. The water in the basin not only symbolized but was "real" Nile water; when it was blessed, the river itself was blessed.[116] In other words, these Christian groups also knew of a Nile water that was not actually taken from the Nile River.

Also instructive is a development which took place in early Christian baptismal practice. According to a variety of sources, the earliest of which is *Didache* 7, the most suitable water for baptism was "living water," i.e., the flowing water found at springs, in rivers, or by the sea.[117] However, with the growing institutionalization of the Christian Church, baptismal ceremonies were conducted out of doors much less frequently. Instead, they normally took place in permanent buildings with fixed facilities. Yet for a long while care was taken to assure a continuity with the old practice of using "living water." For example, in the Latin speaking world the baptismal basin was habitually referred to as a *fons*, i.e., as a spring or source of flowing water. In addition, the designers of these fixed baptismal facilities very often provided a symbolic form of "living water" by arranging for a system of pipes through which the baptismal water flowed into the basin.[118] This type of behavior appears very comparable to the concern within the Isis-Sarapis cult of

Hellenistic times to build structures in which an "imitation" Nile flood took place from time to time. Similarly, just as Christians in later centuries forgot the original significance of "living water" and so no longer designed their baptismal facilities with this in mind—many of them did, however, still require that the water *flow* over the head of the person being baptized—so those in charge of the sanctuaries of Isis and Sarapis ceased to build the complex crypts familiar to the Hellenistic period.

Others who have studied these crypts place less emphasis on their connection with the Nile flood but instead propose a variety of alternative usages. Although some of these are simply outlandish and so have gathered no scholarly support,[119] others appear more realistic possibilities. I therefore would like to turn to a brief consideration of the three principal suggestions.

The first of these, that the crypts were designed as "bathing places" or, to put it in more technical terms, as places for the performance of ritual ablutions, can be dealt with in summary fashion.[120] The problem for this theory is that two of the four sites which have these crypts also have ablution basins above ground. At Gortyn a large basin was found close by the crypt (Fig. 17) while at Pompeii a metal ablution basin was located in the courtyard to the right of the temple. Their presence suggests that the crypt was designed for other purposes.[121]

The other two suggestions require greater attention. In the final analysis, my conclusion that neither of them is valid rests on the fact that all four crypts are examples of a single common type. In designing each of these facilities, the builders must have inculcated whatever structural features were necessary for carrying out the set of purposes common to the type. For example, if one of these facilities lacked any sort of basin, we might wonder if the crypts had actually been primarily intended as water containers. Similarly, if one of these structures proves too small to allow a particular activity, we can safely assume that none of the facilities in the group were designed to have this as a *primary* function. Of course there are limits to this procedure. A particular sanctuary could have employed its crypt for a number of different secondary purposes. My analysis can go no further than to argue that it was not primarily designed for such usages.

Some have argued that the crypts served as places for in-cubation.[122] However, the physical limitations of several of the crypts nullify this theory. At Delos B no floor space at all was available for this purpose if the whole area of the crypt was covered with water. Of the other three sites, the crypt at Pompeii offers the most room. Its floor measures 1.5 × 0.85 m, although part of it is taken up by a base. A would-be sleeper might also have squeezed onto the floor in the crypt at Delos A. This measures 1.15 × 1.10 m and therefore has a diagonal of 1.6 m. Roussel advanced the suggestion that a large stone could have been placed over the water basin to allow more room for the practice of incubation.[123] Yet a large stone indeed would have been required to cover even a portion of the basin, and sufficient supports for such a heavy object have not been found. Finally, the crypt at Gortyn has a floor which measures only 1.10 × 0.64 m. Even a midget might have had problems here! We can therefore safely assume that the Nilometer crypts were not designed for the practice of incubation rites.

Regina Salditt-Trappmann used especially the evidence from Gortyn to argue that the crypts served both as the "lower world" for the initiation rites described by Apuleius[124] and as the place in which the person being initiated underwent a "baptism unto Osiris."[125] This latter ceremony she envisaged as a ritual drowning in the Nile and subsequent apotheosis. The individual descended into the crypt, entered the basin, and then allowed water from the pipe to pour over him (the ritual drowning). While undergoing this and after his ascent from the basin, he beheld divine images (the apotheosis). She believed that the niches in the crypt at Gortyn had been designed to hold statues of the Egyptian gods.

That the crypts could have symbolically represented the realm of Proserpina while at the same time symbolizing the place in which the Nile rose seems a rather harsh juxtaposition of death and life. This aspect of Salditt-Trappmann's theory is therefore not so very attractive. That individuals entered the basins in these crypts to undergo a ritual drowning appears somewhat more credible. Such a ritual might explain why the inflow pipes in the Gortyn and Pompeii crypts are located close to the ceiling. Further, all of the crypts will hold at least two people, although in the case of Delos B everyone who entered would have to stand in water. The chief

problem is access to the basin. At Gortyn this would have been fairly easy—the basin apparently is only 0.40 m deep. The situation at
Delos B also poses no difficulty. However, at Pompeii a person
would have had to climb over a wall 0.65 m high and c. 0.30 m
thick without the aid of a step while at Delos A it would have been
necessary to climb down into a basin 1 m deep. Salditt-Trappmann
refers vaguely to the presence of "eine Stufe" in this latter basin.
Yet a single step would have left a large gap either between itself
and the floor or itself and the bottom of the basin. If these two
basins were entered regularly by individuals undergoing a rite of initiation, we might expect to find steps of some sort to facilitate the
process. Since they are not present, I suspect that the designers of
these facilities did not have such a purpose in mind. I conclude,
therefore, that the crypts were built primarily to allow periodic
recurrences of the Nile flood and to preserve this sacred water for
the needs of the cult.

CHAPTER THREE

OTHER TYPES OF
FIXED NILE WATER CONTAINERS

Sarapis and Isis caused the sacred water of the Nile to flow not only into the Nilometer crypts just described but also into other more simply constructed facilities. Yet their Hellenistic devotees evidently thought that a crypt modeled after the Nilometers of Egypt was the most suitable of all structures to house this great gift from the gods. Five of the six sanctuaries from that period known to have had a fixed Nile water facility had this type of crypt. The only certain exception to the general pattern is the precinct of Sarapis and Isis at Eretria. Cyme may also have had a Nile water container dating from the latter part of this era, but the whole situation there is hedged with so many unknowns that we are left in almost total uncertainty.[1] In short, the picture presented by the available Hellenistic evidence is fairly clear.

In Roman times clarity and order gives way to murkiness and confusion. The first feature to strike the observer is that sanctuaries constructed after the first century BC are far less likely to offer evidence for any sort of permanent Nile water facility. Archaeologists have located the remains of sixteen precincts of Isis and Sarapis which had their origin sometime in the Hellenistic period. Six of them, or thirty-eight percent of the total, are known to have had such a fixed container. For those built during Roman times this figure drops to three out of thirty-one or ten per cent of the total. As we have seen, the ambulatory and cistern arrangement found at one of these sites, Sabratha, does reveal some typological links with the older pattern. However, this is not so clearly the case for the structures found at Frauenberg and at Pergamum. Each of these two Nile water containers has a distinctive design not known to have been imitated elsewhere. We are therefore left with several pressing questions. First of all, if the Roman period facilities are so divergent, how can we be certain that they actually served to hold Nile water? That is, what features define and delineate containers of this sort? Secondly, why are such facilities so much less common in Roman times? Did people no longer care about Nile water? Or did they substitute other less permanent means of preserving it? What follows in this section represents an effort to deal with these various issues. I will begin with descriptions of the physical evidence for those Nile water containers not examined in the previous chapter. In my study of the full array of evidence for all these structures, I found that they shared in common five elements which appear to be typologically significant. These I will set forth and explain in the second and third parts of this chapter. Finally, I believe that a shift within the self-understanding and outlook of the Isis-Sarapis cult is a factor important for understanding the relative absence of permanent Nile water containers in Roman times. The unfolding of this hypothesis forms a fourth and final section.

The Nile Water Containers

1. Eretria

The series of descriptions can best begin with a look at the one clear exception to the general Hellenistic pattern, the Nile water facility found at the sanctuary of Eretria. In the extreme southwest corner of this precinct is a room measuring approximately 3.3 m square (Fig. 20).[2] It was probably roofed over, had an earthen floor, and was possibly surrounded by solid walls on all but its north side. Here in all likelihood a doorway gave admittance to the interior.[3] Inside and just to the left of the door is a well, 0.65 m in diameter. Semi-circular tiles lined its shaft down to an approximate depth of 1.20 m.[4] The well probably was not dug much deeper than this, for water was available not far below ground level. We know this because the excavators dug a trial trench elsewhere on the site and found water just below the sub-surface stratum, a layer of the sand less than a meter thick.[5] Even though the sanctuary is only about 250 m from an inlet of the Euboean Gulf, rain water, not sea water, flowed in at the bottom of the well.[6] Rainfall in this part of Greece averages about 40 cm annually with most of the accumulation occurring during the winter months. Since Papadakis made his measurement of the water table in August,[7] water very likely would have risen much higher in the well toward the latter part of the rainy season.

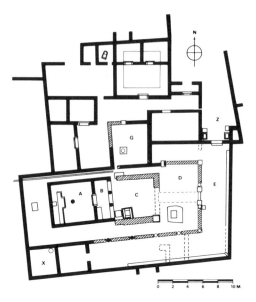

Fig. 20. The Sanctuary of Sarapis and Isis at Eretria. Ground plan. The principal features include: A — Cella; B — Pronaos; C — Enclosed courtyard in front of the central temple; D — Main courtyard; E — A surrounding portico; G — Room for ablutions; X — The Nile water container; and Z — Entrance to the precinct. Most of the rooms to the north of E and G were used for living quarters.

If, as I believe, this facility was a Nile water container, why did the designers of the sanctuary not construct it in the form of a Nilometer crypt? It was not that there was no one associated with the precinct who knew anything about such facilities. The earliest dedication known to have been erected on the site recorded a gift made by "Egyptians" to Isis.[8] Presumably such people knew something of the practices common in the Nile valley during Hellenistic times. Rather, the worshippers of Sarapis and Isis at Eretria may not have had the financial resources to build an underground crypt of the Nilometer type.[9] The water table was quite high, and it would have been necessary to construct a facility which would be watertight at all but a single point. In any event, assuming that this structure has been correctly identified, its builders decided that it was sufficient to tap into the underground sources of Nile water by means of a simple well shaft.

2. *Cyme*

The cistern and water pipe arrangement at Cyme which was described in Chapter I may have been a Nile water container, but there are just too many unknowns and too many alternate possibilities to be sure. This structure may have been built to meet the needs of the original cult of Aphrodite carried on at this site or even to serve various non-cultic purposes. If it can somehow be connected with the cult of Isis known to have had a place here at least during Roman times, if it is actually located right in front of the central temple, and if the water within it rose sharply or "flooded" during the rainy season, then perhaps it did contain the sacred water. This, however, leaves a lot of "ifs" to get around. In our present state of knowledge, we just cannot be sure how this water facility functioned.

3. *Pergamum*

Fortunately, considerably better information is available for the sanctuaries of Pergamum and Frauenberg. The Iseum of Pergamum, located in a huge basilica known locally as the "Red Hall," has a water system more complex than that found at any other of the known sites. One section of it supplied water for ablution rites and so will be treated under that topic. The other, a completely separate sub-system, was constructed as a Nile water facility.[10] A person entering the basilica and walking in the direction of the cult statue would encounter about halfway there a large, flat basin or depression in the floor (Fig. 21 and Pl. VII, 1). This was situated between the columns which originally supported side galleries. It measures approximately 11.30 m from north to south, 5.20 m from east to west, and 0.22 m in depth. Apparently it had no inflow pipe or drain. Beyond it the temple floor continues eastward for another two meters to a point where it then drops off 1.37 m to form a very deep basin which originally had been lined with Egyptian alabaster (Fig. 21 and Pls. VII, 1-2). This is as wide as the previous installation (c. 11.3 m) but is much narrower (1.40 m from east to west). The single inflow or outlet point within it is located in the center of its west wall. This opening, which is quite large, measures 1.00 m high and 0.45 m wide. From it

Salditt-Trappmann traced a water line which ran in a westerly direction to a point "bis vor die Stufen am Eingang."[11]

Such a large water line is a striking feature. Since the basin could hold only about 21 m³ of water, it would hardly have required such a large pipe to drain it. Instead, this sizeable main probably served from time to time to convey considerable quantities of water from outside the temple into the basin, filling it perhaps even to the point of overflowing. This happened, I would further suggest, either when the Selinus River was in flood—assuming that this pipe continued westward to the river[12]—or, much more likely, when a thunderstorm sent water coursing through drains in the courtyard into the big water line.[13] Pergamum receives approximately 60-80 cm of rainfall *per annum*. Three-quarters of this takes place during the five month period from November to March, with December and January being exceptionally wet months.[14] Consequently, there must have been times when a miniature flood occurred in this deep basin. Such an occurrence, I believe, was looked upon as a re-creation of the Nile flood.[15]

The nearby shallow "basin" may have somehow been associated with this Nile water container. Contrary to Salditt-Trappmann, I do not believe that this structure itself was intended to hold water.[16] It is only 22 cm deep and so could have been filled no higher than, say, 16-18 cm. Therefore, its available capacity, about 10 1/2 m³, is not very large. With a surface of almost 59 m² exposed to the air, evaporation would have been relatively rapid, and the pool would have needed rather constant re-supply. Instead, it may have served as an area in which worshippers gathered to receive a sprinkling with water. The space provided by the depression in the floor not only would have served to confine the falling drops of water but also would have demarcated a specific area for the ritual. I tend to believe that such a sprinkling, if it took place, was not carried out with Nile water since we have no evidence that this sacred substance was ever utilized in such a fashion. Instead, the more common ablution water would have been sprinkled over the heads of the people to allow them to approach the cult statue and perhaps also to behold the miracle of the Nile flood.[17]

4. *Frauenberg*

The last of the facilities in this group, the Nile water basin at the sanctuary at Frauenberg (Flavia Solva) in southern Austria, shows still a different design. Directly behind the sanctuary and to its right, W. Modrijan discovered the remains of a structure which he called an "Auffangbecken" or "Sickeranlage," i.e., a "catch basin" or "receiving basin" for water (Fig. 22 and Pl. VIII).[18] It is located somewhat below the temple at a point where the ground begins to slope down at a very steep angle, and its orientation, which differs from that of the temple, is probably a concession to the topography of the site.[19] The basin is almost square—its exterior measures c. 2.9 × 2.6 m—and has rather thick outer walls built up of rubble and mortar.[20] The inside of the basin measures c. 1.9 × 1.5 m; Modrijan gives no indication at what depth its bottom lies. The outer walls of this structure are preserved to a height of approximately 1.5 m above ground level. In the south wall are visible the remains of a rectangular opening, c. 1.6 m wide, through which the water was reached. Such openings may also have existed in the other three walls but no evidence for them now survives. In addition, Modrijan supposed that the entire structure was covered with a hip roof (Pl. VIII). However, no evidence survived on the site which would serve to bolster this purely hypothetical suggestion. All that is certainly known is that the basin had some sort of vertical housing with one or more openings through it.

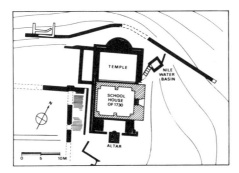

Fig. 22. The Sanctuary of Isis (?) at Frauenberg.
Ground plan of the sanctuary and
other structures found within its vicinity.

A channel, c. 0.80 m wide on its exterior, brought water to the basin through an opening in its south wall. The surviving portion of this channel, which is covered with large sandstone slabs, begins at a point very close to the east wall of the temple and runs northwards down the slope to the basin.[21] Such a wide channel was apparently built to handle, at least at times, fairly large quantities of water. Yet the basin is not all that large and does not have any sort of drain.[22] Therefore the flow of water into it was probably not steady but intermittent. Modrijan at first could offer no suggestion as to where the water might have come from.[23] Later, however, he advanced the view that the channel brought water from the closed area under the pronaos of the temple.[24] How this might have worked is in no way apparent, for there is not a shred of evidence that a spring or source of water existed at any time in this lower area. Instead, the fact that the flow of water to the basin was very probably intermittent suggests that the channel conveyed rain water from the roof of the temple into the basin. The average annual rainfall in southern Austria is fairly ample, about 65 cm, and so it is likely that at certain times water rose high in the basin and perhaps even overflowed. Once again, I suspect that the worshippers who frequented this sanctuary viewed such an event as a recurrence of the Nile flood.

The Typology of Nile Water Containers

The facilities I have just described are unquestionably quite diverse both in comparison with one another and with the Nilometer crypts. The question therefore arises: what factors indicate that all of these various crypts, wells, and basins actually contained Nile water? Despite the numerous differences, I believe that the nine facilities which I have termed ''Nile water containers'' share a number of features which are typologically definitive.

The first of these is one which I have tried to emphasize throughout the preceding discussions. Virtually all of the facilities have been constructed in such a way that at certain times water rose sharply within them or even overflowed. That is, they have been designed to reproduce the phenomenon of ''flooding.'' Admittedly the crypt at Delos B lacks this feature for it was not connected to a source of water. Instead, given the clear parallels in design between this structure and the crypt found at Delos A, the flood waters from the Inopus-"Nile" which certainly supplied the one basin probably supplied the other as well. The difference was that in the latter case the water had to be brought up by hand to fill the basin. What created this persistent determination to design facilities capable of reproducing the Nile flood in some symbolic fashion was the conviction that only this type of water was truly sacred and truly efficacious. This and no other was the water of fertility and life.[25]

Eight of the nine facilities in question share a second common feature. In each case some sort of housing surrounded the basin which contained the sacred water and so shielded it from the gaze of the profane. The situation at Pergamum is somewhat different, for here the basin was apparently in full view of anyone entering the temple. Perhaps the temple itself was thought to serve as the housing just as it does in some respects at Delos A and at Sabratha. Further, those who wished to view this basin may have had to stand in the low, flat basin in front of it and there undergo a preparatory sprinkling with ablution water before being allowed to approach more closely.

Thirdly, none of the basins in any of the known Nile water containers has a drain. The absence of such an outlet presumably allowed the water more easily to flood and then to be retained for the needs of the cult. Interestingly enough, a drain is a regular feature in the ablution basins found at the known Isis-Sarapis sanctuaries.

Fourthly, eight of the nine basins in these facilities are constructed below ground—the lone exception to this pattern is found at Frauenberg. This marks a further difference from the ablution facilities, for these are always raised above ground. Of necessity, Nilometers of all periods had their place of access on high ground but were connected with the river by means of a fairly substantial subterranean stairway or well shaft. Perhaps the location of the various Nile water basins at the Graeco-Roman sanctuaries is somehow reminiscent of this arrangement.

The fifth and final distinguishing mark is the particular type of water employed to fill the basins belonging to these containers. Apparently not just any source of water would do. In early Christian practice the proper water for a baptismal rite was that drawn from a spring, a river, or the sea. Various Christians were even of the mind that the Jordan River was the best of all possible places in which to be baptized, a point of view attacked by Tertullian and later by Ambrose.[26] Yet no types of water were positively excluded. The baptismal regulations in the *Didache* specifically allow various substitutions for "living water," and Tertullian goes so far as to say that all water of whatever type is suitable because all water has been sanctified by the Holy Spirit.[27] By contrast, sea water, for example, is not known to have been used as Nile water. Very probably it could never have been used for this purpose since sea water and Nile water are antithetical elements. To illustrate, Nile water makes crops grow while sea water poisons them. Plutarch even knew of a myth which recounted how Egypt came into existence when the Nile forced out the sea and so allowed life to begin.[28] I suspect, in fact, that the devotees of Isis and Sarapis were rather stringent in the types of water they would allow to supply their Nile water containers. To judge from the available evidence, they may well have considered only two types to be suitable: actual water from the Nile itself or from a "Nile-related" river (e.g., the Inopus)[29] and rain water.

Much of Egypt had, for all practical purposes, only one source of water, the Nile River.[30] While the account of the "ibis test" for water purity found in Aelian and in Plutarch suggests that not all Nile water was deemed suitable for religious rites, no other source but the Nile was available except in the area along the Mediterranean coast.[31] The major distinction in Egypt was therefore temporal, i.e., between ordinary Nile water and the "new water" of the flood.[32] It was this flood water which was used for libations, sprinklings of the temple, etc., and which was properly designated as the sacred water.[33]

However, in the world outside of Egypt, a world in which water was more plentiful and of diverse origin, water could be distinguished according to its source. The evidence found at the various Isis-Sarapis sanctuaries tends to indicate that precisely such a distinction was made. To illustrate this point, let me anticipate at least in broad outline some of my findings with respect to the ablution facilities. According to my analysis, nine sanctuaries are known to have had fixed Nile water containers. Those at Delos A and at Delos B received their water from the Inopus while the basin at Frauenberg was probably fed by rain water. However, none of these three sanctuaries revealed the remains of any other water facilities and so they offer no help in this particular instance. At all the others, various ablution facilities came to light and these probably or certainly were supplied by a source of water different from that which supplied the Nile water container. At Pompeii rain water flowing off from the courtyard area above served to fill the crypt. On the other hand, a metal ablution basin found on the site received its water from elsewhere through an overhead pipe. Similarly at Sabratha, rain water supplied the cistern under the ambulatory while the ablution basins received their water from nearby wells. A parallel division is found at Pergamum. The deep basin probably was filled by means of rain water runoff while the system which supplied the ablution basins apparently was fed by an underground spring. Eretria had an ablution facility as well as a room housing a Nile water container. Each was supplied by a different well. At Gortyn the crypt had its own inflow pipe which probably received its water from a nearby aqueduct or from the runoff of rain water within the precinct. Some other source, now unknown, apparently supplied the ablution basin located in the vicinity of the crypt. In all events, I think it rather unlikely that water was regularly hauled up the stairs from the crypt to meet the needs of this rather large facility. Finally, the large number of ablution basins in the Serapeum of Alexandria probably received their water from a reservoir located to the south of them or else utilized rain water that had been collected. They surely were not supplied from the Nilometer on the slope below when there were so many easier ways of bringing water to them. In short, the Nile water containers were differentiated from the ablution basins by their sources of supply, and the proper sources of supply for the former were quite restricted in number.

Nile Water and Rain Water

That water from the Nile River could be used as Nile water hardly provokes comment—it is a tautology. Nor is it so remarkable that a river like the Inopus could have been thought to have had a connection with the Nile, for the ancients had developed a variety of theories about the underground connection of rivers.[34] In fact, however, river water was not utilized all that frequently for supplying the Nile water containers. The preferred substance appears to have been rain water, a state of affairs which requires some explanation.

Sufficient rainfall was certainly a factor critical for the well-being of those who lived in the Mediterranean basin. With respect to the land of Greece Martin Nilsson observed: "...rain is of more consequence than even rivers and springs; upon it depends the fruitfulness of the fields, and it is in Greece sparsely meted out, so that the inhabitants have a lively sense of its importance." This was a major reason why Zeus, the god who ruled over the storm, the thunder, and the rain, attained to such importance—the people depended upon him to grant fertility to their land.[35] *Mutatis mutandis*, the same was true for any of the countries with a Mediterranean climate or with a low annual rainfall. Much of the northeastern United States receives approximately 100 cm of rain each year. By comparison, the Egyptian litoral receives only 5-25 cm, Delos, Eretria, and Sabratha about 40 cm, Gortyn approximately 50 cm, Frauenberg 65 cm, Pergamum around 70 cm, and Pompeii 88 cm.[36] At most of these places between two-thirds and three-quarters of this accumulation occurs during the winter months. In Greece, for example, the wells and rivers often tend to dry up during the hot summers. If a sufficient amount of rain fell in a given year, most of these areas became fertile and delightful places in which to live. In this respect, at least, they are comparable to the Nile valley—a proper rainfall meant a year of well-being just as did a proper Nile flood.

This parallel state of affairs was recognized in a literary motif recurrent throughout the time of antiquity, the "Rivalry between the Nile and Rain." Serge Sauneron cites passages from twelve writers who dealt with this theme, a spectrum of views extending from the fifth century BC to the early fifth century AD.[37] At least eleven other examples could be added to his list.[38] Many of these texts stress the superior situation of those who live in the Nile valley; they do not have to look to Zeus to supply their needs. Yet this very comparison which is repeated so many times makes it clear that the rain does what the Nile does, even if it does so less effectively than that marvellous river.

The next step is fairly easy to imagine. If the gods of Egypt were so powerful and provided so well for their country, would they not do as much for the lands outside of Egypt if their true power over the elements was recognized and if they were accorded due cultic honors? In Roman times, at least, Isis did possess the title "Mistress of the Rain,"[39] and Osiris and Horus were associated with the rain.[40] Perhaps such connections had already been made in Hellenistic times although admittedly I have not yet found any definite evidence to that effect. Such conceptions do not appear to be Egyptian in origin, for most of Egypt experienced less than 5 cm of rain during the year. Instead, they more probably reflect the viewpoint of those non-Egyptians who held that the gods who controlled the Nile flood also had power over the source of moisture which affected their lands.

The phenomenon of the annual summer inundation of the Nile provoked a considerable degree of scientific curiosity in antiquity, and many attempted to set forth theories to explain the origin of such an uncommon occurrence. One of the most widespread and popular of these hypotheses assigned primary causality to rainfall in Ethiopia. The clouds which brought rain to the areas north of Egypt in winter and spring were blown south by the Etesian winds of early summer. There they struck against the high mountains of Ethiopia where they poured out their masses of water and so set the Nile flood in motion.[41] In effect, this explanation linked the Nile's inundation with the rainfall which replaced it in other countries: both ultimately originated from the same physical source. This and the other considerations I have advanced lead me to believe that rainfall was utilized to supply many of the Graeco-Roman Nile water facilities because the worshippers of Isis and Sarapis thought that this type of water had a particularly close relationship with the Nile River and the gods who had power over it.

A Shift within the Ideology of the Cult

The typology I have outlined for the Nile water containers is verified predominantly by examples from Hellenistic times. Sanctuaries founded in the Roman period are proportionately far less likely to have had such facilities. The time has come to ask why this was so. My general response has to be that I do not fully understand this shift. Let us consider for a moment the well-known Isis aretalogy of which many examples survive from late Hellenistic and Roman times.[42] This is an enumeration of many varieties of powerful deeds accomplished by the great goddess. We might assume that any activity which does not appear in such a listing was not of very much interest to those who made use of this form of praise. Consequently, there is at least some question how much Nile flood water might have meant to such people since Isis' specific power over that river is nowhere mentioned. I therefore wonder if certain areas of the cult either never had that much devotional involvement with the sacred water or gradually ceased to be involved with it as the Roman period began to dawn. On the other hand, a whole group of sites reveals considerable and extensive interest in Nile water during this same period.[43] Some of the sites in this group, e.g., Pompeii, possessed a fixed Nile water container but others, e.g., Philippi and Soli, apparently did not. This leads me to believe that some sanctuaries chose to utilize smaller portable containers for the sacred water rather than the fixed facilities more common in the Hellenistic era. It is this choice that I would like to concentrate upon as I try to offer some explanation for the different state of affairs found in the Roman period. There is no need at this point to treat the specific evidence from this grouping of sites; I am here not so much interested in their specific solutions as in the fact that they no longer utilized fixed Nile water containers but yet were very much concerned with this sacred substance. My hypothesis is this: I believe that the shift away from large, fixed facilities to more portable containers was in part caused by a different perception of the gods who had power over Nile water.

What is involved here is the specific relationship of divine beings to the natural phenomenal world. Generally speaking, the gods of ancient Greece were not thought to inhabit natural phenomena but to control them. So, for example, Zeus was the god who hurled the thunderbolt. The thunderbolt therefore became his symbol not because he was present within it but because he had power over it. Similarly, Apollo was not the sun itself but drove the chariot of the

sun, Poseidon was not simply identified with the sea but had power
to arouse its storms and to calm it, Athena was not immanent
within the olive tree which she gave to Athens but did make that object a symbol of her power and wisdom. Of course, Greek religion
was not untouched by animistic tendencies. River gods, nymphs,
dryads, and δαίμονες of all sorts abounded.[44] Certain of the more
important divine figures also were more closely bonded with the
phenomena with which they were associated. Hermes, for example,
never lost his association with the stone heap which gave him his
name. Demeter was not only the goddess who presided over the
harvest but also in some way the spirit abiding in the crops.[45] Yet
even if, as Nilsson remarks, "anthropomorphism has its starting-
point in animism,"[46] this way of conceiving the gods within Greek
religion served to loosen their connection with specific natural
phenomena. Like men, the gods exerted their power over the
physical world and they did so more effectively because they were
stronger and better by far.

I believe that Egyptians viewed their gods rather differently. As Henri
Frankfort put it, "In Egypt all divine power was immanent
power."[47] Take, for example, the phenomenon of sacred animals.
Frankfort comments:

> But there was nothing metaphorical in the connection between god
> and animal in Egypt. It is not as if certain divine qualities were made
> articulate by the creature, in the way the eagle elucidates the
> character of Zeus. We observe, on the contrary, a strange link be-
> tween divinity and actual beast ... it would seem that *animals as such*
> possessed religious significance for the Egyptians.[48]

The same is true of the various cosmic and terrestrial phenomena.
Re was the sun god, Nut was identified with the sky, Shu was the
air, and even Heqt, the toad-goddess who assisted women in
childbirth, was looked upon as a power within nature, not over
nature. Exceptions to this general pattern are few and far
between.[49] Consequently, it is not unfair to say that the gods of
Egypt were present in phenomena while those of Greece were
distinguished from, yet powerful over, the phenomena.

I believe that a shift in emphasis from one to the other of these
theological conceptions may well help to explain the decline in the

use of permanent Nile water facilities. Neither Sarapis nor Isis
(except when she is associated with Osiris) was identified with the
Nile and its flood water by their Graeco-Roman devotees. Instead,
like Greek divinities, they were looked upon as the divine powers
who caused this annual phenomenon.[50] Isis, for example, is the
goddess who "brings back the Nile over the whole land" of
Egypt,[51] or who "impels the golden streaming Nile and leads it up
through the land of Egypt as a source of joy for men."[52] She is the
divinity who is "mistress over the rivers and the winds and the
sea."[53] Sarapis, too, was spoken of as the god who "brings forth the
Nile in summer and recalls it in wintertime."[54] Related to this is
the miracle of Sarapis recorded in *POxy*. 11.1382, a papyrus from
the second century AD, according to which the god brought forth
potable water in the midst of the sea. As Weinreich pointed out, this
miracle was certainly connected with Sarapis' power over the
Nile.[55] While almost all of this evidence dates to the Imperial
period, no contrary picture has survived in any Hellenistic text.[56]

To such a conception of these gods the fixed Nile water facilities
with their emphasis on reproducing the flood aptly correspond.
Each time water rose in these basins, the Egyptian gods demonstrated anew their saving power. In other words, they made
themselves known to mankind not so much in the water but in their
power to cause it to rise, to flood, and thereby to give forth fertility
and life.

Any shift to more portable containers for this sacred water
presumably meant a lessening of interest in reproducing the flood.
Nile flood water surely continued to be treasured and honored at
least among a number of groups of Isis-Sarapis worshippers during
Roman times. If those who venerated this water no longer felt such
a strong need to see the gods' power made manifest in an actual
overflowing of water taking place within the confines of their own
sanctuary, perhaps what was more important to them was the
presence of the divine power within the water. Perhaps they desired
not a divinity who did things for them from afar but a divinity who
was actually and visibly present to them. In other words, perhaps
Egyptian theological conceptions of a more immanent and
animistic nature had begun to take hold.

If Isis and Sarapis normally stood above the Nile as powers superior to it, Osiris regularly appears as the divine power immanent within the Nile, especially within the waters of the flood. Such an understanding, one which goes back into the earliest stages of Egyptian religion,[57] is attested by a number of writers of the Roman Imperial period.[58] Both the existence of the Isis-Osiris myth as narrated by Plutarch and the annual observance of the "Finding of Osiris" festival make it clear that Osiris shared in the fate of the Nile River. He disappeared and was mourned for when the Nile receded to its lowest level; he returned, restored and with renewed vigor, when the waters began to rise once again. To have and to possess these flood waters was to possess the god in his full power and strength.

At least one segment of the cult as it is found in the Roman period associated Nile water very strongly with Osiris. For them, the pitcher containing Nile water was the "summi numinis veneranda effigies," the revered image of the great Osiris.[59] My concern at this point is not to describe the group of materials, all of them associated with Osiris, which led me to conclude that certain sanctuaries of the Roman period shared a common set of practices in relation to Nile water.[60] Here I am content to suggest that perhaps in Roman times Nile water was more often valued as a sign of the presence of the gods rather than of their power. Under such circumstances, there was no need to build facilities in which the flood could be reproduced because what was religiously important was not so much this manifestation of divine might but the water itself, the living presence of the god. Here I am reminded of the shift in Christian Eucharistic practice from ancient and patristic times to the medieval era. The Eucharistic bread, once valued as a substance to be shared in the community and eaten on certain occasions, instead became something to be looked at and adored. In the present instance Nile water primarily became something to be carried about in procession and to be lifted up on high for adoration. For such activities only a small and portable container was necessary. How this water came to be sacred Nile flood water was no longer of great concern. What mattered, if I am correct in this conception, was that it be the genuine article. Therefore the reason we do not find many fixed Nile water containers at the sanctuaries founded in Roman times may in part be due to the fact that the people who designed them were not interested in reproducing flood water but only in having it. I am not prepared to say how far such an ''Egyptianized'' view of Nile water extended. That at least some sanctuaries adopted such a perspective appears certain.

CHAPTER FOUR

WHY NILE WATER?
1. EVIDENCE FROM THE CRYPTS

That the inhabitants of Egypt would manifest a deep reverence, even a religious awe, for the water of the Nile River is not surprising. However, that people in such places as Flavia Solva (Frauenberg), Gortyn, Pergamum, Pompeii, and Sabratha would manifest a similar reverence and awe for this water is in no way self-explanatory. *Mutatis mutandis*, the question of the Biblical official, Naaman the Syrian, is quite applicable: "Are not Amana and Pharpar, the rivers of Damascus, better than all the waters of Israel?"[1] Surely many in Hellenistic and Roman times would have wondered why some of their compatriots treasured water from the Nile above that of the Danube, the Rhine, the Tiber, the Meander, and the other great rivers closer to home. In this chapter and the two to follow I will attempt an explanation of this perhaps somewhat puzzling phenomenon.

Reverential esteem for particular sources of water is amply attested in other religious traditions. Roman Catholic Christians would at once think of Lourdes water while Hindu believers would recall traditions which speak of the Ganges River as a celestial stream which has descended to earth.[2] Further, for many Christians and Jews the Jordan River still retains at least some of the sacred character of which Elisha once spoke to Naaman. This list could easily be extended but the point seems sufficiently established: the Nile as a sacred water source fits easily into known categories of religious phenomenology.[3]

To determine the significance of Nile water for its devotees, I will pursue in the following chapters three lines of investigation. To begin with, the remains of the various known Nile water containers offer a few relevant clues. If the ravages of time have reduced most of these facilities to skeletal structures, the crypts at Gortyn and Pompeii have produced important evidence, and this material, not much attended to in past studies, will be the subject of the present chapter. In the chapter to follow I will set forth what Graeco-Roman writers have said about the Nile in order to see what properties of this river might have inspired the worshippers of Isis and Sarapis to reverence and celebrate its water. A third body of evidence, perhaps the most significant of all, will be examined in Chapter VI. This is a related group of materials which, as I have discovered, has a sharply defined geographical and temporal distribution: the water pitchers, the so-called Osiris-Canopus figures, and the Osiris "cool-water" inscriptions.

Statuettes of Cows from the Crypt at Gortyn

When Gaspare Oliverio uncovered in the crypt at Gortyn broken statuettes of kneeling bovine figures, he assumed that these images had originally been placed above the water basin in the three large niches at the west end of the structure (Pl. IV). I have argued above that these niches were not designed primarily to contain these objects since the niches are very tall. While it is possible that the niches were so re-utilized at a late period, it is more likely that the terracotta figurines were placed in the basin or at its edge, perhaps in the context of some ritual activity. If so, such a ritual took place at the end of the site's cultic history, for the fragments were found in the basin. Only guesses are possible in this matter because Oliverio has provided little information on the state of the finds.[4] Fortuntely, the analysis to follow does not depend on an exact determination of the actual situation.

Oliverio himself identified these objects only as "bovetti," a term equally applicable to male or female cattle. In Salditt-Trappmann's study, however, they have become "kleine Stier-bilder," an interpretation which allowed her to conclude that they probably represented the Apis bull.[5] From what is known of the iconography of Apis, this hypothesis is quite improbable. Instead, Oliverio appears to have unearthed statuettes of a reclining cow, the cow image of the goddess Isis.

G. J. F. Kater-Sibbes and M. J. Vermaseren have recently produced a comprehensive catalogue of the known Hellenistic and Roman plastic and pictorial representations of Apis, some 696 examples in all.[6] Of these, only 25 are said to depict a reclining Apis figure (Pl. IX, 1-2).[7] However, even this low number is deceptive. For seven of these are reliefs depicting a sacred shrine flanked by Isis and Nephthys and born upon a four-wheeled bier. In the shrine is a reclining animal figure, the mummy of the dead Apis.[8] Three other statuettes show Apis lying on a bier and attended by two individuals who bear small shrines. Again, this appears to be a specialized type which depicts the dead Apis bull.[9] In addition to these ten objects, the identification of six other statuettes has been questioned either by the authors of the catalogue or by others.[10] Putting aside all these items, we are left with only eight images of a reclining Apis figure comparable to the statuettes found at Gortyn, i.e., about one per cent of the total Apis evidence.[11] Oliverio could possibly have discovered a group of reclining Apis figures in the Gortyn crypt but there is only one chance in a hundred that he actually did so.

A reclining bovine figure is normally a cow rather than a bull. This is the position taken by W. Weber,[12] by W. Deonna,[13] and, with some hesitation, by G. Roeder.[14] Roeder observes that it is difficult to determine the sex of these kneeling animals since their genitalia are concealed. On balance he is inclined to interpret them as cows, a view with which Kater-Sibbes and Vermaseren apparently concurred since they included none of this group of bronzes catalogued by Roeder in their corpus of Apis images. The identification of these kneeling cows is facilitated by the fact that several examples (e.g., Karlsruhe nr. H 1043a and Kater-Sibbes and Vermaseren nr. 553) have the distinctive crown of Isis, a solar disk set between cow horns with a pair of feathers rising up behind.[15] From the time of the New Kingdom onward Isis regularly had upon her head the cow horns and solar disk which originally had been the attribute of Hathor.[16] This association of cow imagery with Isis persisted, as is demonstrated by abundant literary texts, right down to the last days of her cult.[17]

If then, as seems highly probable, Oliverio found several images of Isis as a cow in the vicinity of the Nile water basin at Gortyn, a significant clue is at hand for determining how devotees of Isis and Sarapis in the Roman Imperial period looked upon this water and even how they might have utilized it. A number of literary sources, all but one from the second century AD, reveal that it was precisely in her cow form that Isis engaged in the search for Osiris.[18] Plutarch describes how this was ritually re-enacted in Egypt:

> ... they say that Osiris disappeared in the month of Athyr when, with the cessation of the Etesian winds, the Nile utterly recedes and the land is denuded. As the nights grow longer, darkness increases and the power of light is diminished and subdued. Then the priests, amid other sad ceremonies, place a black linen cloth upon a gilded cow (βοῦν διάχρυσον) and display this image as a sign of mourning on the part of the goddess (for they consider the cow to be an image of Isis and of the earth) during four consecutive days from the seventeenth of the month [= November 13] .... On the night of the nineteenth day they go down to the sea, and the stolists and priests take out the sacred box (τὴν ἱερὰν κίστην) which has inside a golden casket (χρυσοῦν κιβώτιον). Into this they pour some drinking water which they have obtained, and the people present shout, "Osiris has been found!"[19]

Reinhold Merkelbach and J. G. Griffiths both agree that a second passage from the *De Iside et Osiride* describes another version of the same general rite:[20]

> Further, at the time of the winter solstice they lead the cow (τὴν βοῦν) seven times around the temple of Helios. This circumambulation is called the Search for Osiris since the goddess [surely Isis] longs for water in the wintertime.[21]

Long before the time of Plutarch, Herodotus had seen at Sais a cow image which was said to date back to the Fourth Dynasty. He described it as follows:

> The cow is covered with a purple cloth, all but the head and neck, which are bare and very thickly coated with gold. Between its horns there is a golden disk representing the sun. The figure is not erect but in a kneeling posture and is the size of a large live cow. Once a year at the festival on which the Egyptians beat themselves in honor of that deity whom I must not name in this connection, the cow is taken from the chamber into the sunlight.[22]

If, as Griffiths and others believe, the god who cannot be named is Osiris, Herodotus very probably was referring to an annual celebration of the Search for Osiris.[23] The cow would then have represented Isis.[24]

This group of traditions in turn helps to shed light on a somewhat obscure reference in Martial. A certain Selius, it seems, was wont, though not for the best of reasons, to frequent the "Memphitica templa" at Rome and to station himself before the seats of the "mournful cow."[25] In this context the "cow" can only be the goddess Isis. In her cow form she is sorrowful because she has not found Osiris. Merkelbach also sees a connection between the sequence of divine images in the *Navigium Isidis* procession as described by Apuleius[26] and the myth and ritual of the Search for Osiris.[27] After "Anubis,"[28] says Apuleius, came a cow ("bos in erectum levata"), the "omniparentis deae fecundum simulacrum." Next followed an individual who bore a *cista*; its purpose was to contain the "secreta" of the cult. He in turn was succeeded by another devotee who carried in his arms the sacred pitcher of water, symbol of Osiris. The parallelism between this text with its mention of the Isis cow, the *cista*, and the container for water and the first passage from Plutarch cited above is evident even though Apuleius is not speaking directly of the Search for Osiris.[29] Perhaps, as Merkelbach argues, the *Navigium Isidis* of Imperial times had in its origin a close connection with the older Egyptian ritual of the Search for and Finding of Osiris.[30]

This whole body of evidence strongly suggests that the statuettes found in the Gortyn crypt are to be connected with a "search for Osiris." We can imagine as a possible scenario the clergy of the sanctuary bearing the terracotta cow images of Isis down into the crypt before the onset of the rainy season to set them near or in the empty water basin. Of course, there may not have been an actual Search for Osiris festival celebrated during the Roman period at this Cretan shrine or these images may not have been utilized in that ritual. They could have been, rather, a permanent part of the furnishings of the crypt. Whatever the case, if we assume, as I do, that the statuettes found were cow figures, their interpretation and function must be understood in terms of the theme of Isis' search for Osiris.

The water which flowed into the crypt apparently represented Osiris, at least in this later period. However, it is not as though this god was the only life-giving and fructifying divine principle at work. No, Osiris is found when Isis is present; both together are the ground and source of life. Plutarch implies this when he describes the final ceremony in the Search for and Finding of Osiris:

Then they mingle fertile earth (γῆν κάρπιμον) with water and, having mixed precious spices and incense with them, they fashion a small crescent-shaped image. This they clothe and adorn, indicating that they consider these gods [clearly Isis and Osiris] as the reality behind earth and water (γῆς οὐσίαν καὶ ὕδατος).[31]

This ritual described by Plutarch not only foreshadowed but assured the reality. With the accomplishment in the world of nature of the union of Isis and Osiris at the time of the Nile flood in Egypt or its equivalent elsewhere, life is reborn. In this connection Apuleius revealed the power of the cow image and the "earth-mother" role of Isis when he spoke of this symbol of hers as the "fructifying sign of the goddess who is mother of all."[32] So too, Clement of Alexandria probably had Isis' cow image in mind when he said that for the Egyptians the βοῦς is a sign of the earth and of agriculture and of nurture.[33] Nonnus in relating the myth of Io said that when she came to Egypt, she was transformed from her cow state and became "a goddess of fruitful crops ... Egyptian Demeter," i.e., Isis.[34]

This imagery is largely agricultural because in its origins this was its primary focus. Yet the various elements lent themselves to a broader interpretation even in Pharaonic Egypt. For example, Isis and Hathor in their cow forms also had the task of giving nourishment and health and life to the Pharaoh and, through him, to the people.[35] The devotees who at Gortyn prayed in later Imperial times for the return of the water of Osiris to the crypt and who placed the cow images there probably sought the fertile, life-giving power of these divinities not only for their herds and crops but also, as will become clearer in the next chapter, for their families and for themselves. Earthly life in all its forms was in the hands of these mighty gods. That this life would continue to be available to the worshippers was assured by the renewed union of Isis and Osiris in the sacred crypt.

The Reliefs at Pompeii

I would like now to turn to the second group of evidence, the reliefs on the exterior side walls of the crypt at Pompeii. In Chapter II I briefly described these two stucco reliefs, one of Mars and Venus, the other of Perseus and Andromeda. It is time now to see what these tell us of the crypt and its significance, at least as this was understood after the reconstruction of the sanctuary about 63 AD.

The Mars-Venus panel is on the west side of the crypt building, the side facing the interior of the courtyard (Pl. VI, 2). The divine couple walks arm in arm together while from the left a cupid advances with a long flaming candlestick-like object. At the right a second cupid carries the shield and sword of Mars. Although for reasons of symmetry the second cupid is shown facing the divine couple, he is perhaps carrying the weapons away to hang them up. In all events, the weapons of Mars have passed under the power of Venus and her entourage.[36]

As Margaret Bieber has observed, the motif of Ares and Aphrodite as a divine couple expresses the idea that the god of love has conquered the god of war.[37] The presence of the cupid with the lighted candlestick underscores this: Mars/Ares has been set aflame by the power of Love.[38] If, however, the flaming candlestick is meant to serve as a wedding torch, it would imply that the conquest is to be a permanent one.[39] Such a theme must have harmonized well with the feelings and hopes of all Pompeians in the first century of the Empire.[40] However, those who frequented this sanctuary must have recognized at once in the figure of Venus/Aphrodite their own goddess Isis, for such an identification of the two divinities is encountered not only elsewhere on a wide scale but also here in this very sanctuary.[41] For them it was Isis who was the bringer of peace and harmony.

If Sourdille were correct in identifying Ares with Seth/Typhon, the relief would then have its proper setting in the Isis-Osiris cycle of myths.[42] Griffiths, however, finds this equation of the two gods far-fetched and notes that Month, not Seth, is the Egyptian god who corresponds most closely to Ares.[43] Both this fact and the way in which the relief is composed render the Ares-Seth identification quite improbable. That Isis should be shown walking arm in arm with Seth is an impossible conception. The theme of the composition is more general, the overcoming of war and strife by Isis. I cannot explain how such a concern was directly related to the crypt and its contents, but since the other panels on the crypt housing do demonstrate such a relationship, perhaps it possessed one as well.

Much clearer in this respect is the Perseus-Andromeda panel on the east outer wall (Pl. VI, 3).[44] As indicated above in Chapter II, there was at first some debate about the identity of the figures in this relief. Investigators at length agreed that the two central personages are indeed Perseus and Andromeda.[45] Accounting for the presence of this mythological pair is not easy. Yet to say that they serve only for decoration would be to assert that these figures alone among all the divinities and heroes seen in the sanctuary have no relationship to the circle of gods around Isis. Therefore, the worshippers at this Iseum must have seen some direct link between the Perseus-Andromeda motif and the concerns of their cult.

Traditions do exist which associate Perseus with Egypt. Herodotus reported that the ancestors of this hero, Danaus and Lynceus, had originally come from Chemmis (Panopolis) in Upper Egypt and that Perseus himself had visited this city. Indeed, he had appeared often to its citizens either in the open country or in the precinct which they had dedicated to him. Besides this, they had also established sacred games in his honor.[46] A. B. Lloyd in his study of this passage pointed out that Herodotus had visited this town in the mid-fifth century BC and must have been told of these things by the inhabitants themselves. Lloyd became convinced that Herodotus' informants were Graeco-Egyptians who had adopted a Greek custom, the celebration of gymnastic contests, as a means to honor the local Egyptian divinity whom they had equated with Perseus.[47] Proof exists that such games were celebrated in this town during the early Imperial period. Iconomopoulos located and published a text inscribed on leather which announced the "Sacred, triumphal, ecumenical, olympic games of Perseus Ouranios, held during the Great Paneia festival."[48] The really important point, however, is not the verification of Herodotus' account in all its details. After all, the Roman period games could have been instituted because of older traditions found in Herodotus and perhaps others. Rather, it is the fact that traditions existed in the Greek-speaking world which linked Perseus closely with Egypt.

The list of such accounts can be extended. Diodorus goes Herodotus one better and says that according to tradition Perseus himself was born in Egypt.[49] Herodotus had known of a place on the Egyptian coast called the Watchtower of Perseus.[50] Such a place is referred to by Strabo, though he apparently located it at a different point on the coastline.[51] In addition, the *persea* tree found in Egypt invited speculation. A variety of authors said that the hero himself had planted it in Egypt.[52] Pliny adds in his version that because Perseus had planted this tree at Memphis, Alexander the Great, who claimed Perseus as an ancestor, ordered that victors in the games at Memphis be crowned with wreaths made from its branches.[53] Traditions like these probably explain why in the third century AD the city of Alexandria placed a figure of Perseus with an Egyptian headdress on its coin series.[54] Despite this unusual headdress, the identification of the figure is certain for he is carrying a ἅρπη in his right hand and the head of Medusa in his left. The presence of a small Pan figure to the left may be a reflection of Perseus' ancient association with Chemmis/Panopolis.

By itself, all of this evidence is not that compelling. After all, the various narratives of Perseus and his exploits are associated with many different places: Argos, Seriphos, Ethiopia, Libya, Joppa and the Palestinian coast, Tarsus and the Syrian coast, Persia, etc. The Egyptian traditions are not all that numerous in relation to many of these others.[55] What suggests, however, that this strand of the myth was exploited within the Graeco-Roman cult of Isis and Sarapis is not only the relief found at Pompeii but also the known presence in the Serapeum of Alexandria of a series of statues depicting the heroic exploits of Perseus. In his description of the Serapeum as it existed in the late Roman period, Aphthonius singled these out as a prominent feature of the central courtyard: "The decoration of the courtyard was not a uniform whole, for one section was done one way, another in a different fashion. In one part were representations of the struggles of Perseus."[56] This evidence from two different sanctuaries leads me to conclude that at least some worshippers of Isis and Sarapis identified Perseus and his activities with the concerns of their own cult.

In my judgment, Horus/Harpocrates provided the specific point of focus for this identification. Much of the discussion of Herodotus 2.91 has sought to explain how that writer could have discovered in southern Egypt Greek rites being practiced in honor of a Greek hero. Scholars at first thought that the Greek inhabitants of Chemmis had associated Perseus with Min, the chief god of this town.

Some came to this theory via their belief that linguistic connections could be demonstrated between various titles of Min and the name "Perseus."[57] Others centered their attention on the sacred games celebrated in Perseus' honor and argued that of all the Egyptian gods only Min had a ritual which could be called a γυμνικός ἀγών.[58] A further group of investigators appealed to general characteristics supposedly shared by both Perseus and Min.[59] While Min has no role whatever in the Graeco-Roman cult of Isis and Sarapis, various Egyptian sources indicate a close connection between this divinity and Horus, a state of affairs which led to the interchanging of their respective myths.[60] At a later date Plutarch saw no difficulty in simply affirming that Horus was called Min.[61] If Perseus, then, is to be identified with Min, he is also to be identified with Horus.

On the other hand, A. B. Lloyd has made a compelling case that the Min hypothesis should be abandoned and that Perseus instead should be directly linked with Horus.[62] That the subtle characteristics supposedly shared in common between Perseus and Min should have led Greek settlers in Egypt to identify the two appeared extremely unlikely to him. Rather, they must have based any syncretism between Perseus and an Egyptian god on obvious attributes and deeds shared in common. Lloyd argued that Horus, who was also with Min a leading deity at Chemmis, is a much more likely candidate than the latter god since both Horus and Perseus are conquering warriors and both fight with monsters associated with an evil power.[63] I believe that Lloyd is correct and that the points to follow will only serve to bolster his case further.

It is evident from the frescoes in the northwest room of the precinct, the so-called *Sacrarium* (Fig. 18), that some version of the Isis-Osiris myth played a role at the Pompeii Iseum.[64] The arch-villain of this cycle of stories is, of course, Seth/Typhon.[65] Various texts in Plutarch's *De Iside et Osiride* have led me to believe that the relief of Perseus and Andromeda is to be associated with aspects of this myth. In a number of places Plutarch has recorded traditions which identify Seth/Typhon with the sea. For example, he says in one place that "Typhon is the sea into which the Nile falls and so disappears and is dispersed."[66] Related to this is his notion that the Nile was "eaten up" by the sea.[67] Consequently, as he says, the priests of Egypt abominated the sea and did not put salt on their tables since they thought of it as the "spit of Typhon."[68] They would not greet the pilots of ships and they avoided fish.[69] Plutarch felt that he could speak openly of these priestly observances since, in his words, they were a part of "common tradition."[70]

Griffiths in his commentary on Plutarch's account found this identification of Seth/Typhon with the sea "puzzling" and indicated his own belief that no strong Egyptian antecedents have been established.[71] This is not too important for the argument I am advancing, although it must be said that the picture is not quite so bleak as Griffiths believed.[72] Plutarch's group of "common traditions" makes it clear that at least by the early Imperial period many had come to equate the evil, demon-like Seth/Typhon with the sea.

The struggle of Perseus to free Andromeda was also described in various sources as a struggle with the sea and its ruling divinities. This is first of all revealed in the way the supposed offense of Andromeda and her family is described. According to Apollodorus, Andromeda's plight came about because her mother, Cassiopeia, boastfully claimed to be more beautiful than any of the Nereids. This affront led Poseidon and these goddesses of the sea to send a flood and a monster against Andromeda and her land.[73] Another line of tradition explained Andromeda's predicament better, for here Cassiopeia exalted not her own, but her daughter's beauty over that of the Nereids.[74] In each case the offense is against the ruling powers of the sea and leads them to seek for revenge.

The subsequent response of the sea deities reveals the depth of their involvement. In the Apollodorus account Poseidon and the Nereids join together in the quest for revenge. Lucian tells the story as an effort by the sea goddesses to eliminate their upstart rival, Andromeda.[75] Further, a whole series of vase paintings show the Nereids present while Andromeda stands chained to the rock. They are there, says Konrad Schauenburg, to gloat and to mock.[76] Consequently, when Perseus undertakes his fight against the monster, he is in actuality attacking the fundamental ruling forces of the sea.

Three points have now been established which together will make comprehensible the presence of the Perseus relief at the Pompeii sanctuary. First, the Perseus traditions reveal a connection between the hero and the god Horus. In the second place, Seth/Typhon was fairly commonly identified with the sea at least in Graeco-Roman times. Finally, Perseus' fight with the monster was conceived of in some quarters as a fight against the powers of the sea. I would now like to bring this group of findings together and will turn to the sage of Chaeronea for the central clue. Plutarch in his *De Iside et Osiride* remarks at one point:

> ... one should not reject that tradition that Typhon once had control over the land of Osiris since Egypt was at that time a sea. For that reason many seashells are found even to the present in the quarries and the mountains. Further, all the springs and wells, of which there are many, have salty and brackish water as though a stale vestige of the ancient sea had collected there. In time Horus overpowered Typhon. That is, when a timely abundance of rain took place, the Nile, having forced out the sea, revealed the plain and filled it with its alluvial deposits.[77]

In this text Horus, the inveterate enemy of Seth, is identified with the fresh water of the Nile flood.[78] By his conquering power, which is inherent in the rain and in the subsequent upsurge of water, the sea (Seth/Typhon) is expelled from the valley of Egypt and life can begin to flourish. Death-bringing salt water yields to fructifying fresh water.

This same motif is attested elsewhere. Plutarch himself speaks of it in his account of the ceremony of the Search for Osiris. At one point in the four-day celebration the worshippers went down to the sea (θάλατταν) at night. There the priests drew forth drinkable water and placed it in a gold container. At that the cry arose, "Osiris has been found!"[79] While Osiris alone and not Horus is mentioned, the basic theme is the same: sea water gives way to fresh water.[80] In this connection, Aelius Aristides noted as one of the typical mighty deeds of Sarapis that he had "produced potable water in the midst of the sea."[81] Such traditions were not unknown in first-century Italy. A verse in Lucan's *Pharsalia*, while lacking any direct mythological reference, certainly implies a conflict between river and sea: "at inde/gurgite septeno rapidus mare summovet amnis."[82] "Summovet," a strong word, implies that the river has the power to compel the sea to retreat. Statius, however, specifically mentions the Nereids in this connection. In a passage in the *Thebaid* he tells how at the time of the Nile flood the routed Nereids take refuge in the depths and fear to encounter the flood of sweet water.[83]

When, therefore, the worshippers who frequented the Pompeii Iseum beheld the relief of Perseus, they recognized it as an image of their own god, Horus/Harpocrates, the conqueror of the sea, the victor over the evil power of Seth. Not without reason was this composition placed on the side wall of the Nile water facility. For the coming of Nile water into the basin of the crypt was a renewal of the god's victory. Once again Sea had been conquered, once again the forces of life had triumphed over the powers of evil and death. In short, I believe that a recrudescence of the age-old myth of the struggle between a divine warrior and the Sea can be verified at this Pompeian sanctuary as it was reconstructed in the mid-first century AD.[84] Those who came to this Iseum would not have been interested in such a myth in terms of its bare literal level any more than were those who narrated it in earlier ages. Just as Yamm/Sea "represented the unruly powers of the universe who threatened chaos" and death,[85] so Seth from Saite times onwards was simply the Evil One.[86] When the rains came down and filled the underground Nile water container, it was a sign of the victory of life over destruction and death, a clear indication that the beneficent deities honored here were more powerful than any evil force.

Once Perseus-Horus has triumphed over the sea monster of Seth, he liberates Andromeda from her bonds and unites her to himself. This act of liberation underscores the divine power which resides in the hero and sets him alongside other savior deities. Dionysus, for example, characterized, among other titles, as "The One Who Looses" (Λύσιος), was venerated as a god who freed people both from actual bonds and from the metaphorical bonds of Fate. On this Aristides remarks: "Therefore nothing will be bound so firmly by disease, by wrath, by fortune of any sort, that it will not be possible for Dionysus to loose it."[87] Equally, the myth of Heracles' rescue of Hesione from bonds pointed to that divine hero's power as a liberator and savior.[88] Isis herself is praised in the aretalogies as the one who "looses those in bonds."[89] The act of loosing from fetters was a manifestation of divine power. According to Philostratus, for example, Damis recognized for the first time the divine nature of Apollonius when the latter was able to remove his own leg from the fetters which emprisoned it without his needing to call upon any god to assist him.[90] Less divinely endowed mortals used magical formulae to summon "familiar spirits" who were able to break chains and fetters and to open locked doors. One such formula reads in part: "Let every bond be loosed, let every force be dissolved. Let every iron fetter, every rope, every thong, every knot be burst asunder. Let every chain be unlocked and may no one constrain me for I am X (say your name)."[91]

This motif of liberation from bonds serves in a Graeco-Roman environment to extend this protological myth of cosmic struggle to the needs and concerns of individual devotees. In the present instance, those who frequented this precinct presumably were expected to identify themselves with Andromeda. They looked to Horus and the other Egyptian gods to deliver them in the present and in the future from the monstrous forces of evil and chaos which threatened in the person of Seth.[92] The location of the relief clearly links such expectations with the crypt and its contents. The renewed presence of the sacred Nile water was an assurance of continued saving benefits from the gods of Egypt.

Conclusions

The cows from Gortyn and the relief from Pompeii are different objects of different date and from different sanctuaries. Yet in their significance they reveal certain lines of convergence. In both of them there is a promise of life for the participant in the cult. This is perhaps not life eternal, for the sources of information explored here seem to point more immediately to an improved quality of life in this world: good crops and herds, good health, numerous and vigorous children. Yet in each case, the accent on life goes back primarily to the divine power immanent in Nile water, the power of Osiris or of his son Horus. It may be that some worshippers saw these Nile water rituals as a means to participate in the immortal and glorious existence of the gods. Beyond this, both objects found their interpretation in the Isis-Osiris cycle of myths. I would not be prepared to conclude from this that both sanctuaries shared a common *hieros logos*. What does seem clear is that participants in the cultic activities of these two sites knew and utilized Isis and Osiris traditions.

To be sure, different emphases are also apparent. At Gortyn Isis in her cow image represents a more passive and constant female principle. This is not the Isis of the aretalogies, an active and powerful creator and producer. No, here she is the searcher after her beloved; her own being is defined in terms of Osiris and she shares in his fate. On the other hand, the Perseus relief recalls the exploits of an active and violent male figure. Evil is not to be a part of a larger synthesis; it is to be attacked and destroyed by the over-powering might of the gods of Egypt. However, the artist in his composition did not choose to depict the actual moment of battle but the aftermath of that conflict. He portrayed the victorious hero standing with Andromeda, his wife-to-be. If, as I believe, she is a figure who symbolizes the individual devotee, the relational dimension found at Gortyn between god and god is here expressed in terms of the god and his follower. As a result, the Pompeii relief makes it vividly clear that the god's victory over evil is something that will affect and change the lives of each and every worshipper.

CHAPTER FIVE

WHY NILE WATER?
2. EVIDENCE FROM OUTSIDE THE CULT

If pertinent evidence from the Nile water crypts themselves is relatively limited, there exist abundant literary sources from antiquity which speak of the properties and benefactions of Nile water. In the course of my own investigations I discovered no fewer than fifty-six Classical, Hellenistic, and Roman authors who provide information or theories on this topic.[1] By far the largest number of these sources date from the first century BC or later. Indeed, comments on Nile water survive in works by only three Classical and seven early Hellenistic writers, although it is altogether probable that some of the remarks contained in later writings were ransacked from earlier sources.[2]

Little if any of the evidence to be presented here expressly represents viewpoints of actual participants in the cult. Rather, it reflects the interests, concerns, and fancies of a much wider group of writers and their various audiences. While, therefore, those who took part in Isis-Sarapis worship need not have shared these perceptions, I think it much more probable that for the most part they did. The cult of Isis and Sarapis was in no way defiantly countercultural. To the contrary, Isis normally appears as an upholder of the general culture and its values. For example, the Isis aretalogies depict the goddess as a promoter and defender of the basic structures of Graeco-Roman society. Even Apuleius' Lucius, that renowned devotee, could rejoice in obtaining as the fruit of his many devotional exercises a noteworthy secular career as a lawyer at Rome. In turn, despite evidence for occasional harassments and local persecutions, e.g., at Delos in connection with the founding of Serapeum A and at Rome at the end of the Republic and the beginning of the Empire, epigraphical remains from numerous sanctuaries attest the public acceptance and general recognition of this cult.

A further consideration seems valid at least for the Roman period, the period from which survive most of the observations on Nile water that we have. The expanding number of intellectuals who investigated this phenomenon and other related Egyptological concerns were undoubtedly motivated in no small measure by an increasing general curiosity about Egypt and its ways, a curiosity strongly felt within Graeco-Roman culture at the end of the first century BC and in the first two centuries of the Empire.[3] The books produced by those who studied such matters must then have played a kind of "pre-catechetical" role in preparing people to turn to Isis and the other divinities of Egypt. In turn, the progressive growth in numbers of those who participated in the cult would have helped to arouse greater interest in studies of Egyptian life and practices. Since those within the circle of Isis worshippers do not appear to have been isolated from their culture, it is altogether likely that the reports of contemporary scholars, scientists, and story-tellers helped to condition their cultic perceptions and expectations.

Specific observations of individual writers should not be given undue weight, for such information may simply have been passed along from older sources or may only record idiosyncratic oddities. More likely to indicate what those familiar with the Isis-Sarapis cult thought about Nile water are general emphases and themes supported by a variety of authors.[4] Where such conceptions are congruent with evidence from within the cult, we have reasonable assurance that we are in contact with actual perceptions shared by devotees of Isis and Sarapis.

Let me state my own understanding at the outset. F. J. Dölger believed that people were interested in Nile water for three reasons. It offered them, he said, "Bewahrung vor Krankheit und Gewährung von Gesundheit, Heil und Leben."[5] While he himself was reluctant to interpret "Leben" as including eternal life,[6] many others have assumed that worshippers of Isis did believe that Nile water offered such a hope to them.[7] However, the evidence I will present below supports only the two more general benefactions, "Heil" and "Leben," mentioned by Dölger and only the this-worldly interpretation he assigned to them. Neither healing power nor immortality play any real role among the effective advantages of Nile water enumerated by these ancient authors. This does not exclude the possibility, of course, that within the cult itself additional benefactions were related to it. It does close off this body of data as a means for verifying such an assertion.

General Perceptions

The general attitude toward the Nile River and its water across these centuries is expressed in a series of superlatives. "As a general statement," said Diodorus, "the Nile surpasses all the rivers of the inhabited world in its benefactions to humanity."[8] For Seneca all other rivers are "vulgares aquae" in comparison to the Nile; it is the "most noble" of all watercourses.[9] His contemporary, Pomponius Mela, after relating its benefits to mankind, termed it "amnium in nostrum mare permeantium maximus."[10] In late Roman times the feeling was the same. Arnobius spoke of the Nile as "the greatest of rivers"[11] while Ammianus Marcellinus declared it "a river which is kindly to all."[12] Roman period sources more closely connected with Egypt stressed the sacral character of the Nile. For example, the author of the Hermetic treatise called *Asclepius* addressed an apocalyptic prediction to the Nile and called it the "sanctissimum flumen" and its floodwaters "undae divinae."[13] Documents found at Oxyrhynchus[14] suggest that this mode of speech was common within Egypt.[15]

Because of this esteem and veneration a whole titulature developed in Egypt and became known elsewhere. The Syrian writer Heliodorus records one such list. The Nile, he says, "is called 'Horus,' 'the giver of life' (τὸν ζείδωρον), 'the savior (σωτῆρα) of all Egypt, both Upper and Lower Egypt,' 'the father of Egypt,' 'the creator of Egypt,' 'he who brings new mud each year'."[16]

Of the multitude of literary *topoi* which centered upon the Nile, one of the most popular was, as noted above, the "Causes of the Nile Flood." Another, also widely attested, was the "Rivalry between the Nile and Rain."[17] The existence of a country with perpetually sunny skies which in effect did not need the rain of Zeus for its well-being was a continual source of fascination for intellectuals and ordinary folk alike during all of classical antiquity.[18] Alfred Hermann listed still further *topoi*: descriptions of the Nile, descriptions of the lands and peoples watered by the Nile, accounts of the flora and fauna of the Nile, the reversal of seasons associated with this river, its seven mouths, etc.[19] From all this it is clear that the Nile occupied a very prominent place in the cultural imagination of Graeco-Roman times.

Properties of Nile Water

Valuable as this general evidence is for demonstrating that cultic interest in Nile water would not have been incomprehensible to this age, what is of greater importance is an examination of the specific properties and benefactions of this river. I consider first the former and then the latter, although, as will be seen, the two categories are not entirely unconnected.

Certain properties of Nile water are mentioned only occasionally and probably were of interest only to limited scientific and learned circles, while others occur so frequently that they became in the end common epithets for the water. A good representative of the former type is the unusually low boiling point of Nile water. According to Strabo, Aristotle had reported that to boil Nile water it took only one-half the heat required by any other water.[20] This observation probably only reflects the fact that Nile water was rather warm to begin with. Others observed that the Nile gave off no water vapor or mist, but this property was again one which attracted limited notice.[21] Some also believed that the river and its water had astrological significance. In the twelfth century Eustathius recounted what must have been an ancient tradition: "... the word [Νεῖλος] according to the total numerical value of its letters is able to make up the measure of the year. For Νεῖλος according to the value of the Greek characters which compose it totals the number 365, the number of the days of the year."[22] We do know for certain that in Roman times the Nile itself was sometimes called "the year."[23] This conception not only reflects the rather precise annual recurrence of the flood[24] but also apparently sought to relate it to the magical power of Time.[25] Nilsson notes, however, that "the year" had only limited astrological and religious significance.[26] In addition, as Bonneau points out, it is Ἀβρασάξ and not Νεῖλος which is utilized in the magical texts.[27] I conclude, therefore, that learned speculation rather than popular understanding or practice accounts for this "property."

Aeschylus mentioned as a further property the fact that the Nile water is "untouched by diseases."[28] Even though Dölger believed that one of the benefits of this water was to preserve people from illness and to give health, there is little to support his contention aside from this reference in the *Suppliants* and a single passage in Aelius Aristides. The latter remarks, "We benefit from the healing remedies of the savior gods, of whom one [Sarapis] is synonymous with the Nile."[29] Aristides' proclivities are well-known. Because of his real or imagined illnesses, he tended to be preoccupied with valetudinarian concerns. His attestation, unsupported as it is by contemporary evidence, cannot be taken all that seriously.

Other properties, notably the excellent qualities of this water as a substance for drinking, are abundantly attested. Perhaps the most striking of all reports on the virtues of Nile water as a drink is found in the romance of Achilles Tatius:

> That was the first occasion on which I drank the water of the Nile without mixing it with wine, as I wished to test its excellence as a drink. Wine spoils its character. I filled a transparent glass with it and saw that in the matter of limpidity it vied with, nay, it defeated the vessel that contained it. To the taste it was sweet and cool enough to be delightful.

Therefore, he adds, Egyptians do not care for wine.[30] While the reader might justifiably wonder whether water from a silt-laden river which had passed through hundreds and hundreds of miles of hot desert country could be all that clear and cool, there can be no doubt that the ancients considered Nile water to be a fairly tasty drink.[31] Aeschylus not only called it "holy" but also "good to drink."[32] At the other end of this era Oribasius noted the digestibility and purity of Nile water[33] while Porphyry defined Egyptians as "those who drink the excellent water (τὸ χαλὸν ὕδωρ) of the Nilotic land."[34]

The secret seems to have been the freshness or sweetness of Nile water, a quality which is referred to again and again. For example, Seneca reported that "no river is sweeter to the taste than the Nile"[35] and Aristides indicated that sailors preferred to take Nile water on a sea journey since they believed that it would stay fresh and sweet much longer than other kinds of water.[36] One of the contributors to the *Historia Augusta* remarked, "In fact, the waters of the Nile are so sweet that the inhabitants of the country do not ask for wine.''[37] Various reasons were given for this phenomenon: the tempering of the water by the heat of the torrid zone,[38] the softness of the terrain through which it passed,[39] or the fact that Nile water comes either (as rain) from heaven[40] or from Ocean.[41]

The reputed qualities of this water as a drink no doubt help to explain the existence of traditions that it was bottled and even exported to other countries.[42] Aristides in extolling its qualities says: "And the Egyptians alone of all the peoples we know fill jars with water as others do with wine and keep it at home for three or four or even more years and point with pride to the date as we do in the case of wine.''[43] Epiphanius also had knowledge of such a practice but connected it with a definite annual ritual: "At many locations and sources water changes itself into wine .... Many attest this in Egypt with respect to the Nile. As a consequence, all the people on 11 Tybi (= January 6) draw water [from the Nile] and preserve it both in Egypt itself and in many other countries.''[44] Aside from the religious dimensions of this practice, Epiphanius has pointed out a further aspect: the water thus drawn was in some cases bottled and sent abroad.

There are three much earlier accounts of such an activity but in each case the motivation for it appears to have been other than religious. Herodotus told how Egyptians used the empty wine amphorae after the contents had been consumed:

> Each governor of a district must gather in all the pottery jars from his own town and bring them to Memphis. Those at Memphis must fill them with water and export them from there to those parts of Syria which are waterless. Consequently the pottery containers which are imported and emptied in Egypt are exported to Syria and added to the stock already there.[45]

Although the connection with *wine* jars holds some interest in the light of what has been said above, Herodotus at least saw no religious significance whatever in this whole process. For him it was only a matter of bringing some sort of water to a desert region. For Dinon, a historian of the fourth century BC, the type of water exported assumed central importance. He reported how the Egyptians, when under Persian rule, were required to ship Nile water to the Great King.[46] The water, evidently a symbol for the land of

Egypt, "served as a sort of confirmation of the greatness of the Persian empire and of the universality of its sway."[47] Polybius in turn told how Ptolemy II Philadelphus used to send Nile water to his daughter Berenice after she married Antiochus II of Syria "so that his child would drink water only from this river."[48] Perhaps this, too, was symbolic, an effort to bind Berenice with her country and her dynastic origins, rather than simply a matter of sending her high-quality water to drink.

On the other hand, Juvenal must have known of the practice of exporting Nile water to Rome for religious purposes. At the bidding of Isis-Io, he says, her (overly pious) female devotee will go all the way to Meroe to bring back this water for use in the Campus Martius Iseum at Rome.[49] As Dölger remarks, "Der Untergrund wird aber die Sitte sein, dass tatsächlich Wasser aus dem heiligen Nil zum Sühnewasser gebraucht wurde"—perhaps from the Delta region.[50] If, as Juvenal (and Epiphanius?) apparently indicated, Nile water was put in jars and shipped elsewhere for religious purposes, this would provide still a further explanation for the reduced number of fixed Nile water containers found in Roman times. Under such circumstances a sanctuary no longer needed to prepare its own sacred water since it had water from the actual Nile River. However, this meant that the gods were no longer expected to manifest their power over the water of the Nile within the confines of the local sanctuary—their presence alone in this substance was sufficient.

Benefactions of Nile Water

As observed notably by Diodorus and by Ammianus Marcellinus, the Nile was famed for its benefactions to mankind.[51] In my judgment, the ancient reports of these bring us in closest proximity to the cultic evaluation of this water, and so it is to these that we now turn. As shall be seen, however, links apparently do exist between these effects and at least the chief among the properties discussed above, the freshness and sweetness of the water.

Best known of all these benefits, and one which hardly requires any lengthy comment, was the fruitfulness and abundance which the annual flood gave to Egyptian agriculture.[52] With the proper collection and storage of this water and a proper use of the soil, two or three crops a year were a happy but regular expectation.[53] As Theocritus said, "No land produces as much as Egypt when the Nile floods."[54] A whole variety of Classical and Graeco-Roman sources make it clear how conscious the outside world was of this marvellous richness which the Nile gave. For Aeschylus a proper epithet of the Nile was "feeding many" (πολυθρέμμων).[55] Vergil spoke of the Egyptians as a "gens fortunata" because they dwelt by the Nile which made their country green and productive with its black silt.[56] As a result, Themistius could speak of the Nile as a "father of crops" (ληίων πατήρ).[57] The references to this theme are endless, especially in Roman times when Egypt played such a central role in the agricultural economy of the Mediterranean basin.[58] In this vein, while Nonnus could be swept away with romantic visions of the Nile as a husband passionately embracing and kissing the land with his floods,[59] Libanius could point rather coldly to the harsh economic and political realities that would come about if the Nile ceased to flood. The Christians, he said, would like to abolish the food offerings made to the Nile but have not yet dared to do so because of their fear that the usual harvest would not take place. He dared them either to carry out their secret desire and to bear the disruptive economic and political consequences if grain ceased to be harvested and exported to "all the world" or else to admit that these rituals are in fact efficacious for obtaining an abundant Nile flood.[60] The land of Egypt was preeminently "the fertile land,"[61] and all agreed that it would be unwise to tamper with such remarkable success.[62]

The ancients recognized that the fertility which the Nile gave was not simply due to the water as such but also to the rich silt which it carried. Vergil stressed this in his *Georgics*[63] as did Seneca at some length:

> The Nile brings water and earth to a sandy dry soil .... It leaves all its silt in places which are dried out and full of fissures, depositing all the rich substances carried in suspension by it upon a dry land. By its water and its silt, it renders a two-fold service to the fields .... Egypt owes to the Nile not only the fertility of its land but the very land itself.[64]

The gymnosophists of Ethiopia, according to Philostratus, recognized this dual nature of Nile water in a profound sense.

"They," he reported, "render cultic worship to the Nile in particular, for they consider this river to be both earth and water."[65] In view of his reference to a cult, Philostratus must have depicted these wise men as worshipping this river because it combined in itself two elements fundamental to the generation and growth of the cosmos.

Such an understanding of the richness of the silt suspended in Nile water may very well have led to the conclusion that drinking quantities of this water would lead to rapid growth and weight gain. Not only was Nile water called "rich" and "fat"[66] but it was also said to make those who drink it fat.[67] According to both Plutarch and Aelian, this could even become a problem. The Apis bull, for example, had to have his own special water supply lest by drinking nothing but Nile water he become too fat and overweight.[68]

Perhaps because of this "richness" and because of the evident effects it had on plant life in the Nile valley, the ancients concluded that Nile water fertilized and caused growth in animals as well. Egypt was famed in Graeco-Roman times as the home of a multitude of huge and strange animals.[69] What brought these into being, a variety of ancient scholars agreed, was the Nile. According to Aristobulus, an early Hellenistic historian, "... the Nile is more productive than other rivers and produces huge creatures, among others the amphibious kind."[70] Pomponius Mela in declaring that the waters of the Nile are "efficaces ad generandum alendumque" pointed out that this river not only is teeming with fish but also is the begetter of hippopotami and crocodiles.[71] Consequently, he referred to Egypt as "the richly fecund mother of animals."[72] At a much earlier date Aeschylus, although speaking of the effects of this water on human beings, called it "cattle-producing water" (ἀλφεσίβοιον ὕδωρ).[73] According to Aelian, this had practical implications for animal husbandry as it was carried on in Egypt. Goatherds, he indicated, found Nile water a marvellous aid for promoting the fertility of their flocks:

> There are some Egyptian goats which bring forth quintuplets, while most produce twins. The cause of this is said to be the Nile, for it supplies water which is extremely progenitive (εὐτεκνότατον παρέχων ὕδωρ). As a result, those goatherds who have an eye for fine flocks and who are concerned to take care of their animals use a device to draw as much water from the Nile as possible for them. They do this especially for those animals which are barren.[74]

The same situation held true in the case of human beings. Because of the potency of the Nile, for them, too, Egypt was the "perfecunda generatrix."[75] Aristotle's view was shared widely: "Egypt is a place ... where the women have a reputation for regularly bringing their infants to term. They both bear them and deliver them frequently and with ease. Infants that are born, even those born deformed, are able to live."[76] Birth defects, he believed, occurred more frequently as an unhappy side effect of this rich procreative power: "... in this species (human beings) the occurrence of offspring born deformed is more common in those regions where the women are more prolific (πολύγονοι) as, for example, Egypt."[77] Multiple births were thought to be quite common in the Nile valley. Aristotle noted that women in Egypt bore twins with some frequency and even triplets or quadruplets from time to time.[78] He was even aware of one case in that country in which a woman bore quintuplets. "This," he claimed, "was the limit of human multiple parturition."[79] The Augustan historian Trogus Pompeius, however, reported that seven children had been born at one time from the womb of an Egyptian woman.[80] More than triplets, said Pliny, are considered a portent everywhere except in Egypt where multiple births are much more common.[81] According to some writers, the reason for such fecundity was the Nile. Solinus, for example, remarked: That a woman could give birth to seven children at once as Trogus had reported "is not all that marvellous for Egypt since the Nile makes fruitful with its fertilizing drink not only the fields of the earth but also the wombs of mankind."[82] Seneca was also aware of this theory and added that many believed Nile water to be a good cure for female sterility.[83] Others reported the effects of this water upon pregnant women. Aristotle had heard that children were often born in Egypt after only eight months of gestation and saw this as an illustration of his point that the whole pregnancy period was easier and safer for women in that country.[84] In commenting on this text, Oribasius, a medical writer, insisted that this view was correct for "Egyptians have no still-born infants, yet their women are regularly with children and the rearing of them is continuous, whether this is due to the digestibility of the water—for it is as though Nile water is free from impurities—or due to other causes."[85] Elsewhere the same author adds that Nile water is in

general useful for regulating the female reproductive organs.[86] I
should point out in this connection that according to Theophrastus,
Nile water helped to regulate the internal organs in another way as
well. Because of the soda-like substance it contained (μῖξιν ἔχον
λιτρώδη), it served as a fine laxative![87]

Such an interest in the fertilizing effects of Nile water upon
human beings, a theme so well attested in Hellenistic and especially
Roman times, was in reality of a much more venerable origin. In
the fifth century BC Aeschylus could already refer to the Nile as
"the water from which comes to men life-giving blood in rich abundance."[88] No doubt the concept goes back much further to the early
stages of Egyptian history.[89]

Because the ancients were so impressed by the generative and
nurturing effect that the Nile had upon the flora and fauna with
which it came in contact, they called the river itself "fecund" and
"fructifying." In Greek the epithets frequently applied to it were
γόνιμος and πολύγονος and their variants.[90] Latin authors spoke of it
as *fecundus* or *fertilis*.[91] It was not simply that the Nile fertilized
already existing beings. So potent was its life-giving power that it
even generated living creatures spontaneously. Pomponius Mela
saw this as the most astounding sign of its generative and nurturing
power and described the phenomenon as follows:

> The Nile ... also pours life-forces into the earth and fashions living
> beings from the ground. This phenomenon is clearly seen when the
> river has ceased its flooding and has returned to its bed. In the wet
> fields are found animals which are not yet fully developed but are still
> in process of receiving life. Their bodies are in part clearly formed but
> in part remain still conjoined with the earth.[92]

Several reports indicate that the animals generated in this manner
were mice.[93] The Egyptian writer Horapollo speaks rather of frogs
while Ovid and Joannes Lydus describe the beings thus generated
as exotic and monstrous growths.[94] Diodorus, in relating a tradition
that from time to time great numbers of mice were spontaneously
generated in the Thebaid, insisted that this sort of phenomenon is
verified nowhere else but in Egypt.[95] To this he added:

> For even in our own times throughout the flooded areas of Egypt
> living creatures are clearly seen being generated in the pools of water
> that remain. For when the river begins to recede and the sun has

dried up the surface of the mud, people say that animals are produced, some of them fully formed, but some only half-completed and still actually attached to the earth.[96]

An anonymous lyric fragment cited by Hippolytus apparently also speaks of this marvellous occurrence: "To this day the Nile fattens the Egyptian mud and brings forth creatures enfleshed by means of the watery warmth and gives forth living bodies."[97] The presence of such reports in a variety of sources from the Roman Imperial period probably indicates that many people in that era had heard of this sign of the Nile's exceptional power.[98]

Ancient observers apparently saw some connection between the property of sweetness possessed by Nile water and its generative power. In several cases the two qualities are reported side by side.[99] Plutarch suggests, but does not quite clearly affirm, that the same elements in the water which produce its sweetness also cause its nourishing benefits.[100] In addition, the text in the *Corpus Hermeticum* referred to above would seem to imply a causal relationship of some sort. "I am about to sing a hymn to him who ... has enjoined the sweet water to come forth from the Ocean into the inhabited world and uninhabited land for the support and creation of all men ...."[101] To be sure, the evidence on this point is not very extensive. If it is true, however, that the most frequently mentioned property of Nile water is in fact related to its generative effects, then we may be all the more certain that this benefaction of Nile water was the one which most interested the Greeks and Romans.

Life After Death and Nile Water

Did this life-giving power of the Nile extend to the gift of eternal life? For dynastic Egypt the answer must be yes. As early as the Pyramid texts the "cool water" of the Nile, itself the vital fluid which had issued from the body of Osiris, was said to restore life to the dead Osiris-king.[102] That, however, such a conception was generally known in the Graeco-Roman world is quite difficult to verify.

If writers from this period were aware of such an understanding of this water, they certainly do not reveal it in their extant works. The only possible literary source, a passage from Firmicus Maternus, does not in fact assert that Nile water was believed to offer rebirth: "Frustra tibi hanc aquam quam colis, putas aliquando prodesse. Alia est aqua qua renovati homines renascuntur."[103] There is an obvious claim here by this Christian writer that baptismal water does give renewal and rebirth to Christian believers. In saying this, he is not countering a claim made by devotees of the Egyptian gods that "aqua Nilotica homines renovantur atque renascuntur." Their claims, at least according to him, are much more modest. They simply say that Nile water "will be beneficial at some time" (*aliquando prodesse*), a phrase which points only to some sort of hoped-for benefits. Dölger argues that such words do not look to an other-worldly fulfillment but are firmly situated in empirical realities and expectations.[104] I quite agree. Firmicus Maternus is not saying that baptismal water actually achieves what devotees of the Egyptian gods (falsely) expect from Nile water but that it is a far more powerful substance.[105]

A second set of data requiring attention in this connection are those texts which speak of "apotheosis by drowning in the Nile." According to a variety of Pharaonic and even late Egyptian sources, anyone who drowned in the Nile was divinized in a very special way. Such a person became a *ḥsy*, a "Blessed Drowned Osiris."[106] If such a concept was actually known in the wider Mediterranean world, it managed to leave almost no trace in the literary remains from this area. Herodotus, who had visited Egypt, learned that the corpses of those who drowned or who were eaten by crocodiles were under special taboos. He wrote:

> Whenever either an Egyptian or a foreigner is carried off into the river by a crocodile or drowns in the river and this comes to light, every sort of obligation is upon the inhabitants of the city to whose shore the body has been carried to embalm it, to dress it as finely as possible, and to place it in holy mummy cases. No one is allowed to touch the corpse, not even relatives or friends, except the priests of the Nile, who, because the corpse is something more than human, prepare it for burial with their own hands.[107]

Herodotus himself certainly understood that some sort of divinization took place for a person who died in this manner. His account, however, must have been treated only as an odd bit of anthropological lore, for later non-Egyptian sources show no real awareness of such a practice. Tertullian knew the technical term, *esietus*, but defines such people only as "those whom the waters have slain."[108] Though he places blame for such occurrences upon evil spirits lurking in various bodies of water, he refers not at all to the Nile. For him the term has become generalized; it has lost its specificity. Finally, precisely where we would expect to find this motif, namely, in the accounts of the divinization of Antinoos, the favorite of the Emperor Hadrian, it does not occur. This young man died in 130 AD under strange circumstances as he accompanied Hadrian on a voyage up the Nile. The emperor himself said that the youth had drowned in the river.[109] But contemporaries had other theories. Some said that Antinoos had given up his life out of devotion for Hadrian, perhaps in conjunction with some magical rite,[110] while some related it to an accident caused by some excessive act of passion on the part of Hadrian.[111] The sources are unanimous that Antinoos was then honored as a god but in no case, contrary to Wilcken, is there any suggestion that this occurred *because* he had drowned in the Nile.[112]

There is a third group of evidence, the Osiris "cool water" inscriptions, the so-called Osiris-Canopus figures, and the water pitchers used in the Isis-Sarapis cult. Together, this array of material does provide a more postive indication that the cult of Nile water offered immortality as one of its chief benefactions. Yet, because the texts which speak of these objects do not expressly mention the Nile and because, as will be argued, this evidence occurs only within a limited temporal and geographical confine, I have postponed discussion of it to the following chapter. It is my conviction that this material represents not a general perspective within the cult but only a local development.[113]

Conclusions

Aside, then, from this last group of materials, the evidence from the Graeco-Roman writers is quite clear. Contrary to the wider set of benefactions supposed by Dölger and Bonneau, the actuality depicted by the ancient writings is much more restricted. To be sure, Nile water is imbued with life. But this is almost never conceived of in terms of giving or restoring health (*contra* Dölger) or in terms of endowing a person with immortality (*contra* Bonneau and others). Instead, this water was thought to give fertility and growth to crops, to animals, and to men. A special beneficiary of its powers were women who sought to become pregnant or who were already with child. This is entirely in line with the results set forth in the previous chapter. There I argued on the basis of the available evidence from the sites that the cultic activities which centered upon Nile water offered to their participants an improved quality of life in this world. I cannot here verify what I suggested there that one of these qualities is better health. However, that the cult which was associated with Nile water promised better crops and herbs—or even a better overall financial situation—as well as numerous and vigorous children appears now to be all the more strongly assured.

CHAPTER SIX

WHY NILE WATER?
3. THE OSIRIS EVIDENCE

Of the three groups of objects I wish to examine in this chapter, one in particular, the cultic pitcher (Pl. XI), has received extensive attention during the last hundred years. Scholars perceived it to be a very important utensil in Isis-Sarapis liturgical practice and were able to draw upon descriptions found in several ancient writers for help in interpreting it. The most famous of these is a vivid passage set toward the end of Apuleius' account of a *Navigium Isidis* procession at Cenchreae, the southern port of Corinth. Almost at the end of the line, just before the great priest, marched a cult official bearing such a pitcher:

> Another bore in his blessed bosom the venerable image of the highest deity, an image not like that of any bovine animal nor like that of a bird nor like that of a wild beast nor even like that of man himself, but, having resulted from an ingenious discovery, even in its newness it is an image which should be reverenced as the ineffable sign of a somehow higher worship, one which must be hidden in a great silence. This image was fashioned in shining gold entirely in accord with the following pattern: a small vessel hollowed out with considerable craftsmanship, with a quite round bottom portion. On the outside it was adorned with marvellous images of Egyptian objects. Its mouth was not raised very high but in extending forth to form a channel, it jutted out in a long spout. On its other side was fastened a handle which goes out some distance from the vessel in a sweeping curve. On top of this sat, entwined like a knot, a *uraeus* serpent with his scaly neck lifted high with a streaked swelling.[1]

In the face of such a detailed description and with several other ancient accounts as corroborative evidence,[2] modern scholars have found it easy down almost to the present day to assume that Apuleius is describing a cultic usage found wherever Isis-Sarapis worship had taken root.[3] Only within the last few years have Ladislav Vidman and Françoise Dunand advanced the view that the Graeco-Roman *Navigium Isidis* festival probably originated no earlier than the first century BC.[4] However, this hypothesis says nothing directly about the origin of the cultic pitcher since, as Dunand indicates, it served also in contexts other than this annual festal procession.[5] It is my intention to demonstrate that the use of such a vessel can be verified only within a restricted geographical area and only from about the first century BC onwards.

A second assemblage of materials is closely related to this first group. I refer to those images of Osiris which consist of a decorated jar upon which the head of the god has been placed and which have very often been called Osiris-Canopus figures (Pls. XV, XVI and XVII). This traditional designation or an older variant, "Canopus figure," is based upon a misunderstanding of long duration and is quite misleading since there is no known god named "Canopus," there is no such title of Osiris, and, as far as can be determined, this image had no special connection with the Egyptian seaside town of Canopus.[6] I propose, therefore, to employ instead the nomenclature adopted by J. G. Griffiths and to refer to this iconographic type as an "Osiris Hydreios," that is, as an "Osiris-in-a-jar" or "Osiris *in hydria*."[7] Perhaps the best studies of this rather curious image remain those done by Wilhelm Weber in the years immediately preceding World War I, although certain later investigations are also quite helpful.[8] These studies have succeeded in clearing away a variety of misconceptions and have produced an intelligible explanation of the nature of this object. It now appears quite probable, as will be discussed below, that the Osiris Hydreios statue had its origin about the first century BC and that it is related in form and in significance to the cultic pitcher. What has not been previously observed is that both objects share a rather similar geographical distribution.

A group of about a dozen funerary inscriptions bearing the formula "May Osiris give you cool water" or a variant will constitute the third and final collection of objects pertinent to the present context. These have been the subject of a few specialized studies and are frequently referred to in general works on Isis-Sarapis worship.[9] References to this formula do occur in some of the studies of the cultic pitcher and of the Osiris Hydreios figure, but almost never is the point made that a special relationship might have existed between these latter two items and the "cool water" texts.[10] I intend to clarify and highlight this relationship since I believe it to be significant for the interpretation of all three objects. Beyond this, those who have studied these inscriptions have regularly noted that they are found only in Egypt and in the area around Rome. This point has in fact been made so frequently that a recent writer on the subject has had to remind us that one such "cool water" text was found at Carthage.[11] My argument will be that these inscriptions, the pitchers, and the Osiris statues all show the same geographical and temporal distribution and are interrelated in their significance.

It is my purpose in all of this to show that the three objects formed a single unified cluster related to Osiris. Its component parts came into existence about the same time and spread to the same areas of the Roman Empire. If this proves true, it holds significant implication for the interpretation of those texts found in Apuleius and the other writers of the Roman period to which I referred at the outset. These could no longer be viewed as descriptions of a more or less general liturgical practice within the Isis-Sarapis cult but only of a localized development. In addition, if the "cool water" texts are to be joined with the pitcher and the Osiris Hydreios image, the symbolism involved in all three must have had reference to life after death. Each of these objects has reference, as will be seen, to the water in which Osiris is present, i.e., the life-giving water of the Nile. This means, however, that the Nile water associated with this assemblage of materials was the source not only of a bountiful earthly life but also of a joyous life beyond the grave.

The Cultic Pitcher

The pitcher or "urnula" described by Apuleius in the *Metamorphoses* had a rather unusual form—indeed, Apuleius refers to its "novitas"—and was apparently one of the most sacred symbols of the cult of Isis at Cenchreae.[12] It was gilded or of gold and had a quite round lower portion, the outer surface of which was decorated with images of Egyptian objects.[13] Two features of this pitcher are especially notable. First, its spout was extended out from the body to such a degree that it took on the shape of the long beak of a bird. Secondly, at the top of a large and well-rounded handle the figure of a *uraeus* serpent raised its head and upper body above the pitcher's rim. Apuleius does not indicate the contents of this vessel; this must have been an element of the "deep silence" which, he says, must necessarily surround the fundamental sacred objects of the cult. From other sources, however, it is known that the pitcher held Nile water and that the divinity to which it had reference was Osiris.[14] Although Apuleius here refers to the object as an "urnula" and Vitruvius uses the term "hydria," it apparently was more properly called a "ὑδρεῖον" by Greeks or a "hydraeum" by Latin speakers.[15]

No actual example of this type of cultic pitcher seems to have survived. V. Wessetzky argued that the *hydria* found in 1831 at Egyed, Hungary, did serve as such a vessel and derived originally from the sanctuary at Savaria. For many reasons, however, this hypothesis appears very dubious.[16] On the other hand, a part of such a pitcher may well have been recovered from the central cella of the late Roman period Temple E at Soli, Cyprus. The bronze upper portion of a *uraeus* serpent, 0.102 m long, was found on the floor of this cella and suggests by its presence that a sacred pitcher was in use at this sanctuary.[17] A. Westholm had discovered here in the course of his excavations the headless statue of a female who wore on her upper arms bracelets which terminated in the raised head of the *uraeus*.[18] With this object in mind he concluded that in the central cella he had found the *uraeus* portion of such a bracelet. However, the *uraeus* recovered is much too large to have belonged to an arm bracelet such as is seen on the statue.[19] A much more likely hypothesis is that the object found was broken off the rim or handle of a bronze pitcher and tossed among the rubble in that room. Since the *uraeus* was found among the fragments of statues and other cultic objects lying on the floor of the cella and not in the fill, it is quite possible that worship ceased at the site when, as may be guessed, Christians ransacked the place and, among other things, carried off the valuable pitcher to re-use it. On this view they would have first torn off the hateful demonic symbol of the serpent and tossed it aside with the fragments of the cult statues, etc.[20]

Despite the dearth of actual physical examples, this distinctively-shaped pitcher does grace a fairly large number of frescoes, reliefs, and coin types and is referred to, as has been mentioned, in various literary contexts. The earliest examples date from the end of the first century BC. Vitruvius, writing during the reign of Augustus, provides important information not upon the form of the pitcher but upon its function. Speaking of those "qui sacerdotia gerunt moribus Aegyptiorum," a phrase which certainly would have included non-Egyptians who follow Egyptian ways, he says: "And so when with holy reverence water is brought in a pitcher to the precinct and to the temple, then, prostrating themselves on the ground and with their hands raised to heaven, they give thanks to the divine liberality for the finding of it."[21]

Frescoes found in the so-called *Aula Isiaca*, a room discovered under the palace of Domitian on the Palatine Hill at Rome, offer more precise information on this form of pitcher and its *terminus a quo*. Here on a frieze painted in Egyptianizing style a pitcher of the type described by Apuleius alternates with *uraeus* serpents and other symbols found in connection with Isis worship.[22] Since the paintings in this room are now dated on the basis of their style to c. 20 BC,[23] this type of pitcher must already have been well enough known at the end of the first century to serve as a meaningful symbol in a more secular environment.[24] As a third piece of early evidence, an Alexandrian coin type from the reign of Augustus demonstrates that this pitcher was known in that city in the late first century BC (Pl. XII, 1).[25] Clearly then, this cultic object originated sometime before 20 BC. The absence of any Hellenistic evidence, however, suggests that this date of origin is not to be pushed back very much earlier. Further, the fact that the pitcher appears as an Egyptian symbol in the *Aula Isiaca* points to that country as its place of origin.

That such a pitcher had a significant function at least in certain Isis-Sarapis cultic environments is clear not only from literary sources but also from evidence associated with several known sanctuaries. The Soli fragment and Apuleius' description of what purported to be the pitcher from the Cenchreae Iseum have already been treated. In addition, the Isis sanctuary at Pompeii provides a number of examples. Already described previously was the relief of a large pitcher found above the outer door of the Nile water crypt (Pl. VI, 1). This vessel, which is flanked by two kneeling worshippers, has a large round body, a rather narrow neck, and a large spout. From on-site inspection and from examination of various photographs, it appears to me that a *uraeus* rises by the handle above the mouth of the vessel.[26] Secondly, in the lower right corner of the

"Reception of Io by Isis" fresco found in the *Ecclesiasterion* there stands a pitcher upon a rather irregular stone pedestal.[27] That this pitcher is set so close to Isis and to the Nile river god is no doubt of symbolic importance. Set upon what appears to be a purple cushion,[28] the vessel has a spherical body, a large arching handle, a raised *uraeus* on the rim by the handle, and a long spout which juts out slightly beyond the body of the pitcher.[29] Thirdly, in this same room was discovered a fresco which was at once named the "Temple of the Hydreion." On an altar in the doorway of a shrine stands a pitcher. This vessel has an ovoid body, a tall and narrow neck, an extended spout, and a high arching handle. Around the base is a garland of flowers, perhaps roses.[30] Finally, it is commonly thought that one of the figures forming the procession of cultic officials around the inner walls of the portico bore a pitcher. This personage was described by the excavator—the original painting has not survived—as "an Egyptian priest, entirely clothed in white and wearing sandals. In his hands he carried some object with veneration, but it is not possible to distinguish what it is."[31] While this last item is open to some question, it is clear that at the Pompeii Iseum the pitcher was a very important religious object.

Two sanctuaries at Rome offer some evidence. On the site of the Campus Martius Iseum (Pl. XVIII) were found in the course of the last two centuries several large columns with reliefs carved on their surface.[32] One of these, discovered in 1858, was partially broken and several of its reliefs are rather worn.[33] Wilhelm Weber examined it and indicated his certainty that one of the processional figures depicted on this column bears the long-spouted pitcher described by Apuleius.[34] Also in the small Isis sanctuary found on the Aventine Hill close to the present Church of S. Sabina one of the wall paintings shows a large fluted pitcher with a tall palm branch set in its mouth.[35] This, however, lacks the raised *uraeus* and extended spout so often found on clear examples of the cultic pitcher. Yet in the context the vessel can hardly be anything but religiously significant. Darsy uses stylistic evidence to date this and the other frescoes in the room to the last half of the second century AD.[36]

One more site requires attention. Close to the sanctuary of Isis and Sarapis at Philippi investigators found carved into the natural rock a relief of the goddess with a pitcher near her feet. It dates to the second or third century AD. Isis is portrayed standing in a *naiskos* with a sistrum near her head as an identifying symbol and a small altar on the ground to her right. The pitcher, only faintly visible to her left in the photographs, is also set on the ground. It is in the form of a rather tall and somewhat slender *oenochoe* with a long upturned spout and a high arching handle. No *uraeus* is visible, and indeed the general conformity of this object with the classic type described by Apuleius is slight. Yet its association with Isis and the proximity of the relief to the sanctuary strongly suggest that devotees of the Egyptian gods at Philippi knew the pitcher as a familiar liturgical utensil.[37]

The total body of evidence for these pitchers derives from a limited number of localities.[38] Various Alexandrian coin types from the reign of Augustus up through that of Marcus Aurelius afford by far the largest group of examples.[39] Two reliefs depicting Isis and Sarapis in serpentine form with a pitcher of this general type set between them also seem to have come from Alexandria (Pl. XII, 2). In addition, two coins of this type were struck during the reign of Trajan for the Menelaite nome which is located in the environs of Alexandria. All the rest of Egypt is represented by only a single object, an embroidered tunic of the second century AD which was found at Saqqarah (Fig. 23). This state of affairs suggests that if this pitcher type did indeed originate in Egypt, it was probably first utilized at Alexandria.

Outside of Egypt the only region providing a quantity of such evidence is central Italy. Rome and the Pompeii-Stabiae-

Fig. 23. Saqqarah, Egypt. Detail from an embroidered tunic of the second cen. A.D. A long-spouted cultic pitcher stands upon a stylized offering table. Loaves of bread are to the left; on the right is also bread (?).

Herculaneum area both have produced a number of examples (e.g., Pls. XI and XIII), and single finds were made at Ostia and at Nomentum in Latium. Elsewhere in the Mediterranean basin finds are very scanty. Apuleius, of course, may have been describing an actual pitcher used by Isis worshippers at Cenchreae. There are also the fragment from the Soli Iseum and the rock relief from Philippi which were discussed above. And Plutarch, who speaks of the pitcher used in this cult, may possibly have seen such a vessel utilized in rituals in his native Greece. Be that as it may, only about 10% of the evidence, four out of about forty items, is known to have come from places other than northern Egypt and central Italy.[40]

In the course of his discussion of the well-known fresco from Herculaneum which depicts a priest presenting the sacred water for the adoration of the faithful (Pl. XIV), V. Tran Tam Tinh attempts to fashion a typology of the cult pitchers used in the worship of the Egyptian gods.[41] Though his analysis of the data seems on several points rather problematic, the basic two-fold division he proposes is quite correct. The pitcher described by Apuleius represents one part of this division. Its most notable feature is a long spout which extends well out beyond the body of the vessel and which often tilts or bends downward. I will henceforth refer to this type by a term coined by Weber: *Schnabelkanne*.[42] The other basic type is what I will henceforth call the Vatican Museum relief type or, simply, the Vatican type.[43] In contradistinction to the *Schnabelkanne*, the spout of the vessel which appears on this relief, while somewhat extended, terminates within the horizontal circumference of the body. In relation to the ordinary forms utilized for Graeco-Roman pottery and metal vessels, this type appears more "normal"; Tran Tam Tinh speaks of it as being "plus hellénisée."[44] What appears to have happened is that in certain quarters the original Egyptian form was assimilated to the more familiar *urceus* which was used regularly in Roman sacrificial rites and which appears, for example, on the frieze of the Temple of Vesta at Rome[45] and on a variety of late Republican Roman coins.[46] Far fewer examples of this second type are found and none of them appears to antedate the second century AD. While much of the evidence fits neatly into these two types, four examples (about 10% of the known total) can only be termed "miscellaneous," while eleven items (i.e., about 27% of the total) cannot be categorized because of insufficient data.[47]

What Tran Tam Tinh did not notice is that there is a further division within the *Schnabelkanne* type between those pitchers with high shoulders and those with rounded shoulders. What I mean by the designation "high shoulders" is that the line formed by the top of the body is almost straight and runs parallel to the base. The round-shouldered variety has shoulders which slope downward noticeably from the neck. The body of this second type is almost always rather squat while that of the first is often quite tall.[48] These two varieties of the *Schnabelkanne*, interestingly, show a rather decided geographical split. The high-shouldered type is normal on the coins of Alexandria.[49] The pitcher seen in the frieze of the *Aula Isiaca* at Rome also shows this form, but Malaise has argued on other grounds that the frescoes in this room are Alexandrian in inspiration if not the actual products of Alexandrian-trained painters.[50] The only other *Schnabelkanne* of this type appears in relief on a silver cup which was found in the Palaestra of Pompeii. This cup and a companion piece found with it date from the very beginning of the first century AD. Though in form both cups closely imitate the *terra sigillata* ware of Arezzo and northern Italy, their decorations are purely Graeco-Egyptian in inspiration.[51]

On the other hand, much of the evidence for the round-shouldered *Schnabelkanne* comes from Campania in Italy. The three surviving examples from the Pompeii Iseum are all in this form. A further example from Pompeii is seen in the beautiful frescoes which decorate a small room in the *Casa del Frutteto*.[52] The pitcher, with a purple cushion under it, is set on top of a basin-like structure. Jewels decorate the body of the vessel.[53] On a fresco from Stabiae two women appear bearing this type of *Schnabelkanne* on trays (Pl. XI).[54] The base of each vessel, as frequently, is encircled with a garland of roses. Three male figures who carry *situlae* are seen walking toward the women (to receive some of the sacred water in their small pails?). Two pitchers of this type appear in the central portion of the *Mensa Isiaca*, a bronze table inlaid with designs in silver which was probably produced in a workshop at Rome.[55] Also to be joined to this group is the pitcher described by Apuleius.[56] However, only two instances of the type derive from

Egypt and both apparently are dated no earlier than the second century AD. The tunic found at Saqqarah near Memphis depicts such a round-shouldered pitcher (Fig. 23).[57] The other item is a relief of Isis-Thermouthis and Sarapis-Agathodaimon. Both divinities have serpent bodies, the tails of which are knotted together.[58] Between them is placed a pitcher which is of this type.[59] It is tempting in the light of this configuration of evidence to believe that the round-shouldered type may have had its origin in Italy, not in Egypt. Certainly there is no *a priori* reason to exclude the possibility that reverse influence accounts for the second century examples of this type found in Egypt. I would caution, however, that the overall sample of data is small.[60]

The other basic type of pitcher is the Hellenized Vatican type. The prototype from which the name is borrowed is a superb relief of the Hadrianic period which depicts several members of an Isis procession (Pl. XIII). Very probably it was found at Rome or else certainly somewhere in Italy.[61] The third figure from the right bears a pitcher with a spherical belly, an elegantly curved handle, and a somewhat extended spout. The usual *uraeus* rises from the point at which the handle joins the rim. Closely resembling this pitcher is that found on a grave relief from Ostia (second or third century AD) which commemorates a certain priest of *Isis Ostiensis* and the *Mater deorum Transtiberina*; the pitcher is found on the left side of the relief above a pair of *cistae mysticae*.[62] Besides these examples from Italy, there are the two coins issued by the Menelaite nome which were mentioned above; these depict a cultic pitcher with a shortened spout. Despite differences (e.g., these pitchers have a fluted body), they appear to belong to this classification.[63] These few examples of the type are all second century AD or later. That they appear no earlier than this time suggests, as I indicated above, that this type represents a secondary development from the original *Schnabelkanne*.[64]

How did the cultic pitcher function within Isis worship? To begin with, the various literary references, the Vatican relief, the relief from the Campus Martius Iseum, the Pompeii silver cup, etc., all join in attesting that it was carried in processions as the ''summi numinis veneranda effigies.'' Secondly, as a container for the sacred Nile water, it was the subject of adoration. This is clear from

Vitruvius' discussion of it, from the Herculaneum fresco spoken of above, and from the relief of the pitcher flanked by kneeling devotees which is above the crypt entrance at Pompeii. Both of these functions are well known and need no further comment.

However, I believe that a third function can be demonstrated. The last figure in the procession on the Vatican relief (Pl. XIII) carries in her right hand a sistrum and in her left a long ladle. In a study of the identity of this cultic official, L. Castiglione concluded that she is a *simpulatrix*, i.e., a person who carries the ladle which is called a *simpulum*.[65] Although normally both in Greek and Roman cultic contexts such a ladle was employed for pouring libations, Castiglione rejects this possibility for the cult of Isis and Sarapis since, as he says, the sacred water is an embodiment of Osiris himself.[66] However, I believe that he has made an overly hasty judgment that libations of this sort were impossible. Dunand provides clear evidence of such a sacrificial practice in Ptolemaic Egypt—indeed, this kind of offering could even be made to Osiris himself.[67] That such a practice spread at least to segments of the Graeco-Roman cult is clear from Apuleius' description of the morning ritual at the Cenchreae sanctuary.[68] One of the first things done by the priest after he had opened the curtain in front of Isis' image was to obtain water from the temple cella and to pour a libation to the goddess with a *spondeum* or libation vessel. Given the fact that the priest obtained this water from the inmost part of the temple (*de penetrali*), he probably drew it from the sacred pitcher which was kept in the cella.[69] In the description of a procession supplied by Clement of Alexandria, the person who walked in front of the water pitcher carried a σπονδεῖον.[70] Because he also bore ''the cubit of righteousness,'' very likely the sacred cubit used to measure the Nile flood, this religious functionary, the στολιστής, must have been closely associated with the cultic pitcher and its contents. Presumably the libation vessel which he carried was used for pouring offerings of Nile water from the pitcher. I conclude, therefore, that the ladle carried by the *simpulatrix* in the Vatican relief was also used for the same purpose.[71]

This last assertion is made the more certain by the manner in which the pitcher-bearer is garbed. Castiglione had noted that this individual has his toga pulled up over his head (*capite velato*) but failed to draw the obvious conclusion.[72] In Roman practice such a mode of dress characterized the individual who directed a sacrificial rite.[73] Although the *capite velato* was required only for a genuine *ritus romanus*, its presence here, whether due to a conscious "Romanization" of the cult either by its local practitioners or by the artist, almost certainly indicates that the official who carries the pitcher is about to conduct a sacrificial rite, i.e., a libation of Nile water.

Was the water from this pitcher also consumed as a drink? From the variety of evidence in the last chapter on the efficacy of drinking Nile water, we might well assume that it was. However, while I have found Christian evidence from the Byzantine period which makes it clear that Nile water was ritually consumed even in areas quite far from the Nile valley, I have not been able to discover corresponding evidence from the Isis-Sarapis cult.[74] Heinrich Fuhrmann suggests that the two silver cups found at Pompeii, one of which has the relief of a priest bearing the cultic pitcher, were used "by the faithful during liturgical rites at the sanctuary for drinking the sacred water."[75] Perhaps so. However, these cups, though entirely covered with reliefs which pertain to the cult, were found on the east side of the town near the amphitheater a long distance from the Iseum. That they actually came from the sanctuary is a sheer guess. On the other hand, in the cella of the Pompeii Iseum was found a charred wooden box which contained a tiny gold cup, almost a small version of the communion cups used in some Protestant churches.[76] Conceivably this could have been used in a rite of drinking Nile water but it is very difficult to be certain.

Clement of Alexandria's description of the pitcher-bearer and his accompanying retinue contains one element which raises questions for the present discussion: "After all these comes forth the prophet who in plain sight bears in his arms the cultic pitcher. With him follow those who bear the ἔκπεμψιν of bread."[77] Here bread is clearly associated with the water, but how it is associated rests on how the word ἔκπεμψις is to be interpreted. It might be understood as an "issue," a "giving forth," and thence perhaps a "distribution." However, Derchain believes that Clement's source chose this word to convey peculiarly Egyptian concepts surrounding offertory rites and argues that it must therefore be translated as "offering."[78] Since the scene embroidered on the Saqqarah tunic also depicts the cultic pitcher and several loaves of bread placed on a table in the manner of Egyptian sacrificial practice (Fig. 23),[79] we appear to have in this text further evidence that the sacred water was an element used in sacrifices rather than any suggestion that it was ritually consumed by worshippers.[80]

To sum up, the cultic pitcher very likely originated in the first century BC at Alexandria or in its environs. Its original form was the *Schnabelkanne*, a form presumably with some Egyptian antecedents, although these have not yet been determined with clarity.[81] Its use spread to sanctuaries of Isis at Rome and in central Italy—nowhere is it found in connection with the cult of Sarapis—as well as to a few areas either closely connected with Rome (Corinth-Cenchreae and Philippi) or with Egypt (Soli).[82] Here its form was adapted and even, as time wore on, radically Hellenized. At those precincts which adopted it, the pitcher served as one of the most important cultic symbols. A container for the sacred Nile water, the embodiment of Osiris, it functioned much like a monstrance in Roman Catholic Eucharistic practice. While this water was the subject of great devotion and adoration and while it was also used in sacrificial rites to Isis, a practice which perhaps recalled the fruitful union of Isis and Osiris referred to so frequently in texts cited in earlier chapters, I have not been able to discover any clear evidence that it was shared among the worshippers as a communion element.

The Images of Osiris Hydreios

The second object in question, the Osiris Hydreios statue, is characterized by a number of features. Its body is a high-shouldered jar which is decorated in relief either with a number of Egyptian sacred objects arranged according to a regular pattern, or with a U-neck garment, the opening of which has several horizontal crossbands, or simply with spiral fluting. Its base is regularly surrounded with a garland of flowers. On the top of the jar is set the head of the god; he is sometimes bearded in the Egyptian fashion with a "cylinder" beard, sometimes without a beard. His hair is arranged in the Egyptian style called the *klaft* and on his head is one of several different types of Egyptian crowns. Occasionally the head of Isis or even that of Anubis replaced that of Osiris. This is a secondary development found only where the figure of Osiris Hydreios is also known.[83]

In the course of my investigations I managed to locate some two hundred and twenty examples of this iconographic type including reliefs, large statues, small images, gems, amulets, and a series of about ninety Roman Imperial coin types from Alexandria. At the end of the nineteenth century Petrie excavated a series of tombs at Medinet Gurob in the Faiyum and in one of them found two images which in their general form, although not in their ornamentation, rather closely resemble the Osiris Hydreios.[84] Because he discovered a glass ring from the reign of Ramses II in the same tomb, Petrie was convinced that the origin of this statue type had to go back at least to the New Kingdom. However, although the general grave area apparently dates from Ramesside times and the Ptolemaic burials found by Petrie are said to have been situated at some distance from this older cemetery,[85] the lack of any specific information about the condition and stratigraphy of this tomb plus the entire absence of any similar examples from Pharaonic times stand as barriers to an easy acceptance of Petrie's hypothesis. Even those Osiris Hydreios figures which scholars have dated to ''Ptolemaic'' or ''Hellenistic'' times can only be situated in that era on stylistic grounds.[86] In no case are the conditions known under which these objects were discovered, and so there is no corroborative support from archaeology for the general dating assigned on the basis of stylistic technique. On the other hand, the use of this image on Alexandrian coins of the first century AD certainly demands a previous history of iconographic development, one which leads in all likelihood back into the first century BC. Vogt thought it possible that a coin from the fifth year of Claudius (46 AD) depicted an Osiris Hydreios but his interpretation remains in doubt.[87] However, coins of this city from the reigns of Galba, Otho, and Vitellius certainly do have representations of this figure,[88] and with the advent of the fourth year of Vespasian (73 AD) a long series of such coins began (Pl. XIX) and did not finally cease until at least the fifteenth year of Gallienus (267 AD).[89]

Other early examples of the Osiris Hydreios type can be mentioned briefly. Milne published a grave stele found at Alexandria upon which fourteen Hydreios images with various crowns were inscribed along with an inscription written in fluent and literate Greek. He advanced the opinion that this object was produced in the "early part of the first century A.D."[90] From outside of Egypt there is, first of all, a second silver cup from the Palaestra of Pompeii. Among the various Egyptian scenes in relief upon it is a priest bearing in his veiled hands an Osiris Hydreios. This object cannot postdate the destruction of Pompeii and in fact is probably from the early first century AD.[91] Also at Pompeii in the bottom of a pit located just to the west of the crypt building in the Iseum was found a small and broken Osiris Hydreios. In the same pit were found remnants of burnt fruit and nuts, an iron nail, part of a second Egyptian statue, and a quantity of black ash.[92] This suggests that it served as a repository for waste sacred materials.[93] The *Mensa Isiaca*, which Leospo dates to about the middle of the first century AD, depicts Osiris Hydreios both in the upper vertical border and directly below the image of Isis in the center of the tablet.[94] In both cases the artist has placed the Osiris statue between the outstretched paws of a falcon-headed lion, symbol of Horus.[95] In front of the Osiris in the border is an offering table with a libation pourer on it. Water flows from the twin spouts of the pourer into two cups.[96] A worshipper, accompanied by the god Thot, kneels before this table and presents his offering.

Together, the *Mensa Isiaca* and the other finds point to a date of origin for the Osiris Hydreios image no later than the early first century AD but probably in the first century BC. If, as everyone believes, this object originated in Egypt, there would have had to have been some lapse of time before it spread to Italy. In addition, its presence on the coins of Alexandria in the mid-first century AD also presupposes a previous history of several or perhaps many decades. At the same time, the total or virtually total absence of Hellenistic evidence points to a date not very much earlier than the first century AD.

A. Erman was of the view that this Osiris statue derived from representations of Osiris as a mummy.[97] Since his time, however, there has been a fairly general consensus that the lower part of the statue, though it is always solid,[98] represents a vessel.[99] This vessel, at least in its most common form, is decorated with a group of images that regularly appear on mummy cases.[100] With this in mind, Weber offered the suggestion that two different aspects of Osiris were involved in the composition of the statue. First and most important, the vase iconography stresses Osiris' association with water, especially with the sacred Nile water.[101] The water jar has in effect become the body of the god. Secondly, through the use of decorations found often on mummy cases, those who created this image showed their desire to relate it also to Osiris as lord of the dead.[102]

There is also a rather widespread consensus that this statue took its basic form from the ancient visceral jars, the so-called "Canopic jars," used for the burial of bodily organs from as early as the Fourth Dynasty (Pl. XX).[103] These jars, at least after the Ninth Dynasty, normally were found in groups of four and normally had animal or human-headed covers which represented the "Four Sons of Horus," the guardian deities of the dead. These vessels continued to be utilized in Egypt even down into the late period,[104] though it seems that their purpose shifted from being containers for the major inner organs to serving as images of the divinities who protected the dead person.[105] Given the fact that virtually all the Osiris Hydreios evidence from Egypt for which a definite place of derivation is known is associated with strongly Graeco-Roman places, sites, individuals, etc., I believe it quite probable that this iconographic type was created by the more strongly Hellenized segment of the Egyptian population and found its meaning primarily among this group.[106] The choice of the ancient visceral jars as a prototype for a new image of Osiris and its decoration with images associated with mummy cases served to highlight the lordship of that god over the dead. At the same time, the visceral jars seem also to have been associated with water since, as Weber points out, they were sometimes replaced at burial sites with vases used to contain water.[107] Nonetheless, the new statue type is not normally hollow and so was not designed as a container for water or for anything else. It recalls this dual aspect of the visceral jar only by its shape.

Osiris Hydreios images have been found at five of the known sanctuaries, a fact which indicates the importance of this figure at least for certain groups of Isis-Sarapis worshippers. Two of these are in Egypt (Luxor and Ras el Soda), two in Italy (Pompeii and

Rome: Campus Martius), and one on Cyprus (Soli). Four of the five sites were dedicated principally to Isis and three of the five also provided probable or certain evidence for the use of the cultic pitcher.

At three of the sanctuaries the images found had served as cult statues. Ghoneim discovered a large Osiris Hydreios, 0.80 m high, lying on the cella floor of the small Serapeum at Luxor. He concluded that it had fallen from a pedestal, c. 0.5 m high, directly behind which on the cult platform proper stood a two-meter-high statue of Isis (Pl. XXI, 1-2).[108] Although the Osiris image therefore stood in the center of the cella, both its size and its placement below the cult platform suggest that it was not the principal cult statue. On the other hand, since apparently not even fragments of a Sarapis statue were found, perhaps this image did serve as the local representation of that god. Whatever the case, if Ghoneim's restoration is correct, there was even at this Serapeum a close association between the image of Osiris and that of Isis.[109]

Two large examples of this statue were found in the cella of the small Iseum at Ras el Soda near Alexandria, a precinct founded no earlier than the late second century AD. These originally stood on the cult platform along with three other images. The whole group was arranged as follows: at the far left a statue of Isis (1.85 m high), then the two Osiris figures, then a statue of Hermanoubis (1.32 m high), and finally a statue of Harpocrates (1.27 m high).[110] The Osiris image closest to the statue of Isis, Osiris A according to Adriani's notation, is 1.07 m high (Pls. XVI-XVII). Without its tall crown, found separately and restored by the excavator, this statue would be about the same height as the Luxor example, for which the headdress is missing. Whereas this Osiris A statue conforms to the most common type of Osiris Hydreios images, the "Osiris B," 0.95 m in height, has an unusual miter-like headdress (probably a stylized version of the *atef* crown worn by the mummified Osiris) and its lower portion is decked out in a U-neck garment (Pl. XV). In addition, over its ears are found curled horns, perhaps the emblem of Ammon. The presence of two different types of this image upon the same cult platform suggests that each represented a different aspect of Osiris.

Finally, at the Soli sanctuary a rather large statue, 0.77 m high, was found still upright on the cult platform in the right hand cella (Pls. XXII-XXIII).[111] In his typology of the sculptures found at this site, Westholm assigned this object to his "Style IV" category, which he dated to the very late Roman Imperial period. This helps to explain why this statue, while generally comparable to the more common type, displays a complete lack of cohesion with respect to the reliefs on its body. These are crudely done and show only a limited connection with the forms typical on other images of Osiris Hydreios.[112]

Only the finds from the Campus Martius sanctuary at Rome remain to be discussed since I have already described the example from the Iseum at Pompeii. Three large columns found on the site show relief figures of priests carrying various sacred objects (Pl. XVIII).[113] These individuals do not all proceed in the same direction but stand two by two facing each other. On each of the columns three of the eight priests depicted bear in their veiled hands Hydreios figures. Two of these always form a facing pair while the third is paired off with some other type of bearer. In five of nine cases it is Osiris who is represented in the Hydreios form, but he never appears on both sides of a facing pair. In these cases he faces either Isis (twice) or Anubis. The body of each of these nine Hydreios images is fluted rather than covered with reliefs; this fluting is perhaps an artistic simplification of the Osiris B type found at Ras el Soda.[114] The relationship of the third Hydreios figure on each column to the other member of its pair is probably significant. While on Column C Anubis Hydreios faces the statue of an enthroned Harpocrates and so maintains the pairing of divinities,[115] the two Osiris figures which are not part of a divine pair face objects which probably related directly to this god and his cult. This is clear in one case—the Osiris Hydreios of Column B faces a priest who bears the long-spouted cultic pitcher.[116] In the other case (Column A) the extra Osiris statue faces a priest who bears a palm branch (Pl. XVIII). A palm branch is associated with the pitcher in the fresco from the Santa Sabina Iseum and also on a coin of Alexandria from the reign of Hadrian.[117] Since, as I will argue, this pitcher and the Osiris statue are related, the palm branch may have been ritually linked with both objects. Besides these reliefs, there is also a green stone head (now lost) of an Osiris Hydreios statue which was kept in the sixteenth century in the palace of Cardinal Carpi near the Church of the Minerva, i.e., in the immediate area of the Campus Martius Iseum. Some believe that this object was found in the same neighborhood and so passed into the Cardinal's hands.[118]

The whole body of evidence for these Hydreios figures derives for the most part from a remarkably restricted geographical area. Besides the Campus Martius evidence mentioned above, at least three and perhaps five other finds were made at Rome including a small agate Osiris Hydreios found in a grave.[119] In the environs of Rome several other such finds were made, most notably a group of large statues from the Villa Adriana (Pl. XXIV).[120] Beyond this, other evidence from Italy comes from Pompeii (as discussed previously), from Beneventum (Pl. XXV),[121] and from Cagliari on the island of Sardinia.[122] In all, Italy is the source of twenty-one items or about ten per cent of the whole corpus of known Osiris Hydreios figures.

About seven times as many examples derive from Egypt. Apart from the coin series, the city of Alexandria has yielded the grave stele mentioned above and five terracotta statues, two of which are known to have been found in cemeteries.[123] The suburbs of Alexandria have provided further examples: the two statues from the Ras el Soda sanctuary and two additional statues found at Canopus.[124] Further south, the Faiyum is the source of several of these images.[125] However, outside of these rather Hellenized areas, only three other places in Egypt offer further evidence—Oxyrhynchus (Pl. XII, 3),[126] Hermonthis in the Thebaid,[127] and Antinoopolis.[128] This last is a small terracotta Osiris Hydreios from the tomb of a Greek woman who died in the third century AD; it was one of several guardian images found in the grave. About thirty-four other images of this type, now in various museums, are known certainly or almost certainly to have derived from Egypt.[129] Weber believed that many of the smaller statues in this group must also have come from grave sites.[130]

From the area outside of Italy and Egypt, however, few such pieces are attested. The example from Soli has already been mentioned. A Roman period inscription was found at Tyre (SIRIS 359) which gives in three languages, Egyptian hieroglyphics, Greek, and Latin, the title of a very damaged statue: "Priest (or prophet) bearing Osiris." The statue carried by this official was probably, but not certainly, an Osiris Hydreios.[131] At Knossos on Crete there was discovered a small bronze statue of a weeping woman seated near an Osiris of this type. This is almost certainly a funerary motif.[132] A small Osiris Hydreios is said to have been purchased near the modern city of Belgrade and is thought to have been discovered in the territory of southern Dacia.[133] Another such piece reportedly was found in Dalmatia and then placed in the Museum at Venice; it is now lost. Bernarda Perc comments, "If the information on the find spot is correct, this is the sole example of such a monument found in the Danube region and in the Balkans."[134] Finally, at Rochester in England the head of such a statue seems to have been uncovered sometime in the last few years.[135] In short, the evidence from outside Italy and Egypt is meager: only six items at most, less than three per cent of the total body of evidence. Negative results in connection with certain areas serve to underscore this data. Many images of Osiris have been found in regions such as modern Germany, modern France, and the ancient province of Pannonia as well as on the site of ancient Aquincum, but not a single one has the form of an Osiris Hydreios.[136] I conclude, therefore, that the proper home of this type of image is northern Egypt and central and southern Italy.

The typological analysis of these images, the basic elements of which will be important for the present investigation, can be presented in quite schematic fashion since the fundamental divisions were long ago observed by Wilhelm Weber.[137] Using the coin series of Alexandria as his basic source of evidence, he distinguished between those Hydreios figures which had bodies extensively decorated with symbols in relief (Type A) from those with fluting or strigilation as the chief ornamentation (Type B). I myself would prefer to divide his Type B into two groups. The "strigilation," as we now know from larger examples such as that found at Ras el Soda (Pl. XV), actually represents a U-neck garment, the open neck of which invariably has horizontal bands across it. I will call this Type B. A very few examples, all found in Italy, have bodies decorated with spiral fluting. These I term Type B'. Let me offer several observations about these types. To begin with, of the finds I have examined, about 80% belong to Type A. Secondly, the original type is clearly Type A. I know of no example of a Type B or of a Type B' that is earlier than the reign of Trajan.[138] The only definite examples of Type B' are the Hydreios figures found on the columns of the Campus Martius Iseum (Pl. XVIII) and a large statue of Hadrianic date from the Villa Adriana. This latter item has had its lower portion restored, and neither Weber nor Roullet are certain that this work was executed correctly.[139] It is my own guess that Type B' is an artistic adaptation of the regular Type B body. On this supposition, such specimens should normally date to the second century AD or later.[140] Thirdly, the appearance of both main types as a pair on Alexandrian coins of Trajanic date or later[141] as well as on the cult platform of the Ras el Soda sanctuary suggests, as was pointed out above, that the iconographic difference is more than a matter of artistic taste, at least in Egypt. While Panofsky assumed that the pairs found on the Alexandria coins represented the divine couple, Osiris and Isis,[142] the evidence from Ras el Soda and the fact that at least on some of the coins the two Hydreios figures both have beards or both lack beards raises problems for this hypothesis.[143] I believe it probable that Osiris is being honored under two different aspects.

Weber long ago suggested, as was observed above, that the cultic pitchers and the Osiris Hydreios statues might be related.[144] He pointed out that both objects are frequently depicted being carried in procession by cult officials who have their hands veiled,[145] that both often have bodies decorated with images in relief, and that both are, in part or in whole, vessels associated with water. To this initial list a number of further comparisons may be added. Both often appear with a pillow under them or with a garland of flowers around their base.[146] Both show a variant fluted form in the second century AD. Both appear similarly positioned on reliefs depicting the divine pair, Sarapis-Agathodaimon and Isis-Thermouthis (Pl. XII 2-3). Much more fundamentally, both show precisely the same limited geographical distribution, both originated in Egypt around the same general time, both were special objects of veneration within the cult, and both almost always appear associated with Isis rather than with Sarapis.

As they are found in Egypt throughout the Roman period the two objects show a high degree of parallelism in shape and form. To be sure, the distinctive spout of the pitcher is not seen on the Hydreios figures nor does the head of the god appear atop the pitchers. However, just as the Hydreios figures are always high-shouldered, so almost all of the evidence for pitchers found in Egypt depict this shape of vessel. Secondly, at least three of the earlier coins in the Alexandrian cultic pitcher series show some relief ornamentation on the body of this vessel, though it is not in the same pattern as that found on the Hydreios statues.[147] Thirdly, just when Type B and B' Hydreios images begin to appear on the coins, so at the same time the pitchers begin to show a fluted body.[148] Therefore, with respect to the Egyptian evidence, the formal similarity of the two objects is an additional indicator that people felt them to be closely related.

This similarity in terms of shape and form is not regularly found in the case of material from outside of Egypt until a later stage. The pitchers, whether of the *Schnabelkanne* or of the Vatican type, are normally round-shouldered and with an ovoid or spherical body, features that are virtually never seen in the Hydreios figures.[149] No ornamentation is found on the body of these vessels except that one or two examples had jewels set into the metal surface.[150] This state of affairs suggests that devotees of Isis in Italy and elsewhere who were familiar with these two objects at first did not associate them as closely as did their brethren in Egypt. On the other hand, the known ritual practices surrounding each object appear to have been the same. Both objects were carried in procession, both could normally be held only with veiled hands, both had a place within the temple cella and were frequently presented as objects for veneration. In addition, on the Klein-Glienicke relief, which seems to have come originally from Rome, several members of an Isis procession appear (Pl. XXVI). One of them carries an Osiris Hydreios statue while behind him follows a man carrying a round object which Schede thought might be a σπονδεῖον.[151] If so, libation offerings may have been associated not only with the cultic pitcher but also with this Osiris image. Finally, random chance does not seem to be a sufficient explanation for the fact that in the one case in which the pitcher appears on the surviving columns from the

Campus Martius Iseum, its bearer faces another individual who carries an Osiris Hydreios. At a later period of time this fundamental coherence between the two objects apparently expressed itself also in the form taken by the pitcher. It is not that the shape of the vessel was altered—I have found no evidence for that. Rather, the presence of reliefs of Egyptian figures on the body of the pitcher[152] served, where found, to remind the beholder of the relationship between it and the Osiris statue.

One apparent difference between the two objects requires closer inspection. Various examples of the Osiris Hydreios statue have been found in graves or in a funerary context. The stele and the two small statues from Alexandria, the small guardian image from Antinoopolis, a gem from an Egyptian grave, and the agate statuette from Rome have already been singled out in this regard. Further, the image of the weeping woman seated by this Osiris figure probably also served some funerary purpose. Commenting on the piece from Antinoopolis, Weber points out that this small figure was placed with statues of other deities beside an image of the dead person in order to protect and guide that individual's soul. He concluded that many of the smaller Osiris Hydreios statues must have been similarly utilized.[153] Even though no pitchers, not even in the form of models, have been recovered from any grave site, I am convinced that even here the cultic pitcher and the statue are related. However, to demonstrate this I must introduce the third and final group of objects to be treated.

The Osiris "Cool Water" Inscriptions

Twelve examples of this final group, the "Cool Water" inscriptions, are known to exist.[154] Six of these were found in Egypt, five in Alexandria or its environs and one at Saqqarah near ancient Memphis. All but one of the remaining six items came from Italy, four from Rome and one from Hipponium, a town in the Bruttium region. The twelfth and final inscription was discovered somewhere on the site of Carthage, a city which had been resettled as a Roman *colonia*. Consequently, the geographical distribution of this third group shows the same pattern as in the previous cases: northern Egypt, central (and southern) Italy, and places closely associated either with Egypt or with Rome.[155]

Dates have been assigned to six of these inscriptions either on the basis of letter typology or internal evidence. None of these are earlier than the end of the first century AD, the date assigned to one of the texts found at Rome. While the underlying concepts were familiar in Egypt long before this, the particular formula probably did not come into existence before, say, the beginning of the first century AD. Thereafter it slowly grew in popularity—many of the surviving datable stones come from the third century or, more generally, "late Imperial" times. What all this means is that this Osiris formula came into existence roughly about the time when the cultic pitchers and the Osiris Hydreios statues were first being utilized.

In the late nineteenth century Erwin Rohde argued that this funerary petition was developed in Egypt by Greeks who derived it principally from a Hellenistic Greek formula attested at various places (e.g., Petelia in Bruttium and Eleuthernai on the island of Crete).[156] The Petelia inscription reads in part:

> You [the dead person] will find another water source, namely, cool water (ψυχρὸν ὕδωρ) flowing forth from the lake of Memory. Guardians are in front of it. You must say, 'You are the child of Earth and of starry Heaven. I too am of the heavenly race. This you guardians also know. But I have a parching thirst and am perishing. Quickly give me then the cool water (ψυχρὸν ὕδωρ) flowing forth from the lake of Memory.'[157]

As for the association of Osiris with this "cool water," Rohde viewed it as only a secondary feature in the total scheme of development.

He cannot be correct. For while the formula "May Osiris give you cool water" seems never to have been found on any monument of purely Egyptian origin, the concept that the dead need life-giving water, the concomitant ritual practice of pouring libations of water for the dead, and the association of this water with Osiris all developed very early in Egypt[158] and became quite popular in Ptolemaic times.[159] As Isidore Lévy has suggested, conceptions such as these much more likely passed over from native Egyptians to the Greek population which then took them and reformulated them in the light of its own traditions. This would explain the constant presence of ψυχρόν in the formula, a word which, at least according to Lévy, has no true parallel in Egyptian sources. The water requested from Osiris in this prayer formula is always "*cool water*" because that is the type of water which was spoken of in Greek funerary traditions.[160] This would mean that the formula is fundamentally Egyptian in its origin but influenced by familiar formulations found on Greek funerary monuments.[161]

Without exception these texts appear in a funerary context. Indeed, a few of them were even discovered *in situ* at the tombs to which they belonged. We have already observed that a number of the smaller Osiris Hydreios statues were also found in tombs. Malaise and Deonna have both suggested that these two items might be related in some way to one another.[162] Malaise even thought that the Hydreios statue might have contained the "cool water."[163] This, however, is certainly incorrect since these images are solid and have no provision for holding a liquid. Yet the fact that both statue and formula not only shared a common funerary function and a common association with Osiris but also a similar geographic and temporal distribution is a strong indication that they probably were related to one another.[164]

If the Hydreios statues are not vessels, the cultic pitchers are. I have already tried to demonstrate that the statue type is related to the pitcher and imitates it and recalls it both in its form and in its function. Since no pitchers have been recovered from grave sites, it is reasonable to suppose that the Hydreios statues which were found there served to represent the cool Nile water provided eternally by Osiris. Consequently, there was no need to place containers of water in the graves. The presence of Osiris Hydreios, i.e., the special form of the god which emphasized the gift of himself in life-giving water, guaranteed that this "cool water" would continue to be provided to the dead person just as the pitcher of Nile water, also the symbol of Osiris, provided this guarantee to living worshippers in the context of the cult.

Scholars have generally agreed that the water spoken of in these Osiris inscriptions offered life and immortality to those dead who shared in it.[165] If, then, the association of these texts with the Hydreios statues and the cultic pitchers is valid, the water referred to in all three cases was considered to be a source of life after death. In short, it is my contention that the circle of Isis worshippers who utilized these cultic objects viewed Nile water not only as a source of fertility and growth for plants, animals, and human beings but also as a means by which they might conquer death.

Conclusions

To conclude, then, these three groups of data, the pitchers, the Hydreios figures, and the "Cool Water" inscriptions, objects all from the same limited geographical range and all from the same general time period, converge to form a single unified configuration. Each of the three groups has reference to Osiris, each stresses his watery aspect, and each relates the symbol of water to the hope and promise of life beyond the grave. It is my belief that where one of these objects is found, the other two very likely were present as well. Together they form the external evidence for a particular cultic tradition within the much broader spectrum of Isis-Sarapis worship. In areas such as Asia Minor, much of Greece, and most of northern Europe where in other respects abundant evidence for the worship of the Egyptian gods has been found, no trace of this configuration has yet appeared. It cannot therefore be assumed that practices attested in connection with this data also took place in these other areas. For example, the fresco found at Herculaneum which depicts a priest holding up a vessel of sacred Nile water for adoration reflects a practice almost certainly connected with this assemblage of cultic objects. However, it is impossible to verify that such a ritual also took place, say, at Pergamum, Eretria, Delos, or Philae or that it could be found even at Rome or Alexandria before the end of the Hellenistic period. Processions in honor of Isis in which a pitcher of water was carried by a cult official are abundantly attested for northern Egypt and central Italy in the Roman period. Elsewhere, evidence is quite limited: Plutarch and Apuleius may provide an indication that this type of rite was practiced in parts of Greece. But within what might be called in shorthand fashion the Rome-Alexandria axis it is clear that a major element in the cult of Isis was the worship of Osiris under these particular aspects.

This configuration of materials also provides evidence that a more Egyptian theological perspective influenced those who made use of them. When Vitruvius describes the ritual surrounding the cultic pitcher, he does so in categories familiar to Greek religious thought: the priests raise their hands to heaven and give thanks to the divine liberality for having helped them to obtain the sacred water.[166] Apuleius' comments are somewhat closer to an Egyptian perspective. Yet, just as he very carefully stops short of affirming Isis' direct presence in the cow which walks along in the *Navigium Isidis* procession, so the pitcher remains for him the "summi numinis veneranda effigies."[167] Such a stance is not unexpected if Apuleius is trying to make the cult of Isis intelligible to outsiders. According to Plutarch, however, the water in this cultic vessel is the "emanation" (ἀπορροήν) of Osiris, i.e., that by which the god is made visible.[168] Although this is not quite an assertion that the god is simply immanent in the water, the Egyptian point of view, it is very different from saying that he is "lord" (κύριος) of all moisture, Plutarch's way of describing the corresponding role of Dionysus, Osiris' Greek counterpart.[169]

The various objects just discussed in this section appear to fit best into the religious context described by Plutarch. In the case of the Osiris Hydreios statue, the water jar is in effect the body of the god. Such an iconographic conception must have intended to express a very close bond between the god and the contents of the jar. Such an image reminded devotees that here was a god who had full possession of the waters of life. Beyond this, the formula "May Osiris give you cool water" only superficially appears to move toward a more Greek conception of this god as lord and ruler over the water. As indicated above, such water in Egyptian religious thought has too close an association with Osiris and his son Horus to allow it here to have a separate identity apart from the god. Instead, in giving this water Osiris gives himself. For this reason, it is not surprising that no pitchers or models of pitchers but only Osiris Hydreios images have been recovered from grave sites. The presence of Osiris in his *hydria* form was itself the gift of "cool water."[170]

Such an understanding helps to explain why processions and ceremonies of adoration played such an important role among those who made use of these cultic objects. Since the sacred contents of the pitcher represented the "real presence" of the god, such liturgical rites served to make that presence available to his devotees. Such people apparently were less interested in a deity who did things for them from afar; they wished instead to behold their god in his visible presence. In their sanctuaries they may have continued to utilize the older Nile water crypts, but there is no evidence that they ever built brand-new facilities of this type. For them the crucial thing was the presence of the god, whether this be in the pitcher of Nile water, in the Hydreios image, or in the "cool water." Such a presence was for them not only, as probably everywhere within the Isis-Sarapis cult, a promise of good things in this life but also of a happier and better existence beyond the grave. Such an ideology and such liturgical practices may have existed elsewhere in Isis-Sarapis worship under somewhat different form. However, the unified character of this particular group of material remains points to the existence of an identifiable sub-group more Egyptian in inclination within this general cult as it existed in Roman times.

CHAPTER SEVEN

ABLUTION FACILITIES AND RITUALS

If religious interest in Nile water is a feature distinctive of the cult of Isis and Sarapis, the use of water for ablutions is a practice which it shares with numerous other cults and religious movements. Lustration rites are a virtually ubiquitous aspect of the various religions of the world, and those conducted with water nearly so. The desire for a proper "sacred disinfectant," as Nock calls it,[1] to remove whatever impedes a person from entering into the sphere of the holy is a profoundly felt need among most segments of the human family. This removal process is often looked upon as akin to the act of cleansing away physical dirt. Because most cultures find water so useful in ordinary life for this purpose, it has become within a great many of them the preferred medium for purging individuals of ritual or moral defilement.[2]

Given the general human propensity for elaborating all such activities into organized patterns of behavior, we would assume, at least *a priori*, that the water ablution rituals of the Isis-Sarapis cult would have their own characteristic configurations. In my judgment, this is indeed the case both with respect to the type of facilities utilized and the ritual gestures involved. To support this first point, I offer a typological analysis of the existing evidence for ablution facilities. As to the second assertion, I believe that I can demonstrate that at least certain segments of this cult performed these purification rituals by sprinkling or pouring water over people's heads, a practice which appears to have had clear Egyptian antecedents.

If the "what," the "where," and the "how" of these rites can be determined to some degree, the "why" presents many more difficulties. Mere physical data such as that unearthed by archaeologists cannot explain to us the reasons that participants in this cult had for performing such-and-such a ritual. What is needed are "native informants" or their equivalent, written sources which provide such information. For the cult of Isis and Sarapis such sources are almost entirely lacking. Only two or three sentences in Apuleius and a few other scattered fragments break through an otherwise impenetrable veil of silence. Consequently, the meaning that such practices had for the most part can only be guessed at.

The "Sprinkling Basins"

In Greek religion a variety of water ablution rituals were performed.[3] The most common of these leads us to a class of facilities attested also at several of the known sanctuaries of Isis and Sarapis. Most sacred precincts in the Greek world had at their various entrances basins of lustral water called "sprinkling basins" (περιρραντήρια). Those wishing to enter were first required to sprinkle themselves with water from one of these containers.[4] A statement in the *Onomasticon* of Pollux expresses the significance of these facilities rather well: "The area inside of the περιρραντήρια is possessed by the gods, sacred, consecrated, and inviolable while that outside is open to ordinary use."[5] The use of such ablution water was not just required of those who felt themselves under some present guilt or pollution. Rather, it served as the medium which everyone had to make use of in order to attain to the proper state of ritual purity necessary for approaching the gods.

Such facilities were also in use in Egypt during Graeco-Roman times. According to Heron of Alexandria, "In the temples of the Egyptians near the doorposts ... are basins of lustral water (περιρραντήρια) so that those who enter may sprinkle themselves (περιρραίνεσθαι)."[6] A very fine pair of these basins has survived at the entrance to the Temple of Sebek and Renenutet (= Ermouthis-Isis) at Madinet Madi in the Faiyum, a sanctuary in which Greek-speaking devotees have recorded various dedications and prayers (Pl. XXVIII). On either side of the doorway leading into the outer vestibule is a round, shallow basin, c. 0.85 m in diameter, placed upon a low, squat supporting column.[7] The top of each basin is about 0.70 m above ground level.[8] A. Erman and W. Otto, who follows Erman, appear to have assumed that such basins were a regular feature at all Egyptian temples.[9] This is doubtful. The evidence listed by Erman derives, as he himself admits, only from Hellenized areas of Egypt. In addition, a key item referred to both by Erman and by Otto, a group of basins discovered at the Temple of Min and Isis at Koptos, served not as sprinkling basins but as foot baths.[10] I am inclined to believe, therefore, that the sprinkling basins found in Egypt represent some sort of Graeco-Roman religious influence either on the rite of ablution itself or at least on the type of facility used to supply water for it.

Because the Graeco-Roman sanctuaries of Isis and Sarapis represent a fusion between Egyptian and Greek religious traditions, it is not surprising that several of them are known to have had such basins. To begin with, fragments of a marble basin which was probably of this type—Papadakis called it a "basin for sprinkling" (λεκάνη περιρραντηρίου)—were found in the south wing of the portico at Eretria (Fig. 20).[11] Just outside the west wall of the central temple the excavators also came upon a base of the type normally used to support such a basin.[12] Since neither basin nor stand were discovered *in situ*, the precise use of these objects within the sanctuary cannot be determined with certainty.

Serapeum C on Delos also produced inscribed fragments of various stone basins. However, the scanty remains make it difficult to reconstruct the original appearance of these basins with any degree of certainty.[13] Perhaps some of them once served as sprinkling basins for the sanctuary. This possibility was somewhat enhanced by the discovery of an inscription at the south end of the site near one of the principal entrances to the sanctuary. This text recorded the fact that in 116 BC Dionysius, son of Dionysius, of Sphettos, a priest of the sanctuary, donated a κρήνη.[14] While the term "κρήνη" could refer in Christian usage to a lustral basin set in the atrium near the entrance to the church, we cannot be certain that such a usage prevailed within the Isis-Sarapis context four centuries earlier.[15] However, the fact that no other type of permanent water facility was found in this area may mean that Dionysius did actually donate a sprinkling basin.

A number of nineteenth and twentieth century scholars report that two rectangular marble basins for ablutions were found by the main entrance to the Iseum at Pompeii and are now in the Museum at Naples.[16] One of these, they say, was inscribed *LONGINUS·II·VIR*.[17] This report would stand without question except for the fact that these objects are not mentioned either in the original archaeological report, a work done with some care, or in the writings of other early witnesses.[18] In the mid-nineteenth century Theodor Mommsen investigated the whereabouts of the Longinus inscription and discovered that an object inscribed with this dedicatory formula had been found in the vicinity of the large theater behind the Iseum. What he did not then realize was that the excavators had recorded the discovery of such an object but termed it an altar and not a basin.[19] Consequently, even though an actual basin inscribed with the name of Longinus is in the possession of the Museum at Naples, no early sources connect that basin with the Iseum. As Mommsen later suggested, the tradition which posited this link may have derived from popular sources. The presence of such basins at this sanctuary would not be surprising but it cannot be demonstrated with certainty from the available evidence.

As indicated in Chapter I, a basin on the outside of the sanctuary of Aphrodite at Soli may have served the needs of the Iseum (Temple D) just to the southwest of it. If Strabo indeed refers to this group of temples in his description of the Soli area, the two goddesses actually shared a common precinct.[20] Consequently, the exterior basin (Fig. 4), a facility 1.75 m wide, 1.80 m long, and with walls at least 0.75 m high, may well have served one or both of the sanctuaries as a sprinkling basin.[21]

Also mentioned in Chapter I was a basin located in front of the Serapeum at Luxor. This may also belong to this class of purification facilities, but I am less convinced. The published reports indicate only that this structure is made of brick, that it is about one meter deep, and that it is located between the Serapeum and the sacred way leading from Luxor to Karnak (Fig. 2).[22] Unless it is an elevated basin—and it appears not to have been such—it probably served the needs of pilgrims passing along the road rather than those who entered the sanctuary.

A somewhat similar basin has been recently discovered 12.5 m in front of the small temple in the State Agora at Ephesus (Fig. 24). Although this basin is clearly related to the temple—it is situated precisely on the extended east-west axis of the latter—the temple's association with the cult of Isis remains problematic (see Appendix 1). Measuring 1.20 by 1.50 m., the basin is 0.18 m in depth and had both an inflow pipe and a drain. It appears to have been con-

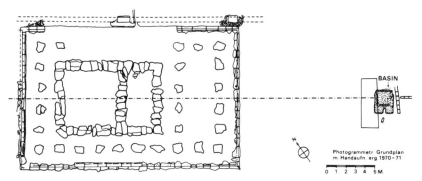

Fig. 24. The Sanctuary of Isis (?) in the State Agora of Ephesus. Ground plan
showing present remains.

structed about 200 AD, and evidence for any earlier basin is entirely lacking. In all likelihood this facility served the precinct as a kind
of sprinkling basin.[23]

A very large cistern located under the east portico of the sanctuary at Sabratha may have served to supply sprinkling basins set
by the doorway leading into the courtyard.[24] No other finds have
survived from the site which would offer any additional support for
this rather hypothetical suggestion. However, if such basins had
once stood in this area, they would surely have been destroyed
when a large wall for defense purposes was constructed in late
Roman times across this end of the precinct (Fig. 19).

Two wells are in the courtyard of the Serapeum at Leptis
Magna.[25] One of these is situated just to the right as one passes
from the main entrance in the direction of the temple (Fig. 25). Like
the cistern at Sabratha, this well may have supplied water for one or
more sprinkling basins set at the entryway into the courtyard.

The Iseum at Pergamum may also have had one or more
sprinkling basins. An inscription found in the "Lower City" of
that town mentions among other offerings made to Isis the repair of
the sprinkling basin (περιραντήριον) which stood "in front of the
gateway."[26] If this text does not refer to the sanctuary now known,
it certainly speaks of some precinct of Isis located at Pergamum.[27]

We therefore have evidence that at least some Isis-Sarapis sanctuaries both in Hellenistic and in Roman times made use of this
Greek type of purification facility. From this it does not necessarily

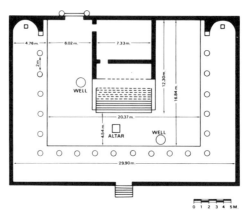

Fig. 25. The Serapeum at Leptis Magna. Ground plan.

follow that the manner of ablution was the same as that proper to the sanctuaries of the traditional Greek divinities. What is clear is that this class of basins has Greek rather than Egyptian ancestry.

Ablution Basins for the Ministers of the Cult

Much more the result of Egyptian influence is a second group of basins found at a fairly large number of the known Isis-Sarapis sanctuaries. These facilities are not placed by the entrances to the precinct but are situated close to the central temple, an arrangement which has led me to designate them as "temple basins." Three features normally distinguish these objects: they are constructed above ground at a height sufficient to allow a person while standing to make use of them with ease, they regularly have a drain, and they are located to the right of the temple cella or cult statue. Because of their placement well inside the precinct and close to the temple, they were probably utilized only by certain individuals rather than by all who entered the general sanctuary area.

A good example of this type of basin is found at the sanctuary of Isis and Sarapis at Gortyn. To the right rear of the temple and behind the crypt building is a basin which measures in its interior 1.67 m wide, c. 2.80 m long, and c. 0.80 m deep (Fig. 17).[28] Its floor, which is set about 0.10 m below ground level, is made out of brick which was then covered over with a mortar plaster which curves upward at the outer edges to join with the surrounding walls. This coating of plaster is the chief indication that this facility was meant to hold water, for neither a water inflow pipe nor a drain has been discovered.[29] Only two of the side walls, those which abut the temple and the crypt housing, have survived to any great height. A few portions of the south wall remain in place, but the east wall, which was probably aligned with the rear wall of the temple, has disappeared altogether. The interior of all these walls was plastered over with a colored stucco revetment (imitation marble?) to a height of c. 0.80 m. It is this evidence which allows us to estimate the probable height of the basin.

The sanctuary at Sabratha has two long basins situated at the west end of the courtyard to either side of the central temple. The larger of the two, located to the right of the temple, measures in its interior 5.70 m long, 0.85 m wide, and 0.42 m deep; the top of it is 0.55 m above the courtyard floor (Fig. 19).[30] Its sides and base were constructed of small, irregular stones bonded together with a mortar made out of lime. These surfaces were then completely covered on both sides with a thick layer of plaster. Evidently water to supply this basin came from a well located in the courtyard floor immediately to the south of it.[31] A hole, 0.06 m in diameter, at the bottom center of the east wall of the basin must have served as a drain.[32] The second basin, which is set against the south portico steps, is separated from the southwest corner of the courtyard by an altar and another well.[33] This latter facility undoubtedly provided water for the basin. The interior of this basin is 2.28 m long, 1.08 m wide, and 0.45 m deep; the distance from the top of it to the courtyard floor is 0.60 m. The construction technique employed in this instance differs considerably from that used for the larger basin. The builders bonded large semi-hewn stones of varying sizes together with mortar and then covered them over with a thick layer of cement plaster (*calcestruzzo*). At the north end of the basin a drain hole, 0.07 m in diameter, allowed waste water to flow out into a catch basin. An opening, 0.06 m in diameter, in one side of this structure then allowed the water to flow into a drain which ran in an easterly direction along the courtyard floor. The catch basin also has an overflow outlet, 0.06 × 0.04 m, which likewise led into the drain. This whole arrangement suggests that the flow of water from the main ablution basin was usually, but not always, moderate. Perhaps the main basin functioned more like a sink. That is, water may have been drawn from the well and then poured over people's hands or heads. It would have splashed down into the main basin and then have flowed out via the catch basin and drain. If several jars of water were poured out at once, the overflow mechanism in the catch basin would have prevented the waste water from slopping over its sides and onto the courtyard floor. If, on the other hand, the main basin were filled to the top with water and its drain then unplugged, the resulting flow of water would probably have overwhelmed the catch basin despite its own rather large drain hole and overflow outlet.

Pesce believed that the relatively coarse construction of the two basins pointed to a date of origin in the late Roman period.[34] Given the different types of masonry employed, I doubt that the two basins were themselves built at the same time. If "coarseness of construction" is the operable norm, the basin to the left of the temple was constructed later. Yet it was located beside a well which Pesce believed to have been dug before the construction of the sanctuary.[35] Consequently, some small degree of uncertainty remains. What does seem clear is that at some period the sanctuary found it needed two large elevated basins for its cultic rites. Because of its greater size, the basin to the right of the temple may have been the more important and the more regularly used of the two facilities.

The excavators at Pompeii reported finding a lead basin, 0.56 m high and 0.43 m in diameter, behind and to the right of the temple in the extreme northwest corner of the courtyard.[36] This object, which has entirely disappeared, is now known only through the archaeologist's description of it:

> This basin is ornamented on its upper edge with an interwoven pattern and with some images that are entirely Egyptian in character. A lead pipe supplied water to this basin. It runs along one side of the courtyard and then goes up the pillar in the corner to a point above the basin. The flow of water through this pipe was regulated by a bronze valve which was found in place. The small pipe through which the water finally flowed into the basin has a total diameter (including its rather thick metal walls) of 1.8 cm, and the end of it is cut on an angle.[37]

Presumably the basin must also have had some sort of drain, although the report does not mention this. In all events, the whole arrangement must have been quite comparable to a modern-day sink.

From evidence discovered on the site, no fewer than six "temple basins" once stood to the right of the central temple in the courtyard of the Serapeum at Alexandria (Fig. 26). Each of these basins were connected by means of open drains to a complex system of water channels.[38] Rowe discovered *in situ* part or all of the flooring for three of these basins. From these remains he determined that they had been built sometime in the Roman period. He was able to ascertain the size and location of the other basins from the depressions which remained in the courtyard floor and from the arrangement of the drains. All six of these basins had a large floor surface.[39] However, since no upper walls have survived, their original depth remains unknown. They probably were not shallow, for the size of the drain pipe utilized, c. 0.50 m on the outside, is an indication that they were meant to handle fairly large quantities of water.[40] Rowe found a number of reservoirs, all seemingly of Roman date, located close to these basins below the courtyard floor. These probably supplied the ablution basins and the so-called "baths" (?) found in the area.[41] The basins in question are clustered in a rather irregular fashion to the west and south of the

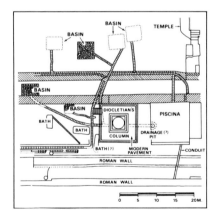

Fig. 26. The Serapeum at Alexandria. Plan of the
ablution basins and their drainage system.

Column of Diocletian and the great pool known as the "Piscina."[42] This irregularity of arrangement is puzzling; it would appear much too casual for the courtyard of a great and famous sanctuary. However, since part of the drainage system passes under the Column of Diocletian, it must have been constructed before that lofty monument was erected (c. 297 AD). The basins and their drains therefore belong to the period when Sarapis was worshipped here and not to the Christian era.

Connected to the back of the small sanctuary of Sarapis at Corinth is a room, 3.8 × 3.2 m, which was used as a collection tank for rain water flowing off the nearby roofs (Fig. 27).[43] That the room served in this fashion is indicated not only by its watertight floor but also by the discovery within it of several terracotta downspouts which had fallen from the surrounding roofs.[44] The floor of the room is not level but slopes downward so that its east end, which is at the normal floor level, is 0.45 m lower than its west end. The resulting 9° angle of declination would cause whatever water accumulated to flow toward the east side, the side closest to the sanctuary. Between this room and the shrine area was an opening, 0.91 m wide. Whether a low cross wall blocked the bottom portion of the opening cannot be positively decided on the basis of the physical remains alone.[45] However, given the angle of the floor, something either of a portable or permanent nature had to have been placed here to block the flow of water or else the cultic area would have been flooded after every rainstorm. Near the northeast corner of this "water room" is an opening leading into a drain

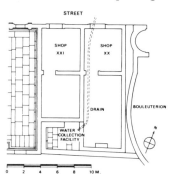

Fig. 27. The Serapeum in the South Stoa of the
Agora at Corinth. Ground plan.

which is made out of tile pipes measuring 0.19 m wide and 0.10 m high. This drain ran under the floor of the sanctuary due north to some point in the Agora outside.[46] While this whole arrangement, as Broneer himself apparently believed, may only have served to supply water to areas within the Agora, the presence of an opening into the "water room" from the Serapeum strongly suggests that some of the water was used within this shrine regardless of whatever else was done with it. I have previously argued that Nile water containers were designed to reproduce the Nile flood and were often fed by rain water. These conditions are verified here. Yet if this is to be a Nile water container, the drain is an anomaly. Not only is such a drain not found in connection with containers of this sort, but this drain would have allowed the sacred water to flow out into a profane area. Therefore, because of the drain and because of the location of this water source to the right of the cult statue, I believe this facility should be included in the list of "temple basins."

These examples from the sanctuaries at Gortyn, Sabratha, Pompeii, Alexandria, and Corinth provide solid evidence for the special type of temple basin which I described at the beginning of this section. To this basic list I would also add several more doubtful installations, those found at Priene, Eretria, and Pergamum, and, though with some reservation, that at Cyrene. Water facilities found at Leptis Magna and Industria will also be dealt with here, although they do not fit the temple basin typology very well and their actual function remains unclear.

In my analysis in Chapter I of the evidence from the sanctuary at Priene, I concluded from the location of a drain (Fig. 9) that a basin had very probably once stood to the right of the great altar. Such a basin must have been elevated above ground level. Waste water from it was conveyed by the drain to the street outside. If I am correct in my assumption that such a basin once was located here, it would have corresponded perfectly in type to the group of temple basins I have been describing.

Despite Philippe Bruneau's very detailed argumentation to the contrary, I believe that Room G at the sanctuary of Sarapis and Isis at Eretria was directly connected with the precinct and served it for an extended period as a place for ablution rituals (Fig. 20). In his re-examination of the material remains of this sanctuary, Bruneau came to a number of conclusions with respect to this room.[47] To begin with, he was convinced that Room G did not exist during the first period of the sanctuary in anything like the form in which it now survives, a statement which appears incontrovertible.[48] At some later date but before the mid-second century BC this area was remodeled so that it took on the shape now seen in Fig. 20. A door, 0.80 m wide, linked it on its south side with the sanctuary while a second doorway or opening at its northwest corner led into the northern complex of rooms.[49] Probably at this time or shortly afterwards, Room G received a watertight floor made out of broken tile and mortar. This slopes down toward the southwest to allow water to flow off from it into a drain which runs from the south entrance of the room along the floor of Courtyard D and out through the back wall of the precinct. The principal feature of this room is a well, 0.50 m in diameter, which was dug no later than the time when the broken tile flooring was laid.[50] This floor surface appears to be earlier in date than the pebble flooring of Courtyards C and D, a surface which was put in place, as Bruneau has now determined, in the second half of the second century BC.[51] Consequently, at some point before this date Room G was constructed to serve as an establishment in which water somehow played an important role. It remained in this form until the time when Wall 6 was constructed. This wall, of very poor construction, left an opening only 0.28 m wide between Room G and the sanctuary. This was sufficient to allow the drainage of water from G but excluded free passage into it. Bruneau apparently believes—and here is a key point at issue—that this blocking wall was constructed around the second half of the second century BC[52] but can prove only that it is later than the paving of Room G.[53] He is in any case unwilling to admit that this room served the sanctuary for ablution rites.[54] Instead, he argues that first Pit f and then later Pit k held water for this purpose.[55]

What Bruneau has presented is essentially a "short chronology." That is, he had tended to push both the remodeling efforts which converted Room G into a "water room" and the subsequent blocking off of this area from the sanctuary very close to the middle of the second century BC.[56] I disagree with him on two counts. First of all, I do not believe that he has made his short chronology any more likely than a "long chronology." According to this latter perspective, Room G would have been constructed in its present form after the building of the main sanctuary but not too much later. Bruneau has not proven that the walls surrounding this room were built in the second century but only that they were not built at the same time as the original precinct. Further, he has not proven that the blocking wall between this room and the sanctuary (Wall 6) was built in the second century but only that it was put in place later than the watertight floor upon which it rests. I think it could just as well have been constructed in the first century BC after the site had ceased to serve cultic purposes. My second reason for disagreeing with him is that his hypothesis does not take account of the doorway in the side wall of Courtyard C almost directly opposite the entrance leading from the sanctuary into Room G. This doorway was put in place when Courtyard C was enclosed in the mid-second century. I would guess that the officials of the sanctuary desired to retain easy access from the central temple to Room G. The arrangement of the two doors certainly suggests some connection between the "water room" and the rites carried on in the temple and its forecourt. For these two reasons I am inclined to believe that Room G supplied water for the cult from sometime after the origin of the sanctuary until the time when cultic worship ceased on the site.

The drain which empties into the area outside the precinct is sufficient, in my judgment, to show that this room was not a Nile water facility. Instead, it almost certainly served for ablution rites.[57] Perhaps a raised basin stood in the southwest corner of G between the well and the drain. Otherwise, water may have been drawn from the well and then poured over the various cultic ministers as they stood on the floor. It would then have run off the sloping surface and into the drain. If this area did serve as an ablution place for the sanctuary, its location immediately to the right of the central temple conforms precisely to the pattern verified for the facilities described above.

The Iseum at Pergamum probably also had such ablution facilities. Under the cult platform in the area in front of the base for the cult statue is a cistern which is over 4 m in depth.[58] Water is still found in this facility, and Salditt-Trappmann noted that its level remains constantly at 2 m in winter and in summer alike. We do not presently know from where it obtains this water, although perhaps it is somehow linked with an underground spring.[59] On the south side of the cult platform Salditt-Trappmann discovered an arched opening (Fig. 21) through which she could not only see the water in the cistern but also a similar arch with two outlets below it in the interior wall on the opposite side. These outlets must be the explanation for the constant level of the water. That is, one or both of them must function as an overflow drain. From the description provided by Salditt-Trappmann I would assume that water was drawn out from the cistern via the opening on the south side, i.e., the side to the right of the cult statue, for there apparently was no other means of access to the water. Very likely one or more ablution basins stood to the right of the cult platform and were supplied by water drawn out through the opening on this side. These would have fit the temple basin category which I have been describing.[60]

In Chapter I, I argued that a basin may have stood in front of the cult statue in the small sanctuary of Isis in the Apollo precinct at Cyrene. What led me to this conclusion was the position of the drain found within the cella (Fig. 10). If such a basin actually had been located in the center right in front of the cult platform, it would have been situated in a manner quite unlike the normal group of temple basins. I myself find it somewhat difficult to imagine that ablutions would have been performed directly in front of the principal image of the goddess, but I have no alternative explanation to suggest—unless, of course, the drain only served to remove waste water from the floor.

Facilities found at Industria and at Leptis Magna may have served a cultic purpose of this type, but the extant remains, especially in the case of the sanctuary at Industria, leave a great deal of room for doubt. As noted in Chapter I, there may have been a drain below ground level at the right rear of the central temple at Industria (Fig. 6).[61] The supposed drain has been badly damaged since it was unearthed in 1812 and so it is not very clear what it originally was or even whether it has any relationship with the sanctuary. Perhaps further investigations will clarify matters, although for my own part I think it too large (exterior dimensions: 0.90 × 1.50 m) to have been a drain at all, much less a drain for an ablution basin. At Leptis Magna there is a well located to the *left* of the central temple (Fig. 25); it conceivably could have supplied a now no longer extant basin for ablutions.[62] However, without further information—the site has not yet been published—no further determination can be made.

We are left, then, with eight or nine sanctuaries which probably or certainly possessed a temple basin for ablution rites. These sites, that is, have structures which substantially verify the typology I sketched at the outset. Eight of these ablution facilities were located to the right of the cult statue—only the apparent arrangement at Cyrene stands as an exception. Six of the nine facilities are known to have had a drain. Possibly the basins at Gortyn, Pergamum, and Pompeii also had such drains, but evidence for them either has not been uncovered or has been destroyed. As for the third distinguishing mark in the proposed typology, five of the sites actually now retain or did retain remnants of a basin whose rim was elevated well above ground level, and two other sites (Cyrene and Priene) offer evidence to suggest that they, too, once had such a basin. The situation at Eretria and at Pergamum is less clear, but I suspect that both sanctuaries did make use of actual basins for their ablution rites. If the missing basins were of metal, they would have been ready targets for scavengers of every sort. The removal of the lead basin from the sanctuary at Pompeii is, after all, only a more recent example of what must have been a long-standing practice.

Ablution Practices and Their Historical Antecedents

As I remarked at the outset, very few ancient materials are available which offer any sort of explanation of either the nature or the meaning of the ablution rites conducted within the Isis-Sarapis cult. Of particular value are a few passages found in the *Metamorphoses* of Apuleius, for they offer an indication of the manner in which ablutions were carried out. According to *Metamorphoses* 11.23, before Lucius underwent his initiation, he was led by the priest "to the neighboring public baths" (*ad proxumas balneas*) in order to be purified. Accompanying this expedition from the sacred precinct of Isis was a crowd of worshippers (*religiosa cohors*). Once at their destination, Lucius first had to take an ordinary bath (*prius sueto lavacro traditum*). However, this was only a prelude to a much more important event: after having first invoked the favor of the gods, the priest of the sanctuary sprinkled Lucius thoroughly with water and thereby purified him (*praefatus deum veniam, purissime circumrorans abluit [sacerdos Lucium]*). Then Lucius and the group returned to the precinct, and the priest at once presented the now purified initiate "before the very feet of the goddess."

This ritual both inaugurated a ten day period of preparation for the actual rite of initiation and, as is indicated by the presentation of Lucius before the cult image, served in its own right to bring him into a new relationship with Isis and the mysteries of her cult.[63] This is made clear by Apuleius' statement that Lucius was presented "ante *ipsa* deae vestigia."

This rite is twice foreshadowed in the same book of the *Metamorphoses*. In 11.7 after having received a vision of Isis in a dream, Lucius awoke full of emotion at having been granted the "clear presence" of the goddess. His first action was then to sprinkle himself with water from the sea (*marino rore respersus*) as a preparation for fixing his attention on her divine commands and for recalling the sequence of her admonitions. The act of sprinkling is both a response to the vision and a purification to prepare him to approach the goddess through the recollection of her words. However, even before these events, when Lucius in his uninstructed state made his first approach in prayer to Isis, he prepared himself by plunging his head seven times in the sea.[64]

These three different purificatory washings described in the *Metamorphoses* form an almost Platonic movement from shadow to reality. The first washing is the naive and instinctive gesture of an utterly uninitiated Lucius who yet has a glimmer of reality and who does perform the proper act—he washes his head. After the dream vision Lucius is endowed with a much richer knowledge and presence. Concomitantly, he knows that he must sprinkle himself with water before recollecting the divine words of Isis. Finally, there is the prime analogate, the priest's sprinkling of Lucius in the presence of the community. It is my belief that this sprinkling still principally involved the head just as did the very primitive washing described in *Metamorphoses* 11.1.[65]

It is not simply the internal development within *Metamorphoses* 11 that points to such a conclusion. Within the general range of Greek religious practice, purifications of the head are occasionally attested. For example, a text found in the vicinity of the sanctuary of the Phrygian god Men at Sunium in Attica sets forth the following regulations for those wishing to enter the precinct: "You are to be pure from garlic and pork and women: after washing with water poured over your head you may enter on the same day. Menstruation requires a wait of seven days, contact with a corpse ten days, an abortion forty days before washing and entering."[66] Of course, even this tradition derives from a foreign cult rather than from the worship of the traditional gods. However, in Egyptian religious usage this type of purification is almost universal.

A long series of reliefs found in various temples of Egypt depict the Pharaoh being purified for his coronation. These first appear at the time of the New Kingdom and continue on through Saite, Ptolemaic, and Roman times. In each case the ruler stands between a pair of gods who pour water in two streams over his head (Pl. XXIX, 2).[67] Because the Pharaoh is divine, he is represented as the same size as the divinities who purify him. They therefore stand on low pedestals so that they are able to pour the water over his head. In a parallel series which shows two gods purifying the crown prince, such pedestals are not to be seen, for the prince is physically (and spiritually) much smaller, and so the gods can reach his head much more easily (Pl. XXIX, 1).[68]

There are also a variety of reliefs which depict the ritual purification of a dead person. Here there is never a question of washing, say, the individual's hands or feet. Rather, in every instance ministers pour water in streams over the head of the corpse.[69] The dead person was also thought to receive a purification when he or she arrived at Amentet, the realm of the underworld. Bonnet provides an illustration of the rite which was supposed to occur. In it a figure is seen pouring water over the head of the individual who wishes to enter.[70]

A relief from the Eighteenth Dynasty has survived which shows the purification of a priestess and a priest for temple service (Pl. XXX). The two individuals stand in low, flat basins and have water poured or sprinkled on their heads by some personages (now missing).[71] Although we lack any further illustrations of this type of lustral washing, the ritual gesture seen here is thought to be typical of all such purifications of the clergy.

Such a pattern therefore characterized many different ablution rites in Egypt. Since the people of that country normally bathed by having water poured over themselves, the liturgical ritual represented a symbolic bath.[72] Therefore when Lucius in *Metamorphoses* 11.1 plunges his head in the sea to purify himself, his action is probably a recollection in a Graeco-Roman context of a ritual practice attested for centuries in Egypt.[73] I therefore suspect that a ritual of pouring or sprinkling water over the heads of those to be purified was widespread in Isis-Sarapis worship. Those who made use of the temple basins probably washed not only their hands (the customary Graeco-Roman practice) but also their heads.

Because of the location of these basins well within the sacred area, they probably were not used by everyone who entered the sanctuary but only by a more select group. In my view, that group was most probably the priests of the sanctuary and their attendant ministers. The basins are set to one side of the central temple and its cult images, i.e., the area to which especially the priests and priestesses had access and over which they exercised special control. The ritual purity of Egyptian priests was a byword in antiquity. They were required to wash or sprinkle themselves before entering certain areas within the temple or before engaging in a religious ceremony.[74] With so much washing and sprinkling they came to be called in Egyptian "the washed ones."[75] Not only the Egyptians but also the Greeks marvelled at this assiduous concern for ritual purity. Herodotus reported how the priests of Egypt bathed in cold water twice each day and twice each night.[76] Chaeremon heard that they did this three times a day, i.e., after sleeping, before the noon meal, and before going to bed.[77] In addition, the "ibis test" for water purity to which I have previously made reference involved the procurement of clean water for the ritual purification of priests.[78] There is every reason to assume, therefore, that such a concern for ritual cleanliness on the part of the clergy permeated into at least certain segments of the Isis-Sarapis cult. If so, it probably provided the principal *raison d'être* for the temple basins. Those who had been initiated or those who were members of a special association may also have joined the priests, at least on occasion, for these ablutions. This would explain why certain sanctuaries such as Alexandria and Sabratha needed more than one large basin. Then, too, perhaps those who wished to approach the images of the gods in prayer and adoration (as did Lucius in *Metamorphoses* 11.20) were required to purify themselves in the manner described.[79] No written or pictorial sources shed light on this question, and so I can only suggest in view of the prevailing Egyptian concern for priestly purity that the clergy of those sanctuaries which had these temple basins was the most likely group to have used them.

I have not been able to establish clear patterns of distribution for these temple basins as I was able to do in the case of the fixed Nile water containers. Although a somewhat greater number of these facilities are known to have been constructed in the Roman period, many more sanctuaries survive from this era than from Hellenistic times.[80] Nor does there seem to be any difference in the relative frequency of these facilities at those sites which were dedicated principally to Isis and those which honor Sarapis at their chief god. Since, unlike the περιρραντήρια, the temple basins were very likely the product of Egyptian influence, I wondered if there might be a correlation between their presence at a given site and the presence of overt signs of "Egyptianization" such as Egyptian architectural motifs, artifacts imported from Egypt or closely imitating objects from that country, cultic equipment of a known Egyptian lineage, etc. However, if the sanctuaries at Pompeii and Pergamum do have such basins and do reveal such Egyptian features, those at Corinth and Sabratha, which also have such basins, produced no such signs of "Egyptianization." Further, no basin of this sort has been found at the Iseum at Soli, and yet its architecture strongly reflects Egyptian antecedents. Therefore a clear pattern along this line of "Egyptianization" does not emerge.

A further factor renders such an analysis even more difficult. Certain ablution rites clearly did not require a fixed facility within the sanctuary. Lucius, after all, received the purification which inaugurated his initation not within the precinct of Isis but at a public bath! In addition, his earlier purification in the sea, an action reminiscent of a ritual practiced at Eleusis, may have reflected an actual liturgical practice found in the Isis-Sarapis cult and known to Apuleius.[81] Clearly the absence of a basin at a given site does not mean that ablution rites were not practiced there. If, however, the priests and priestesses were required to have water poured or sprinkled over their heads before they began a ritual in the sanctuary, they probably would have performed such an ablution within the sacred area. Yet they may not have needed a fixed facility for such a purpose. Perhaps a simple basin of water and a pitcher or a lustral branch would have served quite well. Such diversity in respect to these rites is really not so unfamiliar—early Christians also baptized in rivers, in springs, in lakes, in the sea, and in standing water of all sorts.[82] Differences of this sort do not mean that either the Isis-Sarapis cult or early Christianity lacked order and regularity in their ritual washings. Instead, it only indicates that certain features were not considered critical for the proper performance of the rite. With respect to this group of temple basins, therefore, I am willing to advance only two conclusions. First, the construction of a fixed facility like the temple basin represents both a certain amount of stress upon the rite connected with it and a certain degree of institutionalization. Secondly, such an organized emphasis upon ablution rites, especially insofar as this can be connected with the clergy, appears to go back to traditions and practices common within Egyptian religious observance.

CHAPTER EIGHT

EGYPTIANIZING THE CULT OF THE EGYPTIAN GODS

The task which Jean Leclant urged upon investigators of the cult of Isis and Sarapis represents an avenue of research rich with possibilities. He was quite definite in what he proposed—scholars must bend every effort to determine the various "phases of evolution" through which this form of worship has passed.[1] With this in mind I have intended that my own study of the design, typology, and function of the various water facilities utilized within this cult contribute as much as possible to this broader historical enterprise. The most recent general theory of the cult's development is that proposed by Ladislav Vidman in his book *Isis und Sarapis bei den Griechen und Römern* (1970).[2] It is with this hypothesis in particular that I intend to engage in dialogue in the course of the following pages.

Without a doubt the early Imperial period marks a period of considerable transition within the cult. As I noted at the outset of this work, the second century AD is a time when the worship of the Egyptian gods burgeoned forth in an unmistakable fashion. Particularly indicative of this is the large number of new sanctuaries known to have been constructed and the massive increase in the number of votive inscriptions over those dating to the previous two centuries. Pausanias' enumeration of the sanctuaries of Isis and Sarapis located in mainland Greece offers an added indication, at least on a regional level, of the cult's attractiveness and social respectability during this era. Given such expansiveness and vitality, I can only agree with Vidman's view that this century and the previous mark a key period of development in the life of the cult.

Vidman's designation for this particular phase, the "interpretatio romana," is somewhat puzzling, for precious few "Romanizing" elements make their appearance. Instead, most of the characteristic features that he singles out are Egyptian in origin: more permanent colleges of priests in place of annual appointees, a daily ritual of washing and dressing the cult statue, an annual *Navigium Isidis* festival with a colorful public procession, the custom of plaiting the hair of young boys into "Horus locks," and so forth. Vidman is quite well aware of the Egyptian character of these various institutions. Indeed, at times he speaks of a powerful "Egyptianizing wave" which rolled across the entire Mediterranean world. Yet for him this wave obviously had varying impact since he notes that the Greek East was not very much affected by the new developments but clung instead to its more traditional ways. Only the Roman West welcomed these Egyptian influences and tendencies with enthusiasm. Once Vidman has analyzed the early Imperial stage of development in this fashion, he has brought us back to an understanding long accepted by scholars who study this cult—the Roman and western forms of the cult appear to be much more directly dependent on Egypt that do the Hellenistic and eastern forms.

I part company with such an analysis on two counts. First of all, a simple division between the Greek East and the Roman West is not a tenable proposition. Vidman himself hedges somewhat on this when he observes that the East was also affected by some Egyptianizing influences. For my own part I think the matter is more complex. Is there, for example, clear evidence that "Horus locks" and daily washings of the cult statue were in vogue all over the western Empire? And what is to be made of the fact that no sanctuary is known to have imitated traditional Egyptian architectural forms more closely than the Iseum located at Soli on Cyprus? I do not in any way believe that we should abandon the search for "phases of evolution" within the cult. I simply am convinced that the traditional bipartite division does not do justice to the evidence.

Secondly, I am not content with describing the cause for this expansive phase within the history of Isis-Sarapis worship as "an Egyptianizing wave." I do not quarrel with the stress on Egyptian influence. Indeed, quite the contrary! Instead, I look for greater precision. After all, "Egyptianization" might mean a great many different things. The importation of artifacts from Egypt is a feature observed during this period, and yet this does not seem to be the sort of thing which would spark a cultic revival. Even to list, as Vidman does, a series of new observances is to record symptoms rather than causes. I do not pretend to have the answer as to why in early Imperial times a significantly larger number of people suddenly became interested in this cult. Undoubtedly external factors within the general cultural milieu contributed to this process, and at least in theory they might explain it altogether. Yet I believe that Vidman was correct in searching for significant internal shifts as at least a partial explanation for the sudden attractiveness which this form of worship obviously manifested. After all, symptoms for some sort of shifting and change are clearly present. For my own part, I would be much happier if it were possible to determine the ideological underpinnings that made people more interested in new architectural forms, new iconographic types, new liturgical practices, etc. Most religious and cultic groups tend to be notoriously conservative and reluctant to adopt new ways of doing things. Given all the observable changes that take place within various circles of the Isis-Sarapis cult at this time, we can only assume that powerful ideological forces were at work. My objection to Vidman's work is that he does not offer any clue as to what these might have been.

My analysis of the water facilities has enabled me to see that the movement of Egyptianization which takes place during this period is neither a massive wave engulfing all the known centers of the cult nor a series of isolated and localized rivulets. Regional patterns do exist, although more complex boundaries are required than a simple line separating east and west. In addition, what was transmitted was not simply artifacts, not simply isolated practices, but also basic religious perceptions. The available evidence from the water facilities reveals one major aspect of this ideological shift. To put it quite generally, this may be described as a more wholehearted acceptance of an Egyptian view of the gods and their relation to natural phenomena in place of that more typically found within Greek religious contexts.

It is not the ablution facilities which provide evidence for this tradition from one phase in the life of the cult to another. To begin with, the sprinkling basins or περιρραντήρια attested probably for the sanctuaries at Eretria, Pergamum, and Soli (Temple D) and possibly also for those at Delos (Serapeum C), Luxor, Pompeii, and Sabratha have Greek rather than Egyptian ancestry and so fit better

with Vidman's "interpretatio graeca" phase. As a traditional type
of ablution facility customarily found at Greek sanctuaries, they
made their way in time to various temples in Egypt frequented by
Graeco-Egyptians. Perhaps it was via this route that they then came
to be found at the Graeco-Roman sanctuaries of Isis and Sarapis.
Along the way the ritual practices associated with them may have
shifted, but no proof of this is to be had one way or the other. These
basins reveal no discernible pattern of distribution and so of
themselves afford no indication that Isis-Sarapis worship passed
through any stages of development.

The traditional Egyptian emphasis on ritual purity for the
ministers of the cult appears to have been a strong but more remote
influence leading to the installation of ablution basins just to the
right of the central temple or cult statue. This is the class of water
facilities which I prefer to call "temple basins." Their location well
within the precinct close to the area over which the priests and
priestesses exercised special responsibility has led me to suppose
that these basins were intended primarily, although perhaps not
exclusively, for their use. Several texts in the *Metamorphoses* of
Apuleius provide a clue for determining the manner of purification
utilized in this and in other ablution rites. In accordance with the
practice attested for Egyptian ritual washings of every sort, those
who were being purified had to have water poured or sprinkled over
their heads. As for an explanation of the origin of these temple
basins, I cannot point to the existence of parallel types of facilities at
the traditional sanctuaries of Egypt but only to a more general factor, the repeated attestations in both Egyptian and Greek sources of
the importance of purificatory washings for the Egyptian clergy.

Those sanctuaries which took the trouble to build such permanent facilities—Alexandria, Corinth, Eretria, Gortyn, Pergamum,
Pompeii, Priene, Sabratha, and Cyrene: Apollo Precinct probably
or certainly did so—tended by this very act to lay stress upon the
rites connected with them. Yet the absence of such temples basins
at a given site is no indication that the particular sanctuary did not
value such rituals. In a parallel case, Apuleius was perfectly able to
suppose that Lucius could have received his pre-initiation purification and ritual sprinkling at a public bath. No doubt the ablutions
associated with the temple basins could have been performed with

the aid of a portable basin and a pitcher or lustral branch. Consequently, because we have no proof that any particular ablutions within this cult required permanent facilities and because the group of temple basins that does survive reveals no distinctive pattern of distribution, this body of evidence cannot easily be related to any shifts or transitions which took place within the cult.

On balance, this divergence with respect to these ablution facilities is not so surprising. Whenever we encounter such rites within this cult, they are always merely preparatory to some more important ritual act. People sprinkled themselves before entering the temple; priestesses and priests washed before beginning a sacred rite; Lucius purified himself or was purified before praying to Isis, before recalling her appearance to him, and before beginning the actual initiation into her mysteries. Always this purification rite is before something; it is never a central event in its own right as is, for example, the baptismal washing found in Christianity. This becomes all the clearer when we realize that only Christian sources from antiquity try to make it such.[3] In actuality, ablutions were simply too peripheral to the main concerns of this cult to admit of their becoming explanatory causes for a revival of it.

On the other hand, the sacred water of the Nile flood evidently exercised a much more powerful grip on the imaginations both of those within the cult and those outside as well. One indication of this is the amount of discussion of the various properties and potencies of Nile water found in Hellenistic and especially in Roman literary sources. No fewer than fifty or sixty writers pass on various popular traditions, scientific observations, and theories of all sorts relative to this theme. To judge from these various sources, Nile water was one of the great nostrums of the age! Not only did its freshness and sweetness commend it as a drink of extraordinary merit,[4] but as a fertilizing and life-giving agent this marvellous liquid was without peer. It fructified and enriched the crops of Egypt and made that country the breadbasket of the Mediterranean world. It was responsible for the richness and variety of Egypt's fauna and was thought to be quite useful for promoting weight gain and fertility among domestic flocks and herds. It had a powerfully beneficial influence upon human procreation and growth as well. Nile water made women more fertile, promoted multiple births, made pregnancies easier, and reduced the possibility that an infant might be still-born. Because of this fructifying power the Nile and its flood water were regularly called γόνιμος, πολύγονος, *fecundus,* and *fertilis.* There was even a wide-spread view that the Nile flood promoted spontaneous generation. We do not know how far all of these assessments penetrated into the actual cult of Isis and Sarapis. However, from the limited evidence available, Nile water was esteemed becaue it was a promise from the gods of a life in this world blessed by riches and by healthy and numerous children.

To contain this sacred substance many of the Hellenistic sanctuaries of Isis and Sarapis had a crypt designed in the form of a Ptolemaic Nilometer. The prototypes for these crypts are still to be seen at various places up and down the Nile valley and consist basically of a covered stairway which descends, often after making one or two right angle turns, to a depth equal to the local low-water level of the Nile. Water from the river entered at the bottom and was then free to rise and fall within the Nilometer in harmony with the river itself. Although such facilities were frequently located at the major sanctuaries of Egypt, they were primarily intended to measure the height of the rising flood waters of the Nile and to make this information available for the needs of Egyptian agriculture. I have suggested, however, that they may also have supplied Nile flood water for the cultic needs of the sanctuaries with which they were associated.

One such Nilometer is found at the Serapeum of Alexandria. That it was constructed to serve any economic function is rather hard to imagine, for Alexandria lies at the very end of the Nile's long course. Of course, it certainly could have served to make flood water available to this precinct for its liturgical requirements. Yet I believe the real reason that the builders constructed such an installation high on the Rhacotis Hill was their desire to have a visible symbol of Sarapis' power over the Nile and its annual inundation. We know that the sacred cubit certainly had such a significance in later antiquity. Since this object was also a (symbolic) measuring device for the height of the Nile, I suspect that it may well have inherited the symbolic role which the former Nilometer at the sanctuary once had.[5] If this accurately describes its primary function, this Nilometer probably is the link between the economically functional Nilometers of the Egyptian countryside and the Nilometer-like crypts found at Delos A, Delos B, Gortyn, Pompeii, and perhaps also at Delos C and Thessalonica.[6] Although various theories have been advanced for the use of these facilities within the Graeco-Roman cult, I remain convinced that they were designed to serve only two purposes. First, they provided for a periodic re-creation of the Nile flood within these various precincts, an event which would be a visible demonstration of the power of the Egyptian gods over this phenomenon and the fertilizing and life-giving forces associated with it. Secondly, they then made this sacred water available for the various ritual activities of these sanctuaries.

These Nilometer crypts are a peculiarly Hellenistic feature within the Isis-Sarapis cult. Eretria is the only sanctuary built during this period which had a fixed Nile water container not designed according to this precise pattern. In that situation local conditions may have necessitated the construction of a simpler facility, a facility which nonetheless made provision for periodic re-enactments of the Nile flood. On the other hand, of all the known sanctuaries built in Roman times only the precinct of Sarapis and Isis at Sabratha has a crypt which in any way resembles the older Nilometer type. For that matter, only a limited number of Roman period sites (Frauenberg, Pergamum, and Sabratha) are known to have any sort of fixed Nile water container.[7] Possibly certain segments of the cult ceased to be very much interested in this sacred substance and so did not build such facilities. On the other hand, other groups certainly did continue to value it quite highly but also apparently did not build such structures. The shift in practice from Hellenistic to Roman times is startling. Six out of the sixteen sanctuaries known to have been constructed in the earlier period certainly had such a fixed facility and two others probably did so. Yet for the Roman period only three of the thirty-one sites presently known have any remains of such facilities. Evidently something took place within this cult which rendered the building of such containers unnecessary.[8]

One part of the answer as to what did happen emerges from the analysis of a group of materials associated with the god Osiris. These objects, the long-spouted Nile water pitchers, the Osiris Hydreios statues, and the "Cool Water" funerary inscriptions, were not utilized, as some have thought, wherever the Isis-Sarapis cult had taken root but began to appear only at the very end of the first century BC and in the first century AD and only in northern Egypt, in central Italy, and at those places especially associated either with Rome or with Egypt. Seven of the known sanctuaries (Luxor, Philippi, Pompeii, Ras el Soda, Rome: Campus Martius, Rome: Santa Sabina, and Soli: Temple E) provide evidence for the use of one or more of these objects. Of this group, only one site, the Iseum at Pompeii, is known to have had a fixed Nile water container. Such a state of affairs suggests that at least in this restricted geographical area the cultic pitcher substantially replaced the older fixed facilities as a container for Nile water. Although this pitcher of Nile water was normally kept in the cella of the temple,[9] it was brought out either to be borne aloft in public procession or else to be adored by worshippers within the precinct. It very probably also served as a source of water for libation rituals.

The association of this vessel with the Osiris Hydreios iconographic type and with the Osiris "Cool Water" formula is evident from the common pattern of distribution which all three objects shared, from typological similarities, and from the parallel ritual contexts in which they were employed. The statue of Osiris in his *hydria* form took its origin from a type of visceral jar found regularly in Egytian graves and was itself often buried with the dead as a kind of guardian image. Similarly, the "Cool Water" formula was a prayer that Osiris might grant this revitalizing liquid to the dead person. If the life-giving water to which both of these objects make reference was destined to benefit the dead person, clearly the water in the pitcher was also thought to have this potency. Those who made use of Nile water in other sectors of the cult may also have looked upon it as a substance which promised a joyous existence even beyond the grave. However, we have proof for the existence of such hopes only for the more restricted sphere in which these Osiris materials were honored and utilized.

The fixed Nile water containers, as I indicated above, were designed in such a way as to provide for a periodic reproduction of the Nile flood. If in certain sectors of the cult they came to be replaced by containers like the cultic pitcher, those who made such a substitution no longer were concerned that periodic re-enactments of the flood take place within their sanctuaries. The water itself remained of great value to them, for they preserved it in vessels of a special type. What they were not interested in was the reproduction of the process whereby such water came into existence. It is in this change that the underlying ideology to which I made reference at the beginning makes itself felt.

Despite the stubborn survival of a variety of animistic tendencies, Greek religion essentially viewed the gods as rulers over the phenomena, not as immanent within them. Such a conception is operative, for example, when Isis and Sarapis are seen as "summoning" the Nile, as "impelling" it, or as "causing it to rise and to spread over Egypt." According to these conceptions, the power and might of these two gods is made manifest in the annual inundation. Such language even hints that the phenomena have an inbuilt negative resistance and so must be ruled by mighty powers. This is not the view of the Egyptians. Their gods are immanent within natural phenomena and partake in their existence. Osiris, for example, shares in the fate of the Nile, for his power is incarnate in that river. Though Plutarch himself rejected such a conception, he recognized that this was how the Egyptians viewed this divinity—"Among the Egyptians Osiris is the Nile."[10] Consequently, low Nile was actually the disappearance of this god, while the coming of the flood was his revitalization and restoration. Within such a religious perspective, to have and to possess these flood waters was to have and possess Osiris himself in his full might and vigor.[11]

All three of the objects in the Osiris group of materials are expressive of this religious conception. In the iconographic arrangement of the Osiris Hydreios statue the head of the god is set on top of the *hydria*. In effect, the water jar then becomes the body of the god, a very graphic representation of this divinity's incarnate character. Although Apuleius speaks of the cultic pitcher in somewhat more traditional fashion as the "image" (*effigies*) of Osiris, Plutarch notes that Egyptians describe its contents as the "emanation" or "effluence" (ἀπορροή) of this god.[12] If the latter's enunciation of this belief avoids a simple identification of the god with the water, it nonetheless is quite different from a traditional Greek way of speaking. Finally, when the formula "May Osiris

give you cool water'' is inscribed on a grave stele, the hope
expressed is that Osiris will make available to the dead person the
life-giving power that is in himself. For this reason no cultic
pitchers, not even dummy versions, are found in tombs but only
images of Osiris Hydreios. The presence of the god in his *hydria*
form is itself the gift of ''cool water.''

Those who made use of these objects apparently were not interested simply in benefiting from saving deeds which a god might
work from afar. Instead, they desired to have in their midst the
actual and visible divine presence. It is not surprising, therefore,
that the cultic pitcher and the Osiris Hydreios statue are so often
portrayed being carried in the veiled hands of a minister of the cult.
The devotees of Osiris wanted to behold their god as he passed
before them in sacred procession or as he was held on high for their
adoration. Rituals of this sort naturally assumed considerable
importance once ''real presence'' became such a vital religious
concern.

There are some indications that this conception of the gods as
immanent in phenomena may have extended beyond those areas in
which the cultic pitcher and its related objects were in use. The
reclining bovine images which were discovered in the crypt at Gortyn were placed there in the later Roman period and are probably
to be explained in terms of the conceptual framework I have been
describing. Very likely these objects were representations of Isis as
a cow, a form of the goddess associated with her ''Search for
Osiris.'' In the mythical account and cultic re-enactment of this
event Osiris is always identified with the Nile and Isis with the
earth.[13] Just as the one god shares in the fate of the river, so the
other is intimately involved in the experiences of the earth. Isis in
her cow form mourns when life-giving water is absent but rejoices
when the cry goes up, ''Osiris is found!'' Apparently those who
frequented the sanctuary at Gortyn in this later period and who
placed these terracotta figures in the crypt were aware of such an
Egyptianized conception of these gods.

The shift to portable containers for Nile water probably took
place at other Roman period sanctuaries as well, although we do
not know what form these arrangements might have taken. There
are scattered indications that some groups had water brought in

from outside, possibly even from Egypt.[14] All of this could have been motivated by the shift in religious understanding which I have outlined, but positive evidence to prove this remains unavailable.

Nonetheless, beginning in the early Imperial period certain areas of the cult experienced a very radical degree of Egyptianization. The phenomenon I have been describing goes well beyond the adoption of Egyptian architectural forms and Egyptian artifacts. Many of the sites which reveal a significant degree of Egyptianization on this level (e.g., Pompeii, Rome: Campus Martius, and Soli: Temple E) are also those which made use of the cultic pitcher and the Osiris Hydreios statue. On the other hand, Cyme and Pergamum also show signs of this type of Egyptian influence and yet do not appear to have belonged to this Rome-Alexandria group of sites.[15] Furthermore, even though much of the evidence for processions and adoration rituals derives from this sphere of the cult, this Egyptianization process also went beyond the adoption of new ritual practices. Beyond such external manifestations a transformation of religious ideology took place. This shift may well have been a good deal more complex than I have described, for I have restricted my attention to the water facilities and their related rituals. Yet it is to this Egytianization of religious understanding that I am inclined to look in order to explain the attractiveness and renewed vigor of the Isis-Sarapis cult in early Imperial times.

If Vidman's account of this "Egyptianizing wave" therefore needs to be revised and expanded, so does his description of the areas which it influenced. Perhaps even the notion of a single wave emanating out from the Nile valley is too simplified. Through an analysis of the distribution patterns of certain key objects, we can trace the existence of a series of sites in northern Egypt, central Italy, and a few other related localities in Africa and in the East which obviously adopted a common set of traditions and usages from Egypt. The underlying ideology, certainly of Egyptian extraction, also appears elsewhere (e.g., Gortyn) but apparently under a somewhat different guise. On the other hand, some Roman period sites reveal no sign of Egyptianization on any level (e.g., Sabratha: East End). Only a unified pattern of influence will explain the Rome-Alexandria group of sites. Whether the other instances of Egyptianization in connection with the water facilities were the results of separate currents emanating from this group of cult centers or from other sources in Egypt cannot now be determined. What is clear is that a simple division between the Greek East and the Roman West does not adequately describe the facts of the case.

I believe that further progress can be made in tracing the various strands of Egyptian influence which made themselves felt at the beginning of the Imperial age. Just as a determination of the pattern of distribution for the cultic pitchers and their associate objects led to the discovery of a coherent pattern of religious influence from the Nile valley, so also an analysis of this sort might work with other monumental remains, especially those found in relation to known cult sites. The distribution of artifacts known to have been imported from Egypt is one possible line of investigation. Further, the statues and reliefs of boys with "Horus locks," a group of objects carefully catalogued by Victorine von Gonzenbach, might also reveal some points of connection with the lines of Egyptian influence I have described above.[16] Materials from the cult sites will prove most apt for this sort of investigation since they can generally be inserted more readily into a definite temporal and geographical framework. If most of the "Horus lock" materials do not derive from known sanctuaries, they nonetheless can be utilized insofar as their precise temporal and geographical context is able to be established. With such possibilities for future research in view, I remain convinced that archaeology has much yet to say to investigators of the Isis-Sarapis cult.

APPENDIX ONE

SURVEY OF THE SITES

What follows is an effort to provide the reader with necessary background information on the various Isis-Sarapis sanctuaries discussed in this work.[1] There is, first of all, a table of all these sites; this will permit easy reference and comparison. Following this is a brief discussion of each of the sanctuaries listed in which I concentrate particularly on problems of dating and identification, problems which I have in every case investigated anew. For each site I also provide a detailed and critical bibliography.

Because I apply the term "site" only to those definite locations at which at least some architectural remains were discovered *in situ*, I do not include in the following such proposed sanctuaries as Beneventum. In this case a large group of sculptures was indeed found, but these have not yet been linked with the remains of any determined building.

The present survey gives me the opportunity to explain why I have excluded one site with extensive water facilities which is often associated with the Isis-Sarapis cult. This is the so-called "Serapeum" located close to the Commercial Agora at Ephesus. In the last part of this appendix I will argue that no solid evidence supports the hypothesis that this site was dedicated either to Sarapis or to any other of the Egyptian gods.

Table of the Sites

A word is in order to explain the various categories which appear in the following tabular listing. Column 2, "Identification," refers to the degree of certainty that a particular sanctuary did relate to the worship of Isis and/or Sarapis. The divinity accorded principal honors is indicated in Column 3. I have here used abbreviations to indicate the type of evidence supporting this attribution: A = architectural design, DI = dedicatory inscription for the precinct, I = other types of inscriptions, L = literary evidence, and SF =

small finds. Columns 4-6 should be generally self-explanatory. Of
these various dates, certainly the most difficult to determine is that
for the termination of cultic acivities at a particular site. Most of the
dates given under Column 6 are therefore rather hypothetical
unless the excavators carried out a careful stratigraphic analysis
and this produced sufficient data to determine the matter. Major
reconstructions (Column 5) are important to note since they often
provide evidence for the religious vitality of a particular sanctuary.
In Column 7 I provide the dates of any excavations and the names
of the chief individuals associated with these efforts. Finally,
Columns 8-10 aim at giving the reader an idea of the relative worth
of the various sites as sources of information. While the general rule
of thumb is that high number ratings are good, low ratings are bad,
the reader is urged to consult the interpretations of these ratings
given in the notes.[2] It can be, for example, that a site survived in
fairly good condition (a high "State of Site" rating) but was poorly
excavated and/or poorly reported and so is now largely inaccessible
to further investigation (e.g., Cyme). It is also possible that a given
site was not very well preserved but was excavated and published
with great care. Usually such a site will provide quite valuable information despite its condition. The shrine in the Agora at Corinth
and the two sanctuaries at Soli illustrate such a situation very well.

Dating and Identification

This section, designed to provide bibliography, dates, and
attribution for each of the thirty sites listed in the table, involves
certain problems. With regard to determining attribution,
archaeologists often experience a strong *horror vacui* when they
uncover a temple or other major structure. It must at once be given
a name. The data used to justify that name can at times be extraor-
dinarily meager. No matter, the name is given and the site then
passes into more general literature as a "Serapeum" or a "sanctuary of Isis" or whatever. My constant effort has been to examine
these various identifications as rigorously as possible either to verify
or to challenge them. Similarly I have tried to re-examine all the
evidence for the date of foundation and the date or dates for any
remodeling or reconstruction. Here, as in so many other cases, the

1	2	3	4	5	6	7	8	9	10
SITE	IDENTIFI-CATION	CHIEF DEITY	FOUNDED	REMODELED/REBUILT	CEASED	EXCAVATED	STATE OF SITE	EXCAVATIONS	SITE REPORTS
Alexandria	Certain	Sarapis (DI, L)	246-21 BC	late 2nd cen. AD	391 AD	1865 (Mahmoud el-Falaki); 1894-96 (Botti); 1905-06 (Breccia); 1942-49 (Rowe)	4 (POB)	7	5
Ampurias	Possible	Isis & Sarapis (I)	1st cen. BC (prob.)	?	not later than 3rd cen. AD	1907-08 (Puig y Cadafalch)	5	7	6
Argos	Possible	Isis & Sarapis (?) (I)	3rd cen. BC	Roman period (?)	?	1906 (Vollgraff)	4	7	5
Cenchreae	Doubtful	Isis (SF, L)	2nd cen. AD (?)	early 4th cen. AD	?	1963-67 (Scranton)	7	10	10
Corinth: South Stoa	Certain	Sarapis (SF)	late 2nd cen. AD	--	267 AD	1936-37 (Broneer)	6	10	10
Cyme	Probable	Aphrodite; later: also Isis (I)	c. 4th cen. BC	1st or 2nd cen. AD -- for Isis worship	3rd cen. (?)	1925 (Salač)	5	7	2
Cyrene: Apollo Precinct	Certain	Isis (DI)	117-38 AD (?)	211-17 AD	?	c. 1925 (Pernier?)	8 (PR)	7	1

1 SITE	2 IDENTIFICATION	3 CHIEF DEITY	4 FOUNDED	5 REMODELED/REBUILT	6 CEASED	7 EXCAVATED	8 STATE OF SITE	9 EXCAVATIONS	10 SITE REPORTS
Delos A	Certain	Sarapis (DI, I)	210-200 BC	c. 100 BC	c. 88 BC	1911-12 (Roussel)	8	7	7
Delos B	Certain	Sarapis (I)	c. 200 BC	?	c. 88 BC	1910 (Roussel)	4	7	6
Delos C	Certain	Sarapis (I)	200-190 BC	2nd cen. BC (various projects)	1st cen. BC	1881 (Hauvette-Besnault); 1909-10 (Holleaux, etc.); 1953 (Marcadé)	4	7	7
Ephesus: State Agora	Possible	Isis (?) (A, SF)	50-1 BC	c. 200 AD	no later than c. 380 AD	1970 (Alzinger & Karwiese)	5	6	8
Eretria	Certain	Sarapis & Isis (I)	c. 300 BC	150-100 BC; c. 100 BC	c. 50 BC	1914 (Papadakis); 1973 (Bruneau)	5	10	10
Frauenberg	Possible	Isis (I ?)	late 1st-early 2nd cen. AD	?	c. 400 AD	1951 (Modrijan)	5 (POB)	7	6
Gortyn	Certain	Isis & Sarapis (DI, SF)	c. 2nd cen. BC	1st or 2nd cen. AD	3rd or 4th cen. (?)	1913-14 (Oliverio)	7	6	5

SITE	IDENTIFICATION	CHIEF DEITY	FOUNDED	REMODELED/REBUILT	CEASED	EXCAVATED	STATE OF SITE	EXCAVATIONS	SITE REPORTS
Industria	Probable	Isis (?) (A, SF)	2nd cen. AD	3rd cen. AD (?)	c. 350 AD	1811-12 (Morra); 1961-63 (Gullini)	5	7	9
Leptis Magna	Probable	Sarapis (I, SF)	2nd cen. AD	?	late 4th cen. AD	1960 (Vergara-Caffarelli)	6	7	4
Luxor	Certain	Sarapis (DI)	?	Jan. 24, 126 AD	3rd or 4th cen.	1950-51 (Zakaria Ghoneim)	5 (PR)	7	5
Pergamum	Probable	Isis (SF)	early 2nd cen. AD	?	?	1934-35, 1938 (?)	9 (POB)	6	1938:1 1970:7
Philippi	Certain	Isis & Sarapis (I)	2nd cen. AD (?)	?	3rd cen. or later	1920-21 (Renaudin)	5	7	6
Pompeii	Certain	Isis (DI, SF)	2nd cen. BC	c. 63 AD	79 AD	1764-66	10	9	7
Priene	Certain	Sarapis & Isis (I)	3rd cen. BC	Hellenistic additions	after 100 BC	c. 1897 (Wiegand)	6	9	9
Ras el Soda	Certain	Isis (SF)	after 150 AD	--	?	1936 (Adriani ?)	8	7	6
Rome: Campus Martius	Certain	Isis (& Sarapis) (SF, L)	early 1st cen. AD	89 AD; c. 230 AD; c. 300 AD	4th or 5th cen. (?)	various dates	3 (TOB)	3	5

1	2	3	4	5	6	7	8	9	10
SITE	IDENTIFI-CATION	CHIEF DEITY	FOUNDED	REMODELED/REBUILT	CEASED	EXCAVATED	STATE OF SITE	EXCAVATIONS	SITE REPORTS
Rome: Santa Sabina	Certain	Isis (I, SF)	late 2nd cen. AD (?)	--	mid 3rd cen.	1855-57 (Basson); 1936-39 (Darsy)	9	7	5
Sabratha: East End	Certain	Sarapis & Isis (SF, I)	2nd or 3rd cen. AD	--	4th cen. (?)	1934-40 (Guidi & Caputo); 1943-44; 1946-47 (Pesce)	8 (PR)	9	9
Soli: Temple D	Probable	Isis (SF, L)	1st cen. BC	--	late 1st cen. AD	1930-31 (Westholm)	5 (TOB)	10	10
Soli: Temple E	Certain	Isis or Isis & Sarapis (SF)	late 2nd cen. AD	after 250 AD	4th cen. (?)	1930-31 (Westholm)	6	10	10
Thera	Certain	Sarapis & Isis (I)	c. 250 BC	?	2nd cen. BC (?)	1895 (Wilski)	4	7	6
Thessa-lonica	Certain	Sarapis & Isis (I)	3rd cen. BC	"Roman period"	3rd or 4th cen. AD	1921-24; 1939 (Pelekides)	4 (TOB)	3	1
Timgad	Probable	Sarapis (SF)	2nd cen. AD	213 AD	?	1939-55 (Leschi, C. Godet, and R. Godet)	7 ?	7 ?	3

quality of work done by those who excavated the sites sets a limit to the problems that can be solved.

1. *Alexandria* (Fig. 12)[3]

Literary sources, notably Tacitus, *Hist.* 4.84,[4] and a dedicatory inscription to Sarapis found on the site, a stone thought to belong to the first half of the third century BC,[5] indicate that prior to the construction of the great Serapeum uncovered by Botti and Rowe some sort of sanctuary honoring Sarapis and/or Isis stood on the site. Thus far, however, remains of this older precinct have not been located within the complex of ruins on the Rhacotis Hill. Rowe's amazing discoveries during World War II of a multitude of foundation inscriptions proved, first of all, that the known sanctuary and its central temple had been constructed during the reign of Ptolemy III (246-21 BC) and then dedicated to Sarapis.[6] Secondly, one of these discoveries added the additional information that early in his reign Ptolemy IV had dedicated a temple to Harpocrates next to the larger central temple of Sarapis.[7]

Strabo's statement that "within the Canal are the Serapeum and other ancient precincts which have been somewhat abandoned due to the construction of the new sanctuaries in the Nicopolis" is not altogether clear but may indicate that this sanctuary was somewhat in decline in the first century BC and early first century AD.[8] The frequent mention in the papyri of pious visits to this shrine would seem on the face of it to be evidence for the continued vigor of the cult carried on here, although admittedly much of this evidence is from later in the Roman Imperial period. Whatever the case, contrary to Fraser, I do not believe that the almost total reconstruction of the sanctuary which is known to have taken place in the Roman period can be linked with assurance to a revival of devotional interest in Sarapis and Isis. Rather, it is more easily explained by other factors. Until recently this reconstruction was associated with Hadrian's reign. Wace not very convincingly argued that the rebuilding of the sanctuary was necessitated by the devastation caused during the Jewish revolt of 116-17.[9] Rowe appealed for proof of a Hadrianic date to the Alexandrian coin series which depicts the Serapeum facade and to a large black granite bull dedicated in the sanctuary during the reign of this emperor.[10] This latter object proves nothing one way or the other. As for the former item. Handler has convincingly demonstrated that this coin series, which continued to the eleventh year of Marcus Aurelius, does not offer proof for a Hadrianic reconstruction or for any rebuilding before 171 AD.[11] She herself suggests the reign of Caracalla (211-17 AD) as a more probable date since the coins found under the four corners of the great *Piscina* on the east side of the sanctuary courtyard prove that this huge basin was built during his reign. However, Cassius Dio, unless he is merely being malicious and depicting Caracalla as giving dishonor to the gods, indicates that this emperor used the Serapeum as a base of operations against the rebellious Alexandrians.[12] An open and unfinished precinct would hardly have served such a purpose.

Since the archaeological evidence does not provide a precise date,[13] a determination can only be made on other grounds. Several ancient writers refer to a cataclysmic fire at the Serapeum in 181 AD.[14] It is more likely that the reconstruction detected by Rowe was the result of this event. The aftermath of the fire would have offered the opportunity not simply to restore the sanctuary as of old but to enlarge and enrich it.

2. *Ampurias* (Fig. 7)[15]

The habitual identification of this sanctuary as a Serapeum is certainly open to question. It is based entirely on two inscriptions, SIRIS 767 and 768. No collaborative small finds were reported and what remains of the sanctuary reveals nothing that would point with assurance to the Isis-Sarapis cult. SIRIS 767, discovered in fragmentary condition near the city wall in the neighborhood of the precinct, may possibly mention Sarapis.[16] However, if Hübner and Salač are correct in their restoration of line 3 as --- *meni f(ilius)*, the inscription extended ten or twelve letters to the left.[17] Therefore, if [*Sera*]*pi* is to be read at the right end of line 1, Isis' name very probably preceded it. SIRIS 768, found near the site during the 1908 excavations, reads [*S*]*arapi* at the end of line 2 but again has room to the left for another divine name.[18] If the sanctuary is to be identified on the basis of these two inscriptions, it more probably was a temple of Isis and Sarapis.

There is something of a scholarly consensus that the Ampurias precinct was constructed in the first century BC. While García y Bellido argues for this time period (with the early first century AD as a less likely possibility), Puig y Cadafalch and Almagro preferred a date in the late second or the first century BC.[19] The stratigraphy supports this range of dates without allowing further refinement.

3. Argos[20]

Wilhelm Vollgraff excavated a terrace at Argos on the east side of Mt. Larissa and discovered on it some masonry remains "of a late period" (i.e., of Roman date). The terrace itself was supported by an ashlar wall, and close to this was a carefully made stone cross-wall. On the basis of various small finds recovered, Vollgraff identified this complex as the remains of a sanctuary to the Egyptian gods.[21] Of these finds the most significant are an inscription recording a dedication to Isis and Sarapis and dating to the second century AD (SIRIS 41a) and a base, seemingly influenced in its design by Egyptian antecedents, which supported an offering to an unnamed god made by "Agathocles and Thaeis," the latter perhaps an Egyptian woman. The remaining finds are either not distinctive of the cult of the Egyptian gods or not actually from the site. Since the second of the two inscriptions dates to the third century BC, Vollgraff felt certain that the sanctuary dated from that period. However, because this text was found re-used as a stone in a later wall (and so could have come from elsewhere), I prefer to argue the case for a Hellenistic date on the basis of the masonry style of the retaining wall. The later masonry remains may point to a reconstruction in Roman times.

4. Cenchreae[22]

In the course of underwater investigations in the harbor area, Robert Scranton and his team discovered an apsidal room with a mosaic floor of geometric design. In the center of the apse was a fountain. Along the walls of this room were stacked nine crates of opus sectile glass panels; these date to the early fourth century AD and seem to have been placed here prior to the completion of the reconstruction (construction?) of this building. A variety of other small finds were also recovered but these have been only partially published. While Scranton at least at first was somewhat tentative in his identification of the building as a temple and tentative as well in relating it to the Isis cult,[23] others were quite positive that this was not only an Iseum but the very sanctuary described in Apuleius, *Metamorphoses* 11.[24] I myself find it difficult to believe, at least on the basis of the evidence so far published, that this structure was a temple of any sort, much less an Iseum. Those who call it such appeal almost entirely to the "Nilotic themes" found in the *opus sectile* panels. These, however, are not cultic in character and may have served here as elsewhere to embellish rather secular surroundings. Not all Egyptian items found in the West have religious significance! Here at this site no inscriptions were recovered, no cultic or religious objects, not even a base for a cult statue. Nothing renders it probable that this building was an Iseum.[25]

5. *Corinth: South Stoa* (Fig. 27)[26]

This sanctuary was founded in the latter part of the second century AD, a date indicated both by its relationship to the surrounding architecture and by the date of the Sarapis head found by the cult platform.[27] When the Herulians invaded Corinth in 267, it was destroyed by fire and was not rebuilt.[28] The small annex area to the west with its floor sloping at a nine degree angle toward the sanctuary has a drain which led out under the shrine to the Agora. However, there was also an opening between the annex and the shrine which allowed those within the cult area to make use of the water for their own purposes.[29]

6. *Cyme*[30]

The Isis inscriptions and other objects were found carefully stacked in a building which Salač christened "the meeting place of the *mystoi.*"[31] Perhaps this structure served in late Roman times as a sacred treasury for the offerings of the faithful.[32] Salač himself believed that already in the second century BC Isis was receiving cultic honors at what had been a sanctuary to Aphrodite.[33] He apparently arrived at this date because he had concluded that the Isis aretalogy found here dated to that century. This date for the aretalogy has not received general acceptance. Instead, most scholars now refer this stone to the first or second century AD.[34]

Consequently, L. Castiglione rightly questioned the hypothesis that the Egyptian gods had taken up their dwelling in this Greek temple as early as the second century BC.[35] For if the aretalogy is of Roman date, there remains no known Isis material from the site which is earlier than the first or second century AD.[36] It is my own belief that Isis did not replace the earlier cult but, as at the Cyrene Apollo Precinct site, found a place within the Aphrodite sanctuary sometime during the early Imperial period. A final decision on this must await the publication of Salač's papers.

7. Cyrene: Apollo Precinct (Fig. 10)[37]

SIRIS 804, an inscribed block from the reign of Hadrian, apparently preserves the original dedicatory inscription for this small shrine, although a gap in the text leaves open the slight possibility that the priest of Apollo making this offering used funds from the revenues of Apollo to *repair* the structure. A new roof and general renovations were required during the reign of Caracalla.[38] Other features to be observed in this small "side chapel": low benches on either side of the pronaos and a drain which runs from the front center of the cult platform around one side to the rear wall of the temple.[39]

8. Delos A (Fig. 14)[40]

That this sanctuary honored Sarapis as its principal deity is demonstrated not only by the well-known Sarapis aretalogy which the priest Apollonius set up as a dedicatory text for the precinct but also by a decree of the Roman Senate found on the site which dates from about 164 BC and which confirmed the continued existence of the "sanctuary of Sarapis."[41] Consequently Isis, who is mentioned in second place in many of the dedications, did not share equal honors here with Sarapis.

To judge by the date of the aretalogical inscription, this precinct was founded about 210-200 BC.[42] Prior to its construction a small group of Sarapis devotees had met for many years in rented quarters.[43] The room to the left of the central temple (Room D) was recognized by Roussel as a later addition.[44] Two identical inscriptions which date from about 100 BC and which once had been built into a wall were found near the entrance to this room. They perhaps serve to date the partition which separated this area from the courtyard.[45] Both texts warn men in woolen garments and women not to enter. While the two stones may have been placed at the main entrance to the sanctuary—they were found not far from the main stairway—I believe it more likely that they served to restrict a smaller area within the precinct. Room D, perhaps a shrine dedicated to Sarapis, Zeus Kasios, and Isis Tachnepsis, is a very likely candidate.[46] The portico to the right of the temple (Room C) also appears to have been a later addition. At some point, perhaps because of the construction of a water channel for the nearby Inopus River, the inner row of columns was bricked in and became the outer wall of the precinct.[47] No evidence survives that affords any indication that this sanctuary continued in use after the time of Mithridates' attack on Delos in 88 BC.

9. *Delos B* (Fig. 15)[48]

Of the three sanctuaries to the Egyptian gods on the island of Delos, Serapeum B is the least understood. It offers no such abundance of inscriptions as does Delos C and, unlike those texts found at Delos A, those that came to light here are more typical and commonplace. I believe that the site is correctly termed a "Serapeum," although it is just possible that it was jointly dedicated to Sarapis and Isis. Almost all of the dedications are to Sarapis, Isis, and Anubis in that order just as is the case at the other two Delos sanctuaries. However, none of these surviving stones gives the official dedicatory inscription for the sanctuary, even though one of them does commemorate the gift of a roof for one or more of the buildings on the site.[49] Two texts mention a certain scribe who was also a μελανηφόρος, an office usually associated with the cult of Isis. As it happens, one of these turns out to be a dedication by a κοινόν to Isis.[50] However, the other is an offering by the same group of people to what I believe was the "official" group of divinities, Sarapis, Isis, and Anubis.[51] My conclusion is that the cult assocation centered its devotions upon Isis (hence a μελανηφόρος as one of its leaders) while the sanctuary itself was dedicated chiefly to Sarapis.

Roussel and Vallois both date the origin of the site to the last decade of the third century BC.[52] This hypothesis receives some confirmation if *CE* 20 (= *IG* XI.4.1223), an inscription dating to the year 196 BC, originally came from the site. It was discovered in the valley below and was thought to have tumbled down from the sanctuary area up above.[53] The further history of this sanctuary is difficult to trace. Roussel believed that Room B was a later addition and he is probably correct, although when it was constructed remains uncertain.[54] Since three fragmentary inscriptions survive from the period after 166 BC, the sanctuary evidently continued in existence during the period of Roman rule over the island.[55] Probably, since the site was never overbuilt, it survived, if only as a rather somnulent place of worship, down to 88 BC.[56]

10. *Delos C* (Fig. 16)[57]

No one will deny that Delos C has a very oddly shaped ground plan.[58] A major cause of this irregularity is that this precinct is actually the combination of two formerly separate sanctuaries. The older of the two centered around a Metroon (Temple C on the plan by Replat [Fig. 16]) and an Escharon or shrine to the Cabiri (Structure Z).[59] Vallois believes that the cult of Demeter carried on here attracted into its orbit a group of Isis worshippers who erected c. 220 or perhaps somewhat later a small shrine to their own goddess within the Metroon area.[60] To this Vallois adds: "Si je ne m'abuse, c'est à son tour le modeste Isieion issu du Mètrôon qui amena un groupement de Sarapiastes à installer le dieu consort juste au Nord de la terrasse."[61] Because the central temple in this northern area was remodeled and enlarged about 180 BC, Vallois conjectures that it was originally constructed c. 200-190 BC.[62] During the second century this Sarapis temple was gradually surrounded by a variety of other shrines and outbuildings. By mid-century the northern and southern precincts had been joined together to form a single entity.[63] About 140 BC a new dromos was constructed in the southern area and the precinct attained roughly to the form in which it is now known.[64] The sanctuary then continued to function until 88 BC and perhaps even some years later since there are signs that repairs were carried out at least in one temple building sometime after 88 BC.[65] However, despite evidence advanced by Bruneau, there is no real indication that any cultic activities were carried on here during Imperial times.[66]

Sarapis was unquestionably the principal deity honored in the combined sanctuary. In a civic list of the priests of the year 158-57 BC a known priest of this sanctuary[67] was designated as the priest "of Sarapis."[68] A similar nomenclature appears in several inscriptions from the site itself.[69] Such a title makes clear Sarapis' leading role.

11. *Ephesus: State Agora* (Fig. 24)[70]

All that remains of this small peripteral (6 × 10) temple found at the west end of the upper Agora are the foundations. Those who have investigated the remains of the structure have been very tentative in proposing to identify it as a sanctuary of the Egyptian gods. Such hesitancy is quite correct, for the evidence thus far uncovered is tantalizing but inconclusive. The small finds discovered in the rubble above the foundations (i.e., a "small bronze bell" which "possibly" belonged to a sistrum, a terracotta statuette of Alexandrian origin which was too battered to allow identification, and the head from a small imported statue of Amon-Re) offer no clear supporting evidence.[71] The image of Amon-Re, the only object with assured cultic links, may indeed have served to give an Egyptian tone to a sanctuary of Isis or Sarapis but may also have been a votive offering to some other god. Equally, it may have derived from elsewhere and so have been only an accidental deposit in the rubble. A low and almost square basin for water constructed on the main axis of the temple and 12.5 m in front of it perhaps served as an ablution facility for those who entered the sacred area. It was constructed c. 200 AD and no evidence for any earlier basin was uncovered. However, only at the Serapeum at Luxor is a similar type of basin found and it is not clear in that case whether that structure had an actual connection with the cult of Sarapis. I conclude from the evidence thus far available that this temple, built in the last half of the first century BC, cannot yet be identified with any certainty. The small finds are too meager and the architecture does not fall into any established typology.[72]

12. *Eretria* (Fig. 20)[73]

Thanks to Papadakis and especially to Bruneau, the dating for the various phases of this sanctuary has been established with a considerable degree of certainty. SIRIS 73, a dedication offered c. 300 BC to Isis by a group of Egyptians, provides along with supporting stratigraphical evidence a reasonably precise *terminus a quo*.[74] Sometime later, but before the second half of the second century BC, the "water room" (Room G) received the waterproof tile floor now seen on the site.[75] Other modifications of the sanctuary which cannot now be detected may have taken place during the following years. Bruneau has been able to ascertain that a major remodeling was carried out sometime between 150 and 100 BC.[76] Either in the late second century or in the first century BC access from the sanctuary to the rooms north of it was blocked off.[77] The sanctuary itself ceased to be a place of worship about the year 50 BC. Bruneau believes that it was not destroyed but simply abandoned.[78]

More controversial in my judgment is the attribution of the site. Papadakis felt certain that it was an Iseum,[79] and his opinion has been accepted without any real discussion by all subsequent writers.[80] Clearly this attribution is based on SIRIS 73, the earliest of all the inscriptions and a dedication to Isis. That this stone, which was found *in situ* at the left of the entrance to the central temple, was intended as an official dedicatory inscription for the sanctuary is in no way evident. To the contrary, it more probably was a base serving to support some statue which the Egyptians had offered to this goddess.[81] Since the other five inscriptions which mention the Egyptian divinities by name habitually list Sarapis first and then Isis, I believe it more probable that the Eretria sanctuary was dedicated to Sarapis and Isis and therefore should not be called an Iseum.[82] A further text found in the south portico is a simple dedication to Zeus by a certain Demodicus.[83] While Papadakis was convinced that this inscription had been transported to this site from elsewhere, perhaps Demodicus had actually placed it in this sanctuary to honor Zeus Sarapis.[84] If so, it is one more indication that Sarapis may have enjoyed considerable cultic prestige at this site.

13. *Frauenberg* (Fig. 22)[85]

The temple found here has an apse at the rear of its cella, an altar just in front of the steps to the pronaos, and a large water basin outside and to the right rear of the cella. The entire sanctuary was demolished down to its foundations in late antiquity and was further disturbed especially during the construction of the "Old Schoolhouse" in 1730. Consequently, identification of the divinity worshipped here poses a genuine problem. Modrijan's conclusion that it was Isis is based upon a convergence of evidence: the fragmentary inscription SIRIS 650, perhaps a dedication to Isis; a fragmentary relief of a seated female figure (perhaps Isis nursing Harpocrates); and the water facility, probably a Nile water container.[86] From his analysis of the stratigraphy and from other factors, Modrijan has concluded that the temple was built no earlier than the late first or early second century and that it was destroyed with some considerable violence c. 400 AD.[87]

14. *Gortyn* (Fig. 17)[88]

The dedicatory inscription for the reconstructed temple of Roman times (SIRIS 170) was found near the front of that building and provides solid evidence that the sanctuary was dedicated to Isis and Sarapis.[89] Three other inscriptions (SIRIS 166-68), all of Hellenistic date, also mention Isis before Sarapis. Although this goddess therefore enjoyed pre-eminence, her cult statue, at least in the Roman period, did not stand in the center of the cult platform but at the left with Sarapis in the center and Hermanubis on the right.[90] This disposition for the cult statue of the principal deity is observed elsewhere (e.g., at Ras el Soda).

Since no inscription or other datable object is known to be earlier than the second century BC, the sanctuary very likely was founded in that period. SIRIS 170 is clear proof that at least the central temple was rather thoroughly reconstructed in the early Imperial period. That Flavia Filyra was not simply indulging in rhetorical excess when she said that her reconstruction was "from the very foundations" is seen in the remains of the crypt just to the right of the temple. Its upper walls and perhaps also its stairway reveal signs of this rebuilding.[91] It is not generally realized that only the central temple and a portion of the portico in front of it have been excavated; a large section of the precinct is still buried under several meters of soil.[92] Further investigation of this most important site might well yield significant dividends.

15. *Industria* (Fig. 6)[93]

Early in the nineteenth century this site in Liguria was excavated by Morra di Lauriano. Although all of the small finds which relate to the Isis cult were recovered at that time by him, the curved foundations seemed to suggest the remains of the *cavea* of a theater and he so designated the structure. The Italian team which explored the site anew in the nineteen-sixties demonstrated that the architectural remains do not correspond to those required for a theater and argued that Morra had actually discovered a sanctuary. They noted first of all the small finds he had uncovered there: a bronze sistrum, a marble tablet dedicated by a certain Avilia Ambilis and ornamented with two footprints and a sistrum (SIRIS 645), and a bronze statuette of Isis-Tyche.[94] Such a cluster of evidence at one place seems more than fortuitous. In addition, the architectural evidence, they believed, reveals correspondences with certain known sanctuaries of Isis and with features described by Apuleius in *Met.* 11.[95] Some of their arguments here are not so compelling. For example, the stairways on either side of the cella do not lead to "side entrances" on the model of that found at the Iseum of Pompeii but to small temples set at ninety-degree angles to the main cella. Nonetheless, the overall plan of the site does show significant agreement with the portion of the Iseum in the Campus Martius at Rome visible on the *Forma Urbis* map.[96] Quarters for the priests (?) and a well were uncovered in the southwest corner of the site. This area, originally separate from the precinct proper, was attached to it in the course of a later remodeling.[97] Coin evidence and other stratigraphic data suggest that the sanctuary was constructed in the early second century AD and remained operative until about the time of Constantine.[98]

16. *Leptis Magna* (Fig. 25)[99]

A donor who gave statues of Sarapis to this sanctuary after he had been healed by the god in a dream was allowed to record this divine benefaction on both wings of the staircase leading to the pronaos and cella. The prominent position accorded these inscriptions is perhaps the best argument that this sanctuary honored Sarapis as its chief deity. In addition, however, two large statues of Sarapis were recovered at the site. One of these, a large seated image of the god, was thought by the excavators to have been flung out of the temple at the close of the sanctuary's life; it perhaps was the original cult statue. Also recovered were a large statue of Isis, several portrait statues, and various other lesser finds. The sculptural finds date to the second century AD, a date which probably therefore represents the *terminus a quo* for the site. Supporting this dating are the many correspondences between this precinct and that dedicated to Sarapis at Ostia. The founding of this latter sanctuary took place, as is now known with certainty, in the year 127 AD.

17. *Luxor* (Fig. 2)[100]

The identification of this small temple, which is situated in the outermost courtyard of the great Temple of Luxor just about at the point where the sacred way to Karnak begins, is assured by its dedicatory inscription which was recovered on the site. This text also gives a precise date for the dedication of the temple after it had been reconstructed: January 24 (= Hadrian's birthday), 126 AD.[101] No cult statue of Sarapis was found. Leclant mentions the discovery of a large statue of Isis, a large Osiris Hydreios (Canopus) statue, two statues of bulls, a portion of a Sarapis (?) image which had once been placed in a niche on the outside wall of the temple, and a fragment of what may have been a second statue of Isis.[102] The temple itself is largely Graeco-Roman in design (4 × 5 peripteral) but with some Egyptian ornamentation. A basin set close to the sacred way may have had some relationship to the ritual needs of this site.[103]

18. *Pergamum* (Fig. 21)[104]

The "Red Hall," it is generally agreed, was constructed during the reign of Trajan or that of Hadrian.[105] But quite another matter is determining to whom it was dedicated.[106] Evidence from the site pertinent to this question is quite limited.[107] First, there are the fragments of several double atlantid figures found in the south portico. These have Egyptian *klaft* headdresses and other Egyptianizing features and must have been meant to evoke some sort of "Nilotic atmosphere."[108] Secondly, a small terracotta head having what appears to be a *klaft* headdress was found somewhere in the courtyard.[109] Finally, in 1968 in this same courtyard a small head of Isis, 0.06 m high, was discovered apparently as a chance find.[110] That is all. Other evidence cited by Salditt-Trappmann is not from the site and is therefore of limited relevance. Why, given this situation, Salditt-Trappmann then concludes that the structure was a Serapeum is not very clear. The small head is a head of *Isis* and the Egyptianizing materials, while found at several Roman period Isis temples outside of Egypt (Cyme, Pompeii, Rome: Campus Martius; Rome: Regio III; Soli: Temple D), have not been discovered at Serapeums of the same period except at those in the Nile valley.[111] The atlantids especially offer some assurance that this sanctuary was dedicated to an Egyptian divinity, for it is hard to imagine that the builders of a sanctuary to some other god would have used such motifs in the second century AD. That this divinity was Isis rather than Sarapis appears more probable to me, although I would stress that limited data grounds this hypothesis.

19. *Philippi* (Fig. 8)[112]

While it is certain that this sanctuary was built sometime during the Imperial period, arriving at a precise date offers some difficulties. Coins from the first century AD were found on the site but the conditions under which they were discovered were not recorded. Of the other objects recovered, only the five inscriptions (SIRIS 115-18 and 122) provide assistance in determining the chronology.[113] Since all of them date from the second or third century, the former period represents a probable *terminus a quo*.

This precinct has at its east end five cellae in a row. Various rather speculative hypotheses have been advanced as to which god was honored in each of them.[114] Once again, the inscriptions provide the best evidence. Two of the texts are dedications by a "priest of Isis" (SIRIS 115 and 119). However, a further dedication offered by the same individual who dedicated SIRIS 115 gives this donor his full title: ὁ ἱερεὺς τῆς Εἴσιδος καὶ Σαράπιδος (SIRIS 116). Why this oscillation with respect to the title of the priest? I believe "priest of Isis" to be a short-hand version of the proper formal title and one which reflected the *de facto* devotional situation. That is, even though SIRIS 122 was set up by the "cultores deor(um) Serapis Isidis," normally Isis evoked the greater piety and enthusiasm at Philippi. Formally, however, Sarapis shared cultic honors with her.[115]

20. *Pompeii* (Fig. 18)[116]

The basic facts about this sanctuary require no extended discussion. The dedicatory inscription placed over the street door indicates that the *aedes Isidis* which had collapsed in the earthquake of 62 AD was rebuilt, presumably shortly afterwards, from its foundations.[117] This was more than a mere restoration. By a careful analysis of the architecture H. Nissen demonstrated long ago that the original Iseum which had been constructed in the second century BC or at least before the time of Sulla was expanded to the west at the expense of the old Palaestra. The so-called "Assembly Room" (*Ecclesiasterion*) and the "Sacristy" date only from this later period.[118] In addition, those who reconstructed this sanctuary in the first century AD rearranged the portico colonnade and constructed a suite of rooms for resident priests between the theater and the south wall of the precinct.[119] The underground crypt had survived from the earlier Hellenistic sanctuary, but its upper housing shows signs of having been partially reconstructed.[120] In short, a very active Isis community not only rapidly replaced their destroyed sanctuary but even had the political power to be able to enlarge it.

21. *Priene* (Fig. 9)[121]

While Schrader was content on the basis of SIRIS 292 to call this sanctuary a shrine to the Egyptian gods, Vidman thought it could be more precisely designated as an Iseum.[122] No doubt he had in mind SIRIS 291, a lengthy sacred decree found on the site in which, among other things, special requirements for sacrifices to "the goddess" (Isis) are laid down in detail. Yet in the earlier portion of the decree several rules for sacrifices to "Sarapis and Isis" are introduced as well as the procedure for a sacrifice to Apis.[123] Even though the beginning of the decree is lost, I am inclined to believe that the earlier section indicates the true state of affairs: the sanctuary at Priene was dedicated to Sarapis and Isis. The latter obviously had a special place. Her sacrifices required the presence of an Egyptian assistant to carry them out with the necessary skill (SIRIS 291.21-25). However, when her name is mentioned in the decree alongside that of Sarapis, his appears first.[124]

The history of this precinct and its great altar is somewhat difficult to trace. SIRIS 290 points to a date of origin no later than the third century BC. Later additions were the north propylon and an adjoining stoa; Schrader dates these to "pre-Roman times."[125] Evidently the site continued in use until sometime after 100 BC (SIRIS 292). However, there is no evidence that the two fragmentary inscriptions dated to the Roman period which were found on the site had anything to do with the continuing cult.[126]

22. *Ras el Soda* (Fig. 1)[127]

This rather well-preserved podium temple of Roman type was perhaps a private shrine belonging to a wealthy individual.[128] If so, he was probably the Isidoros who dedicated a votive foot to "the Blessed One" who had saved him.[129] That either the rooms found on a higher level behind this temple or those rather hastily excavated on its east side formed part of a larger precinct appears very doubtful.

The identification of this temple is based on the size and relative position of the five cult statues. These were found *in situ*.[130] From left to right on the cult platform stood an Isis statue, the largest of the five; an Osiris Hydreios, Type A; an Osiris Hydreios, Type B; a Hermanoubis, and a Harpocrates. Just as at Gortyn and Philippi, so in this case the statue to the left would appear to represent the principal deity honored here. These statues and the single inscription date no earlier than the second half of the second century AD. The *terminus a quo* is therefore very probably to be set at c. 150 AD.[131]

23. *Rome: Campus Martius* (Fig. 28)[132]

Literary sources provide all the evidence for dating the original construction and subsequent renovations of this sanctuary. This material is familiar and need not be repeated here. It is also clear both from these sources and from the *Forma Urbis* as reconstructed by V. Lundström that Isis was the principal deity throughout the life of the sanctuary. However, although the writers who speak of this cult in the first or second century AD speak only of Isis,[133] beginning with the *Forma Urbis* map and with Cassius Dio it is regularly designated as the *Iseum et Serapeum*.[134] How much can be made of this is not clear. I am tempted, however, in the light of the apparent enthusiasm of Septimius Severus for the cult of Sarapis, to believe that it was only at the time of his reign that this god first joined Isis as a full partner in the Campus Martius precincts.[135] Perhaps such an elevation of Sarapis had something to do with the renovation which took place during the reign of Alexander Severus. Lampridius, however, gives no clue one way or the other that such was the case.[136]

24. *Rome: Santa Sabina* (Fig. 29)[137]

A certain Cosmus, a freedman in the imperial service of Marcus Aurelius, had his house on the lower slopes of the Aventine close to the Tiber. Here in the late second century AD[138] the walls of one of the rooms—Room IV according to Descemet's notation (= my Fig. 29)—were replastered and painted with scenes relating to the cult of Isis.[139] Portions of these walls were then covered with a variety of graffiti, many of which manifest devotion to Isis.[140] Five specifically mention the name of the goddess (*Laus Isidis; Mystes Isidis L--;* E^{isis}_{paphra} [a personal name interwoven with that of Isis]; Tῆ[ι]

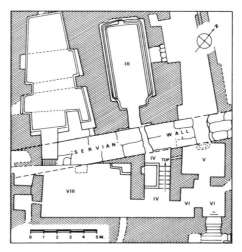

Fig. 29. The Santa Sabina Iseum at Rome. Ground plan of the sanctuary and the rooms around it. A person entering into the area in which the worshippers met (III) had to pass first through Room IV and then through a gap in the Servian Wall. The paintings and graffiti were mostly found in the north corner of Area IV.

ὁσίη[ι] ῎Ισι[141] and *Pamphiliu[s] Isidi et salus ad tuos*) while others seem to refer to rites of initiation. Jupiter is mentioned in a single graffito: [*Laetit*]*ia, salus es Jovis.* In addition, a statue of this god with an eagle by his feet was found in the area.[142] Room IV, where all of these finds were discovered, appears to have been an antechamber to Room III. This latter was probably the gathering place for a "neighborhood confraternity"[143] but its original form does not survive. In the mid-third century the Isis worshippers were uprooted and this room was transformed into part of a bathing establishment.[144]

25. *Sabratha: East End* (Fig. 19)[145]

G. Pesce was convinced that he had discovered an Iseum built in the first century AD.[146] However, both elements in in his assertion need to be questioned. The *terminus a quo* he provided was based primarily on his belief that SIRIS 795 was the dedicatory inscription for the sanctuary. Several years later further portions of this same inscription were recovered, and with these H. Benario was able to demonstrate that the text was actually a lengthy dedication to Vespasian. The various stones had probably come originally from a nearby triumphal arch rather than from the sanctuary.[147] Pesce also appealed to the style of architecture in support of his first century date. He admitted, however, that these forms were common enough in the second century and later; his point seemed to be, rather, that the style did not militate *against* the earlier date.[148] It is my opinion that the sanctuary originated much later, in the second or even the third century. From Pesce's own remarks, the architectural forms employed seem more at home in this later period. Further, the datable statues are virtually all from the third century.[149] Finally, the ornate podium or base found buried under the west portico provides probable confirmation for a later date. If, as Pesce suggested, it was built about the beginning of the present era and if, as I believe, it was *not* related to the Isis cult,[150] it is unlikely that such a finely made object would have been destroyed and buried only a few years after having been built.

Isis was certainly one of the gods honored in this precinct but perhaps not the principal divinity. Pesce found what was probably her cult statue buried in the debris which had fallen into the north crypt directly under the cella.[151] Every indication suggests that the cult platform and the floor, etc., from the cella collapsed at some time into the rooms directly below, the so-called north and south crypts. Under these circumstances, it is noteworthy that the Isis statue was found in the north (i.e., right-hand) crypt and that fragments of a large seated figure which Pesce identified as a cult statue of Sarapis were found in the south or left-hand crypt.[152] This Sarapis figure probably stood originally on the left side of the cult platform and the tall Isis statue on the right. Consequently, the sanctuary must actually have been dedicated to Sarapis and Isis.[153]

26-27 Soli: Temple D and Temple E (Figs. 4 and 5)[154]

When the archaeologists analyzed their data from this site, they confirmed a rather unusual state of affairs: an earlier temple, probably built in the first century BC and dedicated to Isis, had been destroyed in the first century AD and replaced by another structure seemingly non-cultic in character. In the late second century AD this structure was in turn replaced by a second and larger sanctuary to the Egyptian gods built partially on the foundations of its predecessor.[155] The identification of the first sanctuary or "Temple D" as an Iseum is based, first of all, on the discovery of two large Isis heads which date to the first century BC or earlier. These had been reused in the upper walls of one of the later cellae.[156] Secondly, since the other temple found by the Swedish Cyprus Expedition, a structure lying just to the north of this complex, was certainly dedicated to Aphrodite, Westholm argued that a portion of Strabo's description of the Soli area both corresponded to the geographical situation found here and served to identify Temple D as part of a common precinct shared by Aphrodite and Isis.[157] Very little survives of Temple D. Distinctive, however, is the entranceway, apparently a pylon gateway, and a pair of altars in the courtyard, both oriented in an easterly direction at an angle to the general E-SE orientation of the temple.[158]

In my earlier study I spoke of "Temple E," the later of the two temples, as a Serapeum.[159] I now believe this identification to have been incorrect. The central cella[160] was probably dedicated to Sarapis—a large head of this god and two dogs' heads (from a Cerberus group?) were among the finds.[161] In the right-hand cella

Osiris Hydreios was honored—a statue of Osiris in this form was discovered on the cult platform.[162] It is the left-hand cella which is difficult to identify. Westholm thought perhaps that Eros had a cult here since a relief of a "mourning Eros" was found on the cult platform.[163] However, this relief is not so very large[164] and may rather have been a votive dedication to another divinity. I believe this divinity to have been Isis. An Eros dedication would not, of course, have been inappropriate to this goddess, who was very often honored as Isis-Aphrodite. More decisive, in my judgment, are several features found both here and at several Iseums elsewhere. In the courtyard between the cellae and the altar was found a pit filled with burnt pinecones. A similar pit was also found in the Iseum at Pompeii.[165] Further, a huge bronze pinecone (the *Pigna*) seems possibly to have formed a major decorative element at the Campus Martius Iseum at Rome.[166] Secondly, the two temples at Soli, both of which had a pylon gateway, are the only temples outside of Egypt which are known to have imitated major features of traditional Egyptian temple architecture. Such "Egyptianization" is often found at Isis sanctuaries outside of Egypt but rarely, if at all, at Serapeums.[167] Finally, as at Gortyn, Philippi, and Ras el Soda, the image of the chief deity may have been set to the left rather than in the center of the temple. This convergence of evidence suggests both that Isis was the chief deity at Soli and that her cella was on the left-hand side with Sarapis in the center and Osiris Hydreios on the right.[168]

28. *Thera* (Fig. 3)[169]

When the architects of this sanctuary undertook the task of locating it on the slope of a mountain, they determined to reduce the amount of artificial terrace to be constructed by carving the northeast portion of the precinct out of the natural rock. Only this section has survived the ravages of time. Happily, there survived in the lee of this northeast wall a coin box for offerings which, according to an inscription upon it, had been dedicated to Sarapis, Isis, and Anubis by a certain Diocles and a group of Βασιλισταί (= an association of Egyptian soldiers devoted to the Ptolemaic dynastic cult).[170] This object tells us several things: 1) this was a sanctuary dedicated to the Egyptian gods, 2) native Egyptians apparently played a major role in its cultic life,[171] and 3) the site was probably first used as a place of worship in the third century BC.[172] Since no evidence from the site can be dated later than the following century, the sanctuary may well have closed its doors at the same time that Ptolemaic control of the island ceased.[173] While two of the dedications are to Isis alone (SIRIS 141-42), I believe it more likely that the precinct was officially dedicated to Sarapis and Isis. Such is the order of divine names on SIRIS 137, 138, and possibly 139. I would stress, however, that the patterns found in private dedications need not conform to the "official" nomenclature.

29. *Thessalonica* (Fig. 30)[174]

I base the identification of this precinct on *IG* X.83, a dedication of a water facility to "Isis and all the other gods" by a "priest of Sarapis and Isis" in the late first century BC.[175] This text probably accurately reflects the situation in Imperial times as well. The official cult was to Sarapis and Isis but, as in the case of this text, devotional enthusiasm was directed primarily toward Isis.[176] And if religious enthusiasm can be measured by the construction of new edifices, piety abounded here during Roman times. Of the four or more buildings uncovered by Pelekides, three at least were certainly constructed sometime in this period. The fourth, the original structure found in 1921, initially was identified as a structure built in the third century BC.[177] Later, however, Wrede spoke of it as a Roman building constructed on an ashlar foundation.[178] While Hellenistic inscriptions from the third century BC onwards are plentiful from the site, it is not clear that any of the known buildings are from that period. It is my own belief that the Thessalonica precinct was quite large and that the central temple is not among the structures reported to date since none of these are very sizeable.

30. *Timgad*[179]

In the course of excavating the Byzantine fort to the south of Timgad, the French team of archaeologists discovered underneath it the remains of a vast complex dedicated to the *Dea Africa*. Her temple stands in the center at the south end of the precinct. To the right is a second temple in which a yet unidentified god (Diana?) was honored while to the left stands a third temple, similar to the

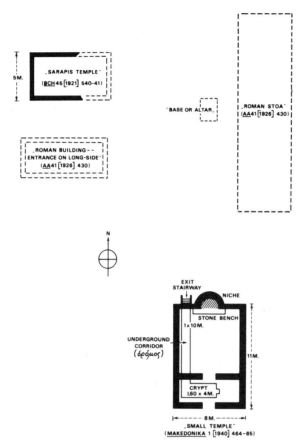

Fig. 30. The Sanctuary of Sarapis and Isis at Thessalonica. Approximate ground plan. This illustrates the various structures mentioned in the reports and their approximate relationship to one another as far as this can be ascertained. Illustrations exist for those architectural elements marked with solid lines.

second, in which Sarapis had his cult.[180] In front of these three buildings is the most noteworthy feature of the sanctuary, a rectangular (7 × 27 m) pool, 1.70 m deep, called the *Aqua Septimiana Felix*.

Small finds constitute the only evidence presently made public that Sarapis received cultic honors in this precinct. Parts of a colossal statue of this god and a head from a slightly smaller statue were found close to the temple area.[181] Additional support for this identification may also have been discovered among the 380 inscriptions and the various other finds from the site. Leschi indicated his belief that Sarapis found a place in this precinct because of his powers as a healing god.[182]

A So-Called "Serapeum"

The single site now to be considered has often been called a sanctuary of the Egyptian gods. I would like to demonstrate here that this designation is incorrect.

Ephesus: Commercial Agora[183]

On the basis of various finds encountered during his investigations in 1926 Josef Keil came to the conclusion that this precinct had been dedicated to Sarapis, a thesis he then maintained in season and out for thirty years.[184] His arguments, excluding those based on materials not found at the site, reduce to four. The strongest derives from a still unpublished inscription—see SIRIS 303 for a partial text—found on a large statue base which had been secondarily placed, probably in the Byzantine period, at the bottom of the staircase leading up to the precinct.[185] Although it was evidently relocated here to help in shoring up the crumbling gateway, Keil argued that it must have originally been situated in the near vicinity. The inscription on the base had been erased at some time. This made reading it very difficult.[186] Keil deciphered it as a dedication to Caesar Caracalla made by a man who had dedicated a statue of the emperor "for those who sacrifice to Sarapis in the presence of the Nile, my god."[187] Such a dedication, he says, would have fit very well into a temple to the Egyptian gods. However, since this base is only secondarily situated by this sanctuary, since the reading of the inscription is so tenuous, and since the dedicant may only have desired, as an Egyptian, to express publicly the devotion of his fellow Egyptians to the emperor, this argument seems quite thin. A parallel base set at the other end of these steps has nothing whatever to do with a cult to Sarapis.[188] Similarly, the discovery in the debris of the sanctuary of a small fragment of a statue in Egyptian granite proves nothing.[189] A fragmentary inscription found in the rubble of the gateway (SIRIS 299) and reading - - ΙΣΤΟΛΟΣΚΑΙΝ - - is interpreted by Keil as

[- - ἀρχ]ίστολος καὶ ν[εωκόρος - -]. Since the word ἀρχίστολος is nowhere else attested[190] and since the text is so fragmentary, Keil's belief that this was part of a dedicatory inscription erected by someone who was an ἀρχίστολος in the Sarapis cult seems fanciful.[191] Finally, though there is no doubt that water facilities are found at many Hellenistic Isis-Sarapis sanctuaries, they are far less common at sites from the Roman period. Certainly no parallel has been found for the particular arrangement seen at this site. I therefore conclude that the identification of this structure as a Serapeum is unfounded.

OTHER TYPES OF CRYPTS ASSOCIATED WITH THE CULT

In my study of the fixed Nile water facilities I described a number of underground enclosed areas properly termed "crypts." Other types of crypts are also found at various precincts honoring Isis and Sarapis. I thought that it would be useful to discuss all of these in a separate section so that the reader can have a proper idea of the diversity of such facilities and can see how the Nile water crypts differ from these other examples. This survey will include the enclosed, windowless structures constructed either underground or above ground on the sites of eight of the known sanctuaries: Alexandria, Miletus, Mons Claudianus, Ostia, Pergamum, Pompeii, Sabratha, and Thessalonica.

A Crypt for Cultic Assembly: Thessalonica

In my view, the most interesting of all these structures is the crypt discovered in 1939 at the sanctuary of Sarapis and Isis at Thessalonica (Fig. 30).[1] In one part of the precinct Ch. Makaronas and S. Pelekides discovered substantial remains of a small Roman temple. Outside and to the rear of this building they found a flight of steps leading down below ground level.[2] A person descending this stairway passed under the north wall of the temple and then came upon a "tunnel-like" corridor which Makaronas termed a "dromos" and which is 10 m long and about 1 m wide. The corridor runs straight south until it reaches a point under the pronaos of the temple. Here a person turned ninety degrees to the left, passed through a doorway, and entered a vaulted chamber, the crypt proper. This room is c. 4.0 m long, c. 1.6 m wide, and c. 1.9 m high from the floor to the highest point of its vaulted ceiling.[3] In the center of the rear wall of this room is a small niche. This contained "a small stele in the form of a herm" set on a marble base. Makaronas described the herm as "a bearded god done in archaizing technique.'' He also noted that there was an accompanying inscription on the base which ''the effects of the humidity on the fragile marble had rendered almost totally illegible.''[4] A person standing in front of this herm stood approximately in line with the central axis of the temple above.

The archaeologists reported that the entrance to the crypt had been sealed with marble slabs. This led them to conclude that they had found the crypt and its corridor ''in their original state.''[5] All well and good if the finds had been fully published. However, S. Pelekides, the leader of the expedition, never found sufficient time to report on these important discoveries even though he had apparently reserved publication rights for himself. Consequently, all that we have is the brief report of Makaronas, and this is largely couched in general terms. Makaronas was Pelekides' chief assistant and took an active role in the excavation of this site. Because he therefore knew more than he could tell, I believe that we must try to read between the lines of his report at several points so as to determine better what was actually found. This, of course, is a speculative venture. Yet the site, which is near the center of modern Thessalonica, has been completely overbuilt, and there is little hope that it will be soon available for any sort of reinvestigation.

Makaronas says that the crypt ''seems to have been a place for mystery cults.''[6] He may simply have said this because he himself was impressed by its eerie and mysterious character[7] and because crypts are supposed to have such a purpose. However, the investigations of 1939 produced two objects which suggest that initiation and/or mystery rites were conducted at this site or close to it. The first of these is a relief with an accompanying inscription which Edson thought was no later in date than the mid-second century BC.[8] The relief depicts a man and a woman sacrificing at an altar. Above and behind the altar is a partially naked young man who is observing the sacred rite.[9] The inscription reads as follows: Ὀσείριδι μύστει Ἀλέξανδρον Δημητρίου καὶ Νίκαιαν / Χαριξένου Δημήτριος τοὺς αὐτοῦ γονεῖς. Parallels for this designation of a god as μύστης are found elsewhere.[10] Here the epithet probably means that Osiris is the prime analogate of all μύσται, the first of all initiates, the one whom all other initiates follow (imitate?).[11] Edson thought that the figure standing behind the altar was Demetrius, the individual who made the dedication. However, given the prominence and centrality of this figure and given his semi-naked attire, I suspect that he represents a divine being. That is, he is probably a very Hellenized Osiris rather than the son of the two figures who stand below him. In all events, the inscription offers some indication that initiation rites took place in the general area, rites in which the initiate was in effect a follower in the footsteps of Osiris.

The second object is also an inscription referring to μύσται.[12] Briefly, this inscription, which is dedicated to the Good Fortune of Zeus Dionysus Gongylos, details the arrangements for a vineyard which had been given to a community of initiates partly by a certain Julius, a βησαρτης, and partly by a large group of initiates. The income from this vineyard is to support a festive meal of bread (ἡ ... ἄρτου ἑστίασις) which is (now) to take place three times a year. The present and future initiates are to swear by the god and by the ὄργια and by the μεσανύκτιον ἄρτου to maintain these observances. A priest named L. Fulvius Felix is listed at the head of the group of donors of the vineyard; he is probably the priest of Zeus Dionysus Gongylos. However, another priest, Straton, son of Epicrates, is recorded as having given permission for the erection of this inscription. G. Daux assumed that both priests served Zeus Dionysus Gongylos and so supposed that there had been a lapse of time between the agreement and its being recorded in stone.[13] I prefer to believe that Straton was instead the priest of Sarapis and Isis, for it is in this precinct where the stone was found.

The inscription may very well have been connected in some way with the herm found in the crypt, and so I should say something more about that image before proceeding further. It portrayed in an archaized form a bearded male deity. But which deity? Sarapis might appear to be a suitable candidate except that he is not known to have been portrayed in this particular manner.[14] Nor is such an iconographic type attested for any other male divinities in the circle of the Egyptian gods. The only male deities remaining whose names appear in the multitude of inscriptions recovered from the sanctuary at Thessalonica are Dionysus and Zeus Dionysus Gongylos.[15] Although the herm may have represented some other deity not attested in these texts, Dionysus was frequently portrayed in the form of a herm.[16] Debate concerning the exact identity of

Zeus Dionysus Gongylos still continues.[17] However, the first two parts of his name suggest that he, too, would have been sometimes represented as a herm. Further than this we cannot go because the herm has never been published. Yet one important fact has emerged—whatever went on in the crypt involved the Egyptian gods only secondarily.

I say "secondarily" because the crypt was located within the sanctuary of Sarapis and Isis. In addition, if the sacred decree recorded by the devotees of Zeus Dionysus Gongylos has anything to do with the crypt and the image found there, the word βησαρτης, the title born by Julius, one of the donors of the vineyard, perhaps indicates some connection with the Egyptian god Bes.[18] Thirdly, if the herm depicted either Dionysus or Zeus Dionysus Gongylos, some reference to Osiris may also have been intended since Dionysus and Osiris were often equated. This leads me to wonder if both of the inscriptions mentioned above may not have referred to a common set of rites which perhaps were carried out in this crypt. In his brief report Makaronas expressed the view that the crypt was used for mystery rites. Perhaps he knew that one or both of these texts had actually been found in conjunction with this structure.[19]

Makaronas called the passageway into the crypt a "δρόμος."[20] This designation is a bit unexpected, a bit too generic. Would not διάδρομος or some similar word have been more precise? While this may only be the matter of an individual choice of words, the fact remains that two inscriptions which refer to a δρόμος were discovered in the sanctuary complex. The first of these, a stone dating to the first or second century AD, reads as follows: ... ΛΟΤ------ / τὸν δρό[μον ἔκτι-]σεν· ἐκ τ[ῶν ἰδίων,] / ἐπὶ ἱερέ[ως ... ’Α-] / χειλίου [------] / ἀρχιν[εοχορούν-] / τος[--------].[21] The second is even more interesting for it appears to relate this structure to the god Osiris: ----- αγένης --- / ... ’Ο]σείριδι --- / [τὸν] δρόμον Ε ---.[22] I am once again led to wonder if Makaronas knew more than he felt he could tell. Perhaps the discovery of one or both of these texts in the general vicinity led him to call the corridor a "δρόμος." This line of speculation leads once again to the god Osiris. If the δρόμος leading into the crypt had been dedicated to Osiris at the time, say, when the temple was built over the crypt, that god surely had some connection with the rites celebrated in the presence of the herm.[23] These rites did not honor

Osiris directly, for the herm did not depict that god. Instead, I would guess that an older mystery cult honoring Zeus Dionysus Gongylos somehow became connected with Osiris and the other Egyptian gods and so was allowed to have a place within the large precinct of Sarapis and Isis at Thessalonica. That is, the cult carried on in the crypt represented a local adaptation rather than a form of ritual activity widespread within Isis-Sarapis worship.

Storage Crypts for Cultic Equipment

At four different sanctuaries, those at Pompeii, Ostia, Miletus, and Mons Claudianus, hollow crypt-like spaces were found under the platforms for the cult statues. These various compartments are somewhat different in design but were probably all intended for the storage of cultic equipment. The oldest of the four is found at Pompeii and dates no later than 63 AD. Along the entire back wall of the temple cella is a high brick podium, 4.82 m long, c. 1.05 m wide, and c. 1.75 m high (Pl. V, 1).[24] Two narrow openings, 0.50 m wide and about 0.90 m high, are found in the front wall of this platform, one at each end. Both provide access to a hollow area which is 4.82 m long, c. 0.80 m wide, and, at a maximum, c. 1.50 m high (Fig. 18). No niches, bases, or other remains of cultic activity are to be seen in this area, and it is not known whether any of the small finds from the cella came from it.[25] While earlier visitors and commentators thought that it had been used for some sort of priestly hocus-pocus, e.g., for concealing someone who would give oracles in the name of the god,[26] its narrow width and the fact that its openings were in full view led later scholars to view it as a storage area for sacred utensils.[27]

A similar area is located under the cult platform of the Serapeum at Ostia, a sanctuary constructed during the reign of Hadrian (Fig. 31). In the center of the front wall of this platform is an opening which is 0.9 m wide and 0.8 m high.[28] This leads first into a kind of vestibule, 1.6 m wide × 1.9 m deep, and then into an inner area, 3.4 m wide and 0.9 m deep. The height of these hollow compartments appears to be about 1.2 m. No small finds, niches, bases, etc., were found that would indicate that this enclosed area served any ritual purpose.

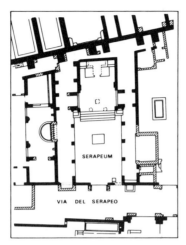

Fig. 31. The Serapeum at Ostia. Ground plan.

A further indication that these hollow spaces were not designed to accommodate ritual activity specific to the cult of Isis and Sarapis is the existence of parallel arrangements at other sanctuaries in central Italy. Long ago Overbeck observed that the Temple of Jupiter in the Forum at Pompeii has several hollow areas not unlike that found under the cult platform in the Iseum of that town.[29] At the Temple of Jupiter a wide and lofty cult platform stretches across the cella. In its front wall are three openings which lead into separate hollow areas under the platform. Overbeck believed that these spaces were designed to contain liturgical equipment such as the ornaments placed on the statues during festivals.[30] A Hellenistic temple at Gabii, a town about twelve kilometers east of Rome, also had a very high cult platform with a hollow interior. Only the lowest portion of the front wall of this platform has survived, but these remains indicate that three doorways gave access to the area under the platform.[31] Probably still further examples have survived in this general region of Italy.

The hollow area found under the cult platform or *bema* in the Serapeum at Miletus is organized rather differently but probably also served the same general purpose (Fig. 32).[32] The platform itself, which is 4.56 m wide and c. 2.7 m deep, was set between two side walls which extended out from the back wall of the sanctuary so as to form a kind of *naiskos*.[33] Apparently a set of six steps, of which

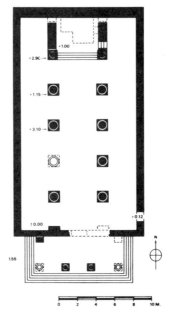

Fig. 32. The Serapeum at Miletus. Ground plan.
The crypt under the cult platform
is indicated with dotted lines.

three still survive, led up to the top of the platform. To judge by the height of the surviving risers for the stairway, the upper surface of the platform, probably a wooden flooring, seems to have been about 1.2 m higher than the floor of the sanctuary.[34] It was supported by an inner masonry structure (still largely in place) consisting of narrow side walls and a large core, 1.30 × 1.24 m, located in the front left corner. The cult statue did not stand on this floor, says Knackfuss, but in a niche in the back wall above the platform.[35] With the aid of the large masonry core the floor of the platform probably supported an altar.

In the wall of the right side below this platform was an opening, 0.50 m wide, leading into a hollow area underneath. This space measures 3.55 × 2.7 m (minus the section taken up in one corner by the masonry core) and probably had about 1.3 m of headroom. Once again no bases, niches, or small finds were noted by the excavators. Both Knackfuss and Salditt-Trappmann suggested that it served as a storage place for the instruments of the cult.[36]

The Serapeum at Mons Claudianus in the quarry district of Egypt near the Red Sea also has such a hollow area under the elevated floor of the temple cella. To judge only by this floor, the lower area measured approximately 3.2 × 4.8 m. Access to it is through an opening cut into the right wall of the cella. The site has been surveyed but not fully excavated, and so no further details are available on the size and character of this room.[37] Very likely, however, it also served for storage purposes.

In short, all of these crypts under the cult platforms probably served the rather ordinary function of housing and protecting the various vessels and implements used in the cult. The openings leading into them were not concealed but could be seen fairly easily. At the same time, they are normally small, low, and difficult to squeeze through. In addition, the hollow areas often have limited headroom and lack niches, bases, and cultic accessories of that sort altogether.[38] All of this, along with the presence of parallel facilities at other sanctuaries in Italy, suggests that these spaces were not designed as places for initiation rites, incubations, and the like.[39]

Apuleius perhaps refers to such a storage area in a passage in the *Metamorphoses*.[40] On one occasion Lucius entered the precinct of Isis at Cenchreae at the time of the morning "opening of the temple" ritual. The priest Mithras led him "to the very doors of the temple" (*ad ipsas fores aedis*) and then, when the rite was completed, went to get certain books "from concealed areas in the cella" (*de opertis adyti*). Perhaps the phrase "concealed areas" refers in actuality to such a storage place under the cult platform.

Various Tunnels and Passageways

Three of the known sanctuaries have various sorts of tunnels or passageways. Theories have been advanced that several of these served for ritual purposes, but I do not believe that any actually did.

The Serapeum of Alexandria boasts two such installations (Fig. 12). The first is a tunnel almost 60 m long which begins in the courtyard of the precinct almost due west of the Column of Diocletian and then wends its way to a very large structure, 27.50 × 24.60 m, which probably once served as a mausoleum.[41] Here it passes through an immense foundation wall, a wall no less than 4.40 m thick, and then begins gradually to ascend to an exit within the structure. No one is certain, but this structure was probably constructed during Ptolemaic times as a tomb for someone of importance. Its extremely thick foundation walls very likely were intended to foil would-be grave robbers.[42] The tunnel therefore would have functioned as a passageway into this mausoleum. Traces of a pavement which appears to be of Roman date were found covering over portions of the tunnel's exit within the tomb, an indication that it was no longer in use during this period.[43] The tunnel itself has thick walls, and its arched ceiling had been buried under a pavement which had been put in place during Ptolemaic times. The passageway inside is c. 1.1 m wide and c. 2.70 m high. I believe it very unlikely that this underground passage and the building to which it was connected ever had any direct connection with the actual cult of Sarapis.

The second tunnel system found at this Serapeum is much more complex.[44] Its discoverer, G. Botti, first came upon a large subterranean room (the "atrium"), an area 9.20 m square. This, he noted, had been "carefully filled in with sand from the seashore." On its walls he discovered two graffiti of Roman date; these recorded "acts of worship" (προσκυνήματα). He also found an inscription dedicated to Hermanubis; fragments of statuettes of this god, of Sarapis, and of Aphrodite; and a variety of lamps, most of which were from Imperial times but a few also of Christian origin. Two lengthy underground galleries are connected to this room. The first, the so-called "North Gallery," begins at the northwest corner of the atrium, runs north toward the central temples for 7 m, and then makes a sharp turn and continues east for another 29 m. The second, the "South Gallery," has an entrance in the southeast corner of the atrium. It then proceeds generally in an easterly direction for some 23 m to a point at which still a further gallery begins. This side branch heads south for 9 m and then continues in an easterly direction for 22 m. The main portion of the South Gallery also continues east for 31 m and then turns toward the south, passes under the Column of Diocletian, and ends 28 m from the point at which it turned. Except for these latter sections of the South Gallery which are somewhat narrower, most of these tunnels are about 2 m wide.

Their height ranges between 2.5 and 3 m. The side walls are honeycombed with a total of almost' seventy niches, the majority of which are about one meter high, one meter wide, and one meter in depth. Some of these are at floor level and some are set higher on the wall. Above the opening to each niche is a small hollow designed to hold a lamp. Inside, Botti found a kind of table with a sloping top in which a single wide groove had been cut.[45] He also discovered fragments of limestone boxes or coffins scattered about in the niches and on the tunnel floor. Not a single box remained intact, and Botti failed to discover any trace of their contents. He suspected, however, that these boxes had once contained the mummified remains of sacred animals. No remnants of these mummies were found because—or so he argued—Christians had purged this entire area of its ancient superstition by breaking into all the coffins and then removing the mummies altogether so that they could be destroyed. As for the tables with their sloping grooved tops which stood in each of these niches, they had been constructed for the reception of libation offerings.[46] In support of Botti's theory, this entire arrangement is quite reminiscent of the burial crypts for sacred animals found at the Serapeum of Memphis and elsewhere in the surrounding area of Saqqarah.[47] The presence of such burial galleries here at the sanctuary of Sarapis at Alexandria indicates that sacred animals were an important aspect of this god's cult at least during Roman times.

Under the Iseum at Pergamum is an extensive network of tunnels as well as a number of underground chambers of considerable size (Fig. 21).[48] The only extant description of all these installations is that provided by Regina Salditt-Trappmann.[49] Without further on-site investigations and an exploration of the numerous segments of the tunnel system which have not yet been excavated, nothing can be added to the facts presented in her report. I will therefore briefly review her findings and then offer some critical observations with respect to her hypotheses.

On either side of the rear portion of the central temple are vaulted underground chambers (D' and E'), measuring 9 × 15 m. The vaulting is supported by columns arranged in a 3 × 3 pattern; the distance from the floor to the top of the vault is c. 4 m.[50] A third underground chamber (H') is located in the southeast corner of the courtyard. It is larger in size, 13 × 15 m, and its vaulting is supported on a 4 × 4 group of columns.[51] Probably a similar room exists under the northeast corner of the precinct (A), but this area is not accessible to investigation. No small finds have been reported from any of these areas, although it is not clear how carefully they have been explored.[52]

In antiquity the only means of access to these underground areas was the tunnel system, and this is quite complex. Three entrances to it are presently known: a stairway leading down from the portico next to the south wall of the central temple (l), a second stairway close to the cult statue (n), and a covered circular ramp (s) in the south round temple (G). A similar ramp is probably located in the north round temple (B), but this building is now a mosque and is closed to archaeological investigation. Once in the tunnel system a person could travel underground without great difficulty—the tunnels are all about 2 m high and their width varies from 0.45 to 1.4 m.[53] Temples B and G, the underground rooms, the area close by the cult statue in the main temple, and shafts in both of the towers at the west end of this building were all linked into the system. The shafts in the towers have steps cut into them and apparently served as a means of access to the roof. The section under the cult platform of the main temple seems to have been designed to provide access into the cult statue itself, for beginning at the left of the cult platform (o) the tunnel inclines sharply upwards until it connects with a vertical shaft, 1.5 m square, located in the center of the base which supported the statue. The vertical shaft may have been designed to allow a person to climb up inside this statue, although alternatively it perhaps is only the hole into which the bottom of the statue fitted. The tunnel to the south of point v has not yet been explored to its end—perhaps it extends all the way to the river. If so, this would be the only direct connection the tunnel system had with any water source. Salditt-Trappmann was not aware of any small finds from the underground passages, but in the section u-v-w near the south tower of the central temple she observed several interesting features. In section v-w she saw "pieces of colored stucco" and just a few centimeters to the north of point v she encountered niches on either side of section u-v. These had been cut out of the rock and are in the form of three steps set one atop the other.[54] Whether these supported lamps or images or some other type of object is not easy to determine, since Salditt-Trappmann has not supplied their exact dimensions. Whatever the case, this area around the south tower stands apart from the general drabness of the rest of the tunnel system.

According to Salditt-Trappmann, one function of the system was to allow a priest or priestess to climb into the presumably hollow cult statue of the god and to cause it to "speak."[55] While it is quite possible that this whole arrangement aimed only at providing a private peep hole through which someone could look and make sure that all was in readiness before summoning the ministers of the cult to enter the temple via Stairway n for the start of a ceremony, what Salditt-Trappmann has suggested remains a viable hypothesis. Perhaps it was not a question of making the statue speak but only of having a noise of some sort emanate from it.[56]

Her second suggestion is that the tunnel system functioned as a "lower world" for the mystery rites. Those being initiated would wander about in darkness fulfilling various tasks. As they went, they would behold scenes painted on the walls of the tunnel and would view dramatic portrayals of scenes from the myths in the larger underground chambers. Finally, after all of this, they would ascend from subterranean darkness into the light of day.

I have four problems with such a hypothesis. First, the duplicate arrangement of the tunnel system on the north and south sides of the main temple is inexplicable unless we suppose, for example, that the poor initiate had to climb twice to the roof! Secondly, the system is by no means a labyrinth with one entrance, one exit, and many blind alleys. Instead, there are many entrances and no demonstrable blind alleys. What would have caused initiates to move in proper sequence from one revelatory scene to the next? Could the clergy have allowed these initiates to blunder about and perhaps even to discover their secret arrangements under the cult statue? However, even if we suppose that each initiate was led by a mystagogue, there is yet a third problem. The underground rooms with their multitude of thick supporting columns are not very suitable for dramatic portrayals. If these are thought to have been carried out by two or three people in a single open section between the columns, why then are these rooms so large? Fourthly, Salditt-

Trappmann's theory that representational scenes were painted in the tunnel corridors is entirely dependent upon the few fragments of colored stucco she observed. These need not have come from an actual fresco but could have belonged to panels of solid color or of imitation marble. Some sort of religious activity may have taken place in the area in which these fragments and the niches were found, but this does not allow us to conclude that the tunnel system as a whole served for initiation rites.

Instead, I believe that these tunnels served the clergy as passageways to the more sacred areas of the sanctuary. The normal entrance into the system may well have been from the portico on the south side of the main temple. Possibly this entire area served as a kind of cloister reserved for the clergy. Like many of the crypts previously examined, the underground rooms very likely served as sacristies and storage areas for cultic equipment. Those partaking in a sacred ceremony could have vested in these areas and then have proceeded even two-by-two via the wider tunnels to the main temple or to the round shrines.[57] The narrower tunnels were probably used less frequently. We can imagine, however, that cultic officials may have wished to go up to the temple roof to hang garlands from the facade, to observe the stars, to offer special sacrifices to the heavenly bodies, to sound a trumpet or some such instrument as an announcement of a festal day, or for many other possible reasons. The tunnel system, in other words, is simply a much larger version of the stairway found at the left rear of the temple at Pompeii (Fig. 18). Both passageways gave the clergy private access to more sacred areas.

In my judgment, the crypt arrangement under the central temple of the sanctuary of Sarapis and Isis at Sabratha served a similar purpose (Fig. 19).[58] The temple itself is constructed upon a platform which rises about 3.5 m above the level of the courtyard. The empty space under the pronaos was filled in with various materials, but below the cella a series of rooms were constructed. At the back of the temple is an entrance into this area, 0.82 m wide and c. 2.55 m high. Here a person passed through the very thick (1.50 m) outer wall of the temple platform, descended two steps, and then reached a U-shaped ambulacrum which extended just inside the west, north, and south exterior walls of the platform.

The width of this corridor ranges from 1.09 to 1.25 m and its height from floor to ceiling was 2.5 m. Within the arms of this ambulacrum are two rectangular rooms which I have labeled the "north crypt" and the "south crypt." The outer walls surrounding these crypts are not as substantial as the platform walls, for they average only 1.00-1.15 m in thickness. The entrance to the north crypt, 0.72 m wide and 2.0 m high, is located at its extreme north-west corner. This area, which measures 5.35 × 2.09 m, has a vaulted ceiling which is almost entirely in place except for a seg-ment, c. 0.90 m wide, at its west end. The maximum height of this area is 2.42 m. The south crypt is entered through a doorway, 0.73 m wide and 2.0 m high, which is located at its extreme southwest corner. This room, whose dimensions are almost iden-tical with those of the north crypt (5.35 × 2.10 m), also had a vaulted ceiling, but only the lowest courses now survive *in situ*. No direct connection exists between the north and south crypts. Although the ambulacrum and the north crypt have the same type of concrete floor found elsewhere on the site and show no trace of any plastering, the south crypt is plastered and has a flooring made of ground pottery (*cocciopesto*) with white marble tesserae set into it to form a series of parallel lines. In addition, just to the north of its entrance is a stairway, 0.84 m wide, which ascends to the cella above. The two lowest steps and part of the substructure survive *in situ*; marks on the plaster indicate the locations of some of the upper steps. Since the surviving risers are 0.18 m high, the stairway must have had about 16 steps.

The walls and the various structures belonging to the temple cella have long since disappeared. Yet much can be learned about its ar-rangement from a study of the fill which Pesce found in the crypts below. Statuary from the cella tumbled into the north and south crypts, but no small finds of any sort were discovered in the am-bulacrum. Those statues found in the fill of the north crypt must have fallen through the gap in the vaulting at its west end. We can imagine either that the cult platform with its statues partially col-lapsed directly from above into this room (perhaps because the stairway from the lower area as it made its ascent to the cella re-quired modifications in the vaulting of the north crypt) or that the statues fell backwards off the platform into the hole.[59] Because of the amount of fill in the north crypt, the former hypothesis is much more likely.[60] Consequently, the stairway in the south crypt was located directly under the cult platform. A person using this means of ascent entered the cella either through an opening in the front wall of the cult platform or through an opening in the floor beyond the north end of this platform.[61]

The utter plainness of the ambulacrum and the north crypt as well as the apparent absence of any niches, bases, or other such objects suggest that neither of these areas had a cultic function. Indeed, the ambulacrum may not have had any special purpose at all. Given the design of the temple above, this lower U-shaped area was probably only the result of architectural necessity. As for the north crypt, Pesce indicated that he recovered a variety of objects from that area. Most of them are clearly identified as having been a part of the fill. However, four items are listed simply as "found in the north room of the crypt": the left hand from a small marble statue of a female, a portion of the head from a small marble statue which depicted either Eros or Harpocrates or a young boy, fragments from the plaster head of a life-size cow, and a group of plaster fragments apparently from a small seated figure.[62] Some or all of these objects may have been stored in this room, although it is also possible that they, too, were in the fill.

The south crypt with its decorated floor, plastered walls, and stairway to the cella provokes greater curiosity. I would note, however, that all small finds from this area were in the fill. Further, the room has no niches, bases, or other direct indications that ritual activity took place there. Although Pesce suspected that this crypt functioned as a sacristy and repository for cultic objects and other valuables,[63] he also wondered if it had been utilized for mystery rites. Using the famous description of the initiation of Lucius which is found in the *Metamorphoses* of Apuleius,[64] Pesce advanced the following hypothesis. The initiate entered the "lower world" through the door in the *west* wall of the temple and *descended* the steps into the crypt area where the nocturnal rites took place. Then in the morning he or she went up the stairs—"remeavi," says Apuleius—into the cella. When the doors were opened the initiate faced east and received the adoration of those assembled in front of the temple.[65] Stressing the hypothetical character of his own explanation, Pesce questioned to what extent Apuleius' description could be generalized.[66] For my own part, I would expect to find some positive indication that the south crypt was used for liturgical purposes (e.g., a niche or a base) if we are to suppose that "nocturnal rites" took place there. Since nothing of this sort was found beneath the fill, I prefer to suppose that this area was used by the clergy of the sanctuary as a gathering place before they ascended to the cella above.

Conclusions

From this survey of the available evidence, it is clear that the various crypts associated with the known sanctuaries of Isis and Sarapis differ considerably in design and in function. There are crypts for containing the sacred Nile water, crypts for storage purposes, crypt-like areas permitting passage from one place to another, and even one crypt for the burial of sacred animals and another for "mystical rites." To say that a crypt is typologically characteristic of all such sanctuaries or to categorize all these structures under some one religious category is to compare apples with turnips. Crypts are not a necessary feature of Isis-Sarapis sanctuaries—most of the known sites lack any evidence of such structures—and the extant examples reveal considerable variety.

Yet the various crypts can be organized into sub-groupings of which some are more important than others for the history of the cult. For example, the crypt-like areas under the cult platforms at Pompeii and Ostia are apparently a regional architectural feature which cuts across cultic boundaries. The underground passages found at Pergamum and Sabratha seem the result of a "local option," a large-scale architectural extension of the stairway for the clergy built next to the central temple in the Iseum at Pompeii. On the other hand, the burial crypts at Alexandria indicate that sacred animals had their place within this great sanctuary of Sarapis. Most important is the insight provided by the crypt at Thessalonica. By its size, its underground location, and its evident cultic character, it would seem to be just the sort of place in which the secret rites of the Isis-Sarapis cult would have taken place. Yet upon inspection it turns out to have been quite atypical, a purely localized phenomenon. Its cult bore only a secondary relationship to the worship of Isis and Sarapis and its structural design is not paralleled elsewhere. Paradoxically, its existence is probably one of the clearest indications that the initiation rites practiced within the Isis-Sarapis cult did *not* regularly take place in crypts.

NOTES

INTRODUCTION

¹ The following are the major studies of archaeological data done since 1955: Almagro, *CuadEERoma* 8 (1956), 201-12 [Spain]; Balil, *CuadEERoma* 8 (1956), 213-24 [Spain]; García y Bellido, *BRAH* 139 (1956), 293-355 [Spain]; Wessetzky, *ActaArch* 11 (1959), 265-82 = *ArchErt* 86 (1959), 20-31 [Hungary]; Lakatos, *Acta Universitatis Szegedinensis: Acta Antiqua* 4 (1961), 1-31 [Pannonia]; Manganaro, *Siculorum Gymnasium* 14 (1961), 175-91 [Sicily]; Wessetzky, *Ägyptischen Kulte* (EPRO 1; 1961) [Hungary]; Squarciapino, *Culti* (EPRO 3; 1962) [Ostia]; Harris and Harris, *Oriental Cults* (EPRO 6; 1965) [Britain]; García y Bellido, *Religions* (EPRO 5; 1967) [Spain]; Rolley, *BCH* 92 (1968), 187-219 [Thasos]; Perc, *Beiträge* (1968) [Balkan countries]; Müller, *Isiskult* (1969) [Beneventum]; Grimm, *Zeugnisse* (EPRO 12; 1969) [Germany]; Tran Tam Tinh, *Culte/Campanie* (EPRO 27; 1972) [central Italy]; Malaise, *Inventaire* and Malaise, *Conditions* (EPRO 21-22; 1972) [Italy]; Selem, *Godisnjak* 9 (1972), 5-104 [Illyricum]; Sfameni Gasparro, *Culti* (EPRO 31; 1973) [Sicily]; Hornbostel, *Sarapis* (EPRO 32; 1973) [Sarapis evidence]; Kater-Sibbes, *Preliminary Catalogue* (EPRO 36; 1973) [Sarapis evidence]; Tran Tam Tinh and Labrecque, *Isis lactans* (EPRO 37; 1973); Kobylina and Neveron, *Représentations* (EPRO 52; 1976) [Russia: Black Sea area]; Berciu and Petolescu, *Cultes* (EPRO 54; 1976) [Dacia]; Grenier, *Anubis* (EPRO 57; 1977) [Anubis evidence]; Budischovsky, *Diffusion* (EPRO 61; 1977-) [Adriatic sea coast]; Smith, *HTR* 70 (1977) 201-31 [Corinth]; Hölbl, *Zeugnisse* (EPRO 73; 1978) [Ephesus]; Malaise, *HomVermaseren* (1978), 2.627-717 [Italy]; Susini, *HomVermaseren*, 3.1199-1216 [Italy: Emilia]; Malaise, *ANRW* 2.17.2—forthcoming [Western Europe]; Selem, *Religions* (EPRO—forthcoming) [northern Yugoslavia]; Medini, *Egyptian Cults* (EPRO—forthcoming) [Dalmatia]; and Wild, *ANRW* 2.17.2—forthcoming [sanctuaries of the Roman period].

² Schaaffhausen, *Bonner Jahrbücher* 76 (1883), 31-62 [Germany]; Lafaye, *Histoire* (1884) [entire Roman Empire]; Drexler, *Mythologische Beiträge* (1890) [Macedonia and Thrace]; Drexler, *LM* 2 (c. 1895), 373-548 [Isis evidence]; Lafaye, *DAGR* 3 (1900), 577-86 [general evidence for the cult]; Guimet, *RArch* 3.36 (1900), 75-86, 4.20 (1912), 197-210, and 5.3 (1916), 184-210 [France]; Rusch, *De Serapide* (1906) [Greece]; Gsell, *RHR* 59 (1909), 149-59 [northwestern Africa]; Taylor, *Cults* (1912) [Ostia]; Baege, *De Macedonum sacris* (1913); Roussel, *CE* (1916) [Delos]. After World War I scholars interested in this cult were largely concerned with its diffusion. Because of this, they tended to focus on epigraphical remains; archaeological evidence appeared relevant only insofar as it could verify the presence of the cult in such and such a place. For that matter, even such minimal use of archaeological data is relatively rare in this whole period. Notable exceptions: Popesco, *Mélanges de l'Ecole Roumaine en France* 1927, 157-209 [Dacia]; Brady, *Reception* (1935) [provides a list of the known sanctuaries in the eastern Mediterranean area]; Dow, *HTR* 30 (1937), 183-232 [Athens]; Dobrovits, *Budapest Régiségei* 13 (1943), 45-75 [Aquincum]; Schweditsch, "Umwandlung" (Diss. 1951) [Noricum, Rhaetia, and Pannonia]; and Magie, *AJA* 57 (1953), 163-87 [Asia Minor]. Nilsson (*GGR*, 1st ed., vol. 2 [1950]), while more at home with literary and epigraphical

data, also records important archaeological evidence. Undoubtedly the recognition that archaeological remains could help in understanding the diffusion of the cult led to the furious activities of the nineteen-fifties and nineteen-sixties.

[3] Von Gonzenbach, *Untersuchungen* (1957) [images of boys with "Horus locks" and their relation to a rite of consecration]; Tschudin, *Isis* (1962) [typology of Isis-Sarapis sanctuaries]; Tran Tam Tinh, *Essai* (1964) [the religious life and practices of the Isis worshippers at Pompeii]; and Salditt-Trappmann, *Tempel* (EPRO 15; 1970) [rituals carried on at the Isis-Sarapis sanctuaries in Greece and Asia Minor]. For an important review of this latter work see L. Castiglione, *Gnomon* 45 (1973) 521-24. More recent general studies of the cult also make much greater use of archaeological data along with the more usual literary and epigraphical evidence. See for example, Dunand, *Culte d'Isis* (EPRO 26; 1973) and Le Corsu, *Isis* (1977).

[4] Roussel, *REg* NS 1 (1919), 81. See also Pesce, *Tempio*, 74 and several reviews of this work: V. Verhoogen, *AntCl* 23 (1954), 285 and M. F. Squarciapino, *ArchCl* 8 (1956), 239.

[5] Leclant, *Problèmes*, 95. Siegrid Düll (*Ancient Macedonia*, 320) stresses this same concern.

[6] There are forty-seven possible, probable, or certain sites and six others which only doubtfully can be assigned to this cult. In Appendix I below I discuss the attribution and chronology of the thirty known sanctuaries which are particularly pertinent to this present study. Most of the remaining sites receive similar treatment in my "The Known Isis-Sarapis Sanctuaries of the Roman Period," *ANRW* 2.17.2 (forthcoming). For the three sites treated in neither place (Memphis, Seleucia Pieria, and Tauromenium) see the bibliographical references in Appendix I, n. 1.

[7] Lafaye himself (*Histoire*) appears simply to have made a pragmatic decision in limiting his investigation to the cult as it was found "hors de l'Egypte." His successors, however, turned this into a normative procedure.

[8] Most recent general studies continue in this pattern. L. Vidman titled his collection of inscriptions the *Sylloge inscriptionum religionis Isiacae et Sarapiacae* but summarily (p. xi) excluded all the evidence from Egypt. In his *Isis und Sarapis bei den Griechen und Römern* (p. 8) he explains: "Die Entwicklung der ägyptischen Religion in Ägypten, die sehr kompliziert ist, muss den Ägyptologen vorbehalten bleiben." This is rather unsatisfactory since it views all the Isis-Sarapis remains in Egypt as a part of traditional Egyptian religion. Dunand (*Culte d'Isis*) discusses, curiously, the evidence from Hellenistic Egypt but excludes all materials from the Roman period. Exceptions to the general trend: Tschudin, *Isis* and Le Corsu, *Isis*.

[9] Besides the Serapeum at Alexandria, the other known Graeco-Roman sites in Egypt are: Antinoopolis, Luxor, Mons Claudianus, Mons Porphyrites: East Iseum, Mons Porphyrites: Serapeum, and Ras el Soda. There is doubtfully a second Iseum at Mons Porphyrites. The sanctuary at Canopus is well-known from literary sources but its site has not yet been located (E. Breccia, "Le rovine e i monumenti di Canopo", *Monuments de l'Egypte gréco-romaine*, 2 vols., Bergamo, 1930-34, 1.40-41).

[10] The "traditional" sanctuaries of Isis in Egypt and in Nubia are: Aswan, Behbet el-Hagar, Buhen, Contralatopolis (El Hilla), Dabod, Deir el Shelwit, Dendera (the small Isis temple), Koptos, Maharaqah, Meroe, Philae, Qasr Dush, Qurta, and Shanhur. Memphis also belongs primarily to this group but was heavily frequented in its late period by Greek-speakers and reveals in its meager remains signs of Graeco-Roman influence. For bibliographies on these sites see Porter and Moss, *Topographical Bibliography*.

L. Castiglione (*ActaAnt* 15 [1967], 107-52) distinguishes three types of architecture in Roman Egypt: "traditional," "classical" (pure Hellenic), and hybrid. The latter occurs either as a basic Egyptian type with classical elements or the reverse. Since I know of no Isis-Sarapis temple of a purely classical type in Egypt, I am concerned only with this third "hybrid" class. In the case of Isis-Sarapis sanctuaries outside of Egypt, their basic design is usually classical but with Egyptian elements added.

[11] The phrase is that of Leclant (*Problèmes*, 95-96).

[12] Vidman, *Isis und Sarapis*, 167-68.

[13] Ibid., 104, 168-70.

[14] Ibid., 86, 170-72.

[15] Ibid., 170. R. E. Witt (*JRS* 62 [1972], 198-99), whose own book (*Isis*) is a throw-back to the undifferentiated use of evidence found in Lafaye, criticized Vidman for exaggerating the difference between the Hellenistic and Roman periods.

[16] Vidman, *Isis und Sarapis*, 105.

[17] Certain sites can only be dated within a two hundred year period: Argos and Tauromenium (3rd-2nd cen. BC); Cyme, Faesulae, Frauenberg, Miletus (1st-2nd cen. AD); Sabratha: East End and York (2nd-3rd cen. AD). For purposes of this analysis I have adopted the somewhat arbitrary assumption that half the sites in each of the above groups were built in one of the two centuries in question, half in the other.

[18] Sanctuaries to Sarapis were at Athens (Pausanias 1.18.4), Corinth (2.4.6—two different sites), Sparta (3.14.5), Oetylus (3.25.10), Patrae (7.21.13—two sites), and Copae (9.24.1). To Isis: Megara (1.41.3), Cenchreae (2.2.3), Corinth (2.4.6—two sites), Phlias (2.17.7), Troezen (2.32.6), Methana (2.34.1), Bura (7.25.9), and Tithorea (10.32.13-18). To Sarapis and Isis: Hermione (2.34.10), Boeae (3.22.18), and Messene (4.32.6). As usual, Pausanias does not provide a date for most of these. However, he does mention that the Serapeum at Sparta was the newest sanctuary in the city (3.14.5).

[19] According to the enumeration of Pausanias, Heracles had in addition almost an equal number of altars set up at various localities.

[20] Charles Edson, ed., *IG* X.2.1: *Inscriptiones Thessalonicae et vicinae*, Berlin, 1972.

[21] Roussel, *CE*.

[22] Inscriptions from Egypt are not included since there is no comprehensive collection of these. Because the amount of evidence from Delos is so great, it has the effect of skewing the overall pattern of distribution for the Hellenistic period. So that the reader is aware of this, I have indicated in parentheses the portion of the total which derives from Delos.

It is not simply the expansion of the cult in the Roman West which produces the pattern seen in the table. If just the texts from the eastern Mediterranean are considered (exclusive of Egypt and the rest of Africa), the following results are obtained:

4th cen. BC — 2	2nd cen. AD — 72
3rd cen. BC — 66 (Delos: 19)	3rd cen. AD — 43
2nd cen. BC — 262 (Delos: 164)	4th cen. AD — 1
1st cen. BC — 107 (Delos: 34)	Unknown date — 95 (Delos: 31)
1st cen. AD — 34	

CHAPTER ONE

[1] For discussions of these various dates and attributions see Appendix 1 and my article on the sanctuaries of the Roman period (*ANRW* 2.17.2—forthcoming). I do

not include here sites which some scholars have assigned to the Isis-Sarapis cult but for which the evidence is very dubious: Bononia, Cenchreae, Gigthis, Mons Porphyrites: West Iseum, Poetovio, and Seleucia Pieria. On Cenchreae see Appendix 1; the others (except Seleucia Pieria) are considered in the *ANRW* article mentioned above.

[2] Adriani, *Annuaire*, 138. The location of the pottery vessels is apparently indicated on my Fig. 1 (taken from Adriani) by two circles. The drain is seen in the room to the north of the two circles.

[3] This facility at Eretria will be discussed below in Ch. VII.

[4] Leclant, *Orientalia* 20 (1951), 455 = Abdul-Qadar Muhammad, *ASAntEg* 60 (1968), 239. The latter provided a plan of the site but for some unknown reason did not indicate the location of the basin. Since it is described as "between the southeast corner [actually the south corner] of the Serapeum and the roadway," I have indicated an approximate location on my Fig. 2.

[5] The following data is derived from the brief preliminary report of M. Leglay: "Le temple sévérien de l'Aqua Septimiana Felix (Timgad)," *BA* NS 3 (1967), 262.

[6] The measurements are derived from F. Hiller von Gaertringen, *Thera: Untersuchungen, Vermessungen und Ausgrabungen in den Jahren 1895-1902*, 4 vols., Berlin, 1899-1906, 3.84, fig. 70. The depth of the two cisterns is unknown.

[7] Ibid., 87.

[8] Ibid. Cisterns are needed because there is no ground water on Thera.

[9] If the stairway and its path were continued in a straight line following its surviving course, a point would be reached several meters above the northeast end of the larger cistern. I am inclined to believe that this pathway served as a means of access to the sanctuary for worshippers coming from the city above.

[10] Dunand, *Culte d'Isis*, 2.20. Dunand has several errors in her discussion of this site (2.19-20). For example, she reports that a small statue of Harpocrates was found at the site, whereas it actually was uncovered at the bottom of the hill on which the sanctuary is located. Very likely it did not derive from that sanctuary, for its stratigraphical associations render this quite improbable. On this see "Travaux de l'Ecole Française: Argos," *BCH* 83 (1959), 758 and 760.

[11] Vollgraff, *BCH* 82 (1958), 561.

[12] Westholm, *Temples*, 88-89, 93, 143. Temple D was apparently destroyed in the 1st cen. AD. For further details on the history of this site see Appendix 1.

[13] Ibid., 17-18.

[14] The Isis-Aphrodite conjunction is found frequently enough in the Graeco-Roman world. See Drexler, *LM*, 2.494-98 and Dunand, *Culte d'Isis*, 1.80-85 and 3.330 s.v. "Isis-Aphrodite."

[15] Westholm (*Temples*, 64-65) provides a description of this channel and the basins. These facilities were all constructed at the same time as the two temples (Ibid., 89). The water channel itself circles around the side and rear of Temple D.

[16] Ibid., 65. See also his diagram and explanation of the stratigraphy of Section III of the site (Ibid., 67-69). He apparently dates the construction of this well to around the time of the reign of Ptolemy II Philadelphus (Ibid., 148) but since the top of it is about a meter below the walls of Temple A, the Aphrodite sanctuary built in the 3rd cen. BC, perhaps an earlier origin is indicated.

[17] Ibid., 68-69.

[18] Ibid., 145.

[19] On the state of research on this site see Appendix 1, n. 30.

[20] *BCH* 49 (1925), 478.

[21] Paul Knoblauch, "Eine neue topographische Aufnahme des Stadtgebietes von Kyme in der Äolis," *AA* 1974, 285 and Abb. 1.

[22] *BCH* 49 (1925) 476, fig. 11.

[23] Pesce, *Tempio*, 22 and 34.

[24] Barra Bagnasco *et al.*, *Scavi*, 13, 26-27, 34-37.

[25] Ibid., 27 and 35.

[26] Ibid., 36. Barra Bagnasco *et al.* suggest (29-30 and 37-38) that there may have been an earlier sanctuary of Isis and Sarapis on the site. They present, however, no real evidence to verify this hypothesis.

[27] Ibid., 34.

[28] Barra Bagnasco *et al.* (33-34) also mention a U-shaped structure located below ground level at the right rear of the main cella (Fig. 6). Morra di Lauriano *(Rovine della città di Industria presso Monteu da Po (Torino),* Turin, 1843, Tav. i) depicts it as a rectangular structure, 0.90 × 1.50 m, with an east-west wall bisecting it. It seems to have suffered severe damage since his time. Conceivably it served as a drain—the view of Barra Bagnasco *et al.*—but the available evidence is presently far too scanty to allow a judgment. Further investigation of this structure is needed.

[29] J. Puig y Cadafalch, "Els temples d'Empuries," *AIEC* 4 (1911-12), 313.

[30] Ibid.

[31] Collart, *BCH* 53 (1929), 75.

[32] Ibid., 75-76. Collart does not provide an exact indication of the depth at which this pipe was found.

[33] Ibid., 76 and 98.

[34] Ibid., 99.

[35] Collart, *Philippes*, 1.446. He compares the *sous-sol* under the large room to the crypts at Gortyn and Pompeii and "Eretria." As to this latter site, the supposed crypt is the product of nothing more than an erroneous first impression on the part of the excavator, N. Papadakis (*ArchD* 1 [1915], 123), with respect to the area behind the temple cella. This misunderstanding was then transmitted in an article by P. Roussel (*REg* NS 1 [1919], 84). However, Papadakis in his own report corrected his initial view (*ArchD* 1 [1915], 124).

[36] Collart, *BCH* 53 (1929), 99.

[37] Unless this drain is set well below the base of the foundations of the walls under which it passes, it should have been broken up and disturbed by the excavations for those foundations if it pre-existed them. The work done in this excavation was of mediocre quality and was poorly reported. All of this renders the determination of the precise nature of this pipe extremely difficult. We do not know at what depth it was located, in what sort of material it was buried, whether it slopes toward the north or toward the south, or how its south end relates to the retaining wall of the cellae terrace.

[38] T. Wiegand and H. Schrader, *Priene*, Berlin, 1904, 169. No description of this drain is given in this report. Therefore it cannot be determined without a new examination of the site whether this is an open channel or a pipe of some sort. Dimensions are estimated from Ibid., 166, Abb. 158 = my Fig. 9.

[39] This *Schenkelmauer*, as Wiegand and Schrader (Ibid., 169) call it, has a slightly shorter companion wall c. 4.6 m to the north. The excavators suspected that there had been a doorway at this point in the east outer wall and that the two short walls supported a roofed entryway. However, it is possible that the two walls formed the sides of a small chapel. These walls are c. 0.80 m thick, i.e., 0.15-0.20 m thicker than any of the other foundations preserved on the site. In all events, the drain

apparently was not related to whatever structure was encompassed by these *Schenkelmauern.*

⁴⁰ That is, it is 7.3 m from the north end of the altar, 6.8 m from the south end.

⁴¹ Pernier, *Tempio,* tav. iv = Fig. 10.

⁴² L. Pernier, "Campagna di scavi a Cirene nell'estate del 1925," *Africa italiana* 1 (1927), 134.

⁴³ Westholm, *Temples,* 65 and 85.

⁴⁴ At both Delos C and Thessalonica inscriptions were found which mention a ὑδρεῖον—see the discussion in the following chapter. In addition, at Delos C an inscription was found at the south end of the precinct which indicated that in 116-15 BC Dionysius, son of Dionysius, of Sphettos, who was priest of the sanctuary, dedicated a χρήνη (*CE* 113 = *I Délos* 2057). The location of this well, fountain, or ablution place has not been discovered.

⁴⁵ For example, Salditt-Trappmann, *Tempel,* 15.

CHAPTER TWO

¹ G. Jéquier (*BIFAO* 5 [1906], 63-64) notes that the Palermo Stone affords evidence that the Egyptians measured the height of the Nile flood even in predynastic times.

² Pliny, *HN* 5.10.58. I have converted the cubit measurements used by Pliny to metrical dimensions on the basis of 1 m = 2 cubits. Pliny himself refers only to Egypt in general and not specifically to Memphis. However, his figures indicate that his informant was speaking of the situation in that particular area (Bonneau, *Fisc,* 51-53).

³ Diodorus (1.36.11) speaks of this dissemination of information throughout Egypt. He also reports that the only Νειλοσκοπεῖον in Egypt was at Memphis. If this is his term for a Nilometer, he is certainly mistaken. Aside from the examples discovered by various archaeologists, Strabo (17.1.48) knew of and described the Nilometer at Elephantine. I suspect that Diodorus instead refers to a central "Nile observatory office." On this see Bonneau, *Fisc,* 24 and 38.

⁴ Daressy (*MIE* 8 [1915], 207) indicated that Nilometers were a regular feature at all of the important sanctuaries of the Ptolemaic period. The association of these structures with temples is also stressed by Bonneau (*Fisc,* 56).

⁵ A key source for information on the structure and design of late Pharaonic, Ptolemaic, and early Roman Nilometers is Borchardt, *AbhBerlin* 1906, 1.1-55. He discussed the Nilometers found at Philae, Elephantine, Aswan, Edfu, Esna, Luxor, and Karnak as well as a possible example from Kom Ombo. In later articles he corrects a few of his earlier statements (*SBBerlin* 1934, 194-207) and adds descriptions of two Nilometers found at Gebel el Silsila (*ZÄS* 72 [1936], 137-39). For more recent surveys of the literary and archaeological evidence for Nilometers see Toussoun, *Mémoire,* 2.265-359 and Bonneau, *Fisc,* 27-39.

⁶ Pfister (*Revue des arts asiatiques* 7 [1931-32], 123 and plates) describes this type and offers several illustations. An example from the late Roman or Coptic period survives at Kom el Gizeh (G. Daressy, "Le nilomètre de Kom el Gizeh," *ASAntEg* 1 [1900], 91-96 and Borchardt, *AbhBerlin* 1906, 1.38).

⁷ Hermann, *JAC* 2 (1959), 62 and Taf. 6a; Hermann, *ZÄS* 85 (1960), 37-40 and Taf. ii.

⁸ H. W. Fairman, "Worship and Festivals in an Egyptian Temple," *BJRL* 37 (1954), 172. So also Bonneau (*Fisc,* 57).

[9] Both at Philae and at Edfu the entrance to the Nilometer is carefully situated within the precinct even though its stairway passes under and outside of the precinct's outer wall.

[10] Bonneau, *Crue*, 275.

[11] Dölger, *AntChrist* 5 (1936) 155.

[12] Hermann, *JAC* 2 (1959), 32, n. 16.

[13] Bonneau, *Crue*, 276-77; Lindsay, *Men and Gods*, 269.

[14] Ablution basins found at two of these sites apparently were supplied with water from a source other than the crypt. This is a further indication that water from these crypts had a restricted and specific character. These ablution facilities will be discussed in Ch. VII.

[15] Information on this Nilometer is found in the following publications: Rowe, *ASAntEg*, Suppl. 2 (1946), 32 and pl. xii; Rowe-Rees, *BJRL* 39 (1956-57), 492-93; Rowe, *BArchAlex* 35 (1942), pls. xliii-xliv; and Adriani, *Repertorio*, ser. C, vol. 1.98.

[16] Rowe (*ASAntEg*, Suppl. 2 [1946], 32) tested this point and found that the level of water in the basin and in the Canal is about the same.

[17] Ibid.

[18] Engreen, *Medievalia et humanistica* 1 (1943), 5-6; Rowe, *ASAntEg*, Suppl. 2 (1946), 32; Adriani, *Repertorio*, ser. C, vol. 1.98. Bonneau (*Fisc*, 56) observes that measuring scales painted or engraved on the walls of a Nilometer were not the only means of determining the height of the water. It was also possible, for example, to use a portable wooden cubit stick to measure from some fixed point down to the water level.

[19] Bonneau, *Fisc*, 39 and Graph. iv.

[20] Engreen, *Medievalia et humanistica* 1 (1943), 6.

[21] Rowe (*BArchAlex* 35 [1942], 139-40) indicates that the most common means of obtaining fresh water at Alexandria was to sink a pit through the roof of one of the great aqueducts or their subsidiary passages.

[22] On the sacred cubit see K. R. Lepsius, *Die altägyptische Elle und ihre Eintheilung*, Berlin, 1865; Hermann, *JAC* 2 (1959), 33-34; Bonneau, *Fisc*, 22-24.

[23] Bonneau, *Fisc*, 56.

[24] Such "votive cubits" are preserved, for example, in the Louvre (Inv. nr. LP 1271) and in the Turin Museum (Inv. nrs. 6347-49—see A. Fabretti *et al.*, *Regio Museo di Torino*, vol. 2: *Antichità egizie*, Turin, 1888, 244-45). These objects are 0.52-0.525 m long and about 0.03-4 m thick; generally they are inscribed with one or more hieroglyphic texts which give the name of the donor.

[25] Socrates, *Hist. Eccl.* 1.18; Theophanes Conf., *Chronogr.* 16.12-26; Sozomen, *Hist. Eccl.* 5.3.3; Rufinus, *Hist. Eccl.* 11.30.

[26] Clement of Alexandria, *Strom.* 6.4.36.

[27] Socrates, *Hist. Eccl.* 1.18.

[28] This Nilometer probably also was intended to supply Nile flood water for the liturgical needs of the Serapeum.

[29] On the Nilometer by the Temple of Isis Usret and on that found in the West Colonnade area see Lyons, *Report*, 34-39 and Borchardt, *AbhBerlin* 1906, 1.10. Both authors describe the measuring scales found in these facilities.

[30] Lyons (*Report*, 33) describes this facility.

[31] An inscription from the time of the reign of Marcus Aurelius is painted on the roofing block at the entrance to the stairway (Lyons, *Report*, 33). Therefore the Nilometer must antedate the late 2nd cen. AD.

[32] Lyons, *Report*, 39-40.

[33] Borchardt, *AbhBerlin* 1906, 1.10.

[34] Against Borchardt (Ibid.).

[35] Henry G. Lyons (*A Report on the Temples of Philae*, Cairo, 1908, pl. v) designated it as the "Modern Nile Gauge."

[36] F. E. Engreen (*Medievalia et humanistica* 1 [1943], 7) thought that the Nilometers found in Egypt were generally located at sanctuaries dedicated to Isis and Sarapis. This is not the case. The only Egyptian sanctuaries of these gods presently known to have had Nilometers are the Serapeum at Alexandria and the Temple of Isis at Philae.

[37] Roussel (*CE*, p. 20) provides a brief description.

[38] Roussel (Ibid.) says that he was unable to find any indication in the surviving upper portion of the temple as to where precisely the cult statue was situated.

[39] Salditt-Trappmann, *Tempel*, 15-16, n. 36. She also reported the presence of a single "step" at the west end of the basin, a feature not mentioned by Roussel.

[40] This channel is indicated by dotted lines in Fig. 14.

[41] Callimachus 3.171; Lycophron 575-76; Strabo 6.2.4; Pliny, *HN* 2.229; Pausanias 2.5.3.

[42] To carry this project out they had to construct a rather deep basin and a large feeder main over 10 m long. That Roussel was unable to trace this water line all the way to the Lower Reservoir is unfortunate. No one else has since done this; Bruneau (*Recherches*, 459 and 461) is compelled in this matter to rely upon Roussel's hypothesis.

[43] The depth of the basin seems to have allowed water to remain in it even when the Inopus fell to a rather low level.

[44] This is an estimate made from the topographical map of Delos published by Bruneau (*Recherches*, plan A) and from on-site observations. Cayeux (*Description*, 1.213, n. 1) at one time proposed to publish a study of the whole water system of the Inopus and its canalization but his work never appeared.

[45] Since the Inopus is now extensively clogged with debris, its ancient flood stage is difficult to estimate.

[46] The founder, the priest Apollonius, came from Memphis (*CE* 1.37-38 = *IG* XI.4.1299.37-38). His family then continued to govern their house shrine and its subsequent replacement, Delos A, for three or more generations—see Roussel, *CE*, pp. 261-62 and Engelmann, *Delian Aretalogy*, 11-16. While most of the donors of the twenty-eight inscriptions found on the site have Greek names, two stones which date no earlier than the mid 2nd cen. BC indicate that Horus, son of Horus, of Casium (a town in Egypt somewhat to the east of Pelusium) made a dedication "to the Great God, to Zeus Casius, and to Tachnepsis" (= a title of Isis at Casium—*POxy.* 11.1380.74-75). Commentary on these inscriptions (*CE* 16-16 *bis* = *I Délos* 2180-81) is found in Roussel *CE*, pp. 95-97. The same Horus is also mentioned as the ἐπιμελητής of the sanctuary in *CE* 15-15 *bis* (= *I Délos* 2116-17); in *CE* 15 he is also called the τὰς θεραπείας αἰτοῦντος. His active role suggests that Egyptian or Graeco-Egyptian influence remained strong at this sanctuary even during its later history.

[47] No examples of a Nilometer related in this fashion to the central temple have been found in Egypt. Further, even though the Nile water crypts found at the various sanctuaries outside of Egypt are set quite close to the temple, this particular arrangement is not known to have been repeated elsewhere.

Twenty-five years ago P. Gilbert (*La nouvelle Clio* 7-9 [1955-57], 296) made a connection between the crypts found at the sanctuaries on Delos and the Nilometers located, as he saw it, at the "temples à caractère funéraire de l'Egypte" and associated both groups of structures with ritual efforts to obtain rebirth and immortality. Unfortunately, he never had the opportunity to develop this bare suggestion any further.

⁴⁸ For a description of this facility see Roussel, *CE*, pp. 36 and 45.

⁴⁹ Ibid., 36.

⁵⁰ Ibid., 45.

⁵¹ Ibid. Roussel wondered if the crypt might have only served as a repository for some smaller container of Nile water. However, the effort taken to cover the walls and the *floor* with stucco—portions of which remain *in situ*—argues against that. Bruneau (*Recherches*, 461) is therefore correct in calling the structure "une citerne."

⁵² So Roussel, *CE*, p. 45.

⁵³ Ibid., n. 2. If the water then had to be carried up by hand, this is an added reason to suppose that the crypt was roofed over. A roof would have served to reduce evaporation.

⁵⁴ Ibid., 55.

⁵⁵ *CE* 175 A-D = *I Délos* 2617-20. The word ὑδρεῖον is found in *CE* 175 D.1-4 (τοῦ ὑδρείου δωρε[ὰν] / δοὺς παρ' ἑαυτοῦ κα[ὶ] τὴν λιθείαν ἄπασαν / τὴν οὖσαν ἐν τῶ(ι) ...) and appears to have been correctly restored by Roussel in *CE* 175 A.4 (εἰς τὴν το[ῦ ὑδ]ρείου ἐπισκευ[ὴ]ν καὶ τὴν περιχ ----). *CE* 175 B and C perhaps also refer to this structure—see Roussel's commentary (*CE*, pp. 181-86).

⁵⁶ See, for example, Clement of Alexandria, *Strom.* 6.4.37 and SIRIS 531, an inscription from Nomentum. In interpreting this latter text H. Dessau (*CIL* XIV. 3941; *ILS* 4378) believed that the word *hydraeum* referred to "a piece of women's jewelry made in the form of a *hydra* or serpent." Later editors (Vidman, SIRIS, nr. 531; Malaise, *Inventaire*, 65-66) now recognize the word as a term for a (Nile) water container, although Malaise refers it specifically to the *situla* rather than to the cultic pitcher.

⁵⁷ The cultic pitchers begin to appear only at the very end of the Hellenistic period. On this see my discussion in Ch. VI.

⁵⁸ Roussel, *CE*, p. 64.

⁵⁹ *CE* 179 = *I Délos* 2068.

⁶⁰ See Roussel, *CE*, pp. 64 and 190.

⁶¹ Several dedications found in connection with Serapeum C use the word Ὑδρεῖος as a divine title: *CE* 152 = *I Délos* 2155 (105-3 BC), *CE* 173a = *I Délos* 2087 (beginning of the 1st cen. BC), and *I Délos* 2160 (same period). The name very likely means "the god of the ὑδρεῖον." Since the names of Sarapis, Isis, and Anubis appear separately in *CE* 173a, the title cannot refer to them. I believe that only two possibilities remain. First, Ὑδρεῖος may have been a title of Harpocrates, for his name appears directly in front of this word in *CE* 173a. Otherwise, the reference is probably to Osiris.

⁶² *IG* X.2.1.83: [ἔτους] ε [['Αντωνίου]] / [Πόπλιο]ς Σαλάριος Πάμφι / [λος ἱε]ρεὺς Σαράπιδος καὶ / [Ἴσι]δος καὶ Μάνιος Σαλά[ρ]ιος / [Π]οπλίου υἱὸς τὸ ὑδρῆον / Ἴσιδι καὶ τοῖς ἄλλοις θεοῖς / τοῖς ἐντεμενίοις πᾶσι / καὶ πάσαις. Edson believed that the name of Mark Anthony should be restored to the text in line 1. He therefore dated the stone to 37-36 BC.

⁶³ See the discussion in Ch. VI.

⁶⁴ The following data is derived from two brief reports by Oliverio (*ASAtene* 1 [1914], 376-77 and *ASAtene* 2 [1916], 309-11) and from Salditt-Trappmann, *Tempel*, 61-65.

⁶⁵ The fact that the builders constructed a double wall instead of allowing the transverse walls of one structure to abut up against the other is somewhat surprising. Oliverio (*ASAtene* 2 [1916], 309) offers no explanation other than that the two buildings were built at different times. Salditt-Trappmann (*Tempel*, 66) theorizes

on the basis of her explanation of the crypt as a "lower world" into which the initiate descends that perhaps there was a desire to keep the temple building separate from this "lower world."

⁶⁶ Salditt-Trappmann, *Tempel*, 65-66. SIRIS 170, an inscription of the 1st or 2nd cen. AD which was found in the central temple, indicates that a certain Flavia Philyra and her children had the οἶκος rebuilt from its foundations and then dedicated it to Isis, Sarapis, and the other gods in the ναός.

⁶⁷ The masonry construction of the crypt was not described either by Oliverio—he only points out (*ASAtene* 1 [1914], 377) that the north wall of the crypt had been rebuilt—or by Salditt-Trappmann. However, it is readily apparent in my Pl. IV.

⁶⁸ Oliverio, *ASAtene* 2 (1916), 310.

⁶⁹ This inscription, which has been published by Guarducci (*Inscriptiones*, vol. 4, nr. 342), is quite fragmentary.

⁷⁰ SIRIS 166 = Guarducci, *Inscriptiones*, vol. 4, nr. 245. This is a dedication to Isis and Sarapis and dates from the 2nd cen. BC. Oliverio (*ASAtene* 2 [1916], 310) reported that it was in fragmentary condition (not so!) and that it came from the crypt. There is some confusion here, however, since Guarducci reported that it was found "in the south wall of the Iseum," and her source of information may well have been the overall director of the Gortyn expedition, F. Halbherr, whose sketch of the inscription is printed in her book.

⁷¹ These and most of the descriptive details to follow are taken from Salditt-Trappmann, *Tempel*, 61-63.

⁷² Salditt-Trappmann (Ibid., 64-65) has argued that this corridor, which measures in its interior 1.60 m wide × c. 6.5 m long and which appears not to have been enclosed by a wall at its west end, was an assembly room for those who were initiated and also served as a place to hold common meals. A statement by Oliverio (*ASAtene* 2 [1916], 310) that he had found a "small, square base made of stone" in that area prompted this latter conclusion. This object became in her view the base of a table. The room may have been used as a gathering place, though it is somewhat narrow for that purpose. But that meals were held within its limited confines seems quite improbable unless we believe that these were eaten with loins girt and staff in hand!

⁷³ The top step probably served as a threshold for the door of the crypt.

⁷⁴ The upper portion of this niche has not survived.

⁷⁵ The risers on these steps are each 0.26 m high; therefore the total descent from ground level, counting the upper stairs, is 1.80 m.

⁷⁶ Oliverio (*ASAtene* 1 [1974], 377) said that the basin was actually 0.55 m deep and 1.10 m on each side. In general, the few measurements provided by Oliverio are not to be trusted.

⁷⁷ Blue paint still covers almost half the surface of the west wall.

⁷⁸ Luigi Pernier, "Gortina, capitale della 'Provincia Cretae et Cyrenarum'," *AeR* 18 (1915), 64.

⁷⁹ Oliverio, *ASAtene* 1 (1914), 376.

⁸⁰ Oliverio (Ibid., 377) describes this object as "una statuetta fittile mancante della testa—una figura muliebre avvolta in ampio manto."

⁸¹ Salditt-Trappmann (*Tempel*, 66, n. 43) saw a headless female statue of unknown provenance in the museum at Gortyn. She does not say whether this object was made of terracotta.

⁸² Statues of Isis with such a full mantle or cloak do exist, although we can only guess at what precisely Oliverio meant in his description. The cult statue of Isis

from this sanctuary, for example, has a quite full outer garment (Salditt-Trappmann, *Tempel*, Abb. 48). In addition, a headless female statue found in the Praetorium of Gortyn has been identified as a figure of Isis on the basis of its full fringed cloak and its large garland of flowers—see Dunand, *Culte d'Isis*, vol. 2, pl. xxvi. Biagio Pace (*Africa italiana* 1 [1927], 123-25) discusses a similar example found at Cyrene.

[83] Oliverio, *ASAtene* 1 (1914), 377.

[84] Salditt-Trappmann, *Tempel*, 66, n. 43.

[85] Oliverio, *ASAtene* 1 (1914), 377.

[86] Ibid.

[87] For example, such niches were found in the Nilometer at Elephantine (Borchardt, *AbhBerlin* 1906, 1.13) and in two of the Nilometers at Philae (Lyons, *Report*, 34 and 39).

[88] The height and width of each niche in the Nilometer at Elephantine from the uppermost to the lowest are as follows: 0.35 × 0.35 m, 0.35 × 0.35 m, 0.52 × 0.35, 0.35 × 0.35 m. The bottom niche is 0.20 m deep and the others are probably similar. (Measurements estimated from Borchardt, *AbhBerlin* 1906, pt. 1, pl. iii.).

[89] The exception is the niche over the basin which probably could not have held a lighted lamp. Water flowing out from the pipe above the niche would have splashed on its protruding base and would have probably extinguished any flame.

[90] For example, the stucco reliefs on the crypt housing have been much defaced and damaged.

[91] The problems involved here should be made clear. No one has ever published any of the dimensions of the crypt area except for the length and width of the subterranean room. I have therefore utilized various scale drawings of the Iseum in order to provide the approximate dimensions given below. I have visited this installation but did not have an opportunity to take measurements or to determine precisely the features in the subterranean portion of the crypt. Of this part only one drawing has been published (Niccolini, *Case*, 1.2, pl. iii) and that over one hundred years ago. (Gusman [*Pompéi*, ed. 1 (1899)] published a drawing taken from Donaldson and Cooke, *Pompeii*, vol. 1 [1827], unnumbered plate, which was there entitled "Niche in the Temple of Isis." This Gusman thought to be a picture of the interior of the crypt. Realizing his error, he withdrew this plate from the 1906 edition of his book.)

Main sources for evidence on the crypt: *PAH* 1.1.169-72; Hamilton, *Archaeologia* 4 (1776), 166, 173, and plan opposite 173; Jorio, *Plan*, 127; Mazois and Gau, *Ruines*, 4.26-27 and pls. x-xi; Niccolini, *Case*, 1.2.13 and pl. iii and plan; Dyer, *Pompeii*, 141; Breton, *Pompeia*, 51; Overbeck and Mau, *Pompeii*, 108-10 and plan; Lafaye, *Histoire*, 183-84, 191, and plan; Mau, *Pompeii*, 172-73; and Tran Tam Tinh, *Essai*, 34-35.

[92] Like Gortyn and Delos B but unlike Delos A the crypt structure is separate from the temple.

[93] The height to the top of the arch is c. 2.5 m. Hardware for the wooden door was found (*PAH* 1.1.172).

[94] Mazois and Gau (*Ruines*, vol. 4, pls. x-xi) provide very good drawings of these stucco reliefs.

[95] *PAH* 1.1.171 and Dyer, *Pompeii*, 141. Others report that the background was blue (Overbeck and Mau, *Pompeii*, 110; Mau, *Pompeii*, 173; and Tran Tam Tinh, *Essai*, 35). Perhaps weathering explains this divergence.

[96] This is the description provided by the archaeologist (*PAH* 1.1.171). The damage suffered by these figures has rendered some of their details unclear.

[97] This iconographic type of Isis is found with some frequency in the area around Rome—see Roullet, *Egyptian and Egyptianizing Monuments*, nrs. 123 (Villa Adriana), 135 (Villa Adriana), 136, 138, etc. Most of these appear to be Roman imitations of an Egyptian type although nr. 123 is Ptolemaic and dates from the 3rd cen. BC.

[98] Earlier scholars designated the male figure as Mercury and the female as a nymph (Niccolini, *Case*, 1.2.13; Breton, *Pompeia*, 51; Lafaye, *Histoire*, 191). The archaeologist reported (*PAH* 1.1.171) that the male figure carried a caduceus, but William Hamilton (*Archaeologia* 4 [1776], 166), who visited the site shortly after its excavation, said that he carried a Gorgon's head and so called the figure Perseus. The nineteenth century drawings of this figure do not show his left hand. Was the pertinent evidence broken off at some early date? Mau (*Pompeii*, 173), Tran Tam Tinh (*Essai*, 35), Merkelbach (*Latomus* 24 [1965], 146), and Schauenburg (*Perseus*, 71) join in designating the figures as Perseus and Andromeda.

[99] So Lafaye, *Histoire*, 191.

[100] Nissen (*Pompeianische Studien*, 174) noted that the joint between this wall and the west wall of the building has been covered over with stucco. He concluded that one of these two walls is earlier than the other. Probably the guard rail is secondary and was installed when the temple was rebuilt c. 63 AD.

[101] The various plans of the site show from six to nine steps with most indicating eight or nine. Part of the problem is that the stairs disappear under the west wall of the crypt housing, a situation presenting something of a quandary for the draftsmen of the various plans. To have a stair riser of something approaching normal height, about nine steps would be needed. This would give each step a riser height of 0.28 m.

[102] The measurement of the height is estimated from Niccolini, *Case,* 1.2, pl. iii.

[103] The final excavation of this lower area does not seem to have been recorded by the archaeologist in his daybook. His entry for June 8, 1765 (*PAH* 1.1.172) reports the discovery of a ''small stairway leading to a crypt *che ancora non si è potuto riconoscere per motivo della mofeta.*'' This ''mofeta'' or ''foul vapor like the damp of mines'' (Hamilton, *Archaeologia* 4 [1776], 166) impeded visitors to this area for at least several years. However, the crypt must have been excavated before the end of Hamilton's tour of duty as English commissioner in Italy since he confidently states the purpose of this underground room in his article.

[104] Mazois and Gau, *Ruines*, 4.26.

[105] Niccolini, *Case*, 1.2, pl. iii.

[106] Nissen, *Pompeianische Studien*, 174.

[107] While certain earlier writers believed that this facility had a roof, Mau (*Pompeii*, 172), Tran Tam Tinh (*Essai,* 35), and others were of the opinion that it did not.

[108] The following data is taken from Pesce, *Tempio*, 35-36 and 41-42 unless otherwise noted.

[109] Ibid., 9. The width of these doorways is estimated from his Tav. 1 (= my Fig. 19).

[110] The top part of this opening is larger and is squared off. Pesce found a block, 0.52 m square, which he thought may have served as a cover for the opening.

[111] The other end of the cistern is located outside the ambulatory about two meters beyond the south side of the temple. Pesce (Ibid., 63) indicated that these cisterns are non-Roman in design and probably go back to a period before the construction of the sanctuary. The west cistern is 9.40 m long and 1.40 m wide. Its height from floor to top of roof vaulting is 3.78 m. However, the highest water line

left on the plaster is 2.83 m above floor level. The approximate capacity of this tank is therefore about 40 m³ of water.

¹¹² Pesce, *Tempio*, 22-23.

¹¹³ Pesce (Ibid., 22 and 34-35) describes this installation. Its drain later was modified by the addition of several catch basins.

¹¹⁴ Merkelbach, *Isisfeste*, 14-19.

¹¹⁵ In wetter climates floods would have taken place within the crypt more often than once a year. The rainfall at Pompeii, for example, averages about 88 cm per year with much of it concentrated in October, November, and December. Perhaps the first flooding of the winter rainy season had a special significance.

¹¹⁶ Engberding, *OrChr* 37 (1953), 80-81.

¹¹⁷ For a list of other sources on the type of water utilized for baptism in early Christianity see Klausner, *Pisciculi*, 157-61.

¹¹⁸ Klausner (Ibid., 161-62) provides evidence both for the nomenclature of the baptismal font and for its construction.

¹¹⁹ For example, Giuseppe Fiorelli (*Guida di Pompei*, Rome, 1877, 84) thought that the crypt at Pompeii was used by priests when they wished to inspect the entrails of animals in the course of a divination ritual. This was merely a hypothesis; Fiorelli offered no empirical evidence for his views.

¹²⁰ This theory centered on the use of the crypt at Pompeii. It was espoused by Niccolini (*Case* 1.2.13), by Charles Bonucci (*Pompéi* [French tr. of the 3rd Italian ed.; Naples, 1830] 200), and by Breton (*Pompeia*, 51).

¹²¹ These ablution facilities will be examined in Ch. VII.

¹²² E.g., R. Lanciani, "Iscrizioni portuensi," *Bullettino dell'Istituto di Corrispondenza Archeologica* 1868, 229-30; Lafaye, *Histoire*, 183-84.

¹²³ Roussel, *CE*, p. 31.

¹²⁴ Apuleius, *Met.* 11.23.

¹²⁵ Salditt-Trappmann, *Tempel*, 64 and *passim*. Apuleius himself (*Met.* 11.23) separates what Salditt-Trappmann calls the baptism from the initiation rite by several hours.

CHAPTER THREE

¹ For a discussion of this sanctuary and its dating see Appendix 1.

² Papadakis (*ArchD* 1 [1915], 128) provides all the information we have on this area. Bruneau (*Sanctuaire*, 46) has nothing to add to this description. He was unable to re-examine this corner of the site because a modern wall has been built over it. The horizontal dimensions which I supply are estimated from the ground plan supplied by Papadakis (*ArchD* 1 [1915], 118). Also on the site is a larger room with a second well (Fig. 20). I will argue below that this served for ablution rites and had nothing to do with Nile water.

³ Papadakis (Ibid., 117, n. 1) implies that this room was roofed over but does not state it directly. He mentions no special characteristics with respect to its floor surface. Therefore it presumably had a floor of pressed earth just as is normally found elsewhere on the site (Ibid., 126 and 130). The location of the door is a matter of guesswork. Papadakis (Ibid., 128) implies that the room was entered from the south wing of the outer portico (Fig. 20) by way of Room Y. However, since no threshold was found between Room Y and Room X, placing the entry to Room X on its north side is at least as justifiable a hypothesis. Since some sort of barrier separated the inner courtyard from the portico (Ibid., 123), the latter was clearly considered a less sacred area. If the well in Room X had a sacred function, access

to it would probably have been located within the courtyard. An entrance at the north side of Room X would have linked it directly with Area D''', a part of the sanctuary which may have served as a kind of sacristy (Ibid., 124).

⁴ Each of these sections, Papadakis reported, had a hole cut into it so as to form a stepping place. When all the tiles were in place, they formed a ladder which allowed a person to descend, though not with ease, into the well for cleaning it. Papadakis believed this type of arrangement to be not uncommon in Greece.

⁵ Ibid., 119. Papadakis believed that the beach originally extended under the area of the sanctuary and that as the harbor area was silted up a thin layer of soil gradually covered over this sand.

⁶ Papadakis (Ibid., 131) indicates that because the water table was so high in the general area of the site, there was no need to construct cisterns fed by rain water to provide fresh water.

⁷ Ibid., 115.

⁸ SIRIS 73 (late 4th or early 3rd cen. BC).

⁹ Those who joined together to build this sanctuary evidently had limited financial means. The type of masonry employed is one indication of this. Only the lowest portions of any of the buildings were constructed with stone; the remaining portions of the walls were built out of unbaked bricks (Papadakis, *ArchD* 1 [1915], 117).

¹⁰ The physical description of this sub-system is derived from Salditt-Trappmann, *Tempel*, 5-6. Unfortunately she failed to indicate the location of the large water line on this plan.

Separate basins located close to the central temple in the two side courtyards (Fig. 21) form yet a third water system at Pergamum. These probably served only to decorate these courtyards, yet Salditt-Trappmann (Ibid., 17) suggests that they may also have supplied water for cultic needs. I do not believe that she is correct. The large central basin is 11.50 m long, 2.50 m wide, and 0.85 m deep (Ibid., 12-13). No steps lead down either into these two large basins or into the small round basins located at either end of them. These latter facilities are 1.75 m in diameter and 0.85 m deep. Cultic parallels to these basins do not readily come to mind. Large, shallow, T-shaped basins found beside the entrance ramp to the temple at Deir el Bahri in Egypt served for the cultivation of papyrus plants. Near them were circular pits for growing other types of vegetation (*BMetrMus* 19 [1924], pt. 2, pp. 17-18; Dieter Arnold, "Deir el-Bahari III," *LÄ* 1.1013-14 [plan] and 1019). The basins at Pergamum do not imitate this T-shape (a form of basin found elsewhere in Egypt in connection with various cults—see Bonnet, "See, heiliger," *Reallexikon*, 695) and show no indication that they were utilized for growing plants. In other words, Egyptian influence does not seem to account for the presence of these basins at Pergamum.

¹¹ Salditt-Trappmann, *Tempel*, 6. She gives no further details and does not offer any indication how far the water line might have continued beyond the entrance to the temple.

¹² Twin tunnels served to conduct the Selinus River under the immense expanse of the courtyard at this sanctuary. Charles Texier (*Description de l'Asie Mineure*, Paris, 1849, 2. 224 and pl. 125) walked through the length of them to view their construction. With him came half the town of Bergama. They managed, he said, to overcome their fear of the tunnels and came along to see if the mad foreigner had discovered a secret treasure. Texier does not seem to have discovered any water outlets or connections within these tunnels—nor any treasure! For a briefer, less

detailed, and less dramatic description of the tunnels see Salditt-Trappmann, *Tempel*, 1-2.

[13] This arrangement would not be unlike that used to fill the cisterns under the pronaos of the temple at Sabratha. At Pergamum, all elements of a crypt arrangement have disappeared. The top of the cistern, as it were, has been removed, but the location of the resulting basin with respect to the central cult area and the main axis of the temple is comparable to what was found at Sabratha.

[14] At nearby Izmir one-third of the annual rainfall normally occurs during these two months.

[15] Two long and narrow basins in the garden of the House of Loreius Tiburtinus at Pompeii, facilities unquestionably designed to represent the Nile River, share some features in common with the deep basin at Pergamum. (For a description of this house and its related structures see A. Maiuri and R. Pane, *La casa di Loreio Tiburtino e la villa di Diomede in Pompei* [I monumenti italiani, 2.1], Rome, 1947. See also P. Grimal, *Les jardins romains*, 2nd ed., Paris, 1969, 296-98.) Loreius Tiburtinus apparently was a priest of Isis (so Tran Tam Tinh, *Essai*, 43) as was his grandfather. A picture of the latter in full sacerdotal regalia was found on the wall of a room called by later investigators the "sacellum Isidis" (Ibid., 124-25, nr. 5). The installations which Loreius Tiburtinus had constructed at his palatial home about the year 65 AD or somewhat earlier (Maiuri-Pane, *Casa*, 6) consist of two basins set in the form of a T—these have about the same width and depth as the basin at Pergamum—and a number of related buildings: two fountain houses (one with a *biclinium*), two shrine-like structures, and a building called by Maiuri-Pane a "fontana"—for illustrations of this structure see *Casa*, tav. 2 and Michael Grant, *Cities of Vesuvius: Pompeii and Herculaneum*, London, 1971, 124. In actuality it is not a fountain but a close imitation of the central portion of the Tomb of Seti I (= the so-called "Osireion") at Abydos in Egypt. (On the Abydos tomb see E. Naville, "Le grand réservoir d'Abydos et la tombe d'Osiris," *ZÄS* 52 [1914], 50-55 and Henri Frankfort, *The Cenotaph of Seti I at Abydos* [Egyptian Exploration Society, 39], 2 vols., London, 1933.) According to Tran Tam Tinh (*Essai*, 45) the basins were so constructed as to allow the production of an "inondation artificielle" which would submerge the plants, flowers, and statuettes placed in them and would remind the devotees gathered in the garden of the joy and prosperity which the Nile flood brings. While installations in the garden of a private estate are not strictly comparable with those in a sanctuary, nonetheless the Pompeii example indicates that the concept of representing the Nile flood in this manner was known in the early Imperial period.

[16] Salditt-Trappmann, *Tempel*, 5.

[17] On ablution rituals see Ch. VII.

[18] Both these references and the descriptive information to follow are taken from two reports by W. Modrijan: *BlHeim* 26 (1953), 61-62 and *Frauenberg*, 26-27. Many of the dimensions are estimated from Modrijan's ground plan of the site (= my Fig. 22). The structure is situated only 1.25 m from the right side wall of the temple. This location to the right of the central temple is typical within this cult for a type of ablution basin—see Ch. VII. However, other overriding features suggest that what Modrijan found was a Nile water container.

[19] Despite the difference in elevation and orientation, Modrijan (*BlHeim* 26 [1953], 62; *Frauenberg*, 26) is certain that the basin belongs to the same level of construction as the temple.

[20] These walls are 0.5 m thick on the average.

²¹ The top part of the channel was not buried below ground and is slightly higher in elevation than the temple's foundation wall.

²² Modrijan (*Frauenberg*, 26) notes with some surprise the absence of a drain.

²³ Modrijan, *BlHeim* 26 (1953), 62.

²⁴ This is the room now covered by the building constructed in 1730 (Modrijan, *Frauenberg*, 26-27; cf. p. 16). What this area had been like cannot now be ascertained since the cellar of the later building was dug to a depth well below any Roman period floor level. It therefore destroyed whatever might have existed here in Imperial times. No sign of any crypt area remains; neither entryway nor doorways between the various areas below the temple have been found. The stairway cut into the Roman wall on the east side is modern.

²⁵ These themes will be developed in the two chapters which follow.

²⁶ Tertullian, *De Bapt.* 4.3; Ambrose, *Sermo* 38.2. On the desire for baptism in the Jordan and on the later custom of referring to all baptismal fonts as the "Jordan" see F. J. Dölger, "Der Durchzug durch den Jordan als Sinnbild der christlichen Taufe," *AntChrist* 2 (1930), 70-79.

²⁷ *Didache* 7.2-3; Tertullian, *De Bapt.* 4.4.

²⁸ Plutarch, *De Is. et Os.* 40.367 B-C.

²⁹ *POxy.* 11.1380.222-24, a text from the early 2nd cen. AD, indicates that Isis not only ruled over the Nile but also over the Eleutherus in Syria and the Ganges in India. Perhaps some also considered these rivers to be "Nile-related."

³⁰ Annual rainfall in Upper Egypt (below Cairo) often is 0 cm. At Cairo the average is 5 cm. On the Mediterranean coast the accumulation is between 5 and 25 cm per year (Bonneau, *Crue du Nil*, 16). The Nile in Egypt is an exotic river; no tributaries are found north of the juncture with the Atbara River in the Sudan.

³¹ Aelian (*NA* 7.45) and Plutarch (*De soll. anim.* 20.974 C and *De Is. et Os.* 75.381 D) observe that an ibis will drink only from pure water; if the water was tainted or disease-ridden this bird would not even approach it. Consequently, only water from which an ibis had drunk was used by the priests of Egypt for purifying themselves. (In *De Is. et Os.* Plutarch says that the νομιμώτατοι among the priests followed this practice).

³² So Bonneau, *Crue du Nil*, 275. There she gives many references.

³³ Ibid., 277.

³⁴ Bonneau (Ibid., 174-76 and 179) provides a list of sources.

³⁵ Nilsson, *History*, 113.

³⁶ These figures are derived from various standard encyclopedias and reference works. They usually represent either the general rainfall accumulation for the region in which the site is located or that of the nearest large modern city.

³⁷ Sauneron, *BIFAO* 51 (1952), 41-48: Herodotus, Euripides, Aristophanes, Isocrates, Tibullus, Pomponius Mela, Seneca, Martial, Pliny the Younger, Philo, Heliodorus, and Claudian.

³⁸ Deut 11:10-12; Theophrastus, *Caus. Pl.* 3.3.3; Apollonius Rhodius, *Argon.* 4.270; Theocritus, *Id.* 17.77-80; Schol. Pindar, *Pyth.* 4.99; Ovid, *Ars Am.* 1.645-52; Lucan 8.445 and 8.828; Aelius Aristides, *Or.* 36.123 (ed. Keil); Aristaenetus, *De Nili bonis* (cited in Eudocia, *Violar.* 698); Himerius, *Disc.* 1.8; and Schol. Lucan 8.826. Most of these are from Bonneau (*Crue du Nil*, 129, n. 5) but with some additions and corrections.

³⁹ Isis Aretalogy of Cyme, 54 (Peek, *Isishymnus*, 124); Ἐγὼ ὄμβρων εἰμὶ κυρία. This inscription dates to the 1st or 2nd cen. AD. Peek (Ibid., 50) was convinced that this phrase formed a regular part of these aretalogies even though it has not survived in the other fragmentary versions. See also *POxy.* 11.1380.227-30 and 237-39.

⁴⁰ Plutarch, *De Is. et Os.* 34.364 D (Plutarch, at least, understood that one form of Osiris' name, Ὕσιριν, indicated such a connection) and 40.367 B (Horus was linked both with the rain and with the Nile).

⁴¹ This theory goes back at least as far as Democritus of Abdera (5th cen. BC). His opinion is cited in the Anonymous of Florence (3rd cen. BC), in Diodorus Siculus (1.39.1-3), and in Plutarch (*Plac. phil.* 4.1.898 A). The theory is also found in a large number of Hellenistic and Roman writings: Pseudo-Aristotle, *De inundatione Nili (Aristoteles pseudepigraphus*, ed. V. Rose, Leipzig, 1863, 638-39); Callisthenes (cited in the Anonymous of Florence = F. Jacoby, *Die Fragmente der griechischen Historiker*, 124 F 12c); Polybius (cited in Strabo 2.3.2); Lucretius 6.729-37; Pomponius Mela 1.9.53; Pliny, *HN* 5.10.55; Statius, *Theb.* 8.411; Lucan 10.242-44; Plutarch, *De Is. et Os.* 39.366 C; Aelius Aristides, *Or.* 36.19 (ed. Keil); Heliodorus 2.28.3-4; Solinus 32.9; Horapollo 1.21; etc. For a fuller discussion of this whole theory see Bonneau, *Crue du Nil*, 201-8 and Rehm, *RE* 17.1.584-85 and 587-88.

⁴² For literature on this aretalogy and the various theories associated with it see Appendix 1, note 30.

⁴³ See Ch. VI.

⁴⁴ On animism in Greek religion see H. J. Rose, *Religion in Greece and Rome*, New York, 1959, 21-26.

⁴⁵ Nilsson, *History*, 108-9.

⁴⁶ Ibid., 142.

⁴⁷ Frankfort, *Ancient Egyptian Religion*, 19.

⁴⁸ Ibid., 9, 12-13.

⁴⁹ In certain circles the god Ptah was looked upon as the power who created everything by his thought and his word. Frankfort (Ibid., 23) believes this to be the only clear exception to the general pattern.

⁵⁰ Isis does appear in Plutarch (*De Is. et Os.* 32.363 D—see also 38.366 A and 57.374 C) as identified with the earth which is watered by the Nile. However, in this work she is constantly associated with Osiris, the god who best represents the shift I am trying to explain. Such is also the case in Origen, *c. Cels.* 5.38; Heliodorus 9.9; Porphyry, *De imag.* (cited in Eusebius, *Praep. Evang.* 3.11.51); Firmicus Maternus, *Err. prof. rel.* 2.6; Sallustius, *De diis et mundo* 4; Macrobius, *Sat.* 21.11.

⁵¹ *POxy.* 11.1380.125-26 (early 2nd cen. AD).

⁵² Madinet Madi, Hymn to Isis 2.17-18 (Vogliano, *Primo rapporto*, 36). See also 1.11-13 (Ibid., 35). Both of these hymns date to about the 1st cen. BC. Lucian (*Dial. Deor.* 3) also records the tradition that Isis is the divinity who brings forth the Nile flood.

⁵³ Isis Aretalogy of Cyme, 39 (Peek, *Isishymnus*, 124).

⁵⁴ Aelius Aristides, *Or.* 45.32 (ed. Keil). Socrates (*Hist. Eccl.* 1.18) also indicated in late antiquity that this was the belief of the "Greeks."

⁵⁵ Weinreich, *Neue Urkunden*, 16.

⁵⁶ Only in an extremely late source, the *Suidas* (s.v. "Sarapis"), is there a report that "some say that Sarapis is the Nile because he has a modius on his head and carries a cubit."

⁵⁷ Budge, *Gods*, 2.122.

⁵⁸ Tibullus 1.7.27-28; Plutarch, *De Is. et Os.* 32.363 D, 33.364 A, 36.365 B; Aelian, *NA* 10.46; Origen, *c. Cels.* 5.38; Heliodorus 9.9; Porphyry (cited in Eusebius, *Praep. Evang.* 3.11.116); etc.

⁵⁹ Apuleius, *Met.* 11.11.

⁶⁰ See Ch. VI.

CHAPTER FOUR

¹ 2 Kgs 5:12.

² On the Ganges and the mythology which surrounds it see H. Zimmer, *Myths and Symbols in Indian Art and Civilization*, New York, 1946, 109-21.

³ For further discussion see M. Eliade, *Patterns of Comparative Religion*, New York, 1958, 188-215.

⁴ Oliverio, *ASAtene* 1 (1914), 377.

⁵ Salditt-Trappmann, *Tempel*, 66. G. Karo (*AA* 29 [1914], 148) also refers to these objects as "bulls," but his report apparently was entirely dependent upon Oliverio's own accounts and his designation is probably the result of a mistranslation.

⁶ Kater-Sibbes and Vermaseren, *Apis*. Their catalogue has 624 entries but a number of these encompass groups of items. I exclude the coins.

⁷ Ibid., nrs. 66-72, 86, 128, 144-45, 190-91, 278, 281, 292, 325, 350, 389, 465, 494, 522, 553, and Add. 6.

⁸ Ibid., nrs. 66-72.

⁹ Ibid., nrs. 190-91, 494. M. Malaise in a review of this catalogue (*ChronEg* 52 [1977], 104) comments briefly on these various images of the dead Apis.

¹⁰ Kater-Sibbes and Vermaseren are not sure that nrs. 278 and 522 actually depict Apis. Wilhelm Weber (*Terrakotten*, 235) identifies Berlin nr. 8842 (= Kater-Sibbes and Vermaseren nr. 389, though they claim the Berlin inventory number is unknown) as a kneeling cow and insists that Kater-Sibbes and Vermaseren nr. 145 must also be identified in this way since it is identical in iconography. E. Breccia (*Terracotte*, nr. 397), however, called nr. 145 "un bue Apis" but did not choose to explain why he differed from Weber. Perdrizet (*Terres cuites grecques*, 1.53, nr. 155) called nr. 128 (my Pl. IX, 1) an "Apis couché" but W. Deonna (*RArch* 5.20 [1924], 155) apparently considered it a "vache sacrée, couchée." Finally, although Kater-Sibbes and Vermaseren speak of nr. 350 as an Apis figure, Günter Grimm (*Zeugnisse*, 134, nr. 14A) observes that the figure is in a kneeling position and is dedicated to Isis. Therefore, even though there is a crescent moon on the right flank of the animal, Grimm doubts that it represents Apis. On the typology of images of the Apis bull see Roeder, *Ägyptische Bronzefiguren*, 324-33 and Taf. xlvii-xlix, and G. Grimm, "Eine verschollene Apisstatuette aus Mainz," *ZÄS* 95 (1968), 23-24.

¹¹ The identification of several of the remaining eight items (nrs. 86, 144, 281, 292, 325, 465, 553, and Add. 6) is open to serious question. Nrs. 553 and Add. 6 have crowns consisting of a solar disk and twin feathers, a type normally proper to Isis or Hathor (so Malaise, *ChrEg* 52 [1977], 104—see also Roeder, *Ägyptische Bronzefiguren*, 324 and 333). Elsewhere Kater-Sibbes and Vermaseren have recognized that this sort of headdress is unusual on an Apis figure (cf. nrs. 94, 195, 415, 445, and 544—this last said to be "perhaps a Hathor cow"). Consequently, their doubts should have extended to these objects. The two kneeling animals on Flavia Caecilia's grave inscription from Ostia (nr. 292) have often been called Apis bulls, e.g., in SIRIS nr. 532 and in Malaise, *Inventaire*, Ostia nr. 9. However, the accompanying emblems (two sistra, a basket of fruit, and a *situla* with a relief of Harpocrates on it) suggest rather that the animals are cows and represent Isis. I can only say, further, that nr. 325 looks like a rather placid and contented cow—at least to my uneducated urban eye! On the other hand, nrs. 86, 281, and 465 (my Pl. IX, 2) do appear to represent Apis.

¹² Weber (*Terrakotten*, 235) discusses a group of four of these figures: Berlin nr. 8842, Alexandria nr. 23300, Hilton Price Coll. nr. 3279, and Karlsruhe nr. H 1043a.

¹³ Deonna, *RArch*, 5.20 (1924), 155. He catalogues a group of ten terracotta statuettes (Geneva, Mus. d'art et d'hist. = Coll. Forcart nrs. 10242-10250 *bis*) and calls all of them "kneeling sacred cows." Unfortunately he offers neither descriptive details nor illustrations.

¹⁴ Roeder, *Ägyptische Bronzefiguren*, 333-36 and Taf. xlix, b-d, g-h. Roeder lists no kneeling bulls.

¹⁵ Representations of Isis with this type of crown are illustrated in abundance in Dunand, *Culte d'Isis*, vol. 1, pls. vii.1, xviii-xxii, etc.

¹⁶ Hopfner, *Tierkult*, 68-69; Bonnet, "Isis," *Reallexikon*, 328-29.

¹⁷ Apuleius, *Met.* 11.11 is an especially important text. See also Aelian, *NA* 10.27, Diodorus 1.11.4, Herodotus 2.41, Martial 2.14.8, 8.81, 10.48; Ovid, *Ars Am.* 3.393, Plutarch, *De Is. et Os.* 19.358 D and 39.366 E. Of course, the association of Isis with the myth cycle of Io continued as a popular theme down to the end of antiquity. For a list of texts see Hopfner, *Fontes*, 851, s.v. "Io." On the Io myth and its origins see Hicks, *TAPA* 93 (1962), 93-97.

¹⁸ H. Bonnet, ("Kuh," *Reallexikon*, 404-5) provides some Egyptian background on Isis as a kneeling cow. One of the cow divinities from Egypt's earlier history, Shentayet, was normally depicted in a kneeling position. In time this iconographic type came to be understood as a form of Isis in mourning for Osiris. By Graeco-Roman times any vestigial connection of this image with Shentayet was forgotten; it had become simply a representation of Isis. Cf. also Griffiths, *Isis-Book,* 220.

¹⁹ Plutarch, *De Is. et Os.* 39.366 D-F.

²⁰ Merkelbach, *Isisfeste*, 38; Griffiths, *Plutarch's De Iside*, 450.

²¹ Plutarch, *De Is. et Os.* 52.372 C. 17 Athyr (Alexandrian calendar) = 28 Choiach (Sothic calendar). If 28 Choiach is taken as a date in the Alexandrian calendar, it is equivalent to our December 24, i.e., the approximate time of the winter solstice. See Merkelbach, *Isisfeste*, 38.

²² Herodotus, 2.131-32.

²³ Griffiths, *Plutarch's De Iside*, 450; Griffiths, *Isis-Book,* 219-20; Bonnet, "Kuh," *Reallexikon*, 404.

²⁴ Wilhelm Spiegelberg (*Die Glaubwürdigkeit von Herodots Bericht über Ägypten im Lichte der ägyptischen Denkmäler*, Heidelberg, 1926, 42, n. 11) says that this cow probably was an image of Neith. However, long before Herodotus' time, a syncretism had taken place between Isis and Neith. For evidence see Dunand, *Culte d'Isis*, 1.17-18.

²⁵ Martial 2.14.8.

²⁶ Apuleius, *Met.* 11.11.

²⁷ Merkelbach, *Isisfeste*, 40.

²⁸ Dog-headed Anubis may come in the procession right before the Isis cow because of his traditional role as her guide in the search for Osiris. See Diodorus 1.87.3.

²⁹ Griffiths, *Plutarch's De Iside*, 51, 451-52; Griffiths, *Isis-Book,* 219.

³⁰ Merkelbach, *Isisfeste*, 37, 58.

³¹ Plutarch, *De Is. et Os.* 39.366 F. See also 32.363 D.

³² Apuleius, *Met.* 11.11: omniparentis deae fecundum simulacrum. "Fecundum" is closely parallel to Plutarch's χάρπιμον in the text above.

³³ Clement of Alexandria, *Strom.* 5.7.

³⁴ Nonnus 3.279-82.

[35] Tran Tam Tinh and Labrecque, *Isis lactans*, 1-7 and pl. 1.

[36] *PAH* 1.1.171; Hamilton, *Archaeologia* 4 (1776) 166; Mazois and Gau, *Ruines*, vol. 4, pl. x; Niccolini, *Case*, 1.2.13; Breton, *Pompeia*, 51; Lafaye, *Histoire*, 191; Mau, *Pompeii*, 173; Tran Tam Tinh, *Essai*, 35.

[37] Margaret Bieber, *The Sculpture of the Hellenistic Age*, 2nd ed., New York, 1961, 41.

[38] A flaming torch or similar object is a regular attribute of Cupid especially in Hellenistic and Roman times. Usually it is a sign of the small god's power to arouse amorous desire. See A Fürtwängler, "Eros," *LM* 1.1.1364-65, and M. Collignon, "Cupido," *DAGR* 1.2.1601.

[39] The lighted candlestick held by the cupid has the form of a *candelabrum*. This type of candlestick, among other things, was used in wedding precessions. Cf. E. Saglio, "Candelabrum," *DAGR* 1.2.871 and fig. 1083.

[40] The patronal deity both of Pompeii and of the Julian house was Venus.

[41] On evidence for this identification see Drexler, *LM* 2.494-99 and Tran Tam Tinh, *Essai*, 83, n. 3. In the southeast corner of the portico of the Pompeii sanctuary stood a large statue of Venus/Aphrodite Anadyomene. This is described in *PAH* 1.1.165; a drawing of it is found in Gusman, *Pompéi*, 83. In the northeast corner opposite stood a statue of Isis of slightly larger size. The symmetrical placement of these two images in the two corners of the portico behind the central temple strongly suggests their association.

[42] Sourdille, *Hérodote*, 188-89.

[43] J. G. Griffiths, *The Conflict of Horus and Seth*, Liverpool, 1960, 86-89. Month is never spoken of in the Graeco-Roman cult of Isis and Sarapis.

[44] R. Merkelbach (*Latomus* 24 [1965], 146), the only person to suggest a reason why this theme found a place in the sanctuary, believed that it expressed the divine salvation of mankind from the pressures and constraints of life.

[45] See Ch. II, n. 98.

[46] Herodotus 2.91. Herodotus says elsewhere (6.54) that the Persians admitted that they had no bond of kinship with Perseus but that his ancestors, as the Greeks also said, were Egyptians. On Chemmis (Panopolis/Achmim) see J. Karig, "Achmim," *LÄ* 1. 54-55.

[47] Lloyd, *JHS* 89 (1969), 85-86.

[48] Iconomopoulos, "Les jeux gymniques de Panopolis," *REG* 2 (1889) 164-68. Text: Ἱερὸς εἰσελαστικὸς οἰκουμενικὸς ὀλύμπιος ἀγὼν Περσέως οὐρανίου τῶν μεγάλων Πανείων. Wainwright (*JEA* 21 [1935], 157, n. 13) indicates that this text is to be dated c. 100 AD.

[49] Diodorus 1.24.

[50] Herodotus 2.15.

[51] Strabo 17.1.18.

[52] Pliny, *HN*. 15.46. The scholiast on Nicander, *Alexipharmaca* 201 reported that Nicander flew in the face of the common opinion that Perseus had planted this tree in Egypt when he said that it had been planted, rather, at Mycenae.

[53] Pliny, *HN*. 15.46. Traditions linking Perseus with Egypt must have been congenial to the Ptolemaic dynasty with its links both to Alexander and to Egypt.

[54] W. Drexler, "Perseus auf alexandrinischen Kaisermünzen," *Wochenschrift für klassische Philologie* 13 (1896), 28-30. The coins are from the 15th year of Gallienus (= Poole, nr. 2213 and pl. 17), the 1st and 2nd years of Claudius II, the 8th year of Diocletian, and the 8th year of Maximinus.

[55] For a survey of the various Perseus traditions see E. Kuhnert, "Perseus," *LM* 3.2.1986-2060 and, though less complete by far, Woodward, *Perseus*.

⁵⁶ Aphthonius, *Progymnasmata* (ed. Rabe) 48: τῆς μὲν οὖν αὐλῆς οὐχ εἰς ἅπας ὁ κόσμος· ἄλλο μὲν γὰρ ἄλλως ἦν· τὸ δὲ τὰ Περσέως εἶχεν ἀθλήματα.

⁵⁷ G. Maspero, *Histoire ancienne des peuples de l'Orient*, 4th ed., Paris, 1886, 21-22: Min as "the Runner" (*Pehresou*). Serge Sauneron, "Persée, Dieu de Khemmis," *REg* 14 (1962), 55-56: Min as "the Watcher" (*P-ouerche*, which becomes Ποϱσεῦς).

⁵⁸ The rite in question is the "Climbing Ceremony of Min," a ceremony known from various reliefs (H. Gauthier, *Les fêtes du dieu Min*, Cairo, 1931, 142-50). Scholars such as K. Sethe ("Chemmis," *RE* 3.2. 2233), L. Castiglione (*MélMichałowski*, 43) and, though with some hesitancy, C. J. Bleeker (*Geburt*, 53-54) equated this ritual with an athletic contest and so viewed the Perseus games as a "further development" of this ceremony. However, Gauthier (*Fêtes*, 149-50) and Lloyd (*JHS* 89 [1969], 83) point out that the so-called "Climbing Ceremony" is actually the "raising of the *shnt*," i.e., the erection of a hut for the sacred bull of Min.

⁵⁹ Wainwright, *JEA* 21 (1935), 154 and 157: Min and Perseus both sky gods and gods of the thunderbolt. Sourdille, *Hérodote*, 212: Min and Perseus both had contacts with foreign lands. S. Morenz, *FF* 36 (1962), 307-9: Min and Perseus both associated with rain and both struggle against the evil power of the sea. Others who affirm this identification of Perseus with Min: A. Wiedemann, "Perseus in Ägypten," *Philologus* 50 (1891), 179-80 and Lindsay, *Men and Gods*, 341-47. Wilhelm Drexler ("Min," *LM* 2.2.2981-82) also discusses the Min-Perseus hypothesis but is less certain of its validity.

⁶⁰ Wainwright (*JEA* 21 [1935], 156 and 162) and Bleeker (*Geburt*, 11-12 and 15-18) summarize this evidence.

⁶¹ Plutarch, *De Is. et Os.* 56.374 B. For a discussion of this text see Bleeker, *Geburt*, 16-17.

⁶² Lloyd, *JHS* 89 (1969), 79-86.

⁶³ Ibid., 81 and 84.

⁶⁴ Tran Tam Tinh, *Essai*, 143-46 and pls. vii-x.

⁶⁵ In one of the frescoes mentioned above this god is found, it is thought, under the feet of Sarapis. Cf. Ibid., 145 and pl. viii. 1.

⁶⁶ Plutarch, *De Is. et Os.* 32.363 D. This identification of Seth/Typhon with the sea is also found in *De Is. et Os.* 33.364 A and 40.367 A-B.

⁶⁷ Plutarch, *De Is. et Os.* 32.363 E: καταναλισκόμενος.

⁶⁸ Ibid. See also *De Is. et Os.* 5.352 F.

⁶⁹ Ibid., 32.363 F. Elsewhere Plutarch makes it clear that the priests abstained both from sea fish and from all other kinds of fish (*De Is. et Os.* 7.353 D).

⁷⁰ Ibid., 32.364 A: Κοινήν ... τὴν ἱστορίαν.

⁷¹ Griffiths, *Plutarch's De Iside*, 59 and 124.

⁷² Bonnet ("Seth," *Reallexikon*, 712), for example, offers some evidence from Pharaonic times for a connection between Seth and the sea. Nowhere, however, can there be verified for this earlier period the range of practices and beliefs which Plutarch knew as common tradition.

⁷³ Apollodorus 2.4.3. So also Sophocles—see A. Nauck, ed., *Tragicorum graecorum fragmenta*, 2nd ed., Leipzig, 1889, 175-77.

⁷⁴ Antiphilus, *Anth. Pal.* 16.147; Hyginus, *Fab.* 64; Lactantius, *Div. Inst.* 4.19. According to the latter, Andromeda was compared to the Nymphs. This is probably only a carelessly reported version of the same general line of tradition.

⁷⁵ Lucian, *Dial. Mar.* 14.1.

⁷⁶ Schauenburg, *Perseus*, 59-60. J. Woodward (*Perseus*, fig. 31) provides an illustration of this motif found on a South Italian vase of the 4th cen. BC.

⁷⁷ Plutarch, *De Is. et Os.* 40.367 A-B.

⁷⁸ Horus' close connection with the beneficent waters of the Nile is attested in a variety of Ptolemaic sources— see Bonneau, *Crue du Nil*, 274, n. 1. In a later era Heliodorus wrote that the Egyptians call the Nile "Horus" and "life-giving," Ὧρον τε καὶ ζείδωρον (9.22). While the Nile is much more commonly associated with Osiris, it is no surprise that the god who always appears in this period as Osiris' son would be endowed with his powers.

Even as a child Horus (= Harpocrates) was a conqueror of evil powers—see Pl. X. On Harpocrates as a warrior deity see Meeks, *LÄ* 2.1007.

⁷⁹ Plutarch, *De Is. et Os.* 39.366 F.

⁸⁰ Hugo Gressmann (*Tod und Auferstehung des Osiris nach Festbräuchen und Umzügen*, Berlin, 1923, 4) is quite certain that the "sea" to which the group of worshippers descends is the Nile rather than the Mediterranean. Historically this may have been the actual case for the practice recorded by Plutarch—19 Athyr (= November 15) is hardly flood season—but there is every reason to believe that Plutarch himself was thinking of the Mediterranean since his usage of θάλαττα in the surrounding passages clearly refers to that body of water in contrast to the Nile. See Bonneau, *Crue du Nil*, 247.

⁸¹ Aelius Aristides, *Or.* 36.10 and 45.29 (ed. Keil). The account of such a miracle probably appears in *POxy.* 11.1382, a text of the 2nd cen. AD, although too little survives of the narrative to be certain. See O. Weinreich, *Neue Urkunden*, 14-17 and Merkelbach, *Isisfeste*, 35, n. 28.

⁸² Lucan 8.444-45.

⁸³ Statius, *Theb.* 8.358-62: Qualis ubi aversi secretus pabula caeli / Nilus et Eoas magno bibit ore pruinas, / scindit fontis opes septemque patentibus arvis / in mare fert hiemes; paenitus cessere fugatae / Nereides dulcique timent occurrere ponto.

⁸⁴ Frank Moore Cross (*Canaanite Myth and Hebrew Epic*, Cambridge, Mass., 1973, 113) has pointed out how widespread this myth was in the ancient Near East. In its origin, the story of the struggle between Baal and Yamm/Sea, also told as a struggle between Baal and Lotan/Leviathan, the sea dragon, served as a cosmogonic myth (Ibid., 120). Plutarch's account of Horus' victory over Seth/Sea follows precisely this line for it is the story of the creation of the land of Egypt.

Lloyd compares Perseus' struggle against the sea monster with representations of Horus fighting hippopotami and other confederate beasts of Seth. He notes as well that Seth himself is called a "monster" in a text from the Eighteenth Dynasty. (See Lloyd, *JHS* 89 [1969], 84). However, additional evidence from Egypt points to a more direct link with the fundamental myth. The story of Astarte and the Sea, popular in Egypt since the New Kingdom, is a tale which reveals close links with northwest Semitic sources (Ibid., 83; Wilson, *Culture*, 261. For a translation of the story see A. H. Gardiner, *Late-Egyptian Stories,* Brussels, 1932, 76-80). In it *Seth* assumes the role of Baal and fights against the Sea (so also in *PHearst* 11.12-14 and *PBerlin* 3038. xxi. 3, both texts from the New Kingdom). This is intelligible enough since one of Seth's functions before he was downgraded during the last part of the second and first part of the first millenium to his more familiar demonic status (Te Velde, *Seth*, 141-51; Morenz, *FF* 36 [1962], 309) was to serve as guardian deity for seafarers (Te Velde, *Seth*, 122-23; Bonnet, "Seth," *Reallexikon*, 712). At Mt. Kasios, a site east of Pelusium on the northeastern coast of Egypt, Seth, who was there identified with Baal Zephon, originally received honors as the patron of sea travelers. (On the collocation of Seth and Baal see Te Velde, *Seth*, 120-33). However, a transformation, one which must have been repeated elsewhere during the same period, took place there once Seth began to be viewed as a hostile and demonic power. Horus became the chief deity of the sanctuary and assumed these functions while Seth himself became simply identified with the sea (Ibid.). This Mt. Kasios was named after the Mt. Kasios near Syrian Antioch at which Baal Zephon was honored from a very early date and with which the struggle between Zeus and the monster Typhon is also associated (Apollodorus 1.6.3. This tradition may lie behind Homer, *Il.* 2.781-83). It is this Typhon with which, of course, Seth became identified in Graeco-Roman times. I conclude therefore that the Perseus/Horus vs. Seth struggle is only one of the more recent manifestations of a cosmogonic tradition stretching far back into Near Eastern history.

In respect to the evidence from Egypt's Mt. Kasios sanctuary, I would note here that three inscriptions dedicated to Zeus Kasios were found at Serapeum A on Delos. Two of these (*CE* 16 and 16 *bis* = *I Délos* 2180-81) were dedicated by Horus, son of Horus, of Kasion to the Great God, to Zeus Kasios, and to Tachnepsis in perhaps the late 2nd cen. BC. A third (*CE* 17 = *I Délos* 2182) honored Zeus Kasios and was given by Xenophon, son of Dionysus, of Beirut (βηρύτιος). Roussel (*CE*, p. 295) rightly connects Tachnepsis with Isis since this epithet is used in *POxy.* 11.1380.74-75 for the goddess in her cult at Mt. Kasios. While he thinks that the Great God is Sarapis, he offers this only as a guess (Ibid., 98). Although these texts were not found in connection with the Nile water facility in this sanctuary, they do afford further evidence that the myths related to the cult of Horus at Mt. Kasios had found their way into the Graeco-Roman cult of Isis and Sarapis. (A fragmentary list of priests for various cults, mostly Egyptian, turned up at Athens [SIRIS 30]. One of the priests listed in this document of the 3rd cen. AD served Zeus Kasios.)

[85] Cross, *Canaanite Myth and Hebrew Epic*, 116. See also pp. 116-18.

[86] Te Velde, *Seth*, 141-51; Bonnet, "Seth," *Reallexikon*, 712.

[87] Aelius Aristides, *Or.* 11.331 (ed. Keil). On this aspect of Dionysus see H. S. Versnel, "Pentheus en Dionysos," *Lampas* 9 (1976), 22.

[88] See F. Brommer, *Die Königstochter und das Ungeheuer*, Marburg, 1955, 7.

[89] Isis Aretalogy of Cyme, 48 (= Peek, *Isishymnus*, 124): Εγὼ τοὺς ἐν δεσμοῖς λύω. Another aretalogy relates this theme to the compulsion of Necessity: Isis Aretalogy of Andros, 144-45 (= Peek, *Isishymnus,* 21; cf. p. 65): Δεσμῶν δ' ἀέκουσαν ἀνάγκαν ἀνλύω. Cf. also Isis Aretalogy of Andros, 96-97 = Peek, *Isishymnus*, 19.

[90] Philostratus, *VA* 7.38. Related to this, as Reitzenstein (*Hellenistische Wundererzählungen*, Stuttgart, 1963, 120-22) recognized, are several Christian accounts of a miraculous deliverance from prison—see Acts 16:25-27, Acts of Thomas 118-22, etc.

[91] *Eighth Book of Moses* = *PGM* 13.294-96. Cf. also *PGM* 1.101-2, *PGM* 12.160-62, and Philostratus, *VA* 7.34. See O. Weinreich, "Türoffnung im Wunder-, Prodigen- und Zauberglaube," *Religionsgeschichtliche Studien*, Darmstadt, 1968, 281-342.

[92] Possibly such hopes even extended to deliverance from death. Scenes of the rescue of Andromeda by Perseus (as also those of the rescue of Hesione by Heracles) are found in tombs and on sarcophagi—see R. Strong and N. Joliffe, "The Stuccoes of the Underground Basilica Near the Porta Maggiore," *JHS* 44 (1924), 78.

CHAPTER FIVE

[1] Even a larger number of writers showed interest in the question of what caused the Nile flood. Bonneau (*Crue du Nil*, 213) found discussions of this problem in the writings of seventy different authors.

² Classical writers: Herodotus, Aeschylus, and Dinon. Early Hellenistic writers: Aristotle, Aristobulus, Theophrastus, Apollonius Rhodius, Hippys of Rhegium, Theocritus, and Polybius.

³ A good example of this phenomenon is the so-called "Egyptomania" which swept Roman Italy at the end of the 1st cen. BC and during the 1st cen. AD. On this see Baltrušaitis, *Essai* and Köberlein, *Caligula*.

⁴ For this reason my primary focus is upon writings which were intended to be read by an international audience. Non-literary papyrological texts from Egypt, works aimed only at a very localized audience, will enter into the following discussion only in a secondary capacity.

⁵ Dölger, *AntChrist* 5 (1936), 174.

⁶ Ibid., 171.

⁷ Bonneau (*Crue du Nil*, 278-79), for example, argued that for Egyptians the Nile was able to renew not only parched soil but also dead human bodies. This view, she claimed, continued to survive in the Graeco-Roman cult.

⁸ Diodorus, 1.36.2.

⁹ Seneca, *QNat.* 3.1.2; 4a.2.1.

¹⁰ Pomponius Mela 1.9.49.

¹¹ Arnobius, *Adv. Nat.* 4.16.

¹² Ammianus Marcellinus 22.15.3 (ed. Seyfarth): *benivolo omnium flumine Nilo.*

¹³ *C.H., Asclepius* 24 (ed. Nock-Festugière).

¹⁴ *POxy.* 3.486.32 (131 AD) and 12.1409.17 (278 AD): τοῦ ἱερωτάτου Νείλου.

¹⁵ An inscription from Ptolemais published by J. U. Powell (*Collectanea alexandrina*, Oxford, 1925, 138) which records a prayer asking Asclepius to give the city the "everlasting streams of the Nile" (Νείλου δὲ ῥοὰς ... ἀϊδίους) is another illustration of this pattern.

¹⁶ Heliodorus 9.22.

¹⁷ This theme was discussed above in Ch. III.

¹⁸ Aristaenetus (*De Nili bonis* [cited in Eudocia, *Violar.* 698]) described the Nile festival as it was celebrated in Egypt. In the course of it, he said, hymns customarily sung in honor of Zeus were chanted to the Nile because, as they believe, this river does the work of Zeus and waters the land.

¹⁹ Hermann, *JAC* 2 (1959), 52-55.

²⁰ Strabo 15.1.23.

²¹ Pliny, *HN* 5.10.58: *Idem amnis unus omnium nullas expirat auras.* Ammianus Marcellinus (22.15.13) seems to have used Pliny as a source when he says "solusque [Nilus] fluminum auras nullas expirat." A third such statement appears in Heliodorus 2.28.

²² Eustathius, *In Dionysium Periegetam* 222.

²³ Heliodorus 9.22.

²⁴ Achilles Tatius 4.12.2-3. See Bonneau, *Crue du Nil,* 29-33 for a general discussion.

²⁵ See Nilsson, *GGR*, 2.505 and F. Cumont, *Astrology and Religion among the Greeks and Romans*, New York, 1960, 60-63.

²⁶ Nilsson, Ibid., 504-5, n. 4.

²⁷ Bonneau, *Crue du Nil,* 289.

²⁸ Aeschylus, *Supp.* 560: νόσοις ἄθικτον.

²⁹ Aelius Aristides, *Or.* 36.124 (ed. Keil). Both the context provided by 36.123 and a somewhat parallel passage in 45.32 make it clear that Aristides is referring to Sarapis and that he does not consider this god to be a power immanent within the Nile River.

[30] Achilles Tatius 4.18.34. English trans. by S. Gaselee (Loeb Classical Library, London, 1917).

[31] Nile water in fact often had to be filtered before it could be drunk. Receptacles for filtering this water are referred to in Rufinus, *Hist. Eccl.* 11.26 and in Oribasius 5.5.1 (ed. J. Raeder). See also Bonneau, *Crue du Nil*, 105. As for the "coolness" of the water, Diodorus (1.40.4) spoke of how the river was warmed as it passed through the torrid zone and Heliodorus (2.23 and 2.28.5) said that Nile water was luke-warm to the touch. Perhaps like the English, Achilles Tatius liked his drinks fairly warm!

[32] Aeschylus, *PV.* 812.

[33] Oribasius, *Coll. Med.* 22.5 (ed. V. Rose, *Aristotelis qui ferebantur librorum fragmenta*, Leipzig, 1886, p. 219).

[34] Cited in Eusebius, *Praep. Evang.* 9.10.413a. This manner of defining true Egyptians is found already in Herodotus 2.18.

[35] Seneca, *QNat.* 4a.2.30.

[36] Aelius Aristides, *Or.* 36.116 (ed. Keil).

[37] *Hist. Aug., Pescennius Niger* 7.7. The usual terms, γλυκύς or *dulcis*, when used of water, normally refer to its freshness. However, the common motif that Nile water is a replacement for wine introduces a certain ambiguity in this case. Nile water as γλυκύς or *dulcis* is both fresh *and* sweet, i.e., not only not bitter like brackish or salt water but actually tasting sweet like wine.

Others who speak of the sweetness of Nile water: Theophrastus, *On Waters* (cited in Athenaeus 2.15.41e); Diodorus 1.40.4 and 1.40.7; *Anth. Graeca* 9.386.4; Plutarch, *Quaest. conv.* 8.5.725 E; Achilles Tatius 4.12.3; and Heliodorus 2.23 and 2.28.5. *Corpus Hermeticum* 13.17 probably refers specifically to Nile water. Philostratus (*VA* 6.11) makes mention of a tradition that at the time of a certain Nile flood honey was found mixed with the waters of the river. Surely the property of sweetness played a role in the formulation of this story. Philostratus himself seems to have become aware of this miracle from reading or hearing Egyptian accounts. For a further discussion of this legend see Bonneau, *Crue du Nil*, 106, n. 5.

[38] Diodorus 1.40.4. See also, however, 1.40.7.

[39] Plutarch, *Quaest. conv.* 8.5.725 E.

[40] Heliodorus 2.23.

[41] *Corpus Hermeticum* 13.17.

[42] Bonneau (*Crue du Nil*, 108-9) offers a brief discussion of this practice.

[43] Aelius Aristides, *Or.* 36.116 (ed. Keil).

[44] Epiphanius, *Adv. Haeres.* 51.30.3. Epiphanius is the only source I have discovered which speaks of a transformation of Nile water into wine. Perhaps he has heard of, but confused, accounts like those given by Aristides and Achilles Tatius. Merkelbach (*Isisfeste*, 17 and 49) is rather inclined to take seriously the reference to a transformation into wine and appeals to Osiris' identification with Dionysus. While such a link between the two gods is surely pertinent, I do not find the evidence he presents for such expectations very convincing. See also Bonneau, *Crue du Nil*, 291-92.

The time of year for the drawing of this water is odd, and it is not attested elsewhere. Merkelbach (*Isisfeste*, 49) is undoubtedly correct when he says that such a ritual looked to the drawing of water on the day of the Nile flood as its prime analogate. Perhaps, like the "Finding of Osiris" festival in November, this represented a proleptic or even magical gesture to assure a proper Nile flood. I frankly doubt whether water drawn from the Nile at its low January level was utilized for cultic rites at sanctuaries of Isis and Sarapis.

⁴⁵ Herodotus 3.6.

⁴⁶ Dinon, *Persica* (cited in Athenaeus 2.67b and in Plutarch, *Alex.* 36.2).

⁴⁷ Dinon, *Persica* (cited in Plutarch, *Alex.* 36.2). The Egyptians were also required to send a salt called ammoniac but this does not appear to have shared the same significance.

⁴⁸ Polybius (cited in Athenaeus 2.45c).

⁴⁹ Juvenal 6.526-29.

⁵⁰ Dölger, *AntChrist* 5 (1936), 177.

⁵¹ Diodorus 1.36.2; Ammianus Marcellinus 22.15.3.

⁵² On this theme see Bonneau, *Crue du Nil*, 130-31.

⁵³ Wilson, *Culture*, 9.

⁵⁴ Theocritus, *Id.* 17.79-80.

⁵⁵ Aeschylus, *Pers.* 33.

⁵⁶ Vergil, *Georg.* 4.287-92.

⁵⁷ Themistius, *Or.* 24.305d. He says that this is not the reason that *he* marvels at the Nile but because this river flows through the land of the Egyptian philosophers. Apparently others, e.g., Pseudo-Plutarch (*De esu carn.* 1.3.994 B), less moved by such exalted concerns, were happy to allow themselves to marvel at a river which provided more mundane and tangible benefits.

⁵⁸ Virtually all of the discussions of the causes of the Nile flood or of the rivalry between rain and the Nile touch upon this point in one way or another. The Nile's contribution to agriculture is reflected in several epithets attested in writings from the Roman period: Oppian, *Cyneg.* 2.85: "wheat-bearing" (πυροφόρος); *Orac. Sibyl.* 4.74: "nurturer of grain" (σταχυητρόφος); Nonnus 31.37: "grain-endowed" (σταχυώδης); and Pseudo-Plutarch, *De esu carn.* 1.3.994 B: "crop-bearing" (χαρποφόρος).

⁵⁹ Nonnus 26.229-34. For the same sort of imagery see Avienus, *Desc. Orb. Terr.* 340.

⁶⁰ Libanius, *Or.* 30.35-36.

⁶¹ Pomponius Mela 1.9.49; Pliny, *HN* 21.50.86.

⁶² In 392 AD segments of the Christian populace finally nerved themselves to destroy the cult image of Sarapis, the god thought to be responsible for the Nile flood. As Rufinus reported, "Everyone believed that Sarapis on account of the destruction and burning of his cult image [in the Serapeum at Alexandria] would not give the customary Nile flood. But then God, to show that not Sarapis ... but he himself was the one who commands the waters of the river to rise at their proper time, gave a high Nile flood such as previous ages had never witnessed." Only then did the Christians feel strong enough to take the sacred cubit from the Serapeum to a Christian church (Rufinus, *Hist. Eccl.* 11.30). On this see also Socrates, *Hist. Eccl.* 1.18 and Sozomen, *Hist. Eccl.* 7.20. This feeling on the part of the Egyptians is discussed by Hermann, *JAC* 2 (1959) 33-35.

⁶³ Vergil, *Georg.* 4.291.

⁶⁴ Seneca, *QNat.* 4a.2.9-10. So also Servius (*ad Aen.* 9.31) and the Christian author Isidore of Seville (*Etym.* 13.21.7). According to a lyric poem dating from c. 200 AD and quoted by Hippolytus (*Haer.* 5.7.5), it is rather the Nile that fattens and enriches the silt (ἰλύν). The writer almost certainly must mean ἰλύς in the sense of the already existing soil rather than, as more usual, the mud or silt carried by the water.

⁶⁵ Philostratus, *VA* 6.6.

⁶⁶ Vergil, *Aen.* 9.31; Dionysius Periegetes, *Orb. terr. desc.* 221. Seneca (*QNat.* 4a.2.9) called the silt carried by the Nile "pingue."

⁶⁷ Plutarch, *De Is. et Os.* 5.353 A; Aelian, *NA* 11.10; Dionysius Periegetes, *Orb. terr. desc.* 227.

⁶⁸ Plutarch, *De Is. et Os.* 5.353 A; Aelian, *NA* 11.10. Aelian says that because this water is sweet and good for bringing about a weight gain, an animal on a steady diet of it will become fat.

⁶⁹ See, for example, Ammianus Marcellinus 22.15.14: *Exuberat Aegyptus etiam pecudibus multis, inter quas terrestres sunt et aquatiles, aliaeque humi et in humoribus vivunt, unde amphibioi nominantur.*

⁷⁰ Cited by Strabo 15.1.22: καὶ τὸν Νεῖλον δ᾽ εἶναι γόνιμον μᾶλλον ἑτέρων καὶ μεγαλοφυῆ γεννᾶν καὶ τἆλλα καὶ τὰ ἀμφίβια. So also Theocritus, *Id.* 17.98; Diodorus 1.40.7; and Seneca, *QNat.* 4a.2.12.

⁷¹ Pomponius Mela 1.9.52: *[Nilus] ... aestivo sidere exundans ... irrigat, adeo efficacibus aquis ad generandum alendumque, ut praeter id quod scatet piscibus, quod hippopotamos crocodilosque vastas beluas gignit ....*

⁷² Pomponius Mela 1.9.49.

⁷³ Aeschylus, *Supp.* 854-57.

⁷⁴ Aelian, *NA* 3.33.

⁷⁵ Pomponius Mela 1.9.49.

⁷⁶ Aristotle, *Hist. An.* 7.4.584b: Περὶ μὲν Αἴγυπτον ... ὅπου εὔτεκφοροι αἱ γυναῖκες καὶ φέρουσί τε πολλὰ ῥᾳδίως καὶ τίκτουσι, καὶ γενόμενα δύναται ζῆν, κἂν τερατώδη γένηται.

⁷⁷ Aristotle, *Gen. An.* 4.4.770a. I have not seen this particular observation elsewhere in ancient literature.

⁷⁸ Aristotle, *Hist. An.* 7.4.584b.

⁷⁹ Ibid. Cited also in Aulus Gellius, *NA.* 10.2. This latter writer knew of a report that quintuplets had been born to a family outside of Rome in the district near Laurentum.

⁸⁰ Cited in Solinus 1.51. Strabo (15.1.22) attributes this tradition to a report of Aristotle.

⁸¹ Pliny, *HN.* 7.3.33. According to Strabo (15.1.22), births of four children at once were not uncommon in Egypt. Joannes Lydus (*De mensibus* 4.57) reported a story that a certain Egyptian woman was sent to the Emperor Hadrian because she had given birth to four children over a period of four days and then to a fifth infant forty days later.

⁸² Solinus 1.51. So also Pliny, *HN.* 7.3.33: "drinking the water of the Nile causes fecundity" (*fetifer potu Nilus amnis*).

⁸³ Seneca, *QNat.* 3.25.11: *Quare aqua Nilotica fecundiores feminas faciat, adeo ut quarundam viscera longa sterilitate praeclusa ad conceptum relaxaverit?* Seneca reports this popular view in interrogative form; he himself is somewhat sceptical that Nile water will actually work in this fashion.

⁸⁴ Aristotle, *Hist. An.* 7.4.584b.

⁸⁵ Oribasius, *Coll. Med.* 22.5 (ed. V. Rose).

⁸⁶ Oribasius 5.3.15 (ed. J. Raeder).

⁸⁷ Theophrastus, *On Waters* (cited in Athenaeus 2.15.41f).

⁸⁸ Aeschylus, *Supp.* 855-57: ὕδωρ / ἔνθεν ἀεξόμενον / ζωόφυτον αἷμα βροτοῖσι θάλλει.

⁸⁹ The ancient Nile god, Hapi, was considered by Egyptians to be male-female. As male he was a creator figure and as female he was a giver of life and nourishment (Hermann, *JAC* 2 [1959] 32).

⁹⁰ Hippys of Rhegium, *Chronica* (ed. C. Müller, *Fragmenta historicorum graecorum*, Leipzig, 1841-70, 2.13, frag. 1) = Schol. Apollonius Rhodius 4.262: γονιμώτατον;

Maximus of Tyre 25.7: γόνιμος; Porphyry (cited in Eusebius, *Praep. Evang.* 5.7.192c): παρὰ γονίμοις χεύμασι Νείλου; Pseudo-Plutarch, *De esu carn.* 1.3.994 B: γονίμου καὶ καρποφόρου ῥεύματος; Orphic Hymn 55.19: γονιμώδεα λουτρά; Nonnus 6.339-40: Νεῖλος ... ῥοθίῳ γονόεντι. Other sources found in Egypt have the epithet γόνιμος. E.g., *POxy.* 3.425 (2nd-3rd cen. AD); 16. 1830.4-6 (6th cen.); a 4th cen. AD inscription from Achoris (*Sammelbuch griechischer Inschriften aus Ägypten* nr. 6598).

Theophrastus, *On Waters* (cited in Athenaeus 2.15.41f.): πολυγνώτατον; Diodorus 1.10.1: πολύγονον; 1.37.8: πολυγονώτατον ... πάντων τῶν γνωριζομένων ποταμῶν; 1.40.7: πολύγονος.

⁹¹ Pliny, *HN* 5.10.54: *Nilus fecundus;* Statius, *Silv.* 3.2.108: *fecunda licentia Nili;* Rufinus, *Hist. Eccl.* 11.23: *Aegyptus opibus et fecunditate [Nili] pascatur;* Avienus, *Ar. Phaen.* 797-98: *largos segetes quod nutriat Nili anni / arentisque locos unda fecundat alumna.* Tibullus 1.7.22: *fertilis ... Nilus.*

⁹² Pomponius Mela 1.9.52: *Nilus ... glaebis etiam infundat animas, ex ipsaque humo vitalia effingat. Hoc eo manifestum est, quod ubi sedavit diluvia ac se sibi reddidit, per umentes campos quaedam nondum perfecta animalia sed tum primum accipientia spiritum et ex parte iam formata, ex parte adhuc terrena visuntur.*

⁹³ Diodorus 1.10.2; Pliny, *HN.* 9.84.179; Macrobius, *Sat.* 7.16.12.

⁹⁴ Horapollo 1.25; Ovid, *Met.* 1.422-37; Joannes Lydus, *De mensibus* 4.107. The traditional understanding of the frog in Egypt as a symbol of rebirth and of resurrection no doubt is related to such a tradition as Horapollo reports. On this see L. Kákosy, "Frosch," *LÄ* 2.334-36, W. Deonna, "La grenouille et le lion," *BCH* 74 (1950), 1-9, and J. Leclant, "La grenouille d'éternité des pays du Nil au monde Méditerranéen," *HomVermaseren* 2.561-72. There is a whole series of "Frog-lamps"—many of these have the inscription ἐγώ εἰμι ἀνάστασις (Maria L. Bernhard, *Lampki starożytne*, Warsaw, 1955; further bibliography in Grimm, *Zeugnisse*, 127-28).

⁹⁵ Diodorus 1.10.2-3.

⁹⁶ Diodorus 1.10.6-7. The empirical data provided in the first half of this passage does not, of course, prove the popular tradition cited by Diodorus in the second half. While this divergence might rouse our own scepticism, Diodorus himself must have considered both statements as making the same point.

⁹⁷ Hippolytus, *Haer.* 5.7.5 = J. M. Edmonds, ed., *Lyra Graeca* (Loeb Classical Library), Cambridge, Mass., 1967, 3. 486, nr. 131.21-24: Αἰγυπτίαν δὲ Νεῖλος ἰλυν ἐπιλιπαίνων / ζῳογενεῖ μέχρι σήμερον / ὑγρᾷ σαρκούμενα θερμότητι / ζῷα σώματα τ' ἀνδίδωσιν.

⁹⁸ Besides the eight authors mentioned above, there is also a pertinent reference in Servius (*ad Georg.* 3.478).

⁹⁹ Theophrastus, *On Waters* (cited in Athenaeus 2.15.41f.); Diodorus 1.40.7. See also Plutarch, *Quaest. conv.* 8.5.725 E and *Corpus Hermeticum* 13.17.

¹⁰⁰ Plutarch, *Quaest. conv.* 8.5.725 E: ὁ δὲ Νεῖλος ... γλυκύτητος μὲν ἀπολαύει καὶ χυμῶν ἀναπίμπλαται δύναμιν ἐμβριθῆ καὶ τρόφιμον ἐχόντων ....

¹⁰¹ *Corpus Hermeticum* 13.17: ὑμνεῖν μέλλω τὸν τῆς κτίσεως κύριον ... καὶ ἐπιτάξαντα ἐκ τοῦ ὠκεανοῦ τὸ γλυκὺ ὕδωρ εἰς τὴν οἰκουμένην καὶ ἀοίκητον ὑπάρχειν εἰς διατροφὴν καὶ κτίσιν πάντων τῶν ἀνθρώπων. The writer mentions first the earth, then the sky, then water, and finally fire. He therefore addresses the creator divinity who has created the four basic elements. However, the reference to "sweet water coming forth from Ocean," as Bonneau (*Crue du Nil*, 105, n. 4) assumes, points primarily to the Nile as the paradigmatic water. As is well known, a common Egyptian theory for the origin of the Nile was that it came from Nun or Ocean (Frankfort, *Ancient Egyptian Religion*, 112, n. 23; 114; Bonneau, *Crue du Nil*, 143-50).

[102] Blackman (*RecTrav* 39 [1921], 59-62) provides many texts. See also Bonnet, *Angelos* 1 (1925), 118.

[103] Firmicus Maternus, *Err. prof. rel.* 2.5. That this is Nile water is made clear in the sentence which immediately follows.

[104] Dölger, *AntChrist* 5 (1936), 171.

[105] Bonneau (*Crue du Nil*, 279) calls attention to a passage from Porphyry which is quoted by Eusebius (*Praep. Evang.* 9.10.413a) and which in the course of a discussion of "the way of the blessed dead" mentions "those who drink the noble water of the Nilotic land." To her mind Porphyry is saying here that drinking Nile water has something to do with attaining "an infinite condition." She has misunderstood the text. The reference to "those who drink Nile water" is only a way of referring to Egyptians in a context in which five national groups are mentioned as all having wisdom to offer on this topic.

[106] Greek: ἐσιῆς or ἀσιῆς; Latin: *esietus*. Egyptian sources for this belief as well as related texts from the Greek magical papyri are provided by Griffith (*ZÄS* 46 [1910], 132-34) and by Dölger (*AntChrist* 1 [1929], 174-83). See also U. Wilcken, "Die griechischen Denkmäler vom Dromos des Serapeums von Memphis," *JdI* 32 (1917), 201-3; Eitrem, *ClRev* 38 (1924), 69; Gressmann, *Die orientalischen Religionen*, 33-34; Kees, *Studies Presented to F. LL. Griffith*, 402-5; Morenz, *ZÄS* 84 (1959), 140-41; Hermann, "Ertrinken," *RAC* 6 (1963), 375-80; and C. Strauss, "Ertrinken/Ertränken," *LÄ* 2.17-19. A bibliography on this theme is found in André Bataille, *Les Memnonia*, Cairo, 1952, 229-30.

[107] Herodotus 2.90: ὃς δ' ἂν ἢ αὐτῶν Αἰγυπτίων ἢ ξείνων ὁμοίως ὑπὸ κροκοδείλου ἁρπασθεὶς ἢ ὑπ' αὐτοῦ τοῦ ποταμοῦ φαίνηται τεθνεώς, κατ' ἣν ἂν πόλιν ἐξενειχθῇ, τούτους πᾶσα ἀνάγκη ἐστὶ ταριχεύσαντας αὐτὸν καὶ περιστείλαντας ὡς κάλλιστα θάψαι ἐν ἱρῇσι θήκῃσι· οὐδὲ ψαῦσαι ἔξεστι αὐτοῦ ἄλλον οὐδένα οὔτε τῶν προσηκόντων οὔτε τῶν φίλων, ἀλλά μιν οἱ ἱρέες αὐτοὶ οἱ τοῦ Νείλου, ἅτε πλέον τι ἢ ἀνθρώπου νεκρόν, χειραπτάζοντες θάπτουσι.

[108] Tertullian, *De Bapt.* 5: *quos aquae necaverunt*.

[109] Cassius Dio 69.11.2.

[110] Cassius Dio 69.11.3; *Hist. Aug., Hadrian* 14.6; Aurelius Victor, *De Caesaribus* 14.7-8.

[111] *Hist. Aug., Hadrian* 14.6.

[112] Wilcken, *JdI* 32 (1917), 203. That statues exist which depict Antinoos as Osiris (see Wernicke, "Antinoos," *RE* 1.2441) proves nothing. According to later Egyptian belief anyone who died became an Osiris. In any case, Antinoos is much more often depicted as a new Dionysus or Apollo. On the divinization of Antinoos see Hermann, *Mullus*, 155-67 and G. Poethke, "Antinoos," *LÄ* 1.323.

[113] One of the Paris magical papyri speaks of a place "purified" by the inundation of Nile water:

An initiation rite (τελετή). Let the person after having been purified for seven days come on the third day after the new moon to a place recently uncovered by the Nile but before anyone has set foot on the purified area (or, alternatively, to a place that was inundated by the Nile).

Source: *PGM* 4.27-29. This papyrus is assigned to the early 4th cen. AD. The particular practice described here is not mentioned elsewhere.

CHAPTER SIX

[1] Apuleius, *Met.* 11.11: *Gerebat alius felici suo gremio summi numinis venerandam effigiem, non pecoris, non avis, non ferae, ac ne hominis quidem ipsius consimilem, sed sollerti repertu etiam ipsa novitate reverendam altioris utcumque et magno silentio tegendae religionis*

argumentum ineffabile, sed ad istum plane modum fulgente auro figuratum: urnula faberrime cavata, fundo quam rotundo, miris extrinsecus simulacris Aegyptiorum effigiata; ejus orificium non altiuscule levatum in canalem porrectum longo rivulo prominebat; ex alia vero parte multum recedens spatiosa dilatione adhaerebat ansa, quam contorto nodulo supersedebat aspis squameae cervicis striato tumore sublimis.

[2] Vitruvius 8. *praef.* 4; Plutarch, *De Is. et Os.* 36.365 B; Clement of Alexandria, *Strom.* 6.4.37.

[3] The following tacitly or even not so tacitly make this assumption: Lafaye, *Histoire*, 124; Cumont, *Oriental Religions*, 97; Nilsson, *GGR*, 2.625-26; Bonneau, *Crue du Nil*, 281-84; Merkelbach, *Isisfeste*, 39-41, 58; Dunand, *Culte d'Isis*, 3.226; and Witt, *Isis*, 89-90 and 93-94.

[4] Vidman, *Isis und Sarapis*, 171-72; Dunand, *Culte d'Isis*, 3.223.

[5] Dunand, *Culte d'Isis*, 3.229.

[6] The traditional name for this iconographic type goes back to the 17th cen. Jesuit scholar Athanasius Kircher (*Oedipus Aegyptiacus*, Rome, 1652-64, 1.207-12 and 3.435-52). He in turn derived it from a passage in the fifth cen. Christian writer Rufinus (*Hist. eccl.* 11.26) in which that individual described such a statue, gave an account of its purported origins, and indicated his own belief that it depicted a god named Canopus. That this last perception is erroneous has been amply demonstrated by Erwin Panofsky (*GazBA* 57 [1961], 193-201). Even though such a statue may have stood during late Roman times in one of the sanctuaries at Canopus and so have prompted Rufinus' remarks, it in no way follows that this city must have been the place in which this image originated. It is true that two such statues have been found in the Canopus area but similar examples have been recovered at many places around Alexandria. Therefore, contrary to such modern authors as Malaise (*Conditions*, 207) and Dunand (*Culte d'Isis*, 2.45), I believe it simply confusing to refer to Canopus at all in connection with this iconographic type. For this object as an image of Osiris, see Weber, *Drei Untersuchungen*, 37-38.

[7] Griffiths, *Isis-Book*, 227-32.

[8] Weber, *Drei Untersuchungen* and *Terrakotten*, 19-24 and Taf. 1. Other important studies: F. von Bissing, *BArchAlex* 24 (1929), 39-59; 25 (1930) 97-98; and *AO* 34.1-2 (1936), 28-34; Panofsky, *GazBA* 57 (1961), 193-216. Stricker, *OudhMeded* 24 (1943), 1-10 is cited frequently but seems in fact to be a study of lesser importance. See also Tran Tam Tinh (*Culte des divinités*, 34-37), who provides some very useful comments, and Malaise, *Conditions*, 125-26, 205-7, and 307-8. T. Hopfner, "Kanopus," *Reallexikon*, 368-69 is not of much use.

[9] The most important study of these inscriptions is still that of I. Lévy, *JAsiat* 211 (1927), 281-310 but especially 299-308. Other sources of information: Deonna, *RHR* 119 (1939), 53-81; Dölger, *AntChrist* 5 (1936), 169-71; Rohde, *Psyche*, 2.543 and 575-76. For a broader history of religion context see André Parrot, *Le 'refrigerium' dans l'au-delà*, Paris, 1937 = "Le 'refrigerium' dans l'au-delà," *RHR* 113 (1936), 149-87; 114 (1936), 69-92 and 158-96; 115 (1937), 53-89. Of these articles in *RHR*, the latter two are the most pertinent. In more general studies of the Isis-Sarapis cult, see Lafaye, *Histoire*, 96; Cumont, *Oriental Religions*, 102 and nn. 89-90; Bonneau, *Crue du Nil*, 279; Vidman, *Isis und Sarapis*, 13; and Dunand, *Culte d'Isis*, 3.212.

[10] A few writers have hinted that at least the "cool water" formula and the Osiris Hydreios image are related: Weber, *Drei Untersuchungen*, 30 and 39; Breccia, *Terrecotte*, 2.2.33; Deonna, *RHR* 119 (1939) 59; Panofsky, *GazBA* 57 (1961), 195; and, somewhat more strongly, Malaise, *Conditions*, 207. In no case are these inferences or suggestions developed.

[11] Dunand, *Culte d'Isis*, 3.212, n. 5.

[12] Griffiths (*Isis-Book*, 15) believes that Apuleius very likely did witness the ceremonies of the *Navigium Isidis* at Cenchreae and perhaps also had a vivid experience in that town of the saving power of Isis.

[13] Griffiths (*Isis-Book*, 227-28) is misled by these decorations on the outer surface of the pitcher into thinking that Apuleius is presenting some sort of hybrid cross between the cultic pitcher and the Osiris Hydreios statue. He is apparently unaware that pitchers with some designs on their outer surface are depicted on several Roman Imperial coins from Alexandria (e.g., Dattari, nrs. 9 [Pl. XII, 1], 286/287, and 1127).

[14] Plutarch (*De Is. et Os.* 36.365 B) provides the clearest ancient evidence that the pitcher was intended to contain water: "Not only the Nile but all moisture they call simply an emanation of Osiris. And the ὑδρεῖον in honor of the god always goes in procession ahead of the (other) sacred objects." The juxtaposition of the two sentences clearly indicates the contents of the pitcher. (The difference between this processional sequence and that provided by Apuleius may reflect different views as to which place in the order of march was the most honorable.) See also Vitruvius 8. *praef.* 4. Vessels of water appear to have been a symbol of Osiris from at least as early as the Old Kingdom (K. Sethe, *Dramatische Texte zu altägyptischen Mysterienspielen*, 2 vols., Leipzig, 1928, 1.107, 109, 142-43).

[15] Vitruvius 8. *praef.* 4. The technical term is found in Plutarch (*De Is. et Os.* 36.365 B), in Clement of Alexandria (*Strom.* 6.4.37) and in a Latin inscription from Nomentum (SIRIS 531—see above, Ch. II, n. 56).

[16] The Egyed *hydria*, Roman Imperial period in date, is described in Wessetzky, *Ägyptischen Kulte*, 42-45 and Taf. vi-viii as well as in Tran Tam Tinh, *Culte des divinités*, 31-32. On the body of this vessel are gold and silver inlaid images of various Egyptian gods, etc. Aside from these, however, there is no particular agreement in type between this object and the pitcher described by Apuleius and portrayed elsewhere nor with any of its sub-types. Leclant (*Problèmes*, 95), in discussing Wessetzky's book, criticizes its tendency to assume that every Egyptian object found in the West must be related to the cult. As for Wessetzky's guess that the *hydria* came from the Savaria sanctuary, this must be dismissed as pure speculation—Egyed and Savaria are not at all close to one another.

[17] Westholm, *Temples*, 101, nr. 325 and pl. xxvii. 6.

[18] Ibid., 107, nr. 439 and pl. xiii. 3.

[19] The statue is about two-thirds life-size. Even if the statue were life-size, the comparable portion of the *uraeus* would be no more than 3 or 4 cm long.

[20] The people who destroyed this cella were not concerned to collect all the valuable metal objects to re-use them. For, besides the *uraeus* fragment, they left 180 bronze fragments, each 1-5 cm in length, scattered about the floor. Hatred of the cult rather than brigandage was perhaps the principal inspiration for this final destruction.

[21] Vitruvius 8. *praef.* 4: *Itaque cum hydria aqua ad templum aedemque casta religione refertur, tunc in terra procumbentes manibus ad caelum sublatis inventionis gratias agunt divinae benignitati.* The reference here to an "inventio" looks very much like Vitruvius is referring to a "Finding of Osiris" ceremony.

[22] G. E. Rizzo, *Le pitture dell' Aula Isiaca di Caligola* (MPAI, 3.2), Rome, 1936, fig. 32. For further information see Malaise, *Inventaire*, 215-19 and the bibliography supplied there. See also J. Gagé, *'Basileia.' Les Césars, les rois d'Orient et les 'mages'*, Paris, 1968, 57-58.

[23] Malaise, *Inventaire*, 217-19.

²⁴ Since the date of this room has now been moved back to the late 1st cen. BC, Cumont's view ("La salle isiaque de Caligula au Palatin," *RHR* 114 [1936], 127-29) that it had been utilized as an "oratoire luxueux aux divinités de l'Egypte" has been rendered quite improbable. It is difficult to believe that Augustus could ever have admitted such a religious installation into his palace. Malaise (*Inventaire*, 218) observed with respect to the Egyptian symbolism utilized in the decorations that what is Alexandrian in motif need not necessarily relate in a direct sense to the Isis-Sarapis cult.

²⁵ Dattari, nr. 9 = Poole, nr. 11 and pl. xxxi = Geissen, nr. 3. Date: 27 BC-14 AD. See my Pl. XII, 1.

²⁶ The best available photograph of this object, though not entirely clear, is found in Salditt-Trappmann, *Tempel,* Abb. 26 (= my Pl. VI, 1). Line drawings of the facade of this building were published by Mazois and Gau, *Ruines,* vol. 4, pl. xi; by Niccolini, *Case,* vol. 1, pl. ix; and by Mau, *Pompeii,* 179, fig. 82. These illustrations do not agree among themselves nor with the photographs and perhaps are all rather free drawings.

²⁷ This fresco is described by Elia (*Pitture,* 27-30) and by Tran Tam Tinh (*Essai,* 139). Elia has an excellent large reproduction in color (Tav. B).

²⁸ Olga Elia (*Pitture,* 27) believed that the vessel was set upon a crown of roses. However, a crack in the fresco at this point makes it difficult to determine this. I am persuaded more in favor of the cushion because the artist who did an engraving of this fresco soon after it was found seems also to have seen a cushion (Ibid., Tav. 3).

²⁹ In the engraving mentioned in the previous note, the vessel, interestingly, assumes a more conventionally classical form. The engraver seems to have "improved" things a bit.

³⁰ Tran Tam Tinh, *Essai,* 140, nr. 41; Elia, *Pitture,* 35 and fig. 31. Elia speaks of the handle being in the form of a *uraeus* but this is not clear from the engraving by Morelli and Imperato (Elia, fig. 31) which provides the only surviving evidence for the fresco.

³¹ *PAH* 1.1.185. See also Tran Tam Tinh, *Essai,* 138, nr. 37. Malaise (*Conditions,* 117) believes that this figure is the prophet or high priest and that he carries the sacred water pitcher. So also Tran Tam Tinh, *Essai,* 95. The fresco, which was probably on the north wall of the portico, has not survived.

³² The best publication of these columns is that of Sergio Bosticco, *Musei Capitolini,* 27-31 and Tav. vi-viii. His system of enumeration for the various columns and individual reliefs will be followed here. He provides photographs of six of the eight reliefs on Column A (= my Pl. XVIII) and two of the reliefs on Column C. One of the missing reliefs on Column A (A.a.1) and four of the eight reliefs on Column B are depicted in H. Stuart Jones, *A Catalogue of the Ancient Sculptures Preserved in the Municipal Collections of Rome: The Sculptures of the Museo Capitolino,* Oxford, 1912, pl. 92. Anne Roullet, who provides additional brief commentary and bibliography (*Egyptian Monuments,* 58 and pls. xxvi-xxxiv), has excellent photographs of many of the reliefs including, at least in some form, six of the eight reliefs on Column C. An additional column, now in the Museo Archeologico at Florence, was found at Rome probably on this site (Malaise, *Inventaire,* Rome, nr. 386 = Roullet, *Egyptian Monuments,* nr. 16 and pl. xxv). However, the reliefs on this column do not follow the same pattern and are not pertinent for the present study.

³³ Malaise, *Inventaire,* Rome, nr. 363 = Bosticco, Column B.

[34] Weber, *Drei Untersuchungen*, 44. He is referring to the figure designated as d.2. on Column B according to the notation method of Bosticco. Bosticco himself (p. 30) says regarding this figure that it is "completamente erosa," while Weber (p. 43) reported that this personage bore "das teilweise beschädigte aber ganz sichere Schnabelgefäss." Bosticco refers to another figure on the same column as being "completely worn away" while in fact it appears fairly clearly in H. Stuart Jones, pl. 92, nr. 15.1 on the left. Tran Tam Tinh (*Culte des divinités*, 36-37) also says that the pitcher appears among the cult objects seen in these reliefs.

[35] Darsy, *Recherches*, 48-49. He calls the palm branch a "lustral branch."

[36] Ibid., 49. See also p. 41.

[37] This is Rock Relief nr. 142A according to the enumeration of C. Picard (*RHR* 86 [1922], 176 and pl. v). A useful photograph is found in Collart, *Philippes*, vol. 2, pl. lxxx. 3; Dunand (*Culte d'Isis*, vol. 2, pl. xviii. 3) illustrates this relief but the pitcher is not visible in her photograph. Picard (Ibid., 178) believed that Isis is also depicted along with Artemis in Relief nr. 409, which was found in the extreme western part of the city. A pitcher is visible in this relief and possibly also a *situla*. However, the identification proposed is far less certain and its find spot places the relief at a good distance from the sanctuary of the Egyptian gods.

[38] Specific references for these and the various other items mentioned in this section will be provided below when their typology is discussed.

[39] A very late coin (reign of Julian the Apostate) is also known (Drexler, *LM* 2.425).

[40] It should be noted that both Philippi and Corinth were Roman *coloniae*.

[41] Tran Tam Tinh, *Culte des divinités*, 30-31.

[42] Weber, *Drei Untersuchungen*, 44. The oddly shaped spout of this type of pitcher is what led Weber to call it a "bird-beak pitcher." I myself wonder if perhaps this spout was consciously intended as an image of the beak of an ibis. According to Plutarch (*De Is. et Os.* 75.381 D and *De soll. an.* 20.974 C) and Aelian (*NA* 7.45), an ibis will drink only from pure water. If the water is tainted or disease-ridden, this bird will not even approach it. Consequently it was valued by Egyptian priests for locating water that was absolutely pure. On the ibis in Egyptian religion see Dölger, *AntChrist* 5 (1936), 183-87.

[43] For this relief, to be discussed below, see Pl. XIII.

[44] Tran Tam Tinh, *Culte des divinités*, 31.

[45] Michael Grant, *The Roman Forum*, New York, 1970, 54.

[46] C. H. V. Sutherland, *Roman Coins*, New York, 1974, nrs. 80, 122, 127, 162, 174, 184, but especially 107. In the case of nr. 174, a coin of Sextus Pompey (c. 42 BC), the handle of the pitcher ends in such a way that it resembles the raised *uraeus* serpent. Yet the vessel is probably only a variety of the usual *urceus*.

[47] Of these eleven items, three are literary references (Vitruvius 8. *praef.* 4; Plutarch, *De Is. et Os.* 36.365 B; Clement of Alexandria, *Strom.* 6.4.37); all of these refer to processions in which the pitcher is born by a priest. SIRIS 531 is an inscription (now lost) from Nomentum in Latium which speaks of the dedication to Isis and Sarapis of a "hydraeum <g>emmis exornatum et auratum"; it possibly dates to the early Imperial period. Also to this group belong the Soli *uraeus* fragment and the lost fresco from the portico of the Pompeii Iseum (*PAH* 1.1.185), both of which were discussed above. The remaining five items are coins from Alexandria for which I have not been able to obtain photographs: Dattari, nrs. 2646 (5th year of Antoninus Pius: pitcher set on a square base), 2655 (24th year of Antoninus Pius: pitcher placed at the feet of Isis), 3047 (3rd year of Antoninus Pius: *naiskos* with Harpocrates. In front of it is a pitcher set on a column), 3048 (unknown year

of Antoninus Pius: mostly the same as nr. 3047 but here the pitcher is set on a square base), and 3217 (Marcus Aurelius: in a *naiskos* Isis is seated on a throne and suckles Harpocrates. A pitcher stands nearby on a small column).

⁴⁸ An example of the high-shouldered *Schnabelkanne* is seen in Pl. XII, 1 while Pls. VI, 1 and XI show the round-shouldered variety.

⁴⁹ Contrary to Tran Tam Tinh, *Culte des divinités*, 31. Perhaps he did not have access to photographs of the coins. The following coins are of this type: Dattari, nrs. 9 (Augustus: pitcher with long spout and wide handle [Pl. XII, 1]), 286/287 = Geissen, nr. 211 (14th year of Nero: body of pitcher is ornamented with an Egyptian crown of twin feathers, horns, and solar disk—see Dattari, pl. 28), 890 (13th year of Trajan: Euthenia [Isis??] sits on an androsphinx. To the right is a square altar and to the left the pitcher set on a base—see Dattari, pl. 13), 891 (10th year of Trajan: same as nr. 890), 918 (10th year of Trajan: Hermanubis stands holding a caduceus and a palm branch. At his feet is a jackal. To the left is a base with a sacred ship on it and to the right a tripod with a pitcher—see Dattari, pl. 16), 1126 (10th year of Trajan: Dattari, pl. 28), 1127 (11th year of Trajan: same as nr. 1126 but here pitcher's body is ornamented with various figures), 1750 (16th year of Hadrian: Isis nurses Harpocrates. To the left is the pitcher, to the right a palm branch—see Dattari, pl. 17), 1977 (14th year of Hadrian: see Dattari, pl. 28), 2643 (2nd year of Antonius Pius: Isis nurses Harpocrates. To the right is the pitcher set on a circular base).

⁵⁰ Malaise, *Inventaire*, 219.

⁵¹ H. Fuhrmann, *AA* (1941), 595-99 and Abb. 108-15.

⁵² Tran Tam Tinh, *Essai*, 199-200, nr. 4 *ter* and also p. 197. For a detailed study of the wall paintings of this room see France le Corsu, "Un oratoire pompéien consacré à Dionysos-Osiris," *RArch* 1967, 2.239-54. Le Corsu believes that a small house-shrine was located in this room, a possibility which cannot be ruled out. For photographs of the particular fresco in question see Le Corsu, 241, fig. 1 and L. Santini, *Pompeii: The Excavations*, Terni, 1972, 75.

⁵³ This feature was noted above in the case of the *hydraeum* mentioned in the Nomentum inscription (SIRIS 531).

⁵⁴ Malaise, *Inventaire*, 291-92, Stabiae, nr. 1. The trays upon which the pitchers are carried perhaps substitute for the humeral veil normal in other cases.

⁵⁵ Leospo (*Mensa Isiaca*, 44-45 and Tav. vi) briefly describes these pitchers but did not recognize that they are *Schnabelkannen*. On the provenance of this bronze tablet see Ibid., 97-98.

⁵⁶ The phrase "urnula faberrime cavata, fundo quam rotundo" (Apuleius, *Met.* 11.11) suggests this.

⁵⁷ P. Perdrizet, "La tunique liturgique historiée de Saqqarah," *MonPiot* 34 (1934), 97-128 and pls. vii-viii. See also Dunand, *BIFAO* 67 (1969), 35-36 and fig. 9.

⁵⁸ Nock (*Conversion*, 40) points out that Agathodaimon was the patronal deity of Alexandria and was not of importance elsewhere. This suggests that this relief and others like it come from Alexandria. It is now preserved in the Alexandria Museum, inv. nr. 3175. On Sarapis as Agathodaimon see Pietrzykowski, *HomVermaseren* 3.959-66.

⁵⁹ Dunand, *BIFAO* 67 (1969), 11; 33, n. 2; 35; and pl. ii. A. Where precisely this relief was found is not known.

⁶⁰ There are two *Schnabelkannen* whose proper subtype I was unable to determine. On a fresco from Pompeii (found somewhere in the town) is a "vase à long bec," as Tran Tam Tinh (*Essai*, 153, nr. 69) describes it, set between two winged

sphinxes (Museo Nazionale, Naples, inv. nr. 8563). The other is the relief on Column B from the Campus Martius Iseum, Rome. I have not seen either of these two representations.

⁶¹ Malaise, *Inventaire*, Rome, nr. 441 and frontispiece. For additional bibliography see Tran Tam Tinh, *Culte des divinités*, 30, n. 3. Date: see Castiglione, *ActaAnt* 8 (1960), 388.

⁶² On the right side is a rooster standing on top of some sort of urn. For a description and photograph of the object see W. Altmann, *Die römischen Grabaltäre der Kaiserzeit*, Berlin, 1905, 237-38 and fig. 191.

⁶³ Dattari, nrs. 6309-10 and pl. 34 (13th year of Trajan: Harpocrates, with the lower part of his body in the form of a crocodile, is in the center. To the left is a base with a pitcher, which rests on a pillow, set upon it. To the right is a base with a tabernacle or altar upon it).

⁶⁴ The pitcher seen on the rock relief from Philippi which was discussed above is very much like an *oenochoe* of standard shape and is probably a somewhat different Hellenized version. It is taller, narrower, and has a much larger handle than the Vatican type. In addition, it appears to lack the *uraeus* emblem. The fresco of a pitcher found in the Santa Sabina Iseum at Rome presents another Hellenized variety. It lacks the *uraeus*, has a tiny spout, and is footed, an unusual feature indeed for the cultic pitcher. Its body is fluted, a feature attested on several coins in the Alexandrian series (Dattari, nrs. 6309 and 6310 [Trajan], 1977 [Hadrian], and 2643 [Antoninus Pius]).

I know of three variants which do not fit the typology:

1. Alexandria: relief of Isis-Thermouthis and Sarapis-Agathodaimon with a pitcher set between them. The pitcher has a wide neck and mouth and lacks both *uraeus* and a long spout (Dunand, *BIFAO* 67 [1969], 23 and fig. 7). See my Pl. XII, 2.

2. Alexandria: coin from the reign of Julian the Apostate. It depicts Sarapis-Agathodaimon and Isis-Thermouthis with a tall, thin pitcher set between them. This lacks the long spout but has the *uraeus* (Drexler, *LM* 2.425).

3. Herculaneum: fresco showing a priest standing in front of a temple and holding up a golden vase for the adoration of the faithful (Pl. XIV). Possibly the vessel is not a pitcher (Tran Tam Tinh, *Culte des divinités*, 29-38; for a full-color photograph of this fresco see A. Toynbee, ed., *The Crucible of Christianity*, London, 1969, 240-41).

⁶⁵ Castiglione, *ActaAnt* 8 (1960), 396-404. However, he prefers to call the instrument a *kyathos* since a *simpulum* normally does not have such a long handle.

⁶⁶ Ibid., 400.

⁶⁷ Dunand, *Culte d'Isis*, 1.152, n. 4 and 190-91. At Philae Ptolemy XII (80-51 BC) is depicted offering incense and a libation of water to Osiris (H. Junker, *Der grosse Pylon des Tempels der Isis zu Philae*, Vienna, 1958, 49-50). The Museum of Fine Arts in Boston has in its Egyptian Collection several objects which depict a water libation: nr. 1972-651: a relief from the Tomb of Tja-Wy (18th or 19th Dynasty)—Tja-Wy pours a water libation to a local cobra goddess; nr. 54-993: painted covering for the mummy of a woman (c. 200 AD)—two Isis figures (= the woman?) pour a libation of water to Osiris; etc. Two literary texts also demonstrate that Egyptians were familiar with the practice of offering libations of water. Heliodorus (2.22.5-23.1) indicated that it was a custom for the "wise" among the Egyptians to offer libations of pure water (ἄκρατον τὸ ὕδωρ) to the gods. Porphyry (*Abst.* 4.9) directly connected such a practice with the cult of Sarapis: ἔτι καὶ νῦν ἐν τῇ ἀνοίξει τοῦ ἁγίου Σαράπιδος ἡ θεραπεία διὰ πυρὸς καὶ ὕδατος γίνεται, λείβοντος τοῦ ὑμνῳδοῦ τὸ

ὕδωρ καὶ τὸ πῦρ φαίνοντος, ὁπηνίκα ἑστὼς ἐπὶ τοῦ οὐδοῦ τῇ πατρίῳ τῶν Αἰγυπτίων φωνῇ ἐγείρει τὸν θεόν.

68 Apuleius, *Met.* 11.20: ... *sacerdos, rem divinam procurans supplicamentis sollemnibus, deae de penetrali fontem petitum spondeo libat* ....

69 According to Apuleius (*Met.* 11.17), after the procession the pitcher and the other sacred images were brought into the cella of the goddess, the "cubiculum deae." The text appears to equate this term with "veneranda penetralia" which is found in the same sentence.

70 Clement of Alexandria, *Strom.* 6.4.36.

71 Françoise Dunand (*BIFAO* 67 [1969], 35 and *Culte d'Isis*, 3.219) is one of the only scholars to have offered any hint that this pitcher served for pouring libations of water.

72 Castiglione, *ActaAnt* 8 (1960), 394, n. 20.

73 J. Toutain, "Sacrificium: Rome," *DAGR* 4.2.977-78.

74 Engberding, *OrChr* 37 (1953), 86. The evidence is found in a Syriac version of a Blessing for Nile Water (G. Margoliouth, *The Liturgy of the Nile*, London, 1896, 35). In the Greek version the rubrics are changed; the people are only to be sprinkled with this blessed water.

75 Fuhrmann, *AA* 1941, 601.

76 *PAH* 1.1.174.

77 Clement of Alexandria, *Strom.* 6.4.37: ἐπὶ πᾶσι δὲ ὁ προφήτης ἔξεισι προφανὲς τὸ ὑδρεῖον ἐγκεχολπισμένος, ᾧ ἕπονται οἱ τὴν ἔκπεμψιν τῶν ἄρτων βαστάζοντες.

78 P. Derchain, "Un sens curieux de ἔκπεμψις chez Clement d'Alexandrie," *ChrEg* 26 (1951), 269-79. So also G. W. H. Lampe, ed., *A Patristic Greek Lexicon*, Oxford, 1961, 435.

79 See above, n. 57. Castiglione (*ActaAnt* 5 [1957], 222-26) discusses the use of bread and water in Egyptian offertory rituals.

80 A final suggestion offered by A. A. Barb ("Diva Matrix," *JWCI* 16 [1953], 200-2) is also attractive in light of the materials presented in the previous chapter but is probably not valid. Barb argued that the cultic pitcher is in the form of a magical uterus and therefore was intended to convey divine power which would assist women in childbearing. While it is true that a variety of Roman writers, for example, did link Nile water with human fruitfulness and ease in pregnancies, Barb's comparison of the shape of the *Schnabalkanne* as described by Apuleius with ancient descriptions and representations of the uterus is not all that convincing. (For criticisms of Barb's theory see Griffiths, *Isis-Book*, 230-32.)

81 Dunand (*BIFAO* 67 [1969], 43) believes that the type was known in ancient Egypt but does not offer any evidence for this. Tran Tam Tinh (*Culte des divinités*, 32, n. 5) cites pitcher types from the 18th and 19th Dynasties but the parallels are not striking. These earlier Egyptian pitchers have somewhat extended spouts, though these are not in the tilted "bird-beak" form. Their necks are usually very thin and tall. On this material see Jean Vercoutter, *L'Egypte et le monde égéen préhellénique*, Cairo, 1956, 331-32, nrs. 337-41 and pls. xlv-xlvi.

82 The Soli Iseum, a product of the later Roman period, is strongly Egyptianized. It is, for example, the only such sanctuary to have a pylon facade in the manner of the temples of Ptolemaic and Roman Egypt.

83 For a more detailed description of this form of Osiris statue see Weber, *Drei Untersuchungen*, 32-33, a description based principally on types found on coins of Alexandria. Also see Von Bissing, *AO* 34.1-2 (1936), 29-31.

84 Petrie, *Kahun*, 36 and Pl. xxiv. 7 and 8. L. Kakosy in a recent review (*ZDMG* 127 [1977], 92) has called attention to these finds.

[85] Petrie, Ibid. 37 and 33.

[86] Daressy, (*Statues*, 214-15 and pl. xliii) said that nrs. 38861 and 38864 in the Cairo Museum are from the Ptolemiac period but gives no reasons for this opinion. Vogt (*Terrakotten*, 2 and 85 and pl. ii. 4) believed that stylistic criteria required a similar date in the case of a terracotta statuette found at Alexandria. Finally, Hill (*Catalogue*, 65, nr. 137 and pl. 5) appealed to similar criteria in assigning to the Hellenistic period a bronze statuette of a priest who probably, but not certainly, bore an Osiris Hydreios in his veiled hands. As in the case of three or four bronzes of similar type, the object carried by the priest has been lost. Charbonneaux (*MélPiganiol* 1.407) believed that all of these figures dated to the late Ptolemaic period but also (p. 412) that the priests carried pitchers, not Osiris statues. He offered little or no empirical evidence for these views, however.

[87] Vogt (*Die alexandrinischen Münzen*, 2.6) holds for this interpretation of the coin. But Von Bissing (*BArchAlex* 24 [1929], 55) and Tran Tam Tinh (*Culte des divinités*, 35, n. 5) indicate that there is still considerable uncertainty.

[88] Dattari, nrs. 318 and 331 (= Geissen, nrs. 252 and 253) and Poole, nr. 220 respectively.

[89] Vespasian: Dattari, nrs. 371 (= Geissen, nr. 291), 372, 373.

Domitian: Dattari, nrs. 436/437 (= Geissen, nr. 357), 470, 471 (= Geissen, nr. 371), 472-75, 476 (= Geissen, nr. 372).

Trajan: Dattari, nrs. 647, 648 (= Geissen, nr. 574), 649 (= Geissen, nr. 593), 823-25, 826 (= Geissen, nr. 577), 827/828 (= Geissen, nr. 600), 829-30; Poole, nr. 375; Geissen, nr. 511; F. Feuardent, *Collections Giovanni di Demetrio, Numismatique, Egypte ancienne*, vol. 2: *Domination romaine*, Paris, 1872, nr. 1014.

Hadrian: Dattari, nrs. 1310-23, 1325-29, 1649-63, 1949-51; Poole, nrs. 629, 772-73, 877; Feuardent, Ibid., nrs. 1373, 1402, 1484-85.

Antoninus Pius: Dattari, nrs. 2179-81, 2496-504.

Marcus Aurelius, Lucius Verus, Faustina: Dattari, nrs. 3433-40, 3568-70, 3618-23, 3702-4, 3798-99; Lederer, *Deutsche Münzblätter* 56 (1936), 201-7 and Taf. 165, nr. 1.

Gallienus: Dattari, nrs. 5233-35; G. MacDonald, *Catalogue of Greek Coins in the Hunterian Collection*, Glasgow, 1905, vol. 3, nr. 926.

[90] J. G. Milne, *Greek Inscriptions* (Cat. gén. Caire, 18), Oxford, 1905, 48-50, nr. 9267 and pl. vii.

[91] Fuhrmann, *AA* 1941, 598-601 and Abb. 112-15. On the back side of this cup is seen a statue of a crocodile with a pitcher set upon his back—a symbol of the Nile River?

[92] This statue, which is not mentioned in the catalogue of Tran Tam Tinh (*Essai*) nor in any other modern study, is described in *PAH* (1.1.172) as follows: "In the bottom of this pit was found ... an Egyptian idol which does not have any legs and which was broken in a number of pieces. From the belt-line downwards it is ornamented with many hieroglyphics. On the basis of the remnants this seems to be a Canopus. It is c. 0.154 m high [literally: 7 ounces high—the measuring scale being Neapolitan palms] ... and is made of marble."

[93] *PAH* 1.1.172. The pit is no longer visible at the site. A second pit containing similar finds was found in the northeast corner of the open couryard (*PAH* 1.1.182).

[94] For detailed photographs and a complete description of this object see Leospo, *Mensa Isiaca*. I follow here the date she has assigned to it (pp. 98-100).

[95] Bonneau (*Crue du Nil*, 268) incorrectly interprets the Horus-sphinx as a dog and then attempts to associate the *Mensa Isiaca* with the Sothic year of 139 AD. On

the two Osiris Hydreios images and their associated figures see Leospo, *Mensa Isiaca*, 37, 74, and Tavv. vi and xx-xxi.

⁹⁶ Jagged lines, the hieroglyphic symbol for water, extend from the spouts of the pourer. Of the many offering scenes on the *Mensa Isiaca*, only here does water serve as the gift. Its association with Osiris and Horus is noteworthy.

⁹⁷ Erman, *Handbook*, 226-27.

⁹⁸ I know of only one exception, the large (0.49 m high) alabaster Osiris Hydreios in the collection of Queen Juliana of the Netherlands (inv. nr. 33). On this see H. P. Blok, "Een onuitgegeven exemplaar van het zogenaamde 'Heilige Beeld van Canopus'," *BABesch* 6 (1931), 25-28 and figs. 1-3 and Schneider, *BABesch* 50 (1975), 8-9 and fig. 11. Schneider thinks it possible that this statue, originally in the Vatican collections, is from the Villa Adriana.

⁹⁹ The chief problem with the mummy theory, as Weber (*Drei Untersuchungen*, 38) pointed out, is that the Hydreios statues never (despite the interpolated passage in Rufinus, *Hist. Eccl.* 11.26 to the contrary—see Panofsky, *GazBA* 57 [1961], 198-200) have feet, even "pedes perexigui"! On the other hand, no mummy types without feet are known.

There is interesting confirmatory evidence for the vessel or *hydria* theory over against the mummy theory from a group of magical curse tablets found buried by the Via Appia just outside of Rome. Admittedly this evidence is from a late period—it dates to c. 390-420 AD. These tablets have been published by R. Wünsch (*Sethianische Verfluchungstafeln aus Rom*, Leipzig, 1898). In these texts there is frequent reference to a god addressed as "dee phrugia" (or: "phudria"), "dee Nymphee Eidonea" (Tablet nrs. 16.14 and 53; 17.5; 19.4; 20.1 and 55; 21.1; 22.9 and 14; etc.). It is Wünsch's view (p. 86) that this god must be Osiris, a divinity who is mentioned by name quite frequently in the tablets. The phrase *dee phudria/dee phrugia* seems to be a Latinized Greek form of *theos eph' hydria*, the god on top of the *hydria*. Further, on two of the tablets just above this form of address to the god is the figure of a head set on top of what certainly looks like a jar (see my Pl. XXVII). From the crudely drawn head comes forth two curved lines which perhaps represent a headdress or crown. The object appears to be placed inside a large rectangular box so that only the upper half of what I would call the Osiris Hydreios figure is visible. But perhaps the "box" is actually a base. (Wünsch himself [p. 85] believed this figure to be a mummy set in some sort of shrine; he did not relate the figure to the *dee phudria* title.) All of this would seem to prove that at least in this late period the base of this statue was understood to be a jar (*hydria*).

¹⁰⁰ Weber, *Drei Untersuchungen*, 38.

¹⁰¹ Ibid., 48. See also Von Bissing, *AO* 34.1-2 (1936), 32 and Griffiths, *Isis-Book*, 42.

¹⁰² Weber, *Drei Untersuchungen*, 38-39. Stricker (*OudhMeded* 24 [1943], 6) treats both motifs as of equal weight but Von Bissing (*BArchAlex* 24 [1929], 43) points out that the Osiris Hydreios type in which the body of the vessel is fluted rather than decorated with reliefs serves to highlight the primacy of the water vessel motif.

¹⁰³ Panofsky, *GazBA* 57 (1961), 193-96; Weber, *Drei Untersuchungen*, 29-30.

¹⁰⁴ For further information on these jars see Budge, *The Mummy*, 194-201. Panofsky (*GazBA* 57 [1961], 194, fig. 1) illustrates a set of four of these jars from the Twelfth Dynasty. Panofsky himself worried that though there was an obvious typological similarity between the visceral jars and the Hydreios figures, the former—or so he thought (pp. 194 and 196)—were not used after the period of the New Kingdom. This is not the case. For example, the Museum of Fine Arts, Boston, has a set of four visceral jars (nrs. 26.895-898) which date to the period

525-304 BC and the Field Museum of Chicago has a "dummy" set—they are solid rather than hollow—which dates from the Ptolemaic period (nrs. 31586-89).

[105] Weber, *Drei Untersuchungen*, 29-30; Von Bissing, *AO* 34.1-2 (1936), 33.

[106] Von Bissing (Ibid.) suggests that the Greek grave stele from Alexandria discussed above may well represent a transitional type between this late use of the visceral jars and the new Osiris iconography. The fourteen images on the stele are arranged in groups of threes and fours, with the two groups of four on the principal sides.

[107] Weber (*Drei Untersuchungen*, 30; see also 39) noted at least one instance of a representation of a burial in which the conventional visceral jars under the bier are replaced by two water containers.

[108] Ghoneim's data was published in brief form by Leclant (*Orientalia* 20 [1951], 454-56). The dimensions given here are estimates based on the photographs provided there and in Kraus, *Christentum am Nil*, fig. 53.

[109] The Osiris Hydreios is the type most frequently found, so-called Type A.

[110] For photographs, detailed descriptions, and comments on the dating of these statues see Adriani, *Annuaire*, 136-48 and pls. 50-59.

[111] Westholm, *Temples*, 140. For his description of the object see pp. 101-2, nr. 329 and pl. xxiii. On its dating see pp. 133 and 144.

[112] Westholm believed that the lower portion of these reliefs may not have been finished.

[113] See note 32 above. With respect to the Hydreios figures, the photographs referred to include all but one, the Anubis Hydreios on Column C (C.d.l).

[114] Panofsky (*GazBA* 57 [1961], 196 and n. 13) discusses this problem. He observes that spiralized fluting such as is found here is not seen on the Alexandrian coins; they reveal only what he calls "vertical strigilation" but what I would term a U-neck garment. The fluting which appears in these reliefs represents, I would say, a development stemming from the U-neck garment type.

[115] No other images of gods save the nine Hydreios figures and this image of Harpocrates are to be seen on these columns.

[116] See Weber, *Drei Untersuchungen*, 44.

[117] At the Santa Sabina Iseum the branch is seen placed in the mouth of the cultic pitcher. The Alexandrian coin is Dattari, nr. 1750 (16th year of Hadrian: Isis nurses Harpocrates. To the left is a pitcher, to the right a palm branch).

[118] Roullet, *Egyptian Monuments*, 98-99, nr. 145. Sixteenth century sources which mention this object are: Ulysses Aldrovandi, *Delle statue antiche che per tutta Roma in diversi luoghi et case si veggono*, Rome, 1562, 203 and Jean-Jacques Boissard, *Romanae urbis topographia et antiquitates*, 4 vols., Frankfurt, 1597-98, 1.108.

[119] The agate statuette is in the Berlin Museum, inv. nr. 21790. See Weber, *Drei Untersuchungen*, 35, n. 38 and Von Bissing, *BArchAlex* 24 (1929), 58. On the Esquiline Hill was found the left half of an Osiris Hydreios (Roullet, *Egyptian Monuments*, nr. 144b). The Klein-Glienicke relief of the 3rd cen. AD (Schede, *Angelos* 2 [1926], 60-61 and Taf. 4 = Roullet, nr. 51 = Malaise, *Inventaire*, Rome, nr. 442a) depicts a procession in which walks a priest who carries in his veiled hands an Osiris Hydreios (Pl. XXVI). The *Mensa Isiaca* mentioned above probably came originally from Rome. Also probably from the same city is a large Osiris Hydreios statue now in the Vatican Museum. Date: 1st cen. AD. See Von Bissing, *BArchAlex* 24 (1929), 55-57 and Roullet nr. 314.

[120] The Villa Adriana finds: Roullet, *Egyptian Monuments*, nrs. 146-48, 315. A large Osiris statue of this type was found at Circeo in Latium (Malaise, *Inventaire*, Circeo, nr. 2). Two other pieces now in the Musée Guimet certainly derive from

Italy and perhaps from the area around Rome (Weber, *Drei Untersuchungen*, 37, n. 42).

[121] At Beneventum were found two headless statues of priests who carry Hydreios images in their veiled hands. These images, both probably of Osiris (the heads are missing), have their bodies clothed in a U-neck garment. Date of the statues: Hadrianic period. They are nrs. 284 and 288 in the catalogue of Müller (*Isiskult*, 95-98, 106, and Tav. xxx).

[122] Malaise, *Inventaire*, Carales, nr. 4.

[123] The terracotta statuettes have been published in the following sources: Vogt, *Terrakotten*, 2 and 85 and pls. ii. 4-6; Breccia, *Terrecotte* 1.43-44, nr. 165 (= Alexandria Museum, inv. nr. 10798) and pl. 49.18; Ibid. 57, nr. 277 (= inv. nr. 16233). Nr. 165 is 0.20 m high and was found in a tomb described as not earlier than the 1st cen. AD. Nr. 277 is only 0.05 m high and is said to have served as the handle of a lamp. It was found in the catacombs of Kom-esh-Shuqafa which date from about the 2nd cen. AD.

[124] Two large statues (E. Breccia, *Monuments de l'Egypte gréco-romaine*, 2 vols., Bergamo, 1926-34, 1.63 and pl. xxix. 6 and 8).

[125] Heracleopolis: a small statue, "very late Roman period" (W. M. Flinders Petrie, *Roman Ehnasya*, London, 1905, pl. 48, nr. 65) and a terracotta relief of the "Sarapis *kline*" type [a pair of Osiris Hydreios images sit in niches below the *kline* at which a number of gods recline] (Ibid., 2 and pl. 47, nr. 45; Castiglione, *ActaAnt* 9 [1961], 298). The other items can only be described as being from the general region: Perdrizet, *Terres cuites grecques*, nrs. 180-81 and pl. xlix; Weber, *Terrakotten*, 1.25 and Taf. 1.4-5 (= Berlin, Aeg. Mus., nr. 9368, "ostensibly from the Faiyum," and nr. 13002, "bought at Medinet el-Fayum"). I am not sure whether the two pieces mentioned by Kaufman (*Gräco-Ägyptische Koroplastik*, 47 and Taf. 17.93-94) are those in the Berlin Museum or still another pair from the Faiyum.

[126] Leiden, Rijksmuseum, inv. nr. F 1960/9.1: a relief, very similar in design to the reliefs from Alexandria mentioned above which depict the cultic pitcher, showing Osiris Hydreios in the center flanked by larger images of Isis-Thermouthis on the left and Sarapis-Agathodaimon on the right. See Hornbostel, *Sarapis*, 297-98 and Abb. 310 and Pietrzykowski, *HomVermaseren* 3.960.

[127] Bronze statuettes of priests who probably carried Osiris Hydreios statues in their veiled hands. One is published by Perdrizet (*Bronzes grecs*, 48-50, nr. 82 and pl. xxii.7), the other by Hill (*Catalogue*, 64-65, nr. 137 and pl. 5). See also Charbonneaux, *MélPiganiol* 1.407-8 and figs. 1, 2, and 8. Charbonneaux (p. 412) believes that these priests bore pitchers of Nile water rather than statues.

[128] A. Guimet, "L'exploration des nécropoles gréco-byzantines d'Antinoe," *Annales du Musée Guimet* 30, pt. 2 (1901), pl. iii.

[129] Berlin, Aeg. Museum, nrs. 8873, 9008, 9140, 9790, 9791, 9839, 9840, 13856 (all mentioned in Weber, *Drei Untersuchungen*, 34, nn. 34 and 36; 35, n. 38—see also Weber, *Terrakotten*, 1.24-25 and Taf. 1), and 14320 (Roeder, *Ägyptische Bronzefiguren*, 486 and Taf. 65L). Cairo Museum, nr. 27525, a statue of a priest who may be carrying an Osiris Hydreios (C. C. Edgar, *Greek Sculpture* [Cat. gén. Caire, 13.1], Cairo, 1903, nr. 27525), and nrs. 38861-64 (Daressy, *Statues*, 214-15 and pl. 43). Alexandria Museum, nrs. 6548, 7647, 7779, 7780, 22225, and 23074 (Breccia, *Terrecotte*, 1.57 and pl. xlviii. 2; 2.33 and pls. xxvii. 180 and 182, xxviii. 188 and 190), and nr. 20274, priest bearing an Osiris Hydreios (Charbonneaux, *MélPiganiol* 1.407-8 and fig. 9). A further example from this museum, the torso of a priest carrying a Hydreios figure, is described by E. Breccia (*Le musée gréco-romaine de l'année 1922/23*, Alexandria, 1924, 21, nr. 5 and pl. 17.2). Budapest, Musée des

Beaux-Arts, inv. nr. 50.139 (E. Borhegyi, *Bulletin de Musée Hongrois des Beaux-Arts* 2 [1948], 8-10, nr. 10). Leiden, Rijksmuseum, nrs. AED 109, 141, and 142 (Stricker, *OudhMeded* 24 [1943], 3 and Afb. 2; Van Wijngaarden, *OudhMeded* 39 [1958], suppl., p. 1). The Hague, Carnegielaan Museum, nr. S-984, a large Osiris Hydreios probably from Egypt (Von Bissing, *BArchAlex* 24 [1929], 39-41). Two Sarapis *kline* reliefs with Osiris Hydreios figures: Berlin, Antiquarium, inv. nr. 31275 and Varga-Castiglione Coll. (Budapest), nr. 123 ("bought in Cairo"). On these see Castiglione, *ActaAnt* 9 (1961), 294-97 and Abb. 1-3. A gem engraved with a Hydreios figure is known to have come from an Egyptian grave, but the precise site has not been recorded (Schläger, *Commentatio de numo Hadriani plumbeo et gemma isiaca in funere Aegyptii medicato repertis*, Helmstedt, 1742, 187—Drexler [*LM* 2.472] lists seven other gems with similar engravings but the find spots of these are apparently unknown). Two glass objects from Egypt decorated with the Osiris Hydreios figure (Abd el-Mohsen el-Khasab, "Représentation du panthéon égypto-gréco-romain sur deux verres gravés," *MélMichałowski*, 111-20). Before 1890 Petrie "bought in Cairo a steatite triad" depicting Isis, Osiris Hydreios, and Harpocrates (Petrie, *Kahun*, 36). The present whereabouts of this object is unknown to me.

[130] Weber, *Drei Untersuchungen*, 35 and n. 38.

[131] Latin: *Sacerdos Osirim/ferens*. Greek: Προφή[της] / ῎Οσειριν κωμ[ά]ζ<ω>[ν].

[132] Weber, *Drei Untersuchungen*, 35, n. 38; Von Bissing, *BArchAlex* 24 (1929), 57-58.

[133] Drexler, *Cultus*, 57. He supplies additional references.

[134] Ibid., 50; Perc, *Beiträge*, 106.

[135] Harris and Harris, *Oriental Cults*, 89.

[136] See the catalogues of Isis-related finds in the following works: Grimm, *Zeugnisse*; Leclant, *Studia aegyptiaca* 1.263-86 (fifty-three images of Osiris found in Gaul—no Osiris Hydreios statues); Lakatos, *Acta Universitatis Szegedinensis: Acta Antiqua* 4 (1961), 1-31; and Dobrovits, *Budapest Régiségei* 13 (1943), 45-75.

[137] Weber, *Drei Untersuchungen*, 31-33. Neither Von Bissing (*BArchAlex* 24 [1929], 48-49) nor any later scholar has seen any reason to deny Weber's basic findings.

[138] The one possible exception is an Osiris Hydreios found in a tomb in the Western Necropolis of Alexandria. The tomb is said by Breccia (*Terrecotte*, 1.43-44) to be no earlier in date than the 1st cen. AD. The typology of the Hydreios image found there would be a factor in pointing to a later date.

[139] Vatican Mus. Eg., nr. 69a. Date: Von Bissing, *BArchAlex* 24 (1929), 43. See Weber, *Drei Untersuchungen*, 37 and n. 43; Roullet, *Egyptian Monuments*, 141, nr. 315.

[140] A cautionary note, however. Once again the iconographic change on the Alexandrian coins of Trajan's reign and later must have been preceded by earlier changes with respect to the statue. Nonetheless, this general observation on the dating of Type B figures may have bearing on the traditional date assigned to the columns from the Campus Martius Iseum which were discussed above. Rather than deriving from the time of Domitian's reconstruction of the sanctuary (the usual theory), they may have been set in place during the course of a later re-modeling. For example, it is known that such a renovation took place at the time of Alexander Severus (*Hist. Aug., Alexander Severus* 26.8).

[141] Dattari, nrs. 826 (my Pl. XIX), 827/828, 829, 830, 1329 (Pl. XIX), 1663, 2500-2 (Pl. XIX), 2504, 3440, 3622, 3798.

[142] Panofsky, *GazBA* 57 (1961), 195.

[143] With respect to the coins see Von Bissing, *BArchAlex* 24 (1929), 49. Examples of coins in which both figures have beards: Dattari, nrs. 1132 and 2500 (my Pl. XIX). Examples of coins in which both figures lack beards: Dattari, nrs. 1949 and 2504. The situation in which the two figures lack beards is, of course, far less probative. However, it suggests that the presence or absence of a beard does not automatically indicate whether Osiris or Isis is depicted.

[144] Weber, *Drei Untersuchungen*, 44.

[145] See also Malaise, *Conditions*, 206.

[146] Ibid., 126.

[147] Dattari, nrs. 9: reign of Augustus (my Pl. XII, 1), 286/287: 14th year of Nero, and 1127: 11th year of Trajan.

[148] Fluted pitchers appear on coins of Trajan, Hadrian, and Antoninus Pius (Dattari, nrs. 6309-10, 1977, and 2643).

[149] A small Osiris Hydreios in the Louvre Museum (Nr. E 22 285 = MG 4 730) has by exception a very rounded, almost spherical belly (Fouquet, *BIFAO* 73 [1973], 63-64 and pl. vi). Fouquet (p. 69) remarks that this object has "à very strong oriental character"; it seems unlikely that it was made in Egypt though its provenance is unknown.

[150] Pompeii, *Casa del Frutetto* fresco; Nomentum inscription (SIRIS 531).

[151] Schede, *Angelos* 2 (1926), 61.

[152] Apuleius, *Met.* 11.11.

[153] Weber, *Drei Untersuchungen*, 35 and n. 38.

[154] I have discovered the following examples of this inscription which is normally in the form δοίη σοι ὁ Ὄσιρις τὸ ψυχρὸν ὕδωρ. This is, to my knowledge, the most complete list yet assembled. Consequently, I include some bibliography (usually the major publication plus references to standard collections) for each text.

From Egypt:

Alexandria:

    1. Wall inscription found on a tomb in the Gabbari area—date: ?

        (G. Botti, "Etudes topographiques dans la nécropole de Gabbari," *BArchAlex* 2 [1899], 50, nr. 2; Lévy, *JAsiat* 211 [1927], 300)

    2. Wall inscription in a tomb in the Kom-esh-Shuqafa catacombs—date: 2nd cen. AD or later

        (G. Botti, "Grafitto orfico nell' ipogeo di Basilissa a Kom-el-Chouqafa," *Revista egiziana* 5 [1893], 271-73; Lévy, *JAsiat* 211 [1927], 300)

    3. Inscription found on the four sides of a square altar which is hollow inside—date: ?

        (E. Breccia, *Iscrizioni greche e latine* [Catalogue général des antiquités égyptiennes du Musée d'Alexandrie], Cairo, 1911, 170-71, nr. 332 and pl. liv.131 and 131a; Lévy, *JAsiat* 211 [1927], 300)

    4. Inscription found in 1877 in the course of digging the foundations of the Bourse de Minet-el Bassal in the "Old City"—date: mid 2nd cen. AD

        (Néroutsos-Bey, *RArch* 3.9 [1887], 1. 201; Lévy, *JAsiat* 211 [1927], 300)

Alexandria ?:

    5. Funerary epigram—date: late Imperial period

        (Bernand, *Inscriptions*, 215-19, nr. 47; Lévy, *JAsiat* 211 [1927], 301; Peek, *Griechische Vers-Inschriften*, vol. 1, nr. 1842)

Saqqarah:

    6. Inscription on the stone cover for a tomb—date: "Roman period"

Formula varies: κατὰ γῆς δῶκε ψυχρὸν ῎Οσιρις ὕδωρ
("Rapport de M. C. Wescher sur sa mission en Egypte," *RArch* NS 10 [1864], 2.222; Lévy, *JAsiat* 211 [1927], 300)
From Italy:
  Rome:
    7. Inscription—date: possibly the 3rd cen. AD
        (G. Zoega, *De origine et usu obeliscorum*, Rome, 1797, 305, n. 25; Lévy, *JAsiat* 211 [1927], 300; *IG* XIV.1488; SIRIS 459)
    8. Inscription on a small, square funerary urn of marble—date: ? The Greek formula is given in Latin letters: *Doe se Osiris to psychron hydor.*
        (Lévy, *JAsiat* 211 [1927], 301; *IG* XIV.1705; *CIL* VI.20616; SIRIS 460)
    9. Inscription which is now lost—date: ?
        (Lévy, *JAsiat* 211 [1927], 301; *IG* XIV.1782; SIRIS 461)
    10. Marble stele—date: end of 1st cen. AD
        (G. Patriarca, "Epitaffio greco recentemente scoperto a Roma," *BullCom* 61 [1933], 211-15; SIRIS 462)
  Hipponium (Bruttium)
    11. Gold plate found in a tomb with an inscription which is restored as follows: [ὁ ῎Οσιρις δοίη σοι τὸ] ψυχρὸν ὕδωρ—date: ?
        (Raoul-Rochette, "Les antiquités chrétiens des catacombes," *MPAIBL* 13 [1837], 577-78; Malaise, *Inventaire*, 311, Hipponium, nr. 1)
From elsewhere:
  Carthage:
    12. Fragmentary inscription: [··· δοίη σοι ὁ ῎Οσι]ρις τὸ [ψυχ]ρὸν ὕδωρ ·· date: ?
        (A. L. Delattre, *BA* 1920, clxxviii; *SEG* IX. 829: SIRIS 778)
[155] There are four inscriptions which are closely related to the "Cool Water" texts and which are often included in lists of those. I give only the pertinent portions of these inscriptions:
Mex (a suburb west of Alexandria). Stele with funerary epigram—date: 2nd cen. AD or later. Text: σοὶ δὲ ᾿Οσείριδος ἁγνὸν ὕδωρ Εἶσις χαρίσαιτο.
    (Néroutsos-Bey, *RArch* 3.9 [1887], 1.199-201, nr. 2; Bernand, *Inscriptions*, nr. 52; Lévy, *JAsiat* 211 [1927], 301)
Luxor area or the south of Egypt. Epitaph for a Greek soldier—date: Imperial period. Text: οὔτ᾿ (᾿Ω) κεανοῦ ψυχρὸν ὕδωρ πίνομαι.
    (P. Jouguet, "Epitaphe d'un grec d'Egypte," *REG* 9 [1896], 433-36; Bernand, *Inscriptions*, nr. 13)
Rome. Funerary epigram—date: 2nd or 3rd cen. AD. Text: ψυχρὸν ὕδωρ δοίη σοι ἄναξ ἐνέρων Αἰδωνεύς.
    (Peek, *Griechische Vers-Inschriften*, vol. 1, nr. 1410; *IG* XIV.1842; Lévy, *JAsiat* 211 [1927], 301. In the late Roman magical curse tablets published by Wünsch (n. 99 above), *Aidōneus* would appear to be Osiris.)
Rome. Metrical funerary inscription—date: ? Text: ... ταύτην τὴν στήλην ἐπύησα Σώτας σε φιλήσας ψυχῇ διψώσῃ ψυχρὸν ὕδ[ωρ] μέταδ[ος].
    (*IG* XIV.1890; Lévy, *JAsiat* 211 [1927], 301)
[156] Rohde, *Psyche*, 2.575-76.
[157] This text, variously dated to the 4th, the 3rd, the 2nd, or even the 5th cen. BC, has been published by Otto Kern (*Orphicorum fragmenta*, Berlin, 1922, 104-5, nr. 32a); by Georg Kaibel (*Epigrammata graeca*, Berlin, 1878, nr. 1037); and in *IG* XIV.638. Text: ... εὑρήσεις δ᾿ ἑτέραν, τῆς Μνημοσύνης ἀπὸ λίμνης / ψυχρὸν ὕδωρ προρέον·

φύλαχες δ' ἐπίπροσθεν ἔασιν. / εἰπεῖν· γῆς παῖς εἰ σ[ὺ] χαὶ οὐρανοῦ ἀστερόεντο[ς. / αὐτὰρ ἐ[γὼ] γένος οὐράνιον· τόδε δ' ἴστε χαὶ αὐτοί / δίψηι δ' εἰμὶ [αὐ]ή χαὶ ἀπόλλυμαι· ἀλλὰ δότ' αἶψα / ψυχρὸν ὕδωρ προρέον τῆς Μνημοσύνης ἀπὸ λίμνης. See also André Parrot, "Le 'refrigerium' dans l'au-delà," *RHR* 115 (1937), 85-86 and Nilsson, *GGR*, 2.237-38.

¹⁵⁸ For example: "This is your libation of water, Osiris; this is your libation of water, N., which had issued from before your son, which went forth from Horus" (Pyramid Text 22—5th Dynasty). For additional evidence see Blackman, *RecTrav* 39 (1921), 59-62 and J. H. Breasted, *Development of Religion and Thought in Ancient Egypt*, New York, 1959, 18-19. Lévy (*JAsiat* 211 [1927], 307) argues that the Egyptian word ordinarily translated "cool water" should be instead "libation of water" (as I give in the text above).

¹⁵⁹ See Lévy, *JAsiat* 211 (1927), 302-3; Ahmed Bey Kamal, *Stèles ptolemaiques et romains* (Cat. gén. Caire), Cairo, 1905, 1.68, nr. 22136.

¹⁶⁰ Lévy, *JAsiat* 211 (1927), 307-8.

¹⁶¹ So also Bernand, *Inscriptions*, 218. C. Mohrmann ("Locus refrigerii," *Etudes sur la latin des chrétiens*, vol. 2: *Latin chrétien et médiéval*, Rome, 1961, 89) does not believe that the Christian concept of *refrigerium* represents any sort of borrowing from the Osiris formula.

¹⁶² Malaise, *Conditions*, 207; Deonna, *RHR* 119 (1939) 59.

¹⁶³ Malaise, *Conditions*, 125. See also pp. 126 and 206-7.

¹⁶⁴ Like the cultic pitcher and the Hydreios statue, the "Cool Water" texts also were probably felt to have a special connection with Isis. A late Roman stele from the Alexandria area (n. 155) has a formula which surely relates to the normal type but which calls upon Isis to give "the sacred water of Osiris."

¹⁶⁵ This is the view, for example, of Cumont (*Oriental Religions*, 102), of Lévy (*JAsiat* 211 [1927], 307-8), of Dölger (*AntChrist* 5 [1936], 171), and, more recently, of Dunand (*Culte d'Isis*, 3.212).

¹⁶⁶ Vitruvius 8. *praef*. 4.

¹⁶⁷ Apuleius, *Met*. 11.11.

¹⁶⁸ Plutarch, *De Is. et Os*. 36.365 B.

¹⁶⁹ Ibid., 34.364 D and 35-36.365 A-B. Plutarch himself (Ibid., 64.376 F) rejects any view of Osiris which would identify him with natural phenomena.

¹⁷⁰ The fact that the Osiris Hydreios statue was accorded the same honors as the actual containers of sacred water fits very well with such an idea.

CHAPTER SEVEN

¹ Nock, *Essays*, 1.97.

² G. van der Leeuw (*Religion in Essence and Manifestation*, 2 vols., New York, 1963, 2.343-49) provides a useful phenomenological account of such purification rites.

³ For various examples of Graeco-Roman purification rites see Nock, *Essays*, 1.98-99 and M. Nilsson, *Greek Piety*, New York, 1969, 14-15.

⁴ Hippocrates, *De morbo sacro* 2. On these sprinkling basins see L. Ziehen, "Perirrantēria," *RE* 19.856-57; A. Bouche-Leclercq, "Lustratio," *DAGR* 3.2.1408 and fig. 4680; Kenner, *ÖJh* 29 (1935), 109-54; and Nilsson, *GGR*, 1.102. For photographs of περιρραντήρια found in the Agora at Athens see H. A. Thompson and R. E. Wycherley, *The Agora of Athens: The History, Shape and Uses of an Ancient City Center* (The Athenian Agora, 14), Princeton, 1972, 118-19 and Pls. 64c and 67a.

⁵ Pollux 1.8. See also Lucian, *De sacrificiis* 13; Heraclitus, *Quaest. Hom.* 3; Iamblichus, *V. Pythag.* 18.83.

⁶ Heron, *Pneumatica* 1.32. The Egyptians also purified themselves by twisting a bronze ring set at the entrance to the temple. Heron suggested that a device be invented whereby when the ring was turned, ablution water would be made available. No evidence for these bronze rings has been found at any of the Graeco-Roman sanctuaries of Isis and Sarapis.

⁷ For a description of these basins see Vogliano, *Primo rapporto*, 17 and tavv. i-iii. The diameter of these basins is estimated from Vogliano, *Secondo rapporto*, plan of the temple. The original column which supported the basin on the left was replaced at some time with two or three random stone blocks.

⁸ This dimension is also estimated from Vogliano's photographs.

⁹ Adolf Erman, "Kupferringe an Tempelthoren," *ZÄS* 38 (1901), 54 and Otto, *Priester und Tempel*, 1.396.

¹⁰ At this temple at Koptos W. M. Flinders Petrie (*Koptos*, London, 1896, 24-25) found a series of small tanks with little stairways leading down into them. These were intended to be set into the ground and, to judge by a foot carved into the bottom of one of them, were designed as ritual foot baths. An inscription on one of the tanks indicates that it was the property of one Aristius Saturninus (Ibid., 25). Further, large "washing tanks" were found inside and to the right of the Third Pylon of this temple (Ibid., pl. 1) as well as by the Gate of Nectanebo in the South Temple complex (Ad.-J. Reinach, "Deuxième rapport sur les fouilles de Koptos," *Bulletin de la Société Française des Fouilles Archéologiques* 3 [1911], 68 and pl. i). No parallels for these foot baths have been found at the sites outside of Egypt.

¹¹ Papadakis, *ArchD* 1 (1915), 144-45 and Bruneau, *Sanctuaire*, 62-63. The outside diameter is 0.75 m while the inside diameter is 0.69 m. Inside depth = 0.18 m.

¹² This stand is also of marble and is 0.61 m high. It has a square hole at the top which almost, but not quite, matches a square protrusion found on the bottom of the basin (Ibid., 145).

¹³ *CE* 184 = *I Délos* 2162 (early 1st cen. BC): five fragments from a basin made of black basalt. It had quite thick walls (0.07 m). *I Délos* 2198: two small fragments of a basin. *I Délos* 2199: a single curved piece of white marble which is said to have come from a basin. Width: 0.15 m, thickness: 0.10 m. If the thickness is any indication, this must have come from a rather large basin.

¹⁴ *CE* 113 = *I Délos* 2057.

¹⁵ In late antiquity Aphthonius (*Progym.* 49) noted that a κρήνη was one of the more noteworthy features in the courtyard of the Serapeum at Alexandria. This water facility was probably the great "Piscina" (Figs. 12 and 26) built around 215 AD rather than a περιρραντήριον of more ordinary dimensions.

¹⁶ Donaldson and Cooke, *Pompeii*, 1.43; E. Gerhard and T. Panofka, *Neapels Antike Bildwerke*, 2 vols., Stuttgart, 1828, 1.43; Dyer, *Pompeii*, 140; Breton, *Pompeia*, 47; G. Fiorelli, *Descrizione di Pompei*, Naples, 1875, 360; Lafaye, *Histoire*, 192; Gusman, *Pompéi*, 88; Tran Tam Tinh, *Essai*, 36. Gusman (p. 89) prints a drawing of a round marble basin set on an ornate column and says that this is the lustral basin from the Iseum. He is in error. The basins attributed to the Iseum are rectangular; they are described in some detail by Gerhard and Panofka (*Bildwerke*, 1.43) and a drawing of one of them appears in *Real Museo Borbonico*, 16 vols., Naples, 1824-57, vol. 7, frontispiece.

¹⁷ This rectangular basin is described by Gerhard and Panofka (*Bildwerke*, 1.43) as 2 1/3 Neapolitan palms wide, 3 1/2 long, and 5 1/2 high (therefore 0.62 × 0.92

× 1.45 m). This last measurement is certainly incorrect if the drawing of this object provided in *Real Museo Borbonico* (vol. 7, frontispiece) is at all in proportion. From this sketch the basin appears to be about 0.90 m high.

[18] There is no mention of these basins in *PAH*, in Hamilton (*Archaeologia* 4 [1776], 160-75), or in Jorio (*Plan*). In other words, they are not mentioned before 1827.

[19] T. Mommsen, *Inscriptiones Regni Neapolitani Latinae*, Leipzig, 1852, nr. 2239. For the archaeologist's description see *PAH* 1.2.53 and 173. Mommsen's report was criticized by scholars such as H. Nissen (*Pompeianische Studien*, 348). His attempted rebuttal to his critics (*CIL* X.1.843) failed to resolve all of the difficulties.

[20] Strabo 14.6.3.

[21] Westholm, *Temples*, 64-65. He indicates that the top part of the walls had been destroyed. From his Fig. 17 it would appear that the basin was set partially below ground level.

[22] Leclant, *Orientalia* 20 (1951), 455.

[23] Hölbl (*Zeugnisse*, 29) provides this data.

[24] Pesce (*Tempio*, 17) gives a full description of this cistern and indicates that it is situated to the north of the main axis of the temple (i.e., close to the main entrance). However, he failed to indicate the precise location of this structure on his plan of the site.

[25] Le Corsu, *Isis*, 246-47. I have no further information on these wells other than their location.

[26] SIRIS 313.7.

[27] Since I believe that this inscription did come from the known Iseum, I prefer to see it dated later in the Imperial period rather than earlier. E. Böringer and F. Krauss (*Das Temenos für den Herrscherkult* [Altertümer von Pergamon, 9], Berlin, 1937, 85) date the stone to the 1st cen. AD (so also Nilsson, *GGR*, 2.341), the century before the founding of the Iseum at the Red Hall. However, Ohlemutz (*Kulte*, 273) believes that a date in the 2nd cen. is also possible. The idiosyncratic character of the lettering makes any certainty in the matter difficult to obtain.

[28] Salditt-Trappmann, *Tempel*, 61-62. For a photograph, though of rather poor quality, see Oliverio, *ASAtene* 2 (1916), 310, fig. 2.

[29] One or both of these may have existed at the east end of the basin. This wall has entirely disappeared, and the excavators dug no further to the east than the outer east wall of the temple and therefore did not verify the absence of pipes in this area.

[30] Pesce, *Tempio*, 32-33 and figs. 17, 18, and 23.

[31] Pesce (Ibid., 32) gives a description of this well and indicates that once it had been cleaned water began again to flow into it.

[32] Pesce (Ibid., 33) notes that the south wall of the basin, the wall by the well, is 0.10 m higher than the other three walls. He also remarks on a base-like block with a deep, 0.14 m square hole in it which is set by the northwest corner of the basin. How this object related to the basin is not clear.

[33] Pesce (Ibid., 31-33) provides a complete description of the altar, the well, the basin, and the accompanying drainage system. See also his Fig. 16.

[34] Since Pesce believed that the sanctuary had been constructed much earlier than it actually was, he supposed (Ibid., 33 and 67-68) that these basins had replaced two earlier versions.

[35] Ibid., 64.

[36] *PAH* 1.1.186. See also Mau, *Pompeii*, 178; Overbeck and Mau, *Pompeii*, 109; and Jorio, *Plan*, 130-31. This basin appears on none of the plans of the Iseum.

[37] *PAH* 1.1.186. I have converted the dimensions in Neapolitan palms given by the writer to metric measurements.

[38] Rowe (*BArchAlex* 35 [1942], 141-43) offers a rather confused and unclear report on these basins and the channels connected to them. More information can be obtained from his detailed plan (Pl. xxxii = my Fig. 26).

[39] The floor of the largest basin measures c. 4.3 × 4.5 m while that of the smallest is c. 2.6 × 2.4 m. In general, the basins approach the larger size. (Dimensions estimated from Ibid., pl. xxxii.)

[40] The smallest basin has a much smaller drain (c. 0.25 m on the outside).

[41] Ibid., 141.

[42] What relation the "Piscina" had to this system of basins is quite uncertain. It is connected to the same drain system but, as an immense and deep pool—its floor measures 10.58 × 10.82 m and is approximately 2.70 m below the level of the courtyard—it seems to have had a different character. For descriptions see Rowe, *BArchAlex* 35 (1942), 142-43 and *ASAntEg*, Suppl. 2 (1946), 61. From coins found at its four corners under the concrete bedding for the floor, Rowe determined that it had been constructed not very long after 215 AD. At its south end is a pit which is 3 m in diameter and 16 m deep; its rim is set below the floor of the Piscina. Water was said to drain into it both from the Piscina and from the ablution basins (Botti, *Fouilles*, 109; Rowe, *BArchAlex* 35 [1942], 141). Botti (*L'Acropole*, 17) found this pit filled with large stones, parts of column bases, a marble Roman eagle, etc. Apparently an earlier pit had been filled in with stones and coarse junk by the Roman engineers—these items would not have prevented water from flowing down—and the floor of the Piscina laid over it. Since Botti (Ibid.) specifically says that he had to probe below the floor of the Piscina before he found the deep pit, perhaps only the ablution basins but not the Piscina actually emptied into it. (Botti [*Fouilles*, 109] reported that the floor of the Piscina slopes toward the north, i.e., in the direction away from the pit.) Such an arrangement would suggest that the ablution basins are earlier than the Piscina.

A large, rose granite scarab (19th Dynasty) measuring 0.89 × 0.62 m at its base was found to the east of the Piscina near the top of the "grand escalier," a designation clearer to Botti (Ibid., 70-71) than to us but probably indicating a find spot about 30 m from the Piscina. Perhaps the scarab had originally been placed close to the Piscina. By the sacred lake at the Temple of Amon at Karnak Amenophis III (18th Dynasty) erected a large stone scarab. This image served to underscore at this site the solar aspect proper to all the sacred lakes of Egypt (Bonnet, "See, heiliger," *Reallexikon*, 695; Blackman, *PSBA* 40 [1918], 88). At a temple at which Sarapis could be addressed as Zeus Helios Sarapis (Wace, *BullFarU* 2 [1944], 25-26), such a solar reference would certainly have been in place. If the scarab did stand close by the Piscina, its presence would have been a sign that this pool of water was the sacred lake for the Serapeum.

[43] See Broneer, *South Stoa*, 136-37 and Smith, *HTR* 70 (1977) 212-14 for a discussion of this facility. The length and width of the room are estimated from Broneer's plan IV; the room is actually wider at its east end (3.3 m) than at its west end (3.1 m).

[44] Broneer, *South Stoa*, 137 and pl. 44.3. The floor of this room is surfaced with large tiles at its west end and with a watertight striated stucco layer over the rest of its area.

[45] Ibid., 136.

[46] Ibid., 136-37. He notes that the construction of medieval cellars and storage pits in the area to the north of the stoa has obliterated the further course of this water channel.

⁴⁷ Bruneau, *Sanctuaire*, 37-42 and 50-52. The room measures approximately 5.5 × 5.3 m.

⁴⁸ Bruneau (Ibid., 51) indicates that Walls 11, 13, and 14 are later than the outer wall of the precinct.

⁴⁹ Bruneau (Ibid.) believes that ''Wall 14'' was only a low stone boundary and not an actual wall. He also argues (p. 126) that the northern rooms were connected to the sanctuary until Wall 6 blocked off access.

⁵⁰ Neither Papadakis (*ArchD* 1 [1915], 131) nor Bruneau (*Sanctuaire*, 51) actually dug to the bottom of the well. Both ask if it might have been a cistern but both finally conclude, Bruneau quite definitely, that it was in fact a well.

⁵¹ Bruneau, *Sanctuaire*, 27-28.

⁵² Ibid., 127.

⁵³ Ibid., 41.

⁵⁴ Ibid., 135-36.

⁵⁵ Even though Bruneau (Ibid., 18) discovered a round opening in the north side of Pit f, it is somewhat unlikely that this structure was designed to hold water for no remains of interior plastering have been found. Pit k is even less likely to have served this purpose, for it is poorly constructed (Ibid., 28), has no drain hole, and also shows no sign of interior plastering.

⁵⁶ In his own words Bruneau (*Sanctuaire*, 136) says that Room G was ''aménagée tardivement et peu de temps avant de cesser d'appartenir au sanctuaire.''

⁵⁷ The door from this room to the northern area does not exclude this possibility. Bruneau argues that the rooms in this area were connected to the sanctuary during much of its existence. They therefore probably served as living quarters for personnel connected with the precinct. Room G would have served not only as a passageway for these individuals but also may have supplied water for ablution rituals carried on in this northern area.

⁵⁸ The description is taken from Salditt-Trappmann, *Tempel*, 15. She provided no other dimensions and did not indicate the location of the cistern on her plan of the sanctuary (= my Fig. 21).

⁵⁹ The Selinus River would often have been too low to maintain such a depth of water in the cistern.

⁶⁰ The cistern cannot have contained Nile water since it was not constructed so as to allow a re-enactment of the flood. Indeed, quite the contrary!

⁶¹ Barra Bagnasco *et al.*, *Scavi*, 33-34. See my Ch. I, n. 28.

⁶² Le Corsu, *Isis*, 246-47. She herself offers no theories about the function of this well.

⁶³ After the presentation before the goddess, the priest imparted certain secret commands to Lucius.

⁶⁴ Apuleius, *Met.* 11.1: *meque protinus purificandi studio marino lavacro trado, septiesque submerso fluctibus capite ... sic apprecabar.*

⁶⁵ If Juvenal (6.523-26) refers to a practice in Isis worship, however exaggerated for the sake of satire, he describes a ritual action parallel to *Met.* 11.1. In this case, a female worshipper plunges her head into the Tiber.

⁶⁶ E. Lane, *Corpus Monumentorum Religionis Dei Menis*, vol. 1: *The Monuments and Inscriptions* (EPRO, 19), Leiden, 1971, 8-10, nr. 13 (= *SIG* 1042). Cf. 7-8, nr. 12 (= *IG* II².1365). Date of both of these inscriptions: late 2nd cen. AD.

⁶⁷ For discussions of these reliefs see Blackman, *PSBA* 40 (1918), 57-66 and 86-91; Bonnet, *Angelos* 1 (1925), 105-9; and especially Gardiner, *JEA* 36 (1950), 3-12. The latter (pp. 4-5) provides a list of thirty-four pre-Ptolemaic examples of this representation. Elsewhere (*JEA* 37 [1951], 111 and *JEA* 39 [1953], 24, n. 4)

Gardiner adds three further examples to his list. To this I can add four later reliefs: Kom Ombo—purification of Ptolemy XI Neos Dionysos (J. de Morgan *et al.*, *Kom Ombos* [Catalogue des monuments et inscriptions de l'Egypte antique, 2-3], 2 vols., Vienna, 1895-1909, vol. 1, pl. 191); Philae—purification of Augustus (Lepsius, *Denkmäler*, Abt. 4, nr. 71a); Dendera—purification of Nero (A. Mariette, *Dendérah: description général du grand temple de cette ville*, 6 vols., Paris, 1870-80, vol. 1, pl. 10); and Kalabsha—purification of Trajan (Lepsius, *Denkmäler*, Abt. 4, nr. 85).

⁶⁸ Examples of this type from Luxor and Deir el Bahri are illustrated in Blackman, *PSBA* 40 (1918), pls. v. 1 and vi. In the Mithraeum of Santa Prisca a pedestal arrangement was also utilized, although in somewhat different fashion, in conjunction with a ritual washing with water. Here, as M. J. Vermaseren and C. C. van Essen (*The Excavations in the Mithraeum of the Church of Santa Prisca in Rome*, Leiden, 1965, 141, figs. 14-15, and Pl. xxxii) reconstruct it, the initiate knelt upon an elevated area located just in front of a cult niche. He would then bend his head over a shallow vessel implanted in the upper surface of this area in such a way that water poured over him would fall into it. Apparently this elevated baptismal area was constructed so that the Father or Heliodromus who performed the rite could easily reach the initiate's head.

⁶⁹ For a list of such representations and for illustrations of several of them see Blackman, *RecTrav* 39 (1921), 53-55. Bonnet (*Angelos* 1 [1925], 110-20; *Reallexikon*, 633-37) also discusses this topic.

⁷⁰ Bonnet, *Angelos* 1 (1925), 119, Abb. 8.

⁷¹ G. Legrain and E. Naville, "L'aile nord du pylône d'Aménophis III a Karnak," *Annales du Musée Guimet* 30 (1902), 12 and pl. xi. B. See also Bonnet, *Angelos* 1 (1925), 109-10.

⁷² Bonnet, *Angelos* I (1925), 105.

⁷³ Long ago Reitzenstein (*Die hellenistischen Mysterienreligionen*, 20-21, 41, and 220-21) observed that there was a link between the ritual sprinkling undergone by Lucius (Apuleius, *Met.* 11.23) and the Egyptian purification of the dead and purification of the Pharaoh. In pointing to this connection I am concerned to compare the manner in which these rituals were conducted rather than their nature and meaning. If these washings had a baptismal character, they nonetheless remain as preparatory rites for more important cultic activities.

⁷⁴ A. M. Blackman, "Purification (Egyptian)," *Encyclopedia of Religion and Ethics*, ed. James Hastings, 13 vols., New York, 1908-27, 10.480.

⁷⁵ A. Wiedemann, "Bronze Circles and Purification Vessels in Egyptian Temples," *PSBA* 23 (1901), 269.

⁷⁶ Herodotus 2.37.

⁷⁷ Chaeremon, *Aegyptiaca* (cited in Porphyry, *Abst.* 4.7).

⁷⁸ Plutarch in particular (*De Is. et Os.* 75. 381 D) makes this clear.

⁷⁹ I have previously suggested that the low, flat basin at Pergamum may have served as a standing place for ablutions of this sort.

⁸⁰ The basins at Eretria and Priene and possibly also those at Gortyn and Pompeii were constructed in Hellenistic times. On the other hand, those found at Alexandria, Corinth, Pergamum, and Sabratha (Gortyn and Pompeii too?) were built during the Roman period.

⁸¹ On purification rites at Eleusis see G. E. Mylonas, *Eleusis and the Eleusinian Mysteries*, Princeton, 1961, 240-41 and 249.

⁸² See especially *Didache* 7.1-3; Tertullian, *De Bapt.* 4.3-4; *Acts of Peter (Actus Vercellenses* 5); *Acts of Thomas* 121; Pseudo-Clement, *Recogn.* 4.32; and *Book of Elchasai* (cited in Hippolytus, *Haer.* 9.15.4).

CHAPTER EIGHT

¹ Leclant, *Problèmes*, 95-96.

² Vidman, *Isis und Sarapis*, 167-72.

³ Tertullian, *De Bapt.* 5.1. Justin (*I Apol.* 62), Firmicus Maternus (*Err. prof. rel.* 2.5), and Sozomen (*Hist. Eccl.* 6.6) provide examples of related category mistakes resulting from polemical concerns. See Nock, *Essays*, 1.98-99.

⁴ However, Theophrastus (*On Waters* [cited in Athenaeus 2.15.41f]) indicated that Nile water also served as a first-rate laxative!

⁵ This Nilometer was filled in during Roman times, and no later replacement has been discovered. Perhaps a Nilometer from the Roman period still lies buried under some unexcavated portion of the site, although I am inclined to believe that the portable sacred cubit simply assumed the chief function of the older structure and so rendered the construction of a replacement unnecessary.

⁶ The Temple of Isis at Philae in southern Egypt had in its late period a number of Nilometers and Nilometer-like structures. The very number of these devices, an unusual state of affairs, perhaps was intended to express the power of Isis over the Nile flood. Of all the sites in Egypt known to have had Nilometers, only this sanctuary at Philae and the Serapeum of Alexandria honored Isis or Sarapis as their principal deities.

⁷ I have determined that five features are characteristic of fixed Nile water containers: they were enclosed in a housing which shielded the sacred water contained within, they were largely situated underground, they lacked any sort of drain, they were fed only by the Nile itself, by Nile-related rivers (e.g., the Inopus), or by rain water, and they were designed in such a way that this water would periodically rise sharply within them or even overflow (the ritual "flooding").

⁸ Given this limited number of fixed Nile water containers at the Roman period sites and given that many of these same sites also lack any evidence of fixed ablution facilities, the view that water facilities are typologically characteristic of Isis-Sarapis sanctuaries cannot be sustained. Proponents of that view include: Weber, *Drei Untersuchungen*, 47; F. Bisson de la Roque, *Rapport sur les fouilles de Médamoud* (Fouilles de l'Institut Français d'Archéologie Orientale du Caire: rapports préliminaires, 9), Cairo, 1931, 45; Josef Keil, "Das Serapeion von Ephesos," *Halil Edhem hâtıra kitabı—In memoriam Halil Edhem*, 2 vols., Ankara, 1947, 1.190-92; and Tschudin, *Isis*, 23, 25, and 30-31. T. Kraus *et al.* (*MDIK* 22 [1967], 180) express some reserve about including this feature in a typology.

⁹ Apuleius, *Met.* 11.17.

¹⁰ Plutarch, *De Is. et Os.* 64.376 F; 32.363 D, 33.364 A, etc.

¹¹ According to my interpretation of the relief of Perseus and Andromeda found on one of the side walls of the crypt housing at Pompeii, this Greek hero undergoes a similar metamorphosis. From an active and aggressive warrior he is converted into a more immanent divine force, the beneficent power of the Nile River which overcomes the demonic might of Sea (Seth) and so brings about fertility and life.

¹² Apuleius, *Met.* 11.11—see also Vitruvius 8. *praef.* 4; Plutarch, *De Is. et Os.* 36.365 B. The word ἀπορροή is a key term in the theory of sense perception developed by Empedocles (Theophrastus, *De sensu* 1-3 and 7-8; Plutarch, *QNat.* 19.916 D). Plato then used it in developing his own theory of color (*Tim.* 67 C-68 D) and also in other contexts (e.g., *Phdr.* 251 B).

¹³ Very often when Isis is associated with Osiris, she is viewed as a divinity immanent in the earth. See Plutarch, *De Is. et Os.* 32.363 D, 38.366 A, 57.374 C; Origen, *c. Cels.*, 5.38; Heliodorus 9.9; Porphyry, *De imag.* (cited in Eusebius,

Praep. Evang. 3.11.51); Firmicus Maternus, *Err. prof. rel.* 2.6; Macrobius, *Sat.* 21.11; etc.

[14] Vitruvius 8. *praef.* 4; Juvenal 6.526-28. See also Epiphanius, *Adv. Haeres.* 51.30.3.

[15] Both of these sites have been poorly reported and have not produced very many small finds.

[16] Von Gonzenbach, *Untersuchungen.* For addenda to this list see Von Gonzenbach, "Der griechisch-römische Scheitelschmuck und die Funde von Thasos," *BCH* 93 (1969), 898. This article (pp. 885-945) comments on a type of hair ornamentation sometimes found in conjunction with the "Horus lock"; her observations were challenged in part by C. Rolley ("Nattes, rubans et pendeloques," *BCH* 94 [1970], 551-65).

APPENDIX ONE

[1] For information on the remaining sites of the Roman period see my "The Known Isis-Sarapis Sanctuaries of the Roman Period," *ANRW* 2.17.2 (forthcoming). Four Hellenistic sites appear neither here in this appendix nor in the *ANRW* article: Argos, Memphis, Seleucia Pieria, and Tauromenium. Bibliographies: for Argos and Tauromenium see SIRIS. On Memphis: M. Guilmot, "Le Sarapieion de Memphis: Etude topographique," *ChrEg* 37 (1962), 359-81. On Seleucia Pieria, a sanctuary site only doubtfully to be associated with the cult of the Egyptian gods: R. Stillwell, ed., *Antioch on-the-Orontes,* vol. 3: *The Excavations, 1937-1939,* Princeton, 1941, 32-34, 260, and Pl. 16, nr. 365; and A.-J. Festugière, *Antioch païenne et chrétien,* Paris, 1959, 59. I am grateful to Dr. Frederick Norris of the Emmanuel School of Religion for bringing this latter site to my attention.

[2] Interpretation of the numerical ratings used in Columns 8-10:

Column 8: State of Site

   1 — general location of site known
   2 — precise location known
   3 — scattered fragments of the architecture found *in situ*
   4 — foundations partially preserved
   5 — foundations substantially or entirely preserved
   6 — foundations and some lower walls preserved
   7 — lower walls substantially preserved
   8 — some upper walls preserved
   9 — site buildings substantially preserved
  10 — site buildings substantially preserved; many small finds recovered *in situ*
  POB = partially overbuilt; TOB = totally overbuilt; PR = partially restored

Column 9: Excavations

   1 — most or all of site impossible to excavate—some random finds
   2 — chance discovery—no record of any systematic exploration
   3 — site probed by scattered trenches
   4 — site sufficiently excavated to determine most of its overall plan
   5 — entire site surveyed in detail but not yet cleared
   6 — central temple of site substantially or entirely cleared
   7 — precinct substantially or entirely cleared
   8 — entire precinct systematically excavated
   9 — site systematically excavated with attention given to minor finds
  10 — site systematically excavated with attention also to stratigraphic analysis

Column 10: Reports

1 — scattered notices only; no actual report
2 — report primarily limited to small finds
3 — notices only, but with more details given
4 — highlights among the discoveries reported; no plan of the site provided
5 — highlights among the discoveries reported; plan of site included
6 — more systematic general report published
7 — still more systematic and more detailed general report
8 — very systematic report provides detailed dimensions and other information on architecture and major small finds
9 — very systematic report provides detailed information on architecture and all small finds. Find spots generally or always indicated
10 — in addition, report offers analyses of pottery finds and stratigraphic remains

[3] A. Adriani, who offers the most useful short assessment of the site (*Repertorio*, ser. C, 1.90-100) underscored the confused state of the publications for this site and called for a complete re-examination of it. Reports by the various excavators: Mahmoud el-Falaki recounted the results of his survey and trenching operations (1862) in his *Mémoire sur l'antique Alexandrie*, Copenhagen, 1872. More important excavations were conducted by G. Botti in 1894-96. Basically he reported his work with care although he includes some rather fanciful reconstructions. See Botti, *L'acropole; Fouilles*; "Fouilles d'Alexandrie en 1896," *BIE* 3.8 (1897), 29-47; and "L'Apis de l'empereur Hadrien trouvé dans le Sérapéum d'Alexandrie," *BArchAlex* 2 (1899), 27-36 (on the black granite statue of a bull dedicated for the welfare of the Emperor Hadrian). In 1905-6 E. Breccia made further soundings on the site; his report, "Les fouilles dans le Sérapéum d'Alexandrie en 1905-1906," *ASAntEg* 8 (1907), 62-76, concentrated on small finds. In his *Iscrizioni greche e latine* ([Cat. gén. ant. ég. du Musée d'Alexandrie, 57], Cairo, 1911) he describes inscriptions from the site—see nrs. 6, 13, 68, 85, 150, 155, 168. His *Alexandrea ad Aegyptum*, Bergamo, 1914, 95-103 (French ed.) gives a guide book survey of the site. By far the most extensive and best-known explorations were carried on by Alan Rowe; his published reports, however, though extensive, are in tumultuous disarray: *BArchAlex* 35 (1942), 124-61 and *ASAntEg*, Suppl. 2 (1946), 1-94. Summary accounts of Rowe's work have been published by P. Jouguet (*CRAIBL* 1946, 680-86), C. Picard (*RArch* 28 [1947], 2.71-72), and A. J. B. Wace (*JHS* 65 [1945], 106-9). Rowe himself later published (with B. R. Rees) an important summation of his findings (*BJRL* 39 [1956-57], 485-520). On the Column of Diocletian: E. Combe, "De la Colonne Pompée au Phare d'Alexandrie," *BArchAlex* 34 (1941), 104-22. Notes on various small finds were published by A. J. B. Wace: "An Altar from the Serapeum," *BArchAlex* 36 (1943-44), 83-97 and Pls. vii-ix and *BullFarU* 2 (1944), 17-26 (inscriptions). For a list of the numerous ancient texts which refer to the Serapeum see A. Calderini, *Dizionario dei nomi geografici e topografici dell' Egitto greco-romano*, Cairo, 1935, 1.140-41 and Rowe-Rees, *BJRL* 39 (1956-57), 513-20. To this can be added *PCairo Zen.* III. 59355.102-3 and *POxy.* 3094. Many papyri refer to acts of supplication performed at Alexandria "before the Lord Sarapis"—e.g., *PAmh.* 136, *BGU* 1680, *PMich.* 492 and 513, *PRyl.* 230. The most important descriptions from antiquity of the (late Roman) sanctuary are: Ammianus Marcellinus 22.16.12-13; Aphthonius, *Progym.* (ed. Rabe, pp. 38-41); and Rufinus, *Hist. Eccl.* 11.23. Studies on the history of the sanctuary: S. Handler, *AJA* 75 (1971), 57-74 (on the date of the Roman reconstruction); A. Bauer and J. Strzygowski, "Eine alexandrinische Weltchronik," *DenkschrWien* 51 (1906),

2.69-75, 122, and Taf. vi (on the destruction of the Serapeum in the late fourth century); Fraser, *OpAth* 7 (1967), 35-40; and Fraser, *Ptolemaic Alexandria*, 1.27-28, 228, 236, 265-70, 274-75 (various aspects).

⁴ Tacitus speaks of a *sacellum Serapidi atque Isidi antiquitus sacratum* which had stood on the site before, as he thought, Ptolemy I replaced it with the present Serapeum. For other ancient texts which suggest the existence of an older sanctuary see Calderini, *Dizionario*, 1.141.

⁵ Wace, *BullFarU* 2 (1944), 18-19, nr. 1 a. See also Breccia, *Iscrizioni*, nr. 6; he reports that a dedication honoring Ptolemy II and Arsinoe was also found on the site. In this text, however, there is no mention of Sarapis and Isis.

⁶ Rowe, *ASAntEg*, Suppl. 2 (1946), 5-11 and 50-51; Rowe-Rees, *BJRL* 39 (1956-57), 509.

⁷ Rowe, *ASAntEg*, Suppl. 2 (1946), 54-58.

⁸ Strabo 17.1.10: ἐντὸς δὲ τῆς διώρυγος τό τε Σαράπειον καὶ ἄλλα τεμένη ἀρχαῖα ἐκλελειμμένα πως διὰ τὴν τῶν νέων κατασκευὴν τῶν ἐν Νικοπόλει. Fraser (*Ptolemaic Alexandria*, 1.274-75) interprets this text as including the Serapeum among the "neglected precincts" and consequently associates its reconstruction in Roman times with a renewal of interest in the cult of Sarapis. However, as Rowe (*ASAntEg*, Suppl. 2 [1946], 3, n. 1) points out, it is not grammatically clear that it *must* be so included.

⁹ Cited in Rowe, *ASAntEg*, Suppl. 2 (1946), 63-64.

¹⁰ Ibid., 62; see Rowe-Rees, *BJRL* 39 (1956-57), 495-96.

¹¹ Handler, *AJA* 75 (1971), 64-68.

¹² Cassius Dio 78.23.2.

¹³ Rowe (*ASAntEg*, Suppl. 2 [1946], 24, n. 1 and 33, n. 2) indicates only that the compressed masonry used by the Romans is from the second century AD or later.

¹⁴ Clement of Alexandria, *Protr.* 4.51; Eusebius, *Chron.* (ed. Schoene, pp. 172-73); and possibly Arnobius, *Adv. Nat.* 6.23.

¹⁵ The excavator, Joseph Puig y Cadafalch, published short annual reports of his finds ("Les excavacions d'Empuries," *AIEC* 2 [1908], 190-93 and "Crònica de les excavacions d'Empuries," *AIEC* 3 [1909-10], 708) and a more lengthy summary article, the single most useful report ("Els temples d'Empuries," *AIEC* 4 [1911-12], 303-22). See also his *L'arquitectura romana a Catalunya*, 2nd ed., Barcelona, 1934, 87-94. E. Gandía compiled a *Diario de excavaciones*—this manuscript was reported to be in the library of the Museum of Barcelona (not seen by me). More recently A. García y Bellido has re-examined the evidence from this site in several publications: *Hispania graeca*, vol. 2, Barcelona, 1948, 36-38 and, of much greater importance, *BRAH* 139 (1956), 313-21. The first part of this latter study is reprinted in abbreviated form in his *Religions orientales*, 125-27. Also important: Martín Almagro, *Les inscripciones ampuritanas griegas, ibéricas y latinas*, Barcelona, 1952, 18, Greek nr. 2; 89, Latin nr. 2; and 94, Latin nr. 5; Fidel Fita, SJ, "El templo de Sérapis en Ampurias," *BRAH* 3 (1883), 124-29 (on the inscriptions); and M. Cazurro and E. Gandía, "La estratificacíon de la cerámica en Ampurias y la época de sus restos," *AIEC* 5 (1913-14), 657-86 (quite important for determining the date of the structure). Martín Almagro provides a street plan of the ancient town (fig. 21), a photograph of a model of the (reconstructed) sanctuary (fig. 22), and a brief survey of the site in his *Ampurias: historia de la ciudad y guia de las excavaciones*, Barcelona, 1951, 92-94.

¹⁶ SIRIS 767 (1st cen. AD): *[Sera]pi aedem*
[sedili]a, porticus
--meni f(ilius)
---ius

¹⁷ On this proposed restoration see Vidman, SIRIS, p. 324.

¹⁸ SIRIS 768 (1st or 2nd cen. AD):   ---us .ACIV

[Σ] αράπι

---ANA

[-Πυριλ?]άνπου Μας -

[σαλιήτης?---]ανίου ['A]λε

[ξαν?]δρεὺς

---εβες ἐπόει

¹⁹ García y Bellido, *BRAH* 139 (1956), 315; Puig y Cadafalch, *AIEC* 4 (1911-12), 319-22; Almagro, *Ampurias*, 94.

²⁰ The principal report on this site was published fifty-two years after the original excavation: Vollgraff, *BCH* 82 (1958), 556-70. Small finds: J. Marcadé and E. Raftopoulou, "Sculptures argiennes (II)," *BCH* 87 (1963), 54-56 (descriptions and photographs of several of the finds) and W. Vollgraff, *Le sanctuaire d'Apollo Pythéen a Argos*, Paris, 1956, 64, fig. 51 (photograph of the Hecataeon found at the site). A small statue of Harpocrates thought by some to have come from the site was actually found at the foot of Mt. Larissa and seemingly at a stratigraphic level lower than that required if the object were to have rolled down from the sanctuary and to have lodged here—see "Travaux de l'Ecole Française: Argos," *BCH* 83 (1959), 758 and 760. Inscriptions: Vollgraff published these both in his original report and in his "Novae inscriptiones argivae," *Mnemosyne* 47 (1919), 166. Short reports: Salditt-Trappmann, *Tempel*, 67; R. A. Tomlinson, *Argos and the Argolid*, Ithaca, NY, 1972, 218; and Dunand, *Culte d'Isis*, 2.19-20 and 161.

²¹ Vollgraff, *BCH* 82 (1958), 559-61.

²² The basic report on this site remains the 1967 article by Robert Scranton and Edwin Ramage: "Investigations at Corinthian Kenchreai," *Hesperia* 36 (1967), 138-52 and pls. 33, 37-45. See also the plans on pp. 126, 128, 131, and 142. [Scranton and his team have now published a final report on their work at Cenchreai: *Kenchreai: Eastern Port of Corinth*, vol. 1: *Topography and Architecture*, Leiden, 1978—I have not yet seen this study]. The same year Scranton also published a more popular presentation of his findings: "Glass Pictures from the Sea," *Archaeology* 20 (1967), 163-73. This includes several useful photographs. These glass panels, certainly a find of major importance, have been published in detail by Scranton in *Kenchreai: Eastern Port of Corinth*, vol. 2: *The Panels of Opus Sectile in Glass*, Leiden, 1976. Brief accounts of the excavations: J. Hawthorne, "Cenchreae, Port of Corinth," *Archaeology* 18 (1965), 197-99; M. Erwin, *AJA* 71 (1967), 298 and pl. 91; R. Bianchi Bandinelli, *Rome: The Late Empire*, New York, 1971, 328-29 and figs. 311-12; Handler, *AJA* 75 (1971), 62; Griffiths, *Isis-Book*, 18-20; R. L. Hohlfelder, "Kenchreai on the Saronic Gulf: Aspects of Its Imperial History," *Classical Journal* 71 (1976), 217-26; and Smith, *HTR* 70 (1977) 200-10. A possible correlation between Pausanias' description of the harbor of Cenchreae and its temples and the discoveries made by Scranton is explored by R. L. Hohlfelder: "Pausanias II, 2, 3: A Collation of Archaeological and Numismatic Evidence," *Hesperia* 39 (1970), 326-31.

²³ Scranton, *Hesperia* 36 (1967), 146; *Archaeology* 20 (1967), 172-73. Scranton did not find any roofing tiles, etc., and so considered it possible that this building had no roof (*Hesperia* 36 [1967], 141).

²⁴ Hawthorne, *Archaeology* 18 (1965), 199; Handler, *AJA* 75 (1971), 62.

²⁵ While the publication of the remaining small finds could conceivably alter this judgment, any objects of cultic significance very likely would have received attention in the earlier reports if they had been found.

²⁶ The principal source of information on this shrine is the very fine publication of O. Broneer (*South Stoa*, 132-39 and pls. iv and xviii). For a very useful discussion of the evidence see Smith, *HTR* 70 (1977) 212-16.

²⁷ Date of the Sarapis head: after 150 AD (Smith, *HTR* 70 [1977]). The head seems to have been specially designed to fit into a (wooden) statue or herm. Probably, therefore, it was made expressly for the shrine to serve as its cult image. For a photograph of this head see Broneer, *South Stoa*, pl. 44.2.

²⁸ Broneer, *South Stoa*, 138.

²⁹ Broneer (Ibid., 136) did not find clear evidence for any sort of barrier across this opening, but there must have been one or every rainfall would have brought water pouring off the surrounding roofs and into the shrine area.

³⁰ A temple to Aphrodite, which later appears to have become (or to have encompassed in its precinct) an Isis shrine, was excavated by Antonín Salač. He managed only to publish some of the major small finds and a few brief notes describing the overall site. His most lengthy description is found in *BCH* 49 (1925), 476-78. (Summary of this in A. M. Woodward, "Archaeology in Greece, 1925-26," *JHS* 46 [1926], 249.) His "Hymnus na počest bohyně Isidy z malasijské Kyme" (*LF* 56 [1929], 76-80) concentrates almost entirely on the Isis aretalogy inscription found on the site but also offers a few additional bits of information regarding the sanctuary (p. 77). Salač discusses the aretalogy and three other inscriptions from the site in "Inscriptions de Kyme d'Eolide, de Phocée, de Tralles et de quelques autres villes d'Asie Mineure," *BCH* 51 (1927), 374-86. All of these have recently been republished by Helmut Engelmann (*Die Inschriften von Kyme* [Inschriften griechischer Städte aus Kleinasien, 5], Bonn, 1976, 97-110, nrs. 41-44 and Taf. 11-14). See also SIRIS 308-10. The aretalogy, as one of the finest examples of this genre, at once received a great deal of scholarly attention. Major works include: Roussel, *REG* 42 (1929), 137-68; Peek, *Isishymnus* (1930); R. Harder, "Karpokrates von Chalkis und die memphitische Isispropaganda," *AbhBerlin* 1943, nr. 14; Festugière, *HTR* 42 (1949), 209-34; Müller, *AbhLeipzig* 53 (1961), Hft. 1; J. Bergman, *Ich bin Isis* (Uppsala, 1968); V. F. Vanderlip, *The Four Greek Hymns of Isidorus and the Cult of Isis* (American Studies in Papyrology, 12), Toronto, 1972, 85-96 and Pl. xv; and Grandjean, *Une nouvelle arétalogie*. For further bibliography see Assmann, *LÄ* 1.425-34. A further inscription from the Cyme discoveries was edited by Roman Haken: "Bronze Votive Ears Dedicated to Isis," *Studia antiqua Antonio Salač septuagenario oblata*, Prague, 1955, 170-72 and pls. xi-xii. Neither the ground survey of ancient Cyme (Jörg Schäfer and Helmut Schläger, "Zur Seeseite von Kyme in der Äolis," *AA* 1962, 40-57) nor Salditt-Trappmann's examination of the site (*Tempel*, 37-38) clarified the outlines or even the location of the sanctuary. Salditt-Trappmann tried without success to locate the small finds in the Izmir Museum. The Haken article (p. 170) suggests that they are at the Charles University in Prague. Paul Knoblauch, however, has not only seen Salač's own plan of the sanctuary—a tiny, almost illegible version appears in his topographic map of the city—but also his notes and other papers ("Eine neue topographische Aufnahme des Stadtgebietes von Kyme in der Äolis," *AA* 1974, 285-91—see p. 285 and Abb. 1). Knoblauch indicates that this material left by Salač will at long last be published.

³¹ Salač, *LF* 56 (1929), 77.

³² So Haken, *Studia Antiqua*, 170.

³³ Salač, *BCH* 49 (1925), 478.

³⁴ Roussel, *REG* 42 (1929), 141, n. 2; F. Hiller von Gaertringen, *IG* XII, Suppl. (1939), pp. 98-99; Festugière, *HTR* 42 (1949), 233; Müller, *AbhLeipzig* 53

(1961), 1.11; Grandjean, *Une nouvelle arétalogie*, 8-9. Nilsson (*GGR* 2.626, n. 5) continues to accept the earlier date.

[35] L. Castiglione, rev. of R. Salditt-Trappmann, *Tempel*, *Gnomon* 45 (1973), 523.

[36] SIRIS 308 apparently belongs to the 2nd cen. AD and 310 to the early 3rd cen. SIRIS 309 (undated) is very fragmentary and its relation to the cult is very questionable. The imported Egyptian *uschebti* found on the site was made in the Saite period (Salač, *BCH* 51 [1927], 384-86) but may well have been brought to Cyme only in Roman times.

[37] This shrine has never received any formal publication. Luigi Pernier, who seems to have directed its excavation, has a few paragraphs of description in his "Campagna di scavi a Cirene nell' estate del 1925," *Africa italiana* 1 (1927), 132-34. A large map of the Apollo precinct published by him (*Tempio*, Tav. iv—cf. also Tav. i) includes a detailed ground plan of the Isis shrine. Pietro Romanelli has a short notice in *La Cirenaica romana*, Verbania, 1943, 223—his fig. 26 is a view of the facade. Vidman (SIRIS, p. 336) does not make it entirely clear that this is a different temple from that found on the acropolis. SIRIS 804-6 come from this site while 803 does not. Oliverio suggests that 806 may have been an architrave block over the cella door (G. Oliverio *et al.*, "Supplemento cirenaico," *ASAtene* NS 23-24 [1961-62], 260, nr. 73). In the same work he also has a photograph (fig. 66) which shows the interior of the shrine and several objects which *may* have been found there: an altar inscribed *LUNAE* and another altar inscribed *MARTIS*. A standing statue of Isis with Horus which is depicted in Enrico Paribeni, *Catalogue delle sculture di Cirene*, Rome, 1959, nr. 418, probably came originally from this site (Oliverio, *ASAtene*, NS 23-24 [1961-62], 260).

[38] SIRIS 805. The M. Aurelius Antonius referred to in this inscription is Caracalla rather than the earlier M. Aurelius according to Groag ("Numisius Marcellinus," *RE* 17. 2.1400) and Vidman (SIRIS, p. 336).

[39] Pernier, *Tempio*, Tav. iv.

[40] General bibliography for the three Delos sites: these sanctuaries received their definitive publication in Pierre Roussel's *Les cultes égyptiens à Délos du IIIe au Ier siècle av. J.-C.*, Paris-Nancy, 1916 = "Les cultes égyptiens à Délos," *Annales de l'est* 29-30 (1915-16), 1-300. Prior to this Roussel had provided a summary of work in progress in his "Fouilles de Délos (Juin-Juillet 1910)," *CRAIBL* 1910, 521-24. He later published a study in which he compared various features found at these sites with those reported by Papadakis for the sanctuary at Eretria: *REg* NS 1 (1919), 81-92. Most of the other general studies are heavily dependent upon the work done by Roussel and his colleagues: Antonio Salač, "Chrámy egyptských božstev na Delu," *LF* 42 (1915), 401-21; Georges Lafaye, "Les cultes égypto-grecs à Délos," *JS* NS 16 (1918), 113-26; and Dunand, *Culte d'Isis*, 2.83-115. While Philippe Bruneau's description of the three sites (*Recherches*, 457-66) likewise offers little new information, his bibliography (pp. 457-59) provides a useful list of publications of various small finds. Bruneau is also supposed to publish *Les cultes orientaux à Délos* in the EPRO series. Roussel was chiefly interested in the large number of inscriptions found and collaborated with F. Durrbach and M. Launey in editing these in various volumes of *Inscriptions de Délos: Actes des fonctionnaires athéniens*, Paris, 1935; *Décrets postérieurs a 166 av. J.-C./Dédicaces postérieurs a 166 av. J.-C.*, Paris, 1937; and *Dédicaces postérieurs a 166 av. J.-C./Textes divers, listes et catalogues, fragments divers postérieurs a 166 av. J.-C.*, Paris, 1937. Before this some inscriptions had been published in *IG* XI. 4 of which *I Délos* represented the continuation. See also SIRIS, pp. 62-87, for a list of inscriptions from these sites and an index of the

offerings mentioned in the inventories. For the topography of the area around these sanctuaries see Cayeux, *Description*.

The principal report on the discoveries at the Serapeum A site is Roussel, *CE*, pp. 19-32 and 71-98. In addition several specialized studies of various features from this precinct have appeared. Helmut Engelmann devoted a monograph to the long Sarapis aretalogy (*IG* XI.4.1299): *Die delische Sarapisaretalogie*, Meisenheim am Glan, 1964 = *Delian Aretalogy*. Unfortunately, this does not shed very much new light on this important text. C. Bonner ("Harpocrates (Zeus Kasios) of Pelusium," *Hesperia* 15 [1946], 51-59) provides useful background information on the references to Zeus Kasios in *CE* 16, 16 *bis*, and 17. Small finds: Perdrizet, *Terres cuites grecques*, 1.60; Marcadé, *Musée*, 433; Alfred Laumonier, *Les figurines de terre cuite* (EAD, 23) Paris, 1956, nr. 274; Grenier, *Anubis*, 140-41 and Pl. 15.

[41] *CE* 1 = *IG* XI.4.1299; *CE* 14 = *I Délos* 1510.

[42] So Engelmann, *Sarapisaretalogie*, 23. Vallois (*L'architecture*, 1.110, n. 1) prefers a somewhat earlier date, c. 220 BC.

[43] *CE* 1.14-18 = *IG* XI.4.1299.14-18.

[44] Roussel, *CE*, p. 31.

[45] *CE* 16 and 16 *bis* = *I Délos* 2180-81. These were dedicated by a certain Horus, son of Horus, of Casium "for the sake of Lucius Granius, son of Poplius, the Roman." This latter individual is mentioned in other texts (*I Délos* 2355 and 2612.7) and lived about 100 BC. Roussel (*CE*, pp. 95-96) preferred to date these texts to the mid 2nd cen. BC but he was not aware of the additional evidence for L. Granius Poplius. Consequently Roussel's view (*CE*, p. 95) that Serapeum A was not used much after 166 BC is problematic.

[46] *CE* 16 and 16 *bis* are dedicated to "the Great God" (probably Sarapis), Zeus Kasios, and Tachnepsis (a title of Isis). A text honoring Zeus Kasios (*CE* 17 = *I Délos* 2182) was found on the floor of Room D.

[47] Roussel, *CE*, p. 22.

[48] There are no studies devoted exclusively to this site. See the general bibliography for Delos listed under note 40 and especially Roussel, *CE*, pp. 33-46 and 98-106. Two small finds from the site, a seated statue, perhaps of Sarapis, and a marble head of the same god, received notice in Marcadé, *Musée*, 427-28 and in Hornbostel, *Sarapis*, 208-9. Besides the inscriptions published by Roussel in *CE*, see also *I Délos* 2202, 2217, and 2655.

[49] *CE* 29 = *IG* XI.4.1246.

[50] *CE* 27 = *IG* XI.4.1229.

[51] *CE* 26 = *IG* XI.4.1228.

[52] Roussel, *CE*, p. 250; Vallois, *L'architecture*, 1.110, n. 1.

[53] Roussel, *CE*, p. 98.

[54] Ibid., p. 36. The south wall of this room partially blocks one of five niches in the eastern wall of the precinct, a probable indication that the former wall was constructed sometime later. This niche, however, is out of symmetry with the other four niches, and so it is hard to imagine how it was originally used.

[55] These inscriptions are *I Délos* 2202, 2217, and 2655.

[56] Virtually all of the datable remains are from the period prior to 166 BC.

[57] Most of the works cited above (Note 40) offer information on this site. See especially Roussel, *CE*, pp. 47-67 and 106-202. Prior to the excavations of 1909-10, A. Hauvette-Besnault had carried out an investigation of the general area in 1881. His report ("Fouilles de Délos: Temple des dieux étrangers," *BCH* 6 [1882], 295-352; cf. also 470-503) concentrated heavily upon the many epigraphical finds. The jumble of architectural remains was not well understood until Maurice Holleaux

and Pierre Roussel undertook their work. Besides Roussel's major site report, shorter summaries of the results were published by Holleaux ("Rapport sur les travaux exécutes dans l'île de Délos par l'Ecole Française d'Athènes pendant l'année 1909," *CRAIBL* 1910, 294-300) and by Georg Karo (*AA* 1910, 166-69 and *ARW* 16 [1913], 279-80). Two later investigations of the site produced important results. Vallois (*L'architecture*, 86-96 and 110) studied the tangle of remains at the south end of the site and was able to produce a convincing history of the development of the sanctuary. About ten years later at the request of Charles Picard, who himself had written a short article on the subject ("A quoi servaient les dromoi des Sarapieia," *RArch* 41 [1953], 206-9), J. Marcadé made several *sondages* under the dromos at Delos C and confirmed that the fill underneath could be dated very precisely to the mid 2nd cen. BC ("Chronique des fouilles en 1953: Délos," *BCH* 78 [1954], 217-20). Epigraphical publications and studies: G. Fougères, "Fouilles de Délos: Avril-Aout 1886: Dédicaces grecques et latines," *BCH* 11 (1887), 274 (= *CE* 44); P. Roussel, "Les Athéniens mentionnés dans les inscriptions de Délos," *BCH* 32 (1908), 303-444; M. Guarducci, "Antichità greche nel Museo di Treviso," *ASAtene* 30-32 (1952-54), 175-93; and L. Vidman, "Quelques remarques sur les inventaires des Sérapées de Délos," *Acta of the Fifth International Congress of Greek and Latin Epigraphy, Cambridge, 1967*, Oxford, 1971, 93-99. Vidman (SIRIS, pp. 78-79) also provides a convenient list of inscriptions probably or certainly from the site which were not published by Roussel in *CE*. For the small finds see Hauvette-Besnault, *BCH* 6 (1882), 305-13; Roussel, *CE*, pp. 64-67; C. Michałowski, *Les portraits hellénistiques et romaines* (EAD, 13), Paris, 1932, 54 and pl. xxxviii; J. Marcadé, "A propos des statuettes hellénistiques en aragonite," *BCH* 76 (1952), 119-20, 125-27, 130-31 and *Musée*, 174, 427-34, 454; P. Bruneau, "Isis Pélagia a Délos," *BCH* 85 (1961), 446 and fig. 1; and J. Leclant and H. de Meulenaere, "Une statuette égyptienne a Délos," *Kêmi* 14 (1957), 34-42.

[58] Care should be taken in using the plan provided by Roussel in *CE*. Its draftsman, M. Replat, proved all too ready to use his imagination to fill out features that in actuality remain uncertain. Consequently, the more jumbled but more accurate plan by Lefèvre should also be consulted (Holleaux, *CRAIBL* 1910, 289; Karo, *AA* 1910, 167-68).

[59] Vallois, *L'architecture*, 87 and 91. The Metroon is mentioned as an active sanctuary in an inscription of 208 BC (*I Délos* 365.2) and is also named in a later inventory of Delos C (*I Délos* 1417 B.1.33—156 BC). The Escharon is mentioned in the account lists of the *hieropes* from 190-80 BC (*I Délos* 440 A.80-83) as well as in *I Délos* 1417 B.1.36-37 where it is clearly understood to be quite close to the Metroon. This is understandable since the cult of the Cabiri appears elsewhere in close association with that of Demeter.

[60] *I Délos* 352.15—however, the reading of this line is rather uncertain. See also *I Délos* 442 A.238 and B.229-31 (179 BC). Vallois (p. 96) suggests that this shrine may have been located in Room V.

[61] Vallois, *L'architecture*, 96.

[62] Ibid., 93 and 110, n. 1.

[63] This is clear from the inventory of sacred objects taken in 156-55 BC (*I Délos* 1417).

[64] On the dating for this sacred way see Marcadé, *BCH* 78 (1954), 220. In the process of joining the two sanctuaries together the Escharon was destroyed and the Metroon became a depository (Vallois, *L'architecture*, 92).

[65] The Isis temple in the northern half of the precinct was certainly rebuilt sometime after (long after?) 88 BC. Hauvette-Besnault found a number of inscrip-

tions from the late 2nd cen. as well as from even the early 1st cen. BC (*CE* 175 D = *I Délos* 2620) reused as building blocks in its cella wall.

⁶⁶ Bruneau (*BCH* 85 [1961], 446 and *Recherches*, 462-63) argues that the discovery on the site of a fragment of a Corinthian lamp of the 2nd cen. AD which depicts Isis Pelagia offers likely evidence that a cult to that goddess continued here in some form. Perhaps so, but in my judgment lamp fragments, even of a type not all that common, hardly prove the existence of a cult. Bruneau stresses the coincidence of finding such an object at this site. Perhaps an individual devotee performed some rite here, but even that I wonder about.

⁶⁷ Cf. *CE* 66-68 = *I Délos* 2114, 2137-38.

⁶⁸ *I Délos* 2605.25-26.

⁶⁹ *CE* 76 = *I Délos* 2042; *CE* 86 = *I Délos* 2044; *CE* 140 = *I Délos* 2063; etc. See also *I Délos* 1417 A.2.158.

⁷⁰ The principal report on this site has been published by W. Alzinger: "Das Regierungsviertel," *ÖJh* 50 (1972-75), Beibl., 283-94. Hölbl (*Zeugnisse*, 27-32 and 57-58) provides no additional archaeological data but does present some useful reflections. Brief notes: Alzinger, "Nachträge: Ephesos B," *RE*, Suppl. 12 (1970), 1601 and M. J. Mellink, *AJA* 75 (1971), 175. For a detailed study of the architectural finds see E. Fossel, "Zum Tempel auf dem Staatsmarkt in Ephesos," *ÖJh* 50 (1972-75), 212-19.

⁷¹ The bell is now lost and the terracotta statuette has not yet been published. On the sculptured head see Alzinger, *ÖJh* 50 (1972-75), Beibl., 287-88 and Abb. 28 and Hölbl, *Zeugnisse*, 57-58 and Taf. vi. This object, 7.75 cm high, would have belonged to a statue c. 40 cm in height.

⁷² G. Hölbl (*Zeugnisse*, 30-31) and S. Karwiese (Ibid.) stress the very Hellenic design of the temple building and ask whether the site was originally dedicated to a Greek deity. Because a large head of (possibly) Mark Anthony was found near the site, Hölbl suggests that Dionysus may have been that deity. He then supposes that Osiris and the Egyptian deities associated with him found a place in the sanctuary and that after 200 AD, the time when the ablution basin in front of the temple was constructed, the cult of these gods became dominant here.

⁷³ Thanks particularly to the efforts of N. G. Papadakis and Philippe Bruneau, the sanctuary at Eretria is one of the best reported of all the known Isis-Sarapis sites. Papadakis, the original excavator, published a detailed account of his discoveries: *ArchD* 1 (1915), 115-90. (Reviewed by E. Ziebarth in *Philologische Wochenschrift* 36 [1916], 385-91.) In recent years Bruneau made further probes and re-examined the entire body of evidence—see Bruneau, *Sanctuaire* (1975). Earlier he had also published a brief but important study of the mosaic found in the other courtyard of the sanctuary: "Eretria 1968: La mosaique de l'Iseion d'Erétrie," *AntK* 12 (1969), 80-82. After Papadakis made his discoveries, P. Roussel attempted a comparison of the Eretria site with those on Delos: *REg* NS 1 (1919), 81-92. However, he made a number of errors in his discussion of the Eretria site and jumped to several false conclusions. Brief treatments: Auberon-Schefold, *Führer*, 139-44 and Salditt-Trappmann, *Tempel*, 67.

⁷⁴ Bruneau, *Sanctuaire*, 45-46, 72, and 115-16.

⁷⁵ Ibid., 41.

⁷⁶ Ibid., 118-21. Auberon-Schefold (*Führer*, 139) argue incorrectly for a reconstruction of the site right after 198 BC.

⁷⁷ Bruneau, *Sanctuaire*, 126. Nothing necessitates that this step took place before the abandonment of the sanctuary. I am inclined to accept a date in the 1st cen. BC while Bruneau (127) holds that the northern rooms were separated from the sanctuary before it ceased to function.

78 Ibid., 132-34.

79 Papadakis, *ArchD* 1 (1915), 116 and 183.

80 E.g., Salditt-Trappmann, *Tempel*, 67; Auberon-Schefold, *Führer*, 139; Bruneau, *Sanctuaire*, 99-100 and 116.

81 No holes or fastenings were found on the top of this block which would demonstrate with certainty that it supported a statue. Yet its size and shape (0.91 × 0.80 m; 0.71 m high) led Papadakis (*ArchD* 1 [1915], 115 and eik. 1) to conclude that it was a "bathron" and Bruneau (*Sanctuaire*, 17) to speak of it as "une base."

82 SIRIS 74, 76, 77, 79, and 82.

83 Papadakis, *ArchD* 1 (1915), 152: Δημόδικος Διί.

84 The stone is rather large (0.45 m high, 0.90 m long, and 0.07 m thick) and would not have been easily moved from one place to another. Bruneau (*Sanctuaire*, 91) thinks that the text may have been incomplete on the right side (thus: Διί ....) but he himself was not able to inspect the stone. Papadakis' own drawing (p. 152) does not suggest that the text is broken off at that point.

85 W. Modrijan published his discoveries first in an article (*BlHeim* 27 [1953], 56-68) and then later in a booklet (*Frauenberg* [1955]). The latter supplements but does not replace the former. Brief accounts: H. Kenner, "Les fouilles celto-romaines en Autriche depuis 1945," *Ogam* 9 (1957), 195-202 and E. Staudinger, "2000 Jahre—Frauenberg bei Leibnitz," (Wegweiser), Leibnitz, n.d. [after 1955]. Werner Knapp ("Buchkogel - Wildon - Kogelberg - Seggau: Eine Kultur-wanderung in Südsteiermark," *Mitteilungen des steirischen Burgenvereines* 3 [1954], 19) tried to argue that what Modrijan had discovered was an eighth or ninth century church. His analysis is quite unconvincing.

86 The inscription: SIRIS 650, which is broken on the right side and is perhaps missing as well a further section on the left, actually reads: --- IŞI[DI] --- /--- C. PRQ ---. (Vidman in SIRIS presents a more certain text than is on the stone.) The relief: Modrijan, *Frauenberg*, 23 and fig. 15; *BlHeim* 27 (1953), 65. The water facility: Modrijan, *Frauenberg*, 26-27; *BlHeim* 27 (1953), 61-62.

87 Modrijan, *Frauenberg*, 22-23; *BlHeim* 27 (1953), 62-63, 67.

88 Brief reports by the excavator, Gaspare Oliverio, were published after each year of work: *ASAtene* 1 (1914), 376-77 and *ASAtene* 2 (1916), 309-11. R. Salditt-Trappmann's observations and photographs (*Tempel*, 54-66, Abb. 47-51, and Plan 6) are also of considerable help for the understanding of this site. Brief reports: William N. Bates, ed., "Archaeological News: Gortyn," *AJA* 18 (1914), 96-97; G. Karo, *AA* 29 (1914), 147-49; Luigi Pernier, "Les travaux de l'Ecole Italienne d'Archéologie d'Athènes en 1913," *JS* NS 12 (1914), 37-39; L. Pernier, "Gortina, capitale della 'Provincia Cretae et Cyrenarum'," *AeR* 18 (1915), 60-61, 64; Biagio Pace, "'Trent' anni di recherche archeologiche italiana in Creta," *Bollettino della Reale Società Geografica Italiana* 56 (1919), 169; Pernier and Banti, *Guida*, 23-24 and Tav. 30; Dunand, *Culte d'Isis*, 2.73-79 and 205-6. The inscriptions from the site were edited with care by Margarita Guarducci (*Inscriptiones*, vol. 4, nrs. 243-49 [= SIRIS 164-70], 290, 342, 362, 391, 501 [?], 554, 558, and 571). An important find, previously unpublished, is reported by L. Castiglione in his "Fragment einer thronenden Sarapis-Statue in dem Sarapieion von Gortyn," *ActaArch* 23 (1971), 229-30.

89 SIRIS 170: Εἴσιδι καὶ Σαραπίδι καὶ θεοῖς συννάοις Φλαβία Φιλύρα μετὰ τῶν / τέχνων Γ. Μετρωνίου Μαξί[μου] καὶ Φιλύρας καὶ Λυσκίας τὸν οἶκον ἐκ θεμελίων / κατασκευάσασ[α] κα[θίδρυ]σεν εὐχὴν καὶ χαριστῆιον. Dated by Guarducci (nr. 249) to the 1st or 2nd cen. AD.

90 Oliverio, *ASAtene* 1 (1914), 376; Pernier and Banti, *Guida*, Tav. 30.

[91] Guarducci, nr. 342, a fragmentary inscription from about the 1st cen. BC, was found reused as one of the steps leading down to the crypt. Oliverio (*ASA tene* 1 [1914], 377) reported that the crypt had been rebuilt. Evidence of this is visible in a photograph provided by Salditt-Trappmann, *Tempel*, Abb. 50 (= my Pl. IV). The ashlar construction of the lower portions of the walls gives way to *opus incertum* in the surviving upper portions.

[92] This was pointed out by Pernier and Banti, *Guida*, 23. Plan 6 (= my Fig. 17) in Salditt-Trappmann, *Tempel*, has an error with respect to the stylobate for the front portico. Oliverio discovered more column bases than she indicates (*ASAtene* 2 [1916], 311).

[93] B. Morra di Lauriano carried out excavations in 1811-12 and reported the results in his *Rovine della città di Industria presso Monteu da Po (Torino)*, Turin, 1843. For a summary of this see G. Casalis, "Monteu da Po," *Dizionario geografico degli Stati di S. M. il Re di Sardegna*, vol. 11, Turin, 1843, 294. The excavations of 1961-63 are reported with considerable care by Marcella Barra Bagnasco et al., *Scavi* (1967); this also provides information on and photographs of most of the small finds. For a brief summary of this more recent work see Malaise, *HomVermaseren* 2.632-33.

[94] Barra Bagnasco et al., *Scavi*, 23-24, 71ff, and Tav. xvi. Other finds which they mention, a dancing infant which they equate with Harpocrates (Tav. xviii, fig. 40) and various images of bulls (Tav. xxvi, fig. 58), are less certainly to be linked with the Isis cult.

[95] Ibid., 24-28.

[96] For convenient drawings of the pertinent portion of the *Forma Urbis*, see Malaise, *Inventaire*, plans 1-2.

[97] Barra Bagnasco et al., *Scavi*, 26-28 and Tav. vii, fig. 9.

[98] Ibid., 38-39. The Italian team argued (Ibid., 29-30 and 37-38) that prior to the Iseum of the second century AD, there had been on the same site temples to Isis and Sarapis. However, from the data they provide, that there were even temples is quite uncertain, to say nothing of the problem of whether they were dedicated to the two Egyptian gods.

[99] Because the excavator of this site, E. Vergara Caffarelli, met an untimely death in 1961, he did not manage to publish his finds in a formal manner. He did place a short notice in *Corriere di Tripoli* (8/8/60) and joined with R. Bianchi Bandinelli and G. Caputo to provide a somewhat more lengthy description in *Leptis Magna*, Rome, 1963, 89-90 and figs. 102-5. Other important sources of information: M. F. Squarciapino, *Leptis Magna*, Zürich, 1966, 116-18 and fig. 88, and Le Corsu, *Isis*, 246-47. The latter provides the only available plan of the site, but this is erroneous at several points. Short notices: P. Romanelli, "Leptis Magna," *Enciclopedia dell' arte antica*, vol. 4, Rome, 1961, 579; H. Sichtermann, *AA* 1962, 501-2; and Hornbostel, *Sarapis*, 245. The statue of an emperor in armor (Marcus Aurelius?) found at the site was published in Hans Georg Niemeyer, *Studien zur statuarischen Darstellung des römischen Kaiser* (Monumenta artis romanae, 7), Berlin, 1968, 30. A variety of inscriptions, all in Greek and from the third century AD, apparently have not yet been published—see Bianchi Bandinelli et al., *Leptis Magna*, 90.

[100] Zacharia Ghoneim's discovery was first made known by Jean Leclant (*Orientalia* 20 [1951], 454-56 and Tab. xlv-xlvii). Leclant (*Orientalia* 30 [1961], 183 and Tab. xxxvi-vii) also reported that the columns and cella walls of the structure had been restored. Largely the same information as that originally provided by Leclant is repeated by Theodor Kraus (*Christentum am Nil*, 103-4 and pls. 52-53) and by

Abdul-Qader Muhammad (*ASAntEg* 60 [1968], 238-40 and pls. v and cvi). The latter author provides for the first time a plan of the site. The dedicatory inscription from over the doorway of the rebuilt temple has received much scholarly attention: A. Merlin, *RArch* 6.40 (1952), 205-6, nr. 159 (the text); J. Schwartz, ''Un préfet d'Egypte frappé de *damnatio memoriae* sous le règne d'Hadrien,'' *ChrEg* 27 (1952), 254-56 (date of the inscription corrected); P. M. Fraser, *JEA* 40 (1954), 125-26, 129; J. Leclant, *Orientalia* 38 (1969), 265; etc.

¹⁰¹ The dedicatory inscription: Ὑπὲρ Αὐτοκράτορος Καίσαρος Τραιανοῦ Ἀδριανοῦ Σεβαστοῦ / καὶ τοῦ παντὸς οἴκου αὐτοῦ Διὶ Ἡλίῳ μεγάλῳ Σαράπιδι Γαίος Ἰούλιος Ἀντωνεῖνος /τῶν ἀπολελυμένων δεκαδάρχων ἐκ τοῦ ἰδίου ἀνοικοδομήσας τὸ ἱερὸν τὸ ζώδιον / ἀνέθηκεν εὐχῆς καὶ εὐσέβειας χάριν ἐπὶ ▇▇▇▇ ἐπάρχου Αἰγύπτου / ὁ αὐτὸς δὲ καὶ νεοκόρος αὐτοῦ τοῦ μεγάλου Σαράπιδος καὶ τὰ κατὰ λοιπὰ ζώδια ἀνέθηκε /l͟i͟ Αὐτοκράτορος Καίσαρος Τραιανοῦ Ἀδριανοῦ Σεβαστοῦ Τυβί x̄θ. The Serapeum at Ostia was also dedicated on January 24.

¹⁰² Leclant, *Orientalia* 20 (1951), 455-56 and Tab. xlvii. The first two statues mentioned were found lying on the temple floor and have now been placed on the cult platform.

¹⁰³ Ibid., 455. This basin has been omitted from the plan given in *ASAntEg* 60 (1968), pl. cvi (= my Fig. 2).

¹⁰⁴ The great ''Red Hall'' in the lower town evoked the interest of various 19th cen. travelers, some of whom wrote descriptions of what they had seen. Of particular interest: Choiseul-Gouffier, Comte de, *Voyage pittoresque dans l'empire Ottoman*, 2nd ed., Paris, 1842, and Charles Texier, *Description de l'Asie Mineure*, vol. 2, Paris, 1849, 224-37 and plates. One of the early projects of the German archaeological team investigating ancient Pergamum was a topographical survey. In reporting this, Alexander Conze and his associates offered a few observations and hypotheses about the Red Hall site (*Stadt und Landschaft* [Altertümer von Pergamon, 1.2], Berlin, 1913, 284). A partial excavation of the site was undertaken in the nineteen-thirties but no reports of this work were published. There were, however, a few brief notices: W. Zschietzschmann, ''Nachträge (Pergamon),'' *RE* 19.1.1242 and 1245; Otfried Deubner, ''Das ägyptische Heiligtum in Pergamon,'' *Bericht über den VI. internationalen Kongress für Archäologie, Berlin, 21.-26. August 1939*, Berlin, 1940, 477-78 (arguments presented for the first time that this was a sanctuary of the Egyptian gods); and Ohlemutz, *Kulte*, 273-76 (survey of Isis-Sarapis material found at Pergumum—very little on the actual site). Somewhat later Erich Böhringer put together a more lengthy description of the remains found here: ''Pergamon,'' *Neue deutsche Ausgrabungen im Mittelmeergebiet und im vorderen Orient*, ed. Deutsches Arch. Institut, Berlin, 1959, 134-38. Credit must be given to Regina Salditt-Trappmann who, after so many years, finally put together a fairly complete and quite useful study of the site: *Tempel*, 1-25. (Cf. L. Castiglione's review, *Gnomon* 45 [1973], 522.) On the date of construction of this site: Wolf-Dieter Heilmeyer, ''Korinthische Normalkapitelle,'' *RM*, Ergänzungsheft 16 (1970), 88-89, 92.

¹⁰⁵ Conze, *Stadt*, 284; Heilmeyer, *RM* (1970), 89 and 92; Salditt-Trappmann, *Tempel*, 1. Whether the site was subsequently remodelled and how long it served as a sanctuary cannot presently be determined.

¹⁰⁶ The excavations in the nineteen-thirties, while little more than an unscientific clearing away of ''debris,'' at least served to make clear that this was not a ''library'' or ''basilica'' or ''public baths''—Conze (*Stadt*, 284) records all of these older hypotheses—but a sanctuary.

¹⁰⁷ Probably a certain amount of smaller material was simply lost when the central temple was cleared. There is still hope of obtaining better data, however.

Salditt-Trappmann (*Tempel*, 20, n. 57) noted the presence of architectural fragments and other ancient materials in unexcavated portions of the tunnel system. This material was probably used as fill in those portions of the underground system over which walls were built during the course of renovations in Byzantine times. In addition, much of the vast courtyard has never been probed.

[108] Salditt-Trappmann, *Tempel*, 13-14 and Abb. 18-20.

[109] Ibid., 24 and Abb. 25.

[110] Ibid., 24 and Abb. 24.

[111] In the courtyard of the Serapeum at Ostia, a mosaic which survives in fragmentary condition depicts hippopotami, crocodiles, water-lilies, ibises, and turtles (Becatti, *Scavi di Ostia,* vol. 4, Rome, 1961, 150-51 and Tavv. 117, 119-21). While this is evocative of the Nile valley, none of it has a directly religious reference. Anne Roullet (*Egyptian Monuments,* 38 and 118-19) believes that two other Egyptian objects are to be connected with this sanctuary. One of these, a stelophorus (Roullet, nr. 215), was found in 1941 "near the Serapeum." The other, simply "a fragment of a leg in black 'basalt'" (Roullet, *Egyptian Monuments,* nr. 217), is said to have been found "near the entrance to the Serapeum." These objects may have come from the sanctuary but could just as well have come from somewhere else in the city. At Thessalonica the sanctuary, which was dedicated, as will be seen, to Sarapis and Isis, yielded as one of the finds a small sphinx (*AA* 1922, 242; *BCH* 45 [1921], 540). The fact that Isis was also honored here *may* explain the presence of this object. Delos C, a Hellenistic site, revealed a number of Egyptian objects. Perhaps their presence at this sanctuary also had something to do with the fact that an ancient shrine of Isis was included in the precinct. It will be argued below that Temple E at Soli, a building constructed with a pylon gateway, was also dedicated to Isis. However, one part of the argument is the use of this Egyptian feature.

[112] The excavation work done here at Philippi was rather unsystematic and leaves a variety of questions unanswered. The failure to investigate fully the evidence at hand (e.g., to explore the full length of the pipe found under a portion of the sanctuary) is reflected in the main report which concentrates more on the overall context at Philippi rather than on the specifics of the site: Collart, *BCH* 53 (1929), 70-100. Earlier notices: *BCH* 44 (1920), 407 and 45 (1921), 544-45. See also Collart, *Philippes,* 1.443-54 and 2, plates. Salditt-Trappmann (*Tempel,* 52-53) has little to add but stresses the present condition of the site and notes that the small finds have disappeared. For a recent summary of the discoveries see Dunand, *Culte d'Isis* 2.191-98. A number of reliefs which apparently, but not certainly, depict Isis have been found carved on the natural rock of the acropolis. Several of these are in the vicinity of the sanctuary. On these see Picard, *RHR* 86 (1922), 119, 173-78 (a further note on the sanctuary is found on p. 180) and P. Ducrey, "Philippes. Reliefs rupestres," *BCH* 94 (1970), 809-11 (a report that two more "Isis" reliefs were found in 1969). Also pertinent: Collart, *Philippes,* vol. 2, pl. lxxx.

[113] SIRIS 119 (2nd or 3rd cen.) was found carved into the natural rock about 4 m from the stairs leading up to the precinct.

[114] Collart, *BCH* 53 (1929), 87-89; Picard, *RHR* 86 (1922), 180; Dunand, *Culte d'Isis* 2.193-95.

[115] The reports (*BCH* 45 [1921], 545 and Collart, *BCH* 53 [1929], 72-74) indicate that the chief deity at Philippi was honored in the second cella from the left. Just as certainly at Gortyn and probably at Ras el Soda and at Soli: Temple E, so here Isis in her status as principal deity was given not the central position on the cultic podium but a place to the left of center.

¹¹⁶ Essential for the understanding of this site is the remarkably well-kept diary of the day-to-day work of excavation kept by the eighteenth-century archaeologists and later edited by Giuseppe Fiorelli: *PAH* (1860-64), 1.1.164-94 and 226; 1.4.149-51. Using this report it is possible to locate the find spots for most of the materials recovered in the excavations of 1764-66. Nonetheless, a variety of questions remain, so much so that a whole new study of this site should probably be undertaken. For example, the various plans published often show differences, architectural dimensions are almost never supplied, objects originally on the site have been destroyed by later tourists, etc. In such a situation the reports written by early visitors take on special significance: D. Migliacci, *Riflessioni sopra il tempio d'Iside in Pompei*, Naples, 1765—not available to me; Hamilton, *Archaeologia* 4 (1776), 160-75 (gives earliest known plan of the site); Giovanni-Battista and Francesco Piranesi, *Antiquités de la Grande Grèce*, vol. 2, Paris, 1804, pls. lviii-lxxii (plan of the site; detailed drawings of selected features; several "romantic" drawings); Donaldson and Cooke, *Pompeii*, vol. 1 (1827) 42-44 and plates; Jorio, *Plan* (1828) 126-31; C. Bonucci, *Pompéi*, French trans. of the 3rd Italian ed., Naples, 1830, 200; Mazois and Gau, *Ruines*, vol. 4 (1838) 24-36 and pls. vii-xi (several important drawings); and Niccolini, *Case*, vol. 1, pt. 2 (1854)—detailed descriptions and plates. Pictures and descriptions of various small finds, some of which have since disappeared, are found in some of the above works. See also: *Real Museo Borbonico*, 16 vols., Naples, 1824-57, vol. 7, frontispiece (the ablution basin) and vol. 9, pl. xi (statue of Dionysus). On the altars in the temple courtyard see Hermann, *Götteraltäre*, 43 and 101-2. Elia, *Pitture* (1942) is a fundamental study of the wall paintings; she provides here a number of excellent color reproductions. See also on these paintings K. Schefold, *Die Wände Pompejis*, Berlin, 1957, 38 and 231-32. Many other accounts of this sanctuary have been published in the last one hundred and twenty-five years but most simply summarize the reports mentioned above. The more important of these are: Reichel, *De Isidis apud Romanos cultu*, 42-45; Dyer, *Pompeii* (1867) 140-43; Breton, *Pompeia* (3rd ed.; 1870) 46-52; G. Fiorelli, *Descrizione di Pompei*, Naples, 1875, 358-62 and *Guida di Pompei*, Rome, 1877, 83-84; Lafaye, *Histoire*, 178-99; Overbeck and Mau, *Pompeii* (4th ed.; 1884) 104-10; Gusman, *Pompéi* (1899) 85-101; Mau, *Pompeii* (2nd ed.; 1908) 174-87 = (Eng. trans. of 1st ed.; 1902) 162-76; Ibid., Anhang (1913) 31-33; H. Thedenat, *Pompéi: Vie publique*, Paris, 1916, 70-77; and R. Etienne, *La vie quotidienne à Pompéi*, 2nd ed., Paris, 1977, 223-30. Heinrich Nissen (*Pompeianische Studien* [1877], 158-61, 170-75, 346-49) re-examined the evidence from the site with great care and was able to determine to some degree how the sanctuary looked before the earthquake of 62 AD. The best known study done in recent years, Tran Tam Tinh, *Essai* (1964), does not provide any new information on the sanctuary itself but, in attempting to catalogue and study all of the Isis-Sarapis evidence from Pompeii, provides a new understanding of the milieu in which it existed. R. Merkelbach (*Latomus* 24 [1965], 144-49) has explored the significance of several artistic motifs found at the Iseum. I was unable to obtain Giuseppe Spano's "Pecularità architettoniche del tempio pompeiano d'Iside," *Studi di antichità classica offerti ... a E. Ciaceri*, Naples, 1940, 288-315 but suspect that it deserves attention.

¹¹⁷ SIRIS 482: *N. Popidius N(umeri) f(ilius) Celsinus / aedem Isidis terrae motu conlapsam / a fundamento p(ecunia) s(ua) restituit. Hunc decuriones ob liberalitatem / cum esset annorum sexs, ordini suo gratis adlegerunt.* This benefaction was in the name of the six-year-old son of N. Popidius Ampliatus. This gentleman and his family donated other objects to the Iseum (SIRIS 483-84).

¹¹⁸ Nissen, *Pompeianische Studien*, 159-61; 173-74.

¹¹⁹ Ibid., 171-72.

¹²⁰ Ibid., 174.

¹²¹ Excavations were carried out at this sanctuary in the eighteen-nineties, and the discoveries were reported with considerable care by Theodor Wiegand and Hans Schrader: *Priene*, Berlin, 1904, 164-70. Two years later F. Hiller von Gaertringen edited all the inscriptions found on the site: *Inschriften von Priene*, Berlin, 1906, nrs. 140, 193-95 (= SIRIS 290-92), 220, 241, 279, 324-26, 348 (= SIRIS 293). Short accounts: Rüstem Duyuran, *Priene Kılavuyu -- A Guide to Priene*, Istanbul, 1948, 22-23 (English summary, p. 48); G. Kleiner, "Priene," *RE*, Suppl. 9, 1201-2; M. Schede, *Die Ruinen von Priene*, Berlin, 1965, 68-69.

¹²² Wiegand and Schrader, *Priene*, 164; Vidman, SIRIS, p. 149.

¹²³ Sarapis and Isis: SIRIS 291.10 and 13. See also 291.8. Apis: 291.71.

¹²⁴ The other inscriptions which mention the names of gods add no decisive evidence. SIRIS 290 (3rd cen. BC) mentions Isis before Sarapis but 292 (c. 100 BC or somewhat later) has the reverse order.

¹²⁵ Wiegand and Schrader, *Priene*, 170.

¹²⁶ Hiller von Gaertringen, *Inschriften*, nr. 220: a fragmentary text on a marble block measuring 0.42 × 0.45 × 0.105 m. The letters are large and carefully made: [ε]ὐτυχῶ[ς]. Nr. 279: fragmentary text, perhaps part of a small base for a statue in honor of someone. The lettering is with apices. No date is given by Von Gaertringen.

¹²⁷ The only publication on this site is that by A. Adriani: *Annuaire* (1940) 136-48 and pls. l-lix. He reported the sculptural finds in detail while giving far less attention to the architecture, especially that of the structures to the east of the shrine.

¹²⁸ Ibid., 148.

¹²⁹ The inscription (Alexandria, Graeco-Roman Museum inv. nr. 25 789): Ῥιφθεὶς ἐξ ἵππων ἀπ' ὀχήματος ἔνθ' Ἰσίδωρος σωθεὶς ἀντὶ ποδῶν θῆκεν ἴχνος μάχαρι. On this text see Adriani, *Annuaire*, 146 and L. Castiglione, "Zur Frage der Sarapis-Füsse," *ZÄS* 97 (1971), 35, nr. 4 and Abb. 2. For general studies of votive feet and votive footprints see M. Guarducci, "Le impronte del *Quo Vadis* e monumenti affini, figurati ed epigrafici," *RendPontAcc* 19 (1942-43), 305-44 and a series of articles by L. Castiglione: "Tables votives à empreintes de pied dans les temples d'Egypte," *ActaOrient* 20 (1967), 239-52; "Vestigia," *ActaArch* 22 (1970), 95-132; and *ZÄS* 97 (1971), 30-43.

¹³⁰ See Adriani, *Annuaire*, pl. lix.1.

¹³¹ Ibid., 147-48.

¹³² A systematic excavation of this site, which is entirely buried under a large area in the heart of Rome, has never been possible. Consequently, investigators have concentrated on three avenues of approach. First, on the classification and analysis of architectural members and small finds recovered accidentally or otherwise in the last four hundred years. M. Malaise (*Inventaire*, 187-214) provides an invaluable summary of this material as well as a useful account of what is known of the general character of the sanctuary. I will not repeat here the bibliographies for the various finds which he so thoroughly has furnished. On the finds which are Egyptian in type see Roullet, *Egyptian Monuments*, 23-35, etc. Malaise's work now replaces the pioneering study of Rodolfo Lanciani, "L'Iseum et Serapeum della Reg. IX," *BullCom* NS 2 (1883), 33-60. A second approach pursued with solid results especially by Gugliemo Gatti ("Topografia dell'Iseo Campense," *RendPontAcc* 20 [1943-44], 117-63) has been to attempt reconstruction of portions of the precinct on the basis of architectural remains which survived *in situ*. Linked to this approach are the various studies of the coin issued during Vespasian's reign (71

AD) which apparently depicts the facade of the pre-80 AD central temple at the Iseum: H. Dressel, "Das Iseum Campense auf einer Münze des Vespasianus," *SBBerlin* 1909, 640-48 and Wilhelm Weber, "Ein Hermes-Tempel des Kaisers Marcus," *SBHeidelberg* 1910, nr. 7, 11-13. Thirdly, various scholars have utilized literary sources and other evidence to determine the general topography of this part of ancient Rome, a task made considerably easier with the discovery of fragments of the *Forma Urbis*, a map of Rome carved on a thin marble slab during the reign of Septimius Severus: Otto Gilbert, *Geschichte und Topographie der Stadt Rom im Altertum*, Leipzig, 1890, 3.110-11; Ch. Hülsen, "Porticus Divorum et Serapeum im Marsfelde," *RM* 18 (1903) 32-47 and 54-57 (important study of the *Forma Urbis* fragments); H. Jordan and Ch. Hülsen, *Topographie der Stadt Rom im Altertum*, vol. 1, pt. 3, Berlin, 1907, 567-72 (largely repeats the findings given in 1903); S. Platner and T. Ashby, *A Topographical Dictionary of Ancient Rome*, London, 1929, 283-85; V. Lundström, *Undersökningar i Roms topografi*, Göteborg, 1929, 110-28 (provides important corrections to Hülsen's work). More general studies on this site: L. Canina, "Tempio d'Iside nella regione IX fra i Septi e le Terme di Caracalla," *AICorrArch* 24 (1852), 348-53; Lafaye, *Histoire*, 216-26; G. Wissowa, *Religion und Kultus der Römer*, 2nd ed., Munich, 1912, 353; Malaise, *HomVermaseren* 2.682-84. Inscriptions found in the area of the sanctuary: SIRIS 382-87. Ancient accounts (see Hopfner, *Fontes*): Josephus, *BJ* 7.123; Martial 2.14.7; Juvenal 6. 528-29; Apuleius, *Met* 11.26; Cassius Dio 66.24.2, 79.10.1; Eusebius, *Chronica: versio lat. Hieronymi* (ed. Helm, p. 191); *Chronicon anni p. Chr. 334* (ed. Frick, pp. 116-17, 121); Eutropius, *Brev.* 7.23.5; *Notitia de regionibus*, reg. IX; *Curiosum urbis Romae*, reg. IX; *Hist. Aug., Alexander Severus* 26.

¹³³ Martial in his reference (2.14.7) to the *Memphitica templa* is probably only employing a poetic phrase and not referring specifically to the sanctuary at Memphis as a Serapeum.

¹³⁴ In 66.24.2 Cassius Dio lists the Serapeum before the Iseum, the only reference in which the Serapeum enjoys this precedence.

¹³⁵ *Hist. Aug., Septimius Severus* 17: *iucundam sibi Alexandrinam peregrinationem propter religionem dei Sarapidis et propter rerum antiquarum cognitionem et propter novitatem animalium vel locorum fuisse Severus ipse postea ostendit.* For bibliography on the interest of the Severi in the cult of Sarapis see M. Leglay, "Un 'Pied de Sarapis' à Timgad, en Numidie," *HomVermaseren* 2.583-84.

¹³⁶ *Hist. Aug., Alexander Severus* 26: *Alexander Severus Isium et Serapium decenter ornavit additis signis et deliacis et omnibus mysticis.*

¹³⁷ A variety of reports exist for the work done in 1855-57. Of these the most important are two publications by Ch. Descemet: *Mémoire sur les fouilles exécutées à Sainte-Sabine (1855-57)*, Paris, 1863, and "Mémoire sur les fouilles exécutées à Sainte-Sabine, 1855-57," *MPAIBL*, Ser. 1: *Sujets divers d'érudition*, vol. 6, pt. 2 (1864), 165-81 and plan iii. Earlier Descemet had also published "Fouilles de S. Sabine," *AICorrArch* 29 (1857), 62-67 (not very useful) and "Note sur les fouilles exécutées à Santa-Sabina," *CRAIBL* 3 (1859), 104-9 (a short preview of his later reports). Also of some use is G. B. de Rossi, "Scavi nell' orto di Santa Sabina," *Monumenti, Annali e Bullettini pubblicati dall' Istituto di Corrispondenza Archeologica* 1855, fasc. 1, pp. xlviii-liv. Félix Darsy completed his re-examination of the area in 1939 but did not produce a full report until 1968: *Recherches*, 30-55. This is the primary publication for understanding all of the discoveries. Prior to this, short accounts of these investigations had been provided by Darsy ("Un sanctuaire d'Isis sur l'Aventin," *RendPontAcc* 21 (1945-46), 8-9 and *Santa Sabina*, Rome, 1961, 52-53) and by Franz Cumont ("Rapport sur une mission a Rome," *CRAIBL* 1945,

396-99). For a summary of the discoveries see Malaise, *Inventaire*, 225-27. Inscriptions: Vidman lists some of the graffiti under SIRIS 390. For a more complete and definitive publication see Darsy, *Recherches*, 30-45.

[138] Darsy (*Recherches*, 54) believes that Isis worshippers assembled here as early as Republican times, but no proof whatever exists for this hypothesis.

[139] Darsy (Ibid., 49) dates these paintings on stylistic grounds to the late 2nd cen. One of the walls covered by these paintings was thought by De Rossi (*Monumenti* 1855, xlviii) to be "perhaps not earlier than the time of Hadrian."

[140] These also date to the end of the 2nd cen. (Darsy, *Recherches*, 41).

[141] The first two words of this graffito are read as nominatives by Darsy (Ibid., 42).

[142] De Rossi, *Monumenti* 1855, xlviii.

[143] Darsy, *Santa Sabina*, 53.

[144] Darsy, *Recherches*, 54.

[145] Work was carried on intermittently at this site from 1934-47. However, the death of one of the chief archaeologists, Giacomo Guidi, and the onset of World War II helped to prevent any effective publication of the many discoveries. Only brief reports appeared: O. Brendel, *AA* 1935, 593; R. Horn, *AA* 1937, 461; *BullCom* 66 (1938), fasc. 4, p. 135; and "The Organization and Work, 1943-48," *Reports and Monographs of the Department of Antiquities in Tripolitania* 2 (1949), 12. In the light of this situation Gennaro Pesce decided to re-examine all of the finds. The result was his *Il tempio d'Iside in Sabratha*, Rome, 1953, a work of great ability. On the subsequent restoration work carried out at this sanctuary see H. Sichtermann, *AA* 1962, 513-14. On the sanctuary's altars see Hermann, *Götteraltäre*, 116. Inscriptions: Pesce, *Tempio*, 47-48; SIRIS 795-96. SIRIS 795 has attracted considerable attention: Joyce M. Reynolds and J. B. Ward-Perkins, *Inscriptions of Roman Tripolitania*, Rome/London, 1952, nr. 15; Ginette di Vita-Evrard, "La dédicace du temple d'Isis à Sabratha: une nouvelle inscription africaine à l'actif de C. Paccius Africanus," *Libya antiqua* 3-4 (1966-67), 13-20 and plates; Herbert Benario, "C. Paccius Africanus at Sabratha," *Epigraphica* 28 (1966), 135-39.

[146] For that matter, Pesce believed that he had discovered two Iseums (Pesce, *Tempio*, 62-64)! But in this belief he was certainly mistaken. Although he had uncovered an older podium or base under the floor of the west portico, an object which he dated to the Augustan period or the early 1st cen. AD (pp. 13-15; 63), he offered not one shred of evidence that this so-called "temple" was dedicated to Isis. Di Vita-Evrard (*Libya antiqua* 3-4 [1966-67], 13) earlier noted the very hypothetical character of this identification.

[147] Vidman, SIRIS, p. 333, concurs with Benario.

[148] Pesce, *Tempio*, 64-65. See also p. 70 on the dating for the capitals.

[149] Ibid., 49-52. A fragment of a Harpocrates statue, dated by Pesce to the 1st cen. AD, is an isolated exception.

[150] See note 146.

[151] Pesce, *Tempio*, 49-50 and fig. 28.

[152] Ibid., 49.

[153] SIRIS 796, possibly of the 3rd cen., is a dedication to Isis which was found in the fill of the crypt area. It provides no evidence for the official character of the sanctuary but only reveals that Isis inspired religious devotion in some particular individual.

[154] Shortly after the Swedish Cyprus Expedition completed its work here, Alfred Westholm published what is probably the finest report on any of the known sites: *The Temples of Soli*, Stockholm, 1936. A large part of this volume was then included

with some revisions in *SCE*, vol. 3 (1937) 399-411, 416-547, 672. In this same volume E. Ekman edited the inscriptions (pp. 623-31). See also Ekman's remarks on the site (pp. 543-47). Westholm had promised that vol. 4 of this series would offer a study of the site from a history-of-religions perspective. This hope, however, did not materialize. Various portions of *SCE*, vol. 4, pt. 3: *The Hellenistic and Roman Periods in Cyprus* (1956) are quite important both for questions of typology and chronology and for the final conclusions of the excavation team. In these some of Westholm's earlier positions undergo modification. For a brief summary of evidence from this site see my ''The Serapeum at Soli, Cyprus,'' *Numina Aegaea* 2 (1975), pt. 3, pp. 1-8. Literary evidence: Strabo 14.6.3 may well be a reference to the earlier temple.

155 Westholm, *Temples*, 148-49. He preferred a *terminus a quo* for Temple E in the mid 3rd cen. However, his own pottery typology points to a somewhat earlier date. Specifically, the fill used for Altar 156 in the left cella (Section viii.6) contained no late Roman pottery fragments (Ibid., 145).

156 Ibid., 100-1, nrs. 314 and 320—cf. pp. 140-41. On the date of these heads of Isis, see also *SCE* 4.3, p. 99.

157 Strabo 14.6.3: εἶτα Σόλοι πόλις λιμένα ἔχουσα καὶ ποταμὸν καὶ ἱερὸν Ἀφροδίτης καὶ Ἴσιδος· κτίσμα δ᾽ ἐστὶ Φαλήρου καὶ Ἀκάμαντος Ἀθηναίων· οἱ δ᾽ ἐνοικοῦντες Σόλιοι καλοῦνται· ἐντεῦθεν ἦν Στασάνωρ τῶν Ἀλεξάνδρου ἑταίρων ἀνὴρ ἡγεμονίας ἠξιωμένος· ὑπέρκειται δ᾽ ἐν μεσογαίᾳ Λιμενία πόλις.

158 Three fragments of sphinxes (Westholm, *Temples*, nrs. 302, 310, and 536) were found in circumstances under which it is likely that they originally came from Temple D.

159 Wild, *Numina Aegaea*, 2.

160 It is also the largest of the three cellae, although the importance of this is diminished by the fact that it is constructed upon the foundations of what had been a left-hand cella in the older sanctuary.

161 Westholm, *Temples*, 100, nrs. 318 and 312-13. Hornbostel (*Sarapis*, 411, n. 3) remarks that the typology of the Sarapis head is somewhat unfamiliar.

162 Westholm, *Temples*, 101-2, nr. 329.

163 Ibid., 104, nr. 407; p. 151.

164 Westholm gives the dimensions of this object as 0.10 × 0.53 m. It must be that he has omitted the width, which, to judge by the photograph (Pl. xx, nr. 4), must have been c. 0.25 m.

165 *PAH* 1.1.172.

166 Ch. Hülsen, ''Porticus Divorum et Serapeum im Marsfelde,'' *RM* 18 (1903), 39-47. See also an Isis relief found at Rome (Malaise, *Inventaire*, 169, nr. 311). Among the cultic objects depicted are two pine cones.

167 See note 111.

168 Perhaps the individual from Soli who honored Isis and Sarapis at Abydos had been a worshipper at this sanctuary: Παύρων Φιλοπίου Σόλιος ἥκω προσκυνῆσαι θε(οὺς) μεγάλους Ἶσιν καὶ Σάραπιν. The date of this graffito is uncertain. See A. H. Sayce, ''The Kypriote Graffiti of Abydos,'' *PSBA* 7 (1884-85), 39.

169 The major report on the excavations carried out at this site was published in two parts by F. Hiller von Gaertringen: *Thera: Untersuchungen, Vermessungen und Ausgrabungen in den Jahren 1895-1902*, 4 vols., Berlin, 1899-1906, 1. 258-64 and 3.84-88. Inscriptions from the site and from a nearby Byzantine church in which such stones were reused as building material have been edited by Hiller von Gaertringen in *IG* XII.3.443-45 (= SIRIS 137-38, 141), 462-63, 1373 (= SIRIS 142), 1388 (= SIRIS 139), and 1389 (= F. Hiller von Gaertringen, ''Inschriften von

Rhodos und Thera,'' *Hermes* 36 [1901], 447 = SIRIS 140). See also Fraser, *OpAth* 3 (1960), 24. A very brief notice on the discoveries made during the excavation is in *AM* 21 (1896), 257-58 and a somewhat longer but largely derivative account is seen in Dunand, *Culte d'Isis* 2.124-29.

170 SIRIS 137. See Fraser, *OpAth* 3 (1960) 24.

171 This fact helps to explain why two dedications honoring Arsinoe were found in the immediate area of the site (*IG* XII.3.462 and Hiller von Gaertringen, *Hermes* 36 [1901], 447) and why a fragment of a scarab in blue faience was discovered on the site itself.

172 None of the inscriptions are earlier, but several others besides SIRIS 137 are from the same century: SIRIS 138, 139 (*very* fragmentary), 140 (also quite fragmentary), and possibly 141.

173 See Fraser, *OpAth* 3 (1960), 24-25.

174 The situation with respect to this site is regrettable. S. Pelekides had the opportunity to explore large segments of what must have been one of the greatest Isis-Sarapis sanctuaries in the Graeco-Roman world but published only two inscriptions out of all his finds: Ἀπὸ τὴν πολιτεία καὶ τὴν κοινωνία τῆς ἀρχαίας Θεσσαλονίκης, Thessalonica, 1934, 3-23. His papers are presently in possession of his family and we may hope that they will allow them to be published. At present we are entirely dependent upon brief reports in various journals: *BCH* 45 (1921), 540-41; *AA* 1922, 242-43; C. Picard "Les dieux de la colonie de Philippes," *RHR* 86 (1922), 179, n. 3; *JHS* 41 (1921), 274; *AA* 41 (1926), 430; and Makaronas, *Makedonika* 1 (1940), 464-65. This last was summarized in *AA* 1940, 260 and 263 and was later translated by Daniel Fraikin, "Note on the Sanctuary of the Egyptian Gods in Thessalonica," *Numina Aegaea* 1 (1974), 1-6. In this article Fraikin also supplies a plan and photographs of the model (now in the Museum at Thessalonica) of the building discovered in 1939. Further brief notes: A. E. Vakalopoulou, Ἱστορία τῆς Θεσσαλονίκης, *315 π. X.—1912*, Thessalonica, 1947, 9 (site now totally overbuilt) and Edson, *HTR* 41 (1948), 181-82. Small finds: T. Krause, *Hekate*, Heidelberg, 1960, 171, n. 14 (a *Hecataeon* found in 1939) and Salditt-Trappmann, *Tempel*, 48-52 and Abb. 42-46. Inscriptions from the site: the long-awaited publication of the eighty or so inscriptions found at the Serapeum (C. Edson, ed., *IG* X.2.1: *Inscriptiones Thessalonicae et vicinae*, Berlin, 1972—cf. Edson's earlier cry of pain at the long delay: "The Greek Inscriptions of Macedonia," *Actes du deuxième congres international d'epigraphie grecque et latin, Paris, 1952*, Paris, 1953, 43-44) has provoked and will continue to provoke considerable interest: Daux, *CRAIBL* 1972, 478-87; Reinhold Merkelbach, "Zwei Texte aus dem Serapeum zu Thessalonike," *ZPE* 10 (1973), 45-54; Jean Bingen, "Sur une dédicace osiriaque de Thessalonique (*IG* X.2.108)," *ChrEg* 47 (1972), 288-91; Dunand, *Culte d'Isis* 2.53-60 and 181-90; Louis Robert, "Les inscriptions de Thessalonique," *RevPhil* 48 (1974), 180-246 (review of the *IG* X volume); F. Sokolowski, "Propagation of the Cult of Sarapis and Isis in Greece," *GRBS* 15 (1974), 441-51; etc. Earlier discussions of the epigraphical evidence: M. N. Tod, "Macedonia VI.—Inscriptions," *BSA* 23 (1918-19), 86-89; Pelekides, 3-23; Benedikt Schwank, " 'Setze über nach Mazedonien und hilf uns!'," *Erbe und Auftrag* 39 (1963), Abb. 3 (photograph of *IG* X.107); and G. Manganaro, "Nuove dediche con impronte di piedi alle divinità egizie," *ArchCl* 16 (1964), 291-93.

175 *IG* X.83: [ἔτους] ε [['Αντωνίου]] / [Πόπλιο]ς Σαλάριος Πάμφι / [λος ἱε]ρεὺς Σαράπιδος καὶ / [Ἴσι]δος καὶ Μάνιος Σαλά[ρ]ιος / [Π]οπλίου υἱὸς τὸ ὑδρῆον / Ἴσιδι καὶ τοῖς ἄλλοις θεοῖς / τοῖς ἐντεμενίοις πᾶσι / καὶ πάσαις. Date: 37-36 BC (?).

[176] Isis is mentioned first (or exclusively) in twenty-one inscriptions while Sarapis is mentioned in this fashion only in ten, most of which are of Hellenistic date.

[177] *BCH* 45 (1921), 541.

[178] *AA* 41 (1926), 430.

[179] The report promised by J. Lassus and M. Leglay (M. Leglay, "Le temple sévérien de l'Aqua Septimiana Felix," *BA* NS 3 [1967], 262) has not yet appeared. Consequently, the only real account of the sixteen years of work carried on at this great sanctuary is a short article by the then director of the work, Louis Leschi: "Découvertes récentes a Timgad: Aqua Septimiana Felix," *CRAIBL* 1947, 87-99. The brief printed summaries of papers given by J. Lassus and M. Leglay ("Le fort byzantine de Timgad," *BA* NS 3 [1967], 260-61) and by Leglay (cited above) clarify a few details but otherwise reiterate information found in Leschi. For a plan of Timgad showing the location of the fort under which the sanctuary was found, see E. Boeswillwald *et al.*, *Timgad, une cité africaine*, Paris, 1905, pl. 1. Small find: M. Leglay, "Un 'Pied de Sarapis' a Timgad, en Numidie," *HomVermaseren* 2.573-74, 580, 589.

[180] Leglay, *BA* NS 3 (1967), 262.

[181] Leschi, *CRAIBL* 1947, 93-94.

[182] Ibid., 98.

[183] Principal sources of information: R. Heberday, "XI. vorläufiger Bericht über die Grabungen in Ephesos, 1913," *ÖJh* 18 (1915), Beibl., 77-88; Josef Keil, "XII. vorläufiger Bericht über die Ausgrabungen in Ephesos," *ÖJh* 23 (1926), Beibl., 265-70; and Salditt-Trappmann, *Tempel*, 26-32. Hölbl, *Zeugnisse* (1978) does not provide any new data about this site.

[184] Josef Keil, *ÖJh* 23 (1926), 267-68; "Das Serapeion von Ephesos," *Bericht über den VI. internationalen Kongress für Archäologie, Berlin, 21.-26. August, 1939*, Berlin, 1940, 473; "Das Serapeion von Ephesos," *Halil Edhem hâtıra kitabı—In memoriam Halil Edhem*, Ankara, 1947, 1.181-92; "Denkmäler des Sarapiskultes in Ephesos," *AnzWien* 91 (1954), 217-28; *Ephesos, ein Führer durch die Ruinenstätte und ihre Geschichte*, 4th ed., Vienna, 1957, 94-96.

[185] Keil, *ÖJh* 23 (1926), 267-68.

[186] Keil apparently had to do a good deal of guesswork to determine a text (*Halil Edhem*, 1.183).

[187] SIRIS 303.14-16: τοῖς ἐπὶ θεοῦ / μου Νείλου Σεράπιδι θύου / σι.

[188] Keil, *ÖJh* 23 (1926), 269-70.

[189] Keil, *Halil Edhem*, 1.183.

[190] Vidman, SIRIS, p. 154.

[191] Keil, *Halil Edhem*, 1.188-89.

APPENDIX TWO

[1] Unless otherwise noted, the physical data for this crypt is from Makaronas, *Makedonika* 1 (1940), 464-65. This has been translated (with the exception of a few lines and several notes) by Daniel Fraikin ("Note on the Sanctuary of the Egyptian Gods in Thessalonica," *Numina Aegaea* 1 [1974], 1-6). He also added a useful plan of this part of the site.

[2] Makaronas did not supply any dimensions for these steps. Since the crypt area is about two meters below ground level in this area, there were probably about 8-10 steps. Apparently there was no direct access to the crypt from within the temple.

³ The height is estimated from a photograph of the model now kept in the Museum at Thessaloniki. The floor of the crypt seems from this to have been about 2.5 m below the floor of the temple.

⁴ Makaronas, *Makedonika* 1 (1940), 464 and n. 4. He provided no other data which would help to determine the character of this inscription. None of the texts published by Edson in *IG* X clearly correspond with this description. *IG* X.2.1.948 is "almost totally illegible" but is probably too large (h., 0.50; w., 0.78; th., 0.43 m) and is made of porous stone rather than of marble.

⁵ Makaronas, *Makedonika* 1 (1940), 465. According to him, the sealing of the crypt was probably carried out by Christians during late antiquity.

⁶ Ibid., 464.

⁷ Ibid., 465.

⁸ *IG* X.2.1.107.

⁹ Benedikt Schwank (" 'Setze über nach Mazedonien und hilf uns!'," *Erbe und Auftrag* 39 [1963], Abb. 3) provides a photograph of the relief and inscription. Makaronas (*Makedonika* 1 [1940], 465) has a description and indicates that this stone was found during the excavations of 1939.

¹⁰ Pausanias (8.54.5) mentions a temple dedicated to Dionysus μύστης, and Artemidorus (2.70) refers to Apollo μύστης.

¹¹ This would be an inscription of great importance if it indicates that initiation rites involving an *imitatio Osiridis* were carried out at Thessalonica. However, this is probably pushing this rather brief text too hard.

¹² *IG* X.2.1.259. This lengthy inscription, which probably, but not certainly, was found in 1939, is not mentioned in Makaronas' report. Because Pelekides did not publish it in the years after 1921 when he and others were making known the best of the finds from that earlier dig and because this text by its museum accession number is grouped with a number of other items known to have been found in 1939, I believe that it was probably discovered in that year and therefore in the vicinity of the crypt. For a preliminary but detailed study of this important text see Daux, *CRAIBL* 1972, 478-87. He also suggests corrections for the readings given in *IG* X. However, Daux's own reference to the date of discovery (p. 478) is erroneous—he appears to be unaware that excavations were also carried out at this site in 1939. On this text see also M. J. Vermaseren, *Cybele and Attis*, London, 1977, 135.

¹³ Ibid., 480. Daux and Edson agree that the inscription dates from the 1st cen. AD.

¹⁴ In a lengthy excursus W. Hornbostel (*Sarapis*, 408-17) raises significant objections to the identification of the one example usually advanced, the archaized herm from Memphis upon which "Demetrius of Phalerum" is leaning. This figure forms a part of a Hellenistic group of sculptures located on the approach to the Serapeum. Aside from a curious double herm found in the Museo Paolino and a possible example in terracotta found from Delos, there are no cases known to Hornbostel in which Sarapis is depicted as a herm (p. 412, n. 5), much less in the archaized form found at Memphis (and at Thessalonica).

¹⁵ *IG* X.2.1.59 and 259. Dedications to Theos Hypsistos (*IG* X.2.1.67-69 and 71) were found *prope Serapeum*. Edson believes that *IG* X.2.1.37 was a dedication to Heros, the Thracian Rider-God, but the reading of this name is uncertain.

¹⁶ S. Eitrem, "Hermai," *RE* 15.705.

¹⁷ Daux (*CRAIBL* 1972, 481) discusses the identity of this deity but without decisive results. Gongylos is perhaps an epithet (the "Round One"?) rather than a reference to an originally independent god. Its presence here in this inscription

renders Schwabl's judgment ("Zeus I. Epiklesen," *RE*, ser. 2, 10A.295) that γογγυλάτης in Lycophron 435 is a simple word play deriving from Aristophanes (*Lys.* 972-76) somewhat less likely. Zeus Dionysus is attested in Thrace and in Phrygia—see Schwabl, Ibid., 299-300—but this inscription may instead refer to another local Zeus. Festugière's explanation (given in Daux, *CRAIBL* 1972, 487, n. 1) that two gods, Zeus-Sarapis and Dionysus-Harpocrates-Bes, are involved is quite strained. The second group would be quite an unusual concatenation of divinities.

[18] βησαρτης is also found as a title in *IG* X.2.1.244. It apparently is not otherwise known.

[19] The early date of the Osiris inscription need not pose any difficulty for this theory. Makaronas believed that the crypt was built sometime earlier than the Roman period temple overhead.

[20] Makaronas, *Makedonika* 1 (1940), 464: ἑνὸς δρόμου σηραγγοειδοῦς; p. 465: ὁ σηραγγοειδὴς δρόμος and ὁ δρόμος τῆς ἐξόδου.

[21] *IG* X.2.1.118.

[22] *IG* X.2.1.111 (c. 2nd cen. AD). *IG* X.111 probably was discovered in the course of the 1939 investigations. It has an accession number (MTh 999) in the Archeological Museum at Thessaloniki which would appear to place it among texts known to have been recovered in that year (MTh 979, 987-90, 996-97, 1009). It therefore probably came from the area of the crypt and temple.

[23] If the temple was constructed over a pre-existing crypt, it may well have been necessary to build a passageway, the δρόμος, to reach the old crypt. *IG* X.2.1.111 may have commemorated the construction of this facility. The date of this stone would then give the approximate date for the construction of the temple (c. 2nd cen. AD).

[24] Tran Tam Tinh (*Essai*, 33) indicates the length and approximate height of the cult platform. Other dimensions are estimated from various plans and photographs of the sanctuary.

[25] The archaeologist (*PAH* 1.1.174) reported the following finds from the cella: a wooden box, partially burned, containing a tiny gold cup, c. 2.2. cm in diameter; a bronze amulet; a small bronze base, c. 2.2 cm in diameter; a tiny crystal vase, c. 4.5 cm in height. A second box, also partially burned, contained a bronze lamp which was about 0.20 m high. This had two wick holes and a chain for suspending it. In this same box were two bronze "candelieri," c. 0.26 m high, with flower-shaped cups at the top. In addition to the boxes the excavators discovered two skulls (used for cultic purposes??) and a marble hand, c. 0.11 m long, which perhaps came from a statue.

[26] Hamilton, *Archaeologia* 4 (1776), 173. Dyer (*Pompeii*, 140-41) spoke darkly of the area being used for "some juggling purposes connected with the worship of the temple."

[27] E.g., Overbeck and Mau, *Pompeii*, 107; Breton, *Pompeia*, 49; Lafaye, *Histoire*, 181-82.

[28] The various dimensions provided are estimated from Squarciapino, *Culti*, 20 (plan) and from various photographs.

[29] Overbeck and Mau, *Pompeii*, 107.

[30] Ibid., 93. For a plan and a brief description of this temple see Heinz Kähler, *Der römische Tempel*, Berlin, 1970, 35-36, Abb. 5, and Taf. 24-25. It was constructed in the 1st cen. BC, was then destroyed in the earthquake of 62 AD, and had not yet been completely rebuilt in 79 AD. Mazois and Gau (*Ruines*, vol. 3, pls. 30-33) provide plans and drawings of the cella area.

[31] Richard Delbrück, *Hellenistische Bauten in Latium*, 2 vols., Strassburg, 1907-12, 2.6-10.

[32] The evidence to follow, unless otherwise indicated, is from Knackfuss, *Südmarkt*, 184-85.

[33] Theodor Wiegand, "Siebenter vorläufiger Bericht über die von den königlichen Museen in Milet und Didyma unternommenen Ausgrabungen," *AbhBerlin* 1911, 1.21.

[34] Salditt-Trappmann (*Tempel*, 35) says that the height of the platform was 1.70 m. This must be a misprint since it contradicts other figures she supplies.

[35] This back wall is twice as thick as the other walls of the building. It was believed to have been constructed in this fashion so as to accommodate a niche with a depth of about 0.70 m. No trace of such a niche has been found, but the back wall survives only to a height of 1.5 m.

[36] Knackfuss, *Südmarkt*, 185; Salditt-Trappmann, *Tempel*, 35.

[37] Kraus *et al.*, *MDIK* 22 (1967), 132, n. 3.

[38] D. Krenker and W. Zschietzschmann (*Römische Tempel in Syrien*, 2 vols., Berlin, 1938, 1.294) argue in similar fashion from the absence of niches, bases, etc., in the many crypts found in the temples of Syria that these areas did not serve a ritual purpose.

[39] Crypts in Egyptian temples were normally used for the storage of cultic images and vessels. They were not used for cultic rituals—often they are simply too small for such a purpose (Erman, *Handbook*, 213; Bonnet, "Krypta," *Reallexikon*, 402).

[40] Apuleius, *Met.* 11.22.

[41] For descriptions of this tunnel see Botti, *Fouilles*, 122-25 and Rowe, *BArchAlex* 35 (1942), 144-46.

[42] Botti and Rowe (*ASAntEg*, Suppl. 2 [1946], 31) both thought that the foundations were those of a temple of Sarapis. A. Adriani (*Repertorio*, C.1.95) calls the structure "the Ptolemaic Mausoleum" but indicates that the meager state of the available evidence leaves much room for doubt.

[43] Rowe, *BArchAlex* 35 (1942), 145, n. 1.

[44] The best descriptions are those provided by Botti: *L'acropole*, 24-26 and plan; *Fouilles*, 111-21. See also Rowe, *ASAntEg*, Suppl. 2 (1946), 35-36; Rowe-Rees, *BJRL* 39 (1956-57), 498-99; and Adriani, *Repertorio*, C.1.95-96.

[45] Botti (*Fouilles*, 116) has a useful illustration.

[46] Ibid., 119. Rowe (*BArchAlex* 35 [1942], 134-35) notes that in the nineteenth century many statues of dogs, jackals, birds, etc., were found on the site. Perhaps these somehow were related to the burial crypts.

[47] Serapeum at Memphis: A. Mariette, *Le Sérapeum de Memphis*, Paris, 1857, and *Le Sérapeum de Memphis*, ed. G. Maspero, Paris, 1882. Guimot (*ChrEg* 37 [1962], 359-81) provides a very useful summary of all the finds. Saqqarah finds: H. S. Smith, "The Sacred Animal Necropolis at North Saqqara," *A Visit to Ancient Egypt*, Warminster, 1974, 21-63—see especially p. 40, fig. 9.

[48] The letters used to designate the various facilities in the description that follows refer to Fig. 21.

[49] Salditt-Trappmann, *Tempel*, 18-22.

[50] Room E', which lies below an area of roughly the same size (E), has in its ceiling two holes, 0.70 m in diameter, which connect it with the room above.

[51] Salditt-Trappmann, *Tempel*, Abb. 22 is a view of the interior of Room H'.

[52] Room H' is presently used as a stable and Room E' apparently still has 2 m of debris piled on top of its original floor.

[53] Salditt-Trappmann reported that 0.45 m was the narrowest width she encountered in the tunnel system. Since her plan (= my Fig. 21) does not always observe precise scale, I am not certain where this very narrow segment is located. Most of the tunnels appear to be at least 0.70 m wide.

[54] Salditt-Trappmann, *Tempel*, 21: "...beidseitig in den Wänden des Ganges, durch regelmässige Aussparung von Steinen gewonnen, je drei übereinanderliegende Tritte." She provides no further details.

[55] Ibid., 6. The text she cites in this connection, Rufinus, *Hist. Eccl.* 11.25, does not refer to the Isis-Sarapis cult.

[56] Salditt-Trappmann (Ibid.) believed that the size of the surviving masonry base, 4.60 m square, indicated the actual size of the base of the cult statue. Consequently, she thought that this image probably was a seated figure. However, the statue's base might very well have been a good deal smaller.

[57] The placement of the exits from the tunnel in the three temples appears designed to facilitate the entrance of cultic officials and others for the performance of rites. The fact that the exit in the main temple is set so close to the cult statue is a further indication that the tunnel system was for the use of the ministers of the cult.

[58] Pesce (*Tempio*, 68) also recognized this as a likely function for the crypt area at Sabratha. The dimensions given in the following description are generally taken from his study of the site (Ibid., 9-11 and 42-43), although a few are based on estimates derived from photographs and plans.

[59] Pesce (Ibid., 70) notes that the upper portions of the temple fell in a westerly direction. He suspected, therefore, that an earthquake caused part of the destruction.

[60] Pesce (Ibid., 49-50) indicates that the fill reached a height of at least 1.5 m above floor level in this crypt.

[61] Pesce believed that the actual cella was situated only over the north and south crypts and not over the ambulacrum, a view with which I concur especially since no small finds were recovered from the latter area. He also believed that the temple was peripteral in form. I suspect, however, that the thickness of the outer platform walls is best explained by assuming that they were designed to support solid masonry and a barrel vault roof. According to my reconstruction, the enclosed area outside the cella would have formed an ambulacrum similar to that found in the Serapeum at Mons Claudianus in Egypt.

[62] Pesce, *Tempio*, 52, nrs. 27 and 31; and 55, nrs. 61-62.

[63] Ibid., 68. Pesce (Ibid., 73, n. 1) notes that other temples at Sabratha (e.g., the so-called Antonine Temple and the Temple of Jupiter) had crypts not unlike that found at this sanctuary. Such crypts served as repositories for various items of value, cultic or otherwise. What is unusual in the present instance is the stairway to the cella.

[64] Apuleius, *Met.* 11.23-24.

[65] Pesce, *Tempio*, 73.

[66] Ibid., 74.

INDICES

I. ANCIENT SOURCES

A. *Literary Texts*

Achilles Tatius
    4.12.2-3   89, 231
    4.18.34   90

Acts of Peter
  Actus Vercell.
    5   255

Acts of Thomas
  118-22   229, 255

Aelian
  NA
    3.33   94
    7.45   62, 222, 239
    10.27   225
    10.46   223
    11.10   94

Aeschylus
  Pers.
    33   93
  PV.
    812   90
  Supp.
    560   90, 230
    854-57   94, 96, 233

Ambrose
  Sermo
    38.2   62

Ammianus Marcellinus
  22.15.3   88, 92, 230
  22.15.14   233
  22.16.12-13   258

Anonymous of
  Florence   223

Anthologia Graeca
  9.386   231

Aphthonius
  Progym. (ed. Rabe)
    48-49   258
    48   79, 227
    49   251

Apollodorus
  1.6.3   229
  2.4.3   81

Apollonius Rhodius
  Argon.
    4.270   222

Apollonius Rhodius, Schol.
  Argon.
    4.262   233

Apuleius
  Met.
    11.1   144, 146, 254
    11.7   144
    11.11   75, 101, 103-4,
        107-9, 127, 157,
        223, 225, 235-37,
        240, 248
    11.17   156, 242
    11.20   111, 147, 242
    11.22   197
    11.23   143-44, 204, 219,
        255
    11.24   204
    11.26   272

Aristaenetus
  De Nili bonis   222, 230

Aristides, Aelius
  Or. (ed. Keil)
    11.331   83
    36.10   82
    36.19   223
    36.116   90-91
    36.123   222, 230
    36.124   90
    45.29   82
    45.32   223, 230

Aristobulus
  Frag.   94

Aristophanes
  Lys.
    972-76   278
Aristotle
  Gen. An.
    4.4.770a   95
  Hist. An.
    7.4.584b   95, 233
  Frag.   89
Arnobius
  Adv. Nat.
    4.16   88
    6.23   259
Artemidorus
    2.70   277
Athenaeus
    2.41f   231, 233-34, 256
    2.45c   232
    2.67b   232
Aulus Gellius
  NA.
    10.2   233
Aurelius Victor
  De Caes.
    14.7-8   235
Avienus
  Ar. Phaen.
    797-98   234
  Desc. orb. terr.
    340   232
Bible
  Deut.
    11:10-12   222
  2 Kgs.
    5:12   224
  Acts
    16:25-27   229
  Book of Elchasai
    Frag.   255
Callimachus
    3.171   214
Callisthenes
    Frag.   223
Cassius Dio
    66.24.2   181, 272
    69.11.2-3   235
    78.23.2   168
    79.10.1   272

Chaeremon
  Aegypt. (frag.)   146
Clement of Alexandria
  Protr.
    4.51   259
  Strom.
    5.7   76
    6.4.36   111, 213
    6.4.37   112-13, 215, 236-
                         37, 239, 242
Corpus Hermeticum
    13.17   91, 97, 231, 234
  Asclepius
    24   88
Didache
    7   50, 62, 255
Dinon
  Persica (frag.)   91-92
Diodorus
    1.10.1-7   96-97, 234
    1.11.4   225
    1.24   78
    1.36.2   88, 92
    1.36.11   212
    1.37.8   234
    1.39.1-3   223
    1.40.4   91, 231
    1.40.7   231, 233-34
Dionysius Periegetes
  Orb. terr. desc.
    221   233
    227   233
Epiphanius
  Adv. Haeres.
    51.30.3   91, 231, 257
Eudocia
  Violar.
    698   222, 230
Eusebius
  Chron.   259, 272
  Praep. Evang.
    3.11.51   223, 256
    3.11.116   223
    5.7.192c   234
    9.10.413a   231, 235
Eustathius
  In Dion. Perieg.
    222   89

Eutropius
Brev.
7.23.5 272

Firmicus Maternus
Err. prof. rel.
2.5 98, 235, 256
2.6 223, 257

Heliodorus
2.22.5-23 241
2.23 91, 231
2.28 223, 230-31
9.9 223, 256
9.22 88-89, 228

Heraclitus
Quaest. Hom.
3 251

Herodotus
2.15 78
2.18 231
2.37 146
2.41 225
2.90 98, 235
2.91 78-80
2.131-32 74
3.6 91
6.54 226

Heron of Alexandria
Pneum.
1.32 130, 251

Himerus
Disc.
1.8 222

Hippocrates
De morbo sac.
2 250

Hippolytus
Haer.
5.7.5 97, 232, 234
9.15.4 255

Hippys of Rhegium
Chron.
frag. 1 233

Historia Augusta
Hadrian
14.6 235
Pescennius Niger
7.7 90-91

Septimius Severus
17 182, 272
Alexander Severus
26 182, 272

Homer
Il.
2.781-83 229

Horapollo
1.21 223
1.25 96

Iamblichus
V. Pythag.
18.83 251

Isidore of Seville
Etym.
13.21.7 232

Joannes Lydus
De mens.
4.57 233
4.107 96

Josephus
BJ
7.123 272

Justin Martyr
I Apol.
62 256

Juvenal
6.523-29 92, 254, 257, 272

Libanius
Or.
30.35-36 93

Lucan
8.444-45 82, 222
8.828 222
10.242-44 223

Lucan, Schol.
8.826 222

Lucian
De sacrificiis
13 251
Dial. deor.
3 223
Dial. mar.
14.1 81

Lucretius
6.729-37 223

Lycophron
  435   278
  575-76   214

Macrobius
  Sat.
    7.16.12   234
    21.11   223, 257

Martial
  2.14.7-8   74-75, 225, 272
  8.81   225
  10.48   225

Maximus of Tyre
  25.7   234

Nicander, Schol.
  Alexipharm.
    201   226

Nonnus
  3.279-82   76
  6.339-40   234
  26.229-34   93
  31.37   232

Oppian
  Cyneg.
    2.85   232

Oribasius
  5.3.15
    (ed. Raeder)   95-96
  5.5.1   95, 231
  Coll. Med.
    22.5   90

Origen
  C. Cels.
    5.38   223, 256

Orphic Hymns
  55.19   234

Ovid
  Ars Am.
    1.645-52   222
    3.393   225
  Met.
    1.422-37   96

Pausanias
  1.18.4   209
  1.41.3   209
  2.2.3   209, 260
  2.4.6   209
  2.5.3   214

  2.17.7   209
  2.32.6   209
  2.34.1   209
  2.34.10   209
  3.14.5   209
  3.22.18   209
  3.25.10   209
  4.32.6   209
  7.21.13   209
  7.25.9   209
  8.54.5   277
  9.24.1   209
  10.32   209

Philostratus
  VA
    6.6   93-94
    6.11   231
    7.34   229
    7.38   83

Pindar, Schol.
  Pyth.
    4.99   222

Plato
  Phdr.
    251B   256
  Tim.
    67C-68D   256

Pliny
  HN
    2.229   214
    5.10.54   234
    5.10.55   223
    7.3.33   95, 233
    9.84.179   234
    15.46   79, 226
    21.50.86   93

Plutarch
  Alex.
    36.2   232
  De Is. et Os.
    5   94, 227
    7   227
    19   225
    32   80-81, 157, 223,
                          225, 256
    33   157, 223, 227
    34   127, 223
    36   108, 127, 157,
                          223, 236-37, 239

38	223, 256
39	74, 76, 82, 223, 225
40	62, 82, 223, 227
52	74
56	80, 227
57	223, 256
64	157, 250
75	146, 222, 239
De soll. anim.	
20	222, 239
Plac. phil.	
4.1	223
Quaest. conv.	
2.15	91, 231
8.5	97, 234
QNat.	
19	256
Pollux	
Onom.	
1.8	130
Polybius	
Frag.	92, 223
Pomponius Mela	
1.9.49	88, 93-95
1.9.52	94, 96, 233-34
1.9.53	223
Porphyry	
Abst.	
4.7	255
4.9	241-42
De imag. (frag.)	223, 256
Frags.	90, 223, 234-35
Pseudo-Aristotle	
De inund. Nili	223
Pseudo-Clement	
Recogn.	
4.32	255
Pseudo-Plutarch	
De esu carn.	
1.3	232, 234
Rufinus	
Hist. eccl.	
11.23	234, 258
11.25	280
11.26	231, 236, 244
11.30	213, 232
Sallustius	
De diis et mundo	
4	223

Seneca	
QNat.	
3.12	88
3.25.11	95, 233
4a.2.1	88
4a.2.9-10	93, 233
4a.2.12	233
4a.2.30	90
Servius	
Ad Aen.	
9.31	232
Ad. Georg.	
3.478	234
Sibylline Oracles	
4.74	232
Socrates	
Hist. eccl.	
1.18	27, 213, 223, 232
Solinus	
1.51	95, 233
32.9	223
Sophocles	
Frag.	227
Sozomen	
Hist. eccl.	
5.3.3	213
6.6	256
7.20	232
Statius	
Silv.	
3.2.108	234
Theb.	
8.358-62	82, 228
8.411	223
Strabo	
2.3.2	223
6.2.4	214
14.6.3	14-15, 132, 184, 274
15.1.3	89
15.1.22	233
17.1.10	167, 259
17.1.18	79
17.1.48	212
Suidas	
s.v. "Sarapis"	223
Tacitus	
Hist.	
4.84	167, 259

Tertullian
  De Bapt.
    4.1   256
    4.3-4   62, 255
    5   99, 235
Themistius
  Or.
    24.305d   93, 232
Theocritus
  Id.
    17.77-80   93, 222
    17.98   233
Theophanes Conf.
  Chronogr.
    16.12-26   213
Theophrastus
  Caus. Pl.
    3.3.3   222

De sensu
  1-8   256
On Waters (frag.) 96, 231, 234, 256

Tibullus
  1.7.22   234
  1.7.27-28   223

Trogus Pompeius
  Frag.   95

Vergil
  Aen.
    9.31   233
  Georg.
    4.287-92   93

Vitruvius
  8. praef. 4   104-5, 111, 127,
                   236-37, 239, 256-
                   57

B. *Papyri*

BGU
  1680   258

PAmh.
  136   258

PCairo Zen.
  3.59355   258

PGM
  1.101-2   229
  4.27-29   235
  12.160-62   229
  13.294-96   84

PMich.
  492   258

POxy.
  425   234
  486   88, 230
  513   258
  1380   68, 214, 222, 229
  1382   68, 228
  1409   88, 230
  1830   234
  3094   258

PRyl.
  230   258

C. *Inscriptions (Principal Collections)*

CE
  1   171, 214, 263
  14   171
  15-15 bis   214
  16-16 bis   171-72, 214, 229,
                   263
  17   229, 263
  20   173
  26   172
  27   172
  29   172
  66-68   265
  76   265

  86   265
  113   131, 212
  140   265
  152   215
  173a   215
  175 A-D   215, 265
  179   215
  184   251

CIL
  VI.20616   249
  X.1.843   252
  XIV.3941   215

I Délos

352	264
365	264
440	264
442	264
1417	264-65
1510	171
2042	265
2044	265
2057	131, 212
2063	265
2068	215
2087	215
2114	265
2116-17	214
2137-38	265
2155	215
2160	215
2162	251
2180-81	171-72, 214, 229, 263
2182	229, 263
2198-99	251
2202	173, 263
2217	173, 263
2355	263
2605	174
2612	263
2617	20, 215
2620	265
2655	173, 263

IG

II².1365	254
X.2.1.37	277
59	277
67-69	277
71	277
83	215, 275
107	191-92, 275, 277
108	275
111	193, 278
118	193
244	278
259	192-93
638	249-50
948	277
XI.4.1223	173
1228-29	172
1246	172
1299	171, 214, 263

XII.3.443-45	274
462-63	274-75
1373	274
1388-89	274
XIV.1488	249
1705	249
1782	249
1842	249

ILS

4378	215

SIG

1042	145

SIRIS

30	229
41a	169
73	175, 220
74	266
76-77	266
79	266
82	266
115-18	179
119	179, 269
122	179
137	185-86, 274-75
138-42	186, 274-75
164-65	266
166	176, 216, 266
167-68	176, 266
169	266
170	176, 216, 266
290-92	180-81, 271
293	271
299	188-89
303	188, 276
308-10	261-62
313	133
382-87	272
459-62	249
482	180, 270
531	215, 237, 239, 248
532	224
539	119-20, 247
645	177
650	176, 266
767-68	168, 259-60
778	249
795-96	183, 273
803-6	171, 262

II. MODERN AUTHORS

Abdul-Qadar, Muhammad   210, 268
Adriani, A.   11, 117, 165, 245, 258, 271, 279
Aldrovandi, U.   245
Almagro, M.   169, 259
Altmann, W.   241
Alzinger, W.   164
Auberon, P.   265
Barb, A. A.   242
Barra Bagnasco, M.   211, 267
Bauer, A.   258
Benario, H.   183
Bieber, M.   77
Bissing, F. von   243-45, 247-48
Blackman, A.   250, 254-55
Bleeker, C. J.   227
Blok, H. P.   244
Böhringer, E.   252, 268
Boissard, J.-J.   245
Bonneau, D.   89, 99-100, 212-13, 223, 228-31, 234-35, 243
Bonnet, H.   145, 225, 227, 254
Bonucci, C.   219
Borchardt, L.   212
Bosticco, S.   238-39
Botti, G.   163, 167, 198-99, 253, 258, 279
Breasted, J. H.   250
Breccia, E.   163, 224, 247, 258-59
Breton, E.   219
Broneer, O.   139, 163, 253, 261
Bruneau, P.   139-41, 164, 173-75, 214-15, 219, 254, 262, 265-66
Budge, E. A. W.   244
Calderini, A.   258-59
Caputo, G.   166
Castiglione, L.   111, 171, 209, 227, 241-42
Cayeux, L.   214
Cazurro, M.   259
Charbonneaux, J.   243, 246
Collart, P.   19-20, 211, 239
Combe, E.   258
Conze, A.   268
Corsu, F. le   208, 240, 254
Cross, F. M.   228
Cumont, F.   238, 250
Daressy, G.   212, 243
Darsy, F.   106, 166, 272-73

Daux, G.   192, 277
Deonna, W.   73, 125, 224
Derchain, P.   112
Descemet, C.   182
Dessau, H.   215
Dölger, F. J.   87, 90, 92, 98-99, 239, 250
Drexler, W.   227
Düll, S.   208
Dunand, F.   14, 101-2, 111, 208, 210, 225, 236, 239, 242, 250
Dyer, T.   278
Edson, C.   191, 215, 277
Ekman, E.   274
Elia, O.   238, 270
Eliade, M.   224
Engreen, F.   31, 214
Erman, A.   115, 130-31
Essen, C. C. van   255
Fairman, H.   26
Falaki, Mahmoud el   163, 258
Festugière, A.-J.   257
Fiorelli, G.   219, 270
Fita, F.   259
Fouquet, A.   248
Fraikin, D.   176
Frankfort, H.   67, 223
Fraser, P. M.   167, 259
Fuhrmann, H.   112
Gandía, E.   259
García y Bellido, A.   169, 259
Gardiner, A.   228, 254-55
Gatti, G.   271
Gau, F.   46, 217, 278
Gauthier, H.   227
Gerhard, E.   251
Ghoneim, Z.   117, 165, 245, 267
Gilbert, P.   214-15
Gonzenbach, V. von   160, 257
Grant, M.   221
Gressmann, H.   228
Griffiths, J. G.   74, 77, 81, 102, 237
Grimm, G.   224
Guarducci, M.   216, 267
Guidi, G.   166, 273
Guilmot, M.   257
Gusman, P.   217, 226, 251
Halbherr, F.   216
Hamilton, W.   218, 252

Handler, S. 168, 258
Hauvette-Besnault, A. 164, 263-64
Hermann, A. 88, 232
Hill, D. 243, 246
Hiller von Gaertringen, F. 13, 271, 274
Hölbl, G. 265
Hohlfelder, R. 260
Holleaux, M. 164, 263-64
Hornbostel, W. 277
Joliffe, N. 229
Jones, H. S. 238-39
Kähler, H. 278
Kaibel, G. 249
Kákosy, L. 234, 242
Karo, G. 224
Karwiese, S. 164, 265
Kater-Sibbes, G. J. F. 72-73, 224
Kaufman, C. M. 246
Keil, J. 188-89, 276
Kern, O. 249
Kircher, A. 236
Klausner, T. 219
Knackfuss, H. 196, 278
Knapp, W. 266
Knoblauch, P. 17, 261
Kraus, T. 267
Krauss, F. 252
Krenker, D. 279
Kuhnert, E. 226
Lafaye, G. 3, 208-9
Leclant, J. 1, 149, 178, 237, 245, 267
Leeuw, G. van der 250
Leospo, E. 115, 240, 243-44
Leschi, L. 166, 188
Lévy, I. 124-25, 250
Lindsay, J. 227
Lloyd, A. B. 78, 80, 227-28
Lundström, V. 181
Lyons, H. 33
Maiuri, A. 221
Makaronas, C. 190-91, 193, 276-78
Malaise, M. 109, 125, 215, 224, 236, 238, 271
Marcadé, J. 164, 264
Mau, A. 218
Mazois, F. 46, 217, 278
Meeks, D. 228
Merkelbach, R. 74-75, 218, 226, 228, 231, 270
Milne, J. G. 114

Modrijan, W. 59-60, 164, 176, 221-22, 266
Mohrmann, C. 250
Mommsen, T. 132, 252
Morenz, S. 226
Morra di Lauriano, B. 177, 211, 267
Mylonas, G. 255
Niccolini, Fausto 47, 218-19
Niccolini, Felice 47, 218-19
Nilsson, M. 64, 67, 89, 207-8, 250, 262
Nissen, H. 180, 218, 270
Nock, A. D. 129, 240, 250
Norris, F. 257
Ohlemutz, E. 252
Oliverio, G. 40-42, 72-73, 164, 215-16, 224, 252, 262, 267
Otto, W. 130-31
Overbeck, J. 195
Pane, R. 221
Panofka, T. 251
Panofsky, E. 121, 236, 244-45
Papadakis, N. 55, 131, 164, 174-75, 211, 219-20, 254, 262, 265-66
Parrot, A. 250
Peek, W. 222
Pelekides, S. 166, 186, 190-91, 275, 277
Perc, B. 120
Perdrizet, P. 224, 246
Pernier, L. 21, 163
Pesce, G. 136, 166, 183-84, 203-5, 218-19, 252, 273, 280
Petrie, W. M. F. 114, 246, 251
Pfister, R. 212
Picard, C. 239, 264
Pietrzykowski, M. 240
Puig y Cadafalch, J. 18, 163, 169, 259
Ramage, E. 260
Reitzenstein, R. 229, 255
Roeder, G. 73, 224
Rohde, E. 124
Rolley, C. 257
Rose, H. J. 223
Roullet, A. 121, 238, 269
Roussel, P. 1, 34-40, 52, 164, 171-73, 211, 214-15, 229, 262-65
Rowe, A. 29, 137, 163, 167-68, 213, 253, 258-59, 279
Salač, A. 17, 163, 168, 170-71, 261

Salditt-Trappmann, R. 34, 41, 52-
53, 58, 72, 141-42, 179, 196, 199-
202, 214-16, 219-21, 254, 261, 267-
69, 278-80
Santini, L. 240
Sauneron, S. 64
Schauenburg, K. 81, 218
Schede, M. 122
Schefold, K. 265
Schneider, H. 244
Schrader, H. 180-81, 271
Schwank, B. 277
Scranton, R. 163, 169-70, 260
Sethe, K. 227
Smith, D. 253
Sourdille, C. 77, 227
Spiegelberg, W. 225
Squarciapino, M. Floriani 278
Stillwell, R. 257
Strong, R. 229
Strzygowski, J. 258
Texier, C. 220
Toussoun, O. 212
Toynbee, A. 241
Tran Tam Tinh, V. 108-9, 218, 221,
239-43, 270, 278
Tschudin, P. 208
Vallois, R. 172-73, 264

Vercoutter, J. 242
Vergara-Caffarelli, E. 165, 267
Vermaseren, M. 72-73, 224, 255
Versnel, H. 229
Vidman, L. 4-5, 101, 149-52, 159,
180, 208-9, 262
Vogliano, A. 251
Vogt, J. 114, 243
Vollgraff, W. 163, 169
Wace, A. J. B. 167, 258
Wainwright, G. 227
Weber, W. 73, 102, 106, 108, 116,
119-21, 123, 224, 239, 244-45, 247
Weinreich, O. 68, 228
Wessetzky, V. 104, 237
Westholm, A. 14, 16, 22, 104, 118,
166, 184-85, 210, 245, 252, 273-74
Wiedemann, A. 227
Wiegand, T. 165, 271
Wilcken, U. 99
Wild, R. 208, 257, 274
Witt, R. E. 209
Woodward, J. 226-27
Wrede, W. 186
Wünsch, R. 244
Zimmer, H. 224
Zschietzschmann, W. 279

III. SUBJECTS

Ablutions 2, 17, 51, 63, 129-48, 151-
53, 174, 178, 256, 265
Ablutions: Basins for Clergy 3, 21,
56, 134-43, 145-47, 152-53, 170,
175, 219, 221, 253
Ablutions: Basins for Worshippers 3,
130-34, 151-52, 174, 178, 250-52,
265, 270
Ablutions: Ritual 3, 23, 58, 61, 129-
31, 136, 141, 143-48, 152-53, 250,
254-55
Abydos (Egypt) 221, 274
Achoris (Egypt) 234
Agathodaimon 240, 244, 249
Alexander Severus 181, 247
Alexander the Great 79, 226
Alexandria, city 29, 31, 79, 105, 107,
109, 113-15, 118-21, 123, 126, 159,
213, 236-37, 239-41, 245, 247-48,
250, 272

Alexandria: Graeco-Roman Museum
240, 246, 271
Altar 20, 38, 107, 132, 135, 139, 175,
181, 184, 187, 191
Αἰδωνεύς 196, 240-41, 248, 252, 258,
262, 270, 273-74
Ambulatory 48-49, 54, 63, 202-4, 280
Amenophis III 253, 255, 286
Amentet 145
Ammon 117
Amon Re 26, 174, 253
Andromeda 3, 46, 76, 78, 80-81, 83-
85, 218, 227, 229, 256
Animals, Sacred 198-99, 205, 279
Animism 67-68, 223
Ankh 46
Antinoopolis 119, 123
Antinoos 99, 235
Antioch (Syrian) 229
Antiochus II 92

Antoninus Pius 239-40, 243, 248
Anubis 38, 44, 75, 114, 118, 172, 185, 215, 225
Anubis Hydreios 114, 118, 245
Aphrodite 14-15, 57, 77, 132, 170-71, 184, 198, 210, 226, 261, 274
Apis, Apis bull 72-73, 94, 180, 224, 258
Apollo 21-22, 66, 171, 235, 262
Apollonius of Tyana 83
Apollonius, priest of Delos 83, 214
Apotheosis 52
Apotheosis by Drowning 98-99, 235
Aqua Septimiana Felix 13, 187
Aqueduct 29, 42-43, 63, 213
Aquincum 120
'Ἀρχίστολος 189
Architecture, Typology 209
Ares 77
Aretalogy, Isis 66, 68, 85
    Aretalogy of Andros 229
    Aretalogy of Cyme 68, 83, 170-71, 222, 229, 261
Arezzo 109
Arsinoe 259, 275
Artemis 6, 239
Artemis Hagia 39
Asclepius 6, 230
Assembly Room, Sacred 45, 106, 170, 180, 190-94, 216, 276-78
Association, Cult 37, 146, 172, 183, 185
Astarte 228
Astrology 89
Aswan 212
Atbara River 222
Athena 6, 67
Athens 209, 229
Athyr, month of 74, 225, 228
Atlantid 178-79
Attica 145
Attis 6
Augustus, Augustan Period 104-5, 107, 238, 240, 255, 273
Aula Isiaca 105, 109
Austria 59-60
Aventine Hill 182
Baal 228
Baal Zephon 228-29
Bab Sidra, Cemetery of 32
Balkans 120

Baltimore: Walters Art Gallery 243, 246
Baptism, Christian 62, 98, 148, 153, 219, 222
Baptism, Isis-Sarapis 52, 144, 152, 255
Baptism, Mithraism 255
Basilica 57, 268
Basins 12, 15-16, 22, 29, 34-35, 37-38, 42, 46-48, 52-53, 57, 59-60, 109, 130-43, 145-48, 151-53, 174-76, 178, 210, 214, 216, 220-21, 250-53, 255, 265, 270
Basins, Catch 59, 135-36, 219
Basins, Sprinkling *see* Περιρραντήριον
Basins, Temple 134-43, 146-48, 152-53, 170, 175, 253
Basins, T-Shaped 220-21
Baths 137, 143, 147, 152, 183, 268
Baths, Foot 131, 251
Belgrade 120
Bench 22, 171, 187
Berenice 92
Bergama (Turkey) 220
Berlin: Ägyptisches Museum 224-25, 245-46
Berlin: Antiquarium 247
Bes 193, 278
βησαρτης 192-93, 278
Births, Multiple 95, 153, 233
Boeae (Greece) 209
Boston: Museum of Fine Arts 241, 244-45
Box, Sacred *see Cista*
Bread 107, 112-13, 192, 242
Bruttium 123-24
Budapest: National Museum 246-47
Bull, image of 42-43, 72, 178, 224-25, 258, 267
Bura (Greece) 209
Cabiri 6, 38, 173, 264
Caduceus 44, 218, 240
Cagliari (Sardinia) 119
Cairo 222
Cairo: Nat. Museum 243, 246
Campania 109
Candlestick 46, 77, 226, 278
Canopic Jars *see* Visceral Jars
Canopus, city 102, 119, 236
Canopus, supposed deity 102, 236, 243

Canopus Statue   *see* Osiris Hydreios
Capite velato   111-12
Caracalla   4, 168, 171, 188, 262
Carpi, Cardinal   119
Carthage   103, 123, 249
Cassiopeia   81
Cella, Temple   18-20, 56, 104, 111,
    117-18, 122, 134, 142, 156, 175, 177,
    179, 184-85, 194-95, 197, 202-4, 211,
    242, 262, 267, 269, 278, 280
Cenchreae, city   113, 260
Cerberus   184
Channel, Water   15, 18, 29, 35, 46,
    60, 137, 172, 210-11, 214, 222, 253
Chemmis (Egypt)   78-80
Chicago: Field Museum   245
Choiach, month of   225
Christianity, Christians   32, 50-51,
    61-62, 69, 71, 93, 98, 104, 112, 131,
    148, 153, 199, 219, 229, 232, 250,
    277
Circeo (Italy)   245
Cista   74-75, 110
Cistern   13-14, 17, 48-49, 54, 63, 133,
    141-42, 210, 215, 218-19, 221, 252,
    254
Claudius   114
Claudius II   226
Coins: Alexandria and Environs   105,
    107, 109-10, 114-15, 120-22, 167-
    68, 237, 239-43, 245, 247-48, 253
Coins: Rome   108, 239, 271-72
Coins: various   177, 179
Collection System, Water   17, 47-49,
    138
Colonia   123, 239
Commodus   4
Constantine   17, 32, 177
Copae (Greece)   209
Corinth   101, 113, 209, 239
Cow, image of   42-43, 73-74, 204,
    224-25
Crete   40, 120
Crocodile   94, 98, 233, 235, 241, 243,
    269
Crypts   2, 20, 28-29, 34-54, 56, 72-
    76, 83-84, 86, 128, 134-35, 139, 154-
    55, 158, 176, 180, 184, 187, 190-
    206, 211, 214-19, 256, 267, 276-80
Cubit, Sacred   32, 36, 111, 154, 213,
    223, 232, 256

Cult Platform, Temple   21, 117-18,
    121, 142, 170-71, 176, 181, 184,
    194-97, 200, 203-5, 269, 278-79
Cupid   45-46, 77, 185, 204, 226
Cursing, magical tablets for   244
Dacia   120
Δαίμονες   67
Dalmatia   120
Danube   120
Dea Africa   13, 186
Deir el Bahri (Egypt)   220, 255
Delos, city   64, 126, 172, 214, 277
Delta (Egypt)   25, 31, 92, 222
Demeter   6, 38, 67, 76, 173, 264
Demetrius of Phalerum   277
Dendera   255
Diana   186
Dining Room, Cultic   22-23, 35, 216
Diocletian   226
Diocletian, Column of (Alexandria)
    138, 197-98, 258
Dionysus   6, 83, 127, 192-93, 229,
    231, 235, 240, 265, 277
Dionysus-Harpocrates-Bes   278
Dioscuri   6
Divination   219
Domitian   105, 243, 247
Drains   1, 11-12, 18-21, 37, 42-43, 47,
    49, 57, 60-61, 132, 134-43, 170-71,
    210-12, 222, 252-54, 256
Dreams   177
Dromos   38, 173, 187, 190, 193, 264,
    278
Drowning, Ritual   52
Dryad   67
Eagle   183, 253
Ears, Votive   261
Edfu   26, 212-13
Egyed (Hungary)   104, 237
Egypt   2-3, 24-25, 36, 50, 62, 65, 88,
    94-95, 103, 108, 110, 113, 115-16,
    119-23, 126, 130-31, 146, 153-54,
    156, 159, 197, 220, 226, 247, 253
Egyptomania   230
Elephantine   43, 212, 217
Eleusis   147, 155, 255
Eleuthernai (Crete)   124
Eleutherus River   222
Empedocles   256
Eretria, city   64, 126
Ermouthis-Isis   24, 130

Eros 77, 185, 204, 226
Escharon 38, 173, 264
Esietus 99, 235
Esna (Egypt) 26, 212
Esquiline Hill 245
Etesian Winds 65, 74
Ethiopia 65, 93-94
Euboean Gulf 55
Eucharist, Christian 69, 112, 113
Euthenia 240
Exedra 38
Faiyum 25, 114, 119, 130, 246
Faustina 243
Fertility, Agricultural 92-94, 100, 126, 153
Fertility, Human 95-96, 100, 126, 153-54, 242
Flavia Solva *see* Frauenberg
Florence: Museo Archeologico 238
Foot/Footprint, Votive 181, 271, 276
Forma Urbis Map 177, 181, 267, 272
Fountain, Water 21-22, 169
France 120
Frauenberg, city 64, 71
Frieze 44, 105, 109
Frogs 96, 234
Funerary Context/Motif 102, 110, 114-16, 119, 123-28, 156, 158, 241, 244-50
Gabbari (Alexandria) 248
Gabii (Italy) 195
Galba 114
Gallienus 114, 226, 243
Games, Sacred 78-80, 226-27
Ganges River 71, 222, 224
Gebel el Silsila (Egypt) 212
Geneva: Musée d'Art et d'Histoire 225
Germany 120
Gongylos 192-94, 277-78
Gorgon 46, 218
Gortyn, city 64, 71
Gortyn: Museum 216
"Great God" 229, 263
Greece 5-6, 55, 64, 108, 126, 220
Gymnosophists 93
Hadrian, Hadrianic Period 5, 99, 110, 118, 121, 167-68, 171, 178, 194, 233, 243, 245-46, 248, 258, 268, 273
The Hague: Carnegielaan Museum 247

Hapi (Nile god) 28, 233
Harpe 79
Harpocrates 79, 83, 117-18, 167, 176, 181, 204, 210, 215, 224, 228, 239-41, 245, 247, 260, 267, 273, 278
Hathor 73, 76, 224
Head, purification of 3, 144-46, 152, 255
Hecate 260, 275
Heqt (divinity) 67
Hera 6
Heracleopolis 246
Heracles 6, 83, 209, 229
Herculaneum 108, 111, 126, 241, 284
Herm 190-94, 261, 277
Hermanubis 117, 176, 181, 198, 240
Hermes 67
Hermione (Greece) 209
Hermonthis (Egypt) 119
Heros (Rider God) 277
Herulians 170
Hesione 83, 229
Hieroglyphics 120, 244
Hieropes 264
Hieros Logos 84
Hipponium (Italy) 123, 249
Hippopotamus 94, 228, 233, 269
Holy Spirit 62
Horus 65, 79-84, 88, 115-16, 127, 223, 228-29, 243-44, 250, 262
Horus, Four Sons of 116
Horus-locks 4, 150, 160, 257
Hydraeum 39, 104, 215, 239-40
Hydreion 39-40, 104, 106, 212, 215
Hydreios (divine name) 215
Hydria 102, 104, 127, 156-58, 237, 244
Ibis 62, 146, 222, 239, 269
Immortality 3, 84, 87, 97-100, 103, 125-26, 128, 156, 230, 235
Incense 241
Incubation 52, 197
Infiltration, Water 25
Initiation Rites 17, 52-53, 143-44, 153, 182-83, 191-94, 197, 201-2, 204-6, 216, 219, 255, 277
Inopus River 35-37, 39, 61-64, 172, 214, 256
Io 76, 92, 106, 225
Isis *passim*

Isis, cow image of 72, 74-76, 84-85, 127, 158, 225
Isis, crown of 73, 224-25
Isis, iconography of 45-46, 218
Isis-Aphrodite 185, 210
Isis Hydreios 114, 118
Isis-Io 92
Isis Pelagia 265
Isis Tachnepsis 172
Isis-Thermouthis 24, 107, 110, 121, 130, 241, 246
Isis-Tyche 177
Isis Usret 33, 213
Italy 2, 4, 107-10, 113, 115, 119-20, 122-23, 126, 156, 159, 195, 197, 246, 249
Izmir 221
Izmir: Museum 261
Jewish Revolt (Alexandria) 167
Jews 71
Jordan River 62, 71, 222
Julian the Apostate 239, 241
Jupiter 183, 195
Karlsruhe: Museum 225
Karnak 26, 212, 253
Karnak, sacred way to 12, 132, 178
Klaft (headdress) 113, 178
Klein-Glienicke Relief 122, 245
Kline 246-47
Knossos 120
Kom el Gizeh (Egypt) 212
Kom-esh-Shuqafa, catacombs 246, 248
Kom Ombo (Egypt) 212, 255, 287
Koptos 3, 24, 131, 251
Κρήνη 131, 212, 251
Kyathos 241
Lake, Sacred 220, 253
Lamps 43, 198-99, 201, 217, 234, 265, 278
Latium 108, 245
Leiden: Rijksmuseum 246-47
Leptis Magna, mosaic at 26
Leviathan 228
Libation Pourer 111, 115, 122, 241
Libation Rituals 111-12, 115, 122, 124, 156, 199, 241-42, 250
Liguria 177
Longinus (Duovir, Pompeii) 131-32
Loreius Tiburtinus (of Pompeii) 221
Lotan/Leviathan 228

Lourdes 71
Lucius Verus 243
Luxor 12, 132, 212, 249, 255
Magic 83-84, 89, 99, 235, 242, 244
Marcus Aurelius 107, 168, 182, 213, 240, 243, 262, 267
Mark Anthony 215, 265
Mars 46, 76-77
Mater Deorum Transtiberina 110
Maximinus 226
Medinet Gurob, tombs at 114
Medusa 79
Megara 209
Μελανηφόρος 172
Memory (divinity) 124, 249-50
Memphis 25, 79, 91, 212, 214
Men (divinity) 145
Menelaite Nome (Egypt) 107, 110
Mensa Isiaca 109, 115, 244-45
Mercury 218
Meroe 92
Messene (Greece) 209
Methana (Greece) 209
Metroon 38, 173, 264
Mex (Alexandria) 249
Min 24, 79-80, 131, 227
Mithra 6
Mithraeum of Santa Prisca (Rome) 255
Mithridates 172
Modius 223
Mons Porphyrites, village 208
Month (divinity) 77, 226
Mosaics 26, 203, 265, 269
Mt. Kasios 228-29
Mt. Larissa 169, 260
Mummy 115-17, 199, 244
Mystery Rites *see* Initiation Rites
Μύστης 191-92, 277
Mycenae 226
Naiskos 107, 195, 239-40
Naples: National Museum 131-32, 241, 251-52
Navarch 4
Navigium Isidis 4, 75, 101, 127, 150, 237, 242
Nectanebo 251
Νειλοσκοπεῖον 212
Neith 225
Neocorus 189, 193, 268
Nephthys 73

Nereids 81-82
Nero 240, 255
Niche 41-43, 52, 72, 178, 187, 190, 194, 196-97, 199-202, 204-5, 217, 255, 263, 279-80
Nile River 24-25, 35, 62-65, 71, 74, 82, 88-100, 106, 153-54, 157, 228, 237, 243, 256, 269
Nile River: Flood 25, 28, 31, 50, 62, 64-65, 69, 76, 82, 88-100, 153-55, 157, 212, 223, 231-32
Nile River: Flood, ritual reproduction of 28-29, 31-53, 58, 60-61, 68-70, 155-57, 219, 221, 254, 256
Nile River: Flood, rituals (various) 50, 93-94, 230
Nile Water 2-3, 20, 24-25, 28-29, 31-76, 82, 113, 121-23, 125-29, 153, 211-12, 214-19, 223, 228, 230-32, 235-43, 250
Nile Water: Containers 2, 54-70, 141, 147, 155-56, 158, 175-76, 190, 256
Nile Water: Crypts 2, 20, 28-29, 34-54, 56, 72-76, 83-84, 86, 128, 134-35, 139, 154-55, 158, 176, 180, 205, 211, 214-19, 256, 267
Nile Water: Exportation of 91-92
Nile Water: Pitcher 2, 39, 44-45, 69, 72, 75, 99, 101-13, 121-23, 125-28, 155-59, 215, 235-42, 250
Nile Water: Ritual connected with 105, 108, 110-13, 126-28, 155-56, 158-59, 241
Nile Water: Significance 3, 50, 61-62, 66, 68-69, 71-72, 75-76, 84-85, 87-100, 103, 125-28, 153-54
Nilometers 2, 25-40, 43-44, 47, 61, 154-55, 212-14, 217, 256
Nilometers:
  Alexandria 29-33, 63, 154-55, 256
  Aswan 212
  Edfu 26, 212-13
  Elephantine 43, 212, 217
  Esna 26, 212
  Gebel el Silsila 212
  Karnak 26, 212
  Kom el Gizeh 212
  Kom Ombo 212
  Luxor 26, 28, 212
  Philae 26-27, 33-34, 212-13, 217, 256

Nomentum 108, 215, 237, 239-40
Nun (divinity) 234
Nut (divinity) 67
Nymphs 67, 218, 227
Ocean 91, 97, 234, 249
Oetylus (Greece) 209
Offering Table 107, 109, 115
Opus incertum 41, 267
Opus sectile 169-70
Oracle 194, 201
Orientation, Sacred 13, 20-21, 34, 41, 184
Orphism 124, 234, 249-50
Osiris 3, 69, 74-76, 82, 111, 113, 115-18, 121, 124-27, 155-58, 191-94, 215, 223, 225, 228, 231, 235-37, 241, 244-45, 248-50, 256, 265, 278
Osiris, Search for and Finding of 74-76, 82, 85, 105, 158, 225, 231, 237
Osiris, water and 68-70, 104, 116, 124, 126-27, 156-58, 237, 250
Osiris, water and: "Cool Water" Inscriptions 2, 72, 97, 99, 102-3, 123-28, 155-58, 236, 249-50
Osiris Hydreios (Canopus) Statues 2, 72, 99, 102-3, 113-28, 155-59, 178, 181, 185, 236-37, 243-48, 250
Ostia, city 108, 110
Otho 114
Oxyrhynchus 119, 283
Palermo Stone 212
Palm Branch 44, 106, 118, 240, 245
Pan (divinity) 79
Paneia Festival 78, 226
Pannonia 120
Panopolis see Chemmis
Papyrus 220
Paris: Louvre Museum 243, 246, 248
Paris: Musée Guimet 245-46
Patrae (Greece) 209
Pergamum, city 64, 71, 126, 268
Περιρραντήριον 3, 130-34, 147, 151-52, 250-52
Persea Tree 79, 226
Perseus 3, 46, 76, 78-83, 85, 218, 226-29, 256
Persia, Persians 91-92, 226
Petelia (Italy) 124
Pharaoh 76, 145, 254-55
Philae, island 126, 212-13, 217, 241, 255

Philippi, city 113, 239
Phlias (Greece) 209
Phrygia 278
Pinecones 185, 274
Pipes, Water 17, 20, 35, 37, 42-43,
  47-49, 57-58, 63, 132, 135-37, 139,
  211, 214, 217, 220, 252, 269
Piscina (Serapeum of Alexandria)
  137-38, 168, 251, 253
Pithos 22
Pompeii, town 64, 71, 107, 195, 219,
  221, 226, 240
Pompeii: *Casa del Frutteto* 109, 248
Pompeii: *Casa di Loreio Tiburtino* 221
Portico 18, 21, 33, 35-37, 40, 47, 56,
  131, 133, 135, 172, 175-76, 178,
  180-81, 187, 200, 202, 219, 238-39,
  267
Poseidon 6, 67, 81
Prague: Charles University 261
Pregnancy, Human 95-96, 100, 154,
  242
Priests, Egyptian (Traditional) 74,
  80, 105, 145-46, 152, 222, 227, 239
Priests, Isis-Sarapis 39, 44, 75, 105-6,
  110-12, 115, 118, 120-21, 126, 131,
  143-44, 146-49, 152-53, 158, 174,
  179, 186, 192, 197, 201-2, 214-15,
  221, 238, 245-46, 275, 280
Priests, living quarters for 18, 45, 56,
  177, 180, 254
Processions 69, 74-75, 101-2, 110,
  118, 121-22, 126-27, 150, 156, 158-
  59, 237, 242, 245
Pronaos 48, 56, 60, 171, 175, 177,
  190, 202, 221
Prophet 120, 238, 247
Proserpina 52
Proskynesis 198, 258, 274
Ptah 223
Ptolemais (Egypt) 230
Ptolemy I 259
Ptolemy II 92, 210, 259
Ptolemy III 167
Ptolemy IV 167
Ptolemy XI 255
Ptolemy XII 241
Purity, Ritual 129-30, 143-48, 153,
  172, 251
Pylon Gate 184-85, 242, 251, 255,
  269

Pyramid Texts 97, 250
Rain, Rainwater 17, 37, 42-43, 49,
  55, 58, 60, 62-65, 75, 82-83, 88, 91,
  138-39, 219, 221-22, 227, 256, 261
Ramses II 114
Raphia, Battle of 4
Re 67
Red Sea 197
Refrigerium 236, 250
Renenutet 24, 130
Reservoir, Water 35-37, 137, 187,
  214
Rhacotis Hill (Alexandria) 154, 167
Ring, Bronze 251, 255
Rochester (England) 120
Rome 86, 103, 105-6, 108-10, 113,
  119, 122-23, 126, 156, 159, 195,
  218, 245-46, 249, 271-72
Rome: Capitoline Museum 238
Rome: Vatican Museum 108, 245,
  247
Sabratha, city 64, 71, 280
Sacrifice 111-12, 115, 122, 124, 156,
  180, 191, 199, 241-42, 250
Sacristy 45, 80, 180, 202, 204-5, 220
Sais (Egypt) 74
Sanctuaries, Egyptian Gods 5, 9-10,
  54, 161-89
Sanctuaries, Egyptian Gods: Graeco-
  Roman:
  Alexandria 2-3, 9, 23-24, 29-32,
    34, 36, 47, 63, 79, 137-39, 147,
    152, 154, 163, 167-68, 190, 197-
    99, 205, 208, 214, 232, 243,
    246, 251, 255-56, 258-59
  Ampurias (Emporion) 9, 18-19,
    163, 168-69
  Antinoopolis 9, 208
  Aquileia 9
  Argos 9, 14, 163, 169, 209, 257
  Beneventum 119, 161, 246
  Bononia [doubtful] 210
  Canopus 208
  Carthage 9
  Cenchreae 101, 103, 105, 108,
    111, 163, 169-70, 197, 209-10
  Corinth 9, 23, 138-39, 147, 152,
    162-63, 170, 255
  Cyme 9, 17, 23, 54, 57, 159,
    162-63, 170-71, 179, 209, 222,
    261-62

Cyrene: Apollo Precinct 9, 21-23, 139, 142-43, 152, 163, 171, 217

Cyrene: Acropolis 9

Delos (all sites) 40, 214, 262-63, 265

Delos A 9, 23, 34-38, 40-41, 47, 52-53, 61, 63, 86, 155, 164, 171-72, 214, 217, 229, 263

Delos B 9, 23, 36-38, 40, 47, 52-53, 60, 63, 155, 164, 172-73, 217

Delos C 9, 23, 38-39, 131, 151, 155, 164, 172-74, 212, 215, 264, 269

Ephesus: Commercial Agora [not a site] 161, 188-89

Ephesus: State Agora 9, 23, 132-33, 164, 174

Eretria 9, 12, 23, 54-56, 63, 131, 139-41, 143, 151-52, 155, 164, 174-75, 211, 255, 262, 265

Faesulae 9, 209

Frauenberg 9, 23, 54, 57, 59-61, 63, 155, 164, 175-76, 209

Gigthis [doubtful] 210

Gortyn 9, 23, 40-44, 47, 51-53, 63, 71-76, 84-85, 134-35, 139, 143, 152, 155, 158-59, 164, 176, 181, 185, 211, 217, 255, 269

Industria 9, 17-18, 139, 142, 165, 177, 211

Lambaesis 9

Leptis Magna 9, 23, 26, 133-34, 139, 142-43, 165, 177-78

Luxor 9, 12-13, 23-24, 26, 28, 116-17, 132, 151, 156, 165, 174, 178, 208

Memphis 199, 208, 257, 272, 277, 279

Miletus 9, 190, 194-96, 209

Mons Claudianus 9-10, 190, 194, 197, 208, 280

Mons Porphyrites: East Iseum 9, 208

Mons Porphyrites: Serapeum 9, 208

Mons Porphyrites: West Iseum [doubtful] 210

Ostia 9, 178, 190, 194-95, 205, 268-69

Pergamum 9, 23, 54, 57-58, 61, 63, 133, 139, 141-43, 147, 151-52, 155, 159, 165, 178-79, 190, 199-202, 205, 220-21, 252, 255

Philippi 9, 19-20, 66, 106-8, 156, 165, 179-81, 185, 241, 269

Poetovio [doubtful] 210

Pompeii 9, 23, 44-47, 51-53, 63, 66, 71, 76-85, 105-6, 109-12, 115-16, 118-19, 131, 136-37, 139, 143, 147, 151-52, 155-56, 159, 165, 177, 179-80, 185, 190, 194-95, 202, 205, 211, 219, 239, 243, 255-56

Priene 9, 20-21, 23, 139, 143, 152, 165, 180-81, 255

Ras el Soda 9, 11-12, 116-21, 156, 165, 176, 181, 185, 208, 269

Rome: Campus Martius 10, 92, 106, 110, 117-19, 121, 123, 156, 159, 165, 177, 179, 181-82, 185, 241, 247

Rome: Regio III 9, 179

Rome: Santa Sabina 10, 106, 118, 156, 166, 182-83, 241, 245

Sabratha: East End 9-10, 17, 23, 48-49, 54, 61, 63, 133, 135-36, 139, 147, 151-52, 155, 159, 166, 183-84, 190, 202-5, 209, 221, 255, 280

Sabratha: Forum 9

Savaria 9, 104, 237

Seleucia Pieria [doubtful] 208, 210, 257

Soli: Temple D 9, 14-16, 23, 66, 132, 151, 162, 166, 179, 184-85, 210, 273-74

Soli: Temple E 9, 15-16, 22, 66, 104-5, 108, 117-19, 147, 150, 156, 159, 162, 166, 184-85, 231, 239, 242, 269, 273-74

Tauromenium 9, 208-9, 257

Thera 9, 13-14, 166, 185-86, 210

Thessalonica 9, 23, 39-40, 155, 166, 186, 190-94, 205-6, 212, 269, 277

Thysdrus 9

Timgad 10, 13, 166, 186-88, 276

Virunum 10

York 10, 209

Sanctuaries, Egyptian Gods: Tra-
ditional:
  Aswan   208
  Behbet el Hagar   208
  Buhen   208
  Contralatopolis   208
  Dabod   208
  Deir el Bahri   220, 255
  Deir el Shelwit   208
  Dendera   208, 255
  Edfu   26
  Kalabsha   255
  Karnak   26, 253, 255
  Kom Ombo   212, 255
  Koptos   3, 24, 131, 208, 251
  Luxor   178, 255
  Madinet Madi   24, 130, 223, 251
  Maharaqah   3, 208
  Meroe   208
  Philae   3, 24, 26-27, 33-34, 47,
    208, 214, 255-56
  Qasr Dush   3, 208
  Qurta   208
  Shanhur   208
Sanctuaries, Other Gods:
  Aphrodite (Cyme)   57, 170-71,
    261
  Aphrodite (Soli)   14-15, 132, 184,
    210, 274
  Apollo (Cyrene)   21-22, 262
  Cabiri (Delos)   38, 173, 264
  Demeter (Delos)   38, 173, 264
  Jupiter (Pompeii)   195, 278
  Jupiter (Sabratha)   280
  Men (Sunium)   145, 254
  Vesta (Rome)   108
Saqqarah (Egypt)   107, 110, 112, 123,
  199, 248, 279
Sarapis   passim
Sarapis-Agathodaimon   107, 110, 121,
  240-41, 246
Sardinia   119
Scarab   253, 275
Schnabelkanne   108-10, 113, 122, 239-
  40, 242
Sea, Sea Water   55, 62, 67, 74, 80-84,
  144, 147-48, 227-29, 254
Sebek   24, 130
Selinus River   58, 220, 254
Senate, Roman   171
Septimius Severus   4, 182, 272

Servian Wall (Rome)   182
Seth   77, 80-84, 227-29, 256
Seti I, Tomb of   221
Sextus Pompey   239
Shentayet   225
Shu (divinity)   67
Simpulatrix   111
Simpulum   111, 241
Sistrum   45, 107, 111, 174, 177, 224
Situla   44-45, 109, 215, 224, 239
Skull, Human   278
Soli, city   113, 132
Sothic Year   243
Sparta   209
Sphinx   115, 240, 243, 269, 274
Spondeum/Σπονδεῖον   111, 122
Spontaneous Generation   96-97, 154,
  234
Springs, Water   13, 50, 60, 63, 82,
  142, 148
Stabiae   107, 109, 283
Stairway   13-14, 20, 25-26, 29-31, 33-
  42, 46-49, 53, 58, 61, 63, 172, 176-
  77, 187-88, 190, 195-96, 202-5, 218,
  222, 253, 276, 280
Stele, Grave   114-15, 119, 158, 245,
  249-50
Stelophorus   269
Στολιστής   111
Sulla   180
Sunium   145, 180
Swedish Cyprus Expedition   184, 273-
  74
Syria   91, 279
Syrian Goddess   6
Tachnepsis   214, 229, 263
Terra sigillata Ware   109
Thebaid   119
Theos Hypsistos   277
Θεραπευταί   39
Thessalonica, city   191
Thessaloniki: Archeological Museum
  277-78
Thot   115
Thrace   278
Thracian Rider God   277
Thyrsus   44
Tiber River   182, 254
Tiberius   12
Time   89
Tithorea (Greece)   209

Tivoli *see* Villa Adriana
Tja-Wy, Tomb of   241
Trajan   5, 107, 121, 178, 240-41, 243, 247-48, 255
Treasury, Sacred   170, 185, 204, 264, 280
Triclinium, Sacred   22-23
Troezen (Greece)   209
Tunnels   190, 197-202, 205, 220, 269, 280
Turin   17
Turin: Museum   213
Tybi, month of   91, 268
Tympanum   44
Typhon *see* Seth
Tyre   119
Uraeus   45, 103-7, 110, 237-39, 241
Urceus   108, 239
Uschebti   262
Uterus   242
Veil, Humeral   115, 118, 121-22, 158, 240, 245-46

Venice: Museum   120
Venus   46, 76-77, 226
Vespasian   114, 183, 243, 271
Vesta   108
Via Appia   244, 286
Villa Adriana   119, 121, 245, 286
Visceral Jars   116, 156, 244-45
Vitellius   114
Water Table   55-56, 220
Wedding Torch   77, 226
Wells, Water   16-18, 26, 47-48, 55-56, 61, 63-64, 82, 133, 135-36, 140-42, 177, 210, 219-20, 252, 254
Yamm/Sea   83, 228
Zeus   6, 64, 66-67, 88, 175, 229-30
Zeus Dionysus   278
Zeus Dionysus Gongylos   192-94
Zeus Helios Sarapis   253, 268
Zeus Kasios   172, 214, 229, 263
Zeus Sarapis   175, 278

LIST OF PLATES

Plate I.

The Sanctuary of Isis at Philae. Cross-section showing the Nilometer by the West Colonnade. Source: Henry G. Lyons, *A Report on the Temples of Philae*, Cairo, 1908, pl. vii (detail).

Plate II.

The Serapeum at Alexandria. The lower portion of the Ptolemaic Nilometer. Source: Rowe, *ASAntEg*, Suppl. 2 (1946), pl. xii.

Plate III, 1.

Serapeum A at Delos. View of the remains of the central temple and of Room D. The entrance to the crypt is plainly visible in the foreground. Source: Roussel, *CE*, fig. 2.

Plate III, 2.

Serapeum B at Delos. View of the Nilometer crypt. Its stairway is in the foreground. Source: Ibid., fig. 6.

Plate IV.

The Sanctuary of Isis and Sarapis at Gortyn. View of the basin of the crypt and two of its niches. The water inflow pipe is faintly visible just above the niche to the left. Source: Salditt-Trappmann, *Tempel*, Abb. 50.

Plate V, 1.

The Iseum at Pompeii. Frontal view of the central temple. A large altar is visible in the left foreground. Source: Malaise, *Inventaire*, pl. 43.

Plate V, 2.

The Iseum at Pompeii. Frontal view of the Nilometer crypt housing. In the foreground stands the same large altar that is visible in Pl. V, 1. Source: Ibid.

Plate VI, 1.

The Iseum at Pompeii. Stucco relief above the entrance to the crypt building. The central design is a cultic pitcher flanked by two kneeling worshippers. Source: Salditt-Trappmann, *Tempel*, Abb. 26.

Plate VI, 2.

The Iseum at Pompeii. Drawing of the stucco relief of Mars, Venus, and two cupids found on the west exterior wall of the crypt building. Source: Overbeck and Mau, *Pompeii*, 109, fig. 59.

Plate VI, 3.

The Iseum at Pompeii. Drawing of the stucco relief of Perseus, Andromeda, and two cupids found on the east exterior wall of the crypt building. Source: Mau, *Pompeii*, 180, fig. 83.

Plate VII, 1.

The Iseum at Pergamum. View of the interior of the central temple. The features indicated are a large, flat basin (a), the Nile water container (b), the platform for the cult statue (c), a higher platform on which the statue itself was placed (d), and the remains of later Byzantine walls (e). Source: Salditt-Trappmann, *Tempel*, Abb. 9.

Plate VII, 2.

The Iseum at Pergamum. View of the interior of the Nile water basin. Source: Ibid., Abb. 10.

Plate VIII.

The Sanctuary of Isis (?) at Frauenberg. Rear view of a model of the (restored) temple. The Nile water basin is to the left. Source: Modrijan, *Frauenberg*, Abb. 10.

Plate IX, 1.

Horbeit, Egypt. Yellow terracotta figure of a kneeling cow or bull lying on a base, sun disk between the horns. Ht. 0.152 m. Formerly Coll. Fouquet. Source: Kater-Sibbes and Vermaseren, *Apis*, vol. 1, nr. 128.

Plate IX, 2.

London, British Museum, inv. nr. 64512. Bronze statuette of Apis lying on a plate, sun disk with uraeus between the horns, triangle on the forehead. The sun disk is supported at the back with a brace. Ht. 0.032 m, L. 0.049 m. Formerly Coll. Acworth. Source: Ibid., vol. 2, nr. 465.

Plate X.

Mit Rahineh, Egypt. Apotropaic magical relief of Horus the Child (Harpocrates) standing upon two crocodiles and gripping in his hands the various noxious animals he has conquered. Now in the Cairo Museum (Cat. gén. Caire, nr. 9402). Source: Dunand, *Culte d'Isis*, vol. 1, pl. vi.

Plate XI.

Stabiae, Italy. Fresco which depicts two women bearing cultic pitchers of the *Schnabelkanne* type. Three men who carry *situlae* approach them. Source: Malaise, *Inventaire*, pl. 53.

Plate XII, 1.

Alexandria, coin of the reign of Augustus. Long-spouted cultic pitcher supported on a cushion. The body of the vessel is decorated with a wreath above three thyrsus wands while the spout is supported by a headdress of Isis (cow horns, disk, and plumes). Source: Poole, pl. xxxi, nr. 11.

Plate XII, 2.

Alexandria, but now in the Berlin Museum, inv. nr. 8164. A relief of Isis-Thermouthis and Sarapis-Agathodaimon with their tails intertwined. Between them is a cultic pitcher. Source: Dunand, *BIFAO* 67 (1969), 23, fig. 7.

Plate XII, 3.

Oxyrhynchus, but now in the Rijksmuseum at Leiden, inv. nr. F 1960/9.1. A relief of Isis-Thermouthis and Sarapis-Agathodaimon with their tails intertwined. Between them is an image of Osiris Hydreios. Source: Hornbostel, *Sarapis*, Taf. cxci, nr. 310.

Plate XIII.

Rome or elsewhere in Italy, now in the Vatican Museum (Cortile del Belvedere, nr. 55). A relief from the period of Hadrian which depicts in stylized fashion an Isis procession. From right to left: woman bearing a *situla*; a sacred scribe who reads from a book; priest with head, arms, and hands veiled who bears a cultic pitcher; woman who carries a sistrum and a ladle (*kyathos*). Source: Malaise, *Inventaire*, frontispiece.

Plate XIV.

Herculaneum. Fresco which is usually entitled "The Adoration of the Water." A priest flanked by two officials who rattle sistrums holds up a golden vessel for the adoration of two choirs of devotees. Source: Ibid., pl. 35.

Plate XV.

The Iseum at Ras el Soda, Egypt. Osiris Hedreios statue from the cult platform. This is an excellent example of a Type B Osiris Hydreios image. Source: Adriani, *Annuaire*, pl. liii, fig. 1.

Plate XVI.

The Iseum at Ras el Soda, Egypt. Frontal view of the Osiris Hydreios statue, Type A, from the cult platform. Source: Ibid., pl. lii.

Plate XVII.

The Iseum at Ras el Soda, Egypt. Side view of the Osiris Hydreios statue, Type A, from the cult platform. Source: Ibid., pl. lii.

Plate XVIII, 1-4.

The Iseum in the Campus Martius at Rome. Reliefs from a single column ("Column A") found on the site; the figures depicted are priests of Isis bearing sacred objects. 1 — Relief nrs. b 1-2 [Bosticco's notation]; 2 — Nrs. c 1-2; 3 — Nr. a 2; 4 — Nr. d 1. Source: Bosticco, *Musei Capitolini*, tavv. vi-vii.

Plate XIX.

Alexandria. Coins depicting Hydreios images.
Nr. 268 = Dattari, nr. 371: Osiris Hydreios
   (Vespasian, year 4 = 71/72 AD)
Nr. 452 = Dattari, nr. 826: pair of Osiris
Hydreios images
   (Trajan, year 15 = 111/12)
Nr. 625 = Dattari, nr. 1328: Osiris Hydreios,
Type B
   (Hadrian, year 9 = 124/25)
Nr. 632 = Dattari, nr. 1329: Osiris Hydreios,
Type A, facing a Type B example
   (Hadrian, year 9 = 124/25)

Nr. 633 = Dattari, nr. 1311: Type B Hydreios image, possibly
of Isis. It has a crown of horns and solar disk
   (Hadrian, year 8 = 123/24)
Nr. 775 = Dattari, nr. 1650: Osiris Hydreios,
Type A
   (Hadrian, year 17 = 132/33)
Nr. 779 = Dattari, nr. 1661: Osiris Hydreios,
Type B, facing a Type A example
   (Hadrian, year 18 = 133/34)
Nr. 1133 = Dattari, nr. 2500: Osiris Hydreios,
Type B, facing a Type A example
   (Antoninus Pius, year 2 = 138/39)
Nr. 1134 = Dattari, nr. 2503: pair of Osiris Hydreios images
born aloft by an eagle
   (Antoninus Pius, year 5 = 141/42)
Nr. 2214 = Dattari, nr. 5234: Osiris Hydreios,
Type A
   (Gallienus, year 9 = 261/62)
Source: Poole, pl. xviii.

Plate XX.
New York, Metropolitan Museum of Art. Three visceral jars
from the Tomb of Princess Sithathoryunet (Twelfth Dynasty).
Source: Metropolitan Museum of Art, *Guide to the Collections*, New
York, 1962, 24, fig. 28.

Plate XXI, 1.
The Serapeum at Luxor. View of the cult platform with statues
of Isis and Osiris Hydreios restored to their original (?) positions.
Source: Leclant, *Orientalia* 20 (1951), pl. 47, fig. 4.

Plate XXI, 2.
The Serapeum at Luxor. The Osiris Hydreios statue. Source:
Ibid., pl. 47, fig. 5.

Plate XXII.
The Sanctuary of Isis at Soli, Cyprus. Frontal view of the statue
of Osiris Hydreios found on the cult platform of the right-hand
cella. Source: Westholm, *Temples*, pl. xxiii.

Plate XXIII.

The Sanctuary of Isis at Soli, Cyprus. Side view of the statue of Osiris Hydreios found in the right-hand cella. Source: Ibid.

Plate XXIV.

Villa Adriana, but now in the Vatican Museum, inv. nr. 39. Large statue of Osiris Hydreios (Type A) in gray basalt. Roman period. Source: Malaise, *Inventaire*, pl. 11.

Plate XXV.

Beneventum, area of the Iseum. Two headless statues of priests who bear in their veiled hands images of Osiris Hydreios (Type B form). The statue to the left is 1.36 m high while that to the right is 1.38 m in height. Source: Müller, *Isiskult*, pl. xxx.

Plate XXVI.

Klein Glienicke, East Germany. A relief showing various figures in an Isis procession. The individual second from the left carries an Osiris Hydreios statue. This relief came originally from Rome or, less likely, from some other part of Italy. Source: Malaise, *Inventaire*, pl. 26.

Plate XXVII.

Rome, Via Appia. Facsimile of a magical curse tablet dating from the end of the fourth century AD which was found in this area. The figure in the upper left-hand corner is the *dee phrugia* or, as I believe, an Osiris Hydreios. The other figures appear to be Typhon and the victim as a mummy enwrapped by venomous snakes. Source: R. Wünsch, *Sethianische Verfluchungstafeln aus Rom*, Leipzig, 1898, 16.

Plate XXVIII.

The Temple of Sebek and Renenutet (= Ermouthis-Isis) at Madinet Madi, Egypt. The photograph shows the end of the sacred way leading to the temple, a vestibule, and the remains of the first pylon. In front of the second pair of sphinxes are "sprinkling basins" for ablutions. Source: Vogliano, *Primo rapporto*, Tav. 1.

Plate XXIX, 1.

The Temple at Luxor. Relief depicting Amenophis III as a child being purified by Atum on the left and Mont on the right (Eighteenth Dynasty). Source: Blackman, *PSBA* 40 (1918), pl. v. 1.

Plate XXIX, 2.

The Temple at Kom Ombo. Relief depicting Ptolemy XI Neos Dionysos being purified by Horus on the left and Thoth on the right. The water is shown in the form of "life" and "authority" signs linked together. Source: Ibid., pl. v. 2.

Plate XXX.

The Temple at Karnak. Fragment of a relief (the left side is missing) showing a priestess (top) and a priest (bottom) standing in low basins and being purified. An accompanying text says that the priests and priestesses descend into the basin of cold water to be purified (Eighteenth Dynasty). Source: G. Legrain and E. Naville, "L'aile nord du pylône d'Aménophis III a Karnak," *Annales du Musée Guimet* 30 (1902), pl. xi.

PLATES I-XXX
AND MAP

PLATE I

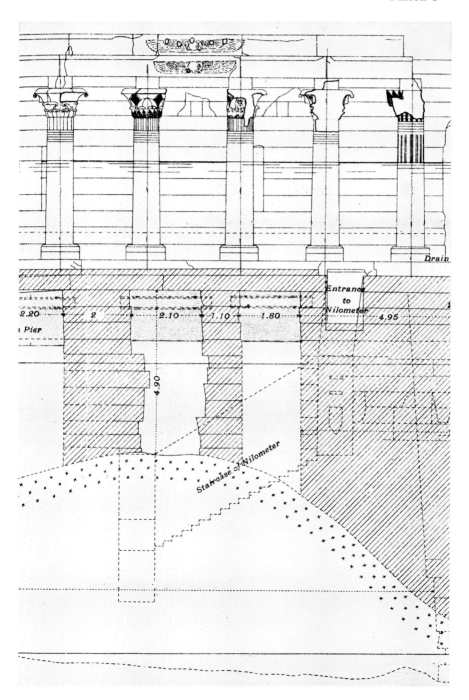

Drain

Entrance
to
Nilometer

2.20 · · · 2 · · · 2.10 · · 1.10 · · 1.80 · · · 4.95

1 Pier

4.90

Staircase of Nilometer

PLATE II

PLATE III

I

2

PLATE IV

PLATE V

1

2

PLATE VI

1

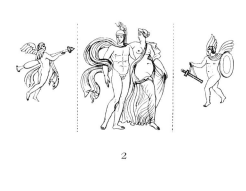

2

3

I

2

PLATE VIII

PLATE IX

1

2

PLATE X

PLATE XI

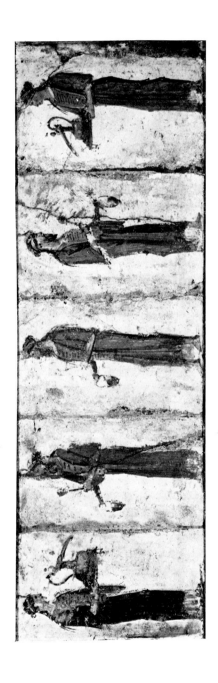

Plate XII

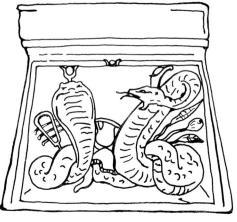

1

2

3

PLATE XIII

PLATE XIV

PLATE XV

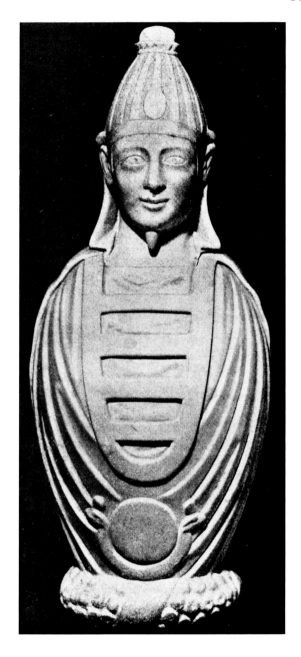

PLATE XVI

PLATE XVII

PLATE XVIII

1

2

3

4

PLATE XIX

268 775 2214 625

779 633 1133

632 452 1134

PLATE XX

PLATE XXI

I

2

PLATE XXII

PLATE XXIII

PLATE XXIV

PLATE XXV

PLATE XXVI

PLATE XXVII

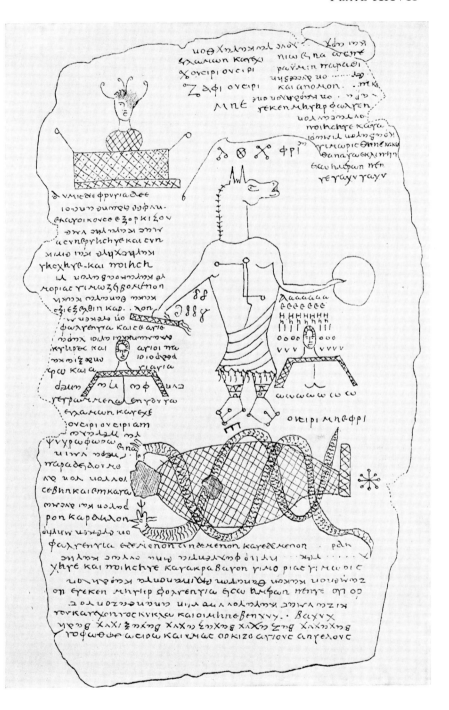

Plate XXVIII

PLATE XXIX

I

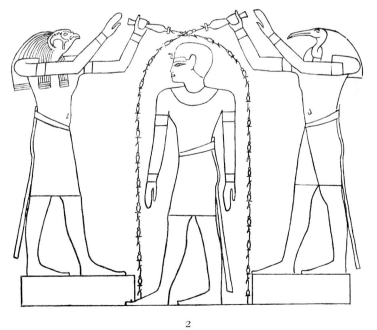

2

PLATE XXX